The Kennedy
Crises

The Kennedy Crises

The Press, the Presidency, and Foreign Policy

Montague Kern
Patricia W. Levering
Ralph B. Levering

The University of
North Carolina Press
Chapel Hill & London

© 1983 The University of North Carolina Press
All rights reserved
Manufactured in the United States of America
Library of Congress Cataloging in Publication Data

Kern, Montague, 1942–
The Kennedy crises.

Bibliography: p.
Includes index.
1. United States—Foreign relations—1961–1963.
2. Press and politics—United States—History—20th
century.   3. Kennedy, John F. (John Fitzgerald), 1917–
1963.   I. Levering, Patricia W., 1946–
II. Levering, Ralph B.   III. Title.   IV. Title:
Kennedy crises.
E841.K468   1983   327.73   83-6899
ISBN 0-8078-1569-1

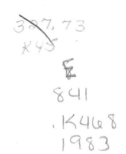

To our children—
Christopher, Alexander, and Deane Kern
Matthew and Brooks Levering—
and to Charles E. Kern II

Contents

Contents

Tables and Figures

Tables

Figures

Preface

When research for this book began in the summer of 1976, it was assumed that the project would include newspaper, magazine, and television news coverage of all major foreign policy issues during the Kennedy years. Although the administration and the public gave primary attention to cold war concerns from Kennedy's inauguration until civil rights became equally important in the summer of 1963, it was thought that the brevity of Kennedy's presidency would make it possible to cover virtually all foreign policy issues in depth.

As is customary during the first few months of research, the project was narrowed both by necessity and by design. Television news was dropped because most of the evening news programs before systematic preservation began in the late 1960s have been destroyed and hence are unavailable to researchers. Some research was done in news magazines and journals of opinion, but it was decided that coverage of foreign policy issues in magazines was a very different subject worthy of separate treatment. Finally, the idea of covering all major foreign policy issues was discarded after it became apparent that substantial effort would be required to cover any one in depth.

The decision soon emerged to focus on press-presidential interaction and on day-to-day coverage in five important newspapers during four major crises in which the Kennedy administration was involved: Laos and Berlin in 1961, Cuba in 1962, and Vietnam in 1963. But, even after the narrowing of focus, this study has involved the systematic study of thousands of news stories, editorials, and columns; numerous interviews with journalists and officials who played important roles during the four crises; and substantial research in previously untapped primary sources at the John F. Kennedy Library and elsewhere. By examining these four crises in detail, we have sought to present new insights into the press-presidential relationship during foreign policy crises.

Although based largely on practical considerations, the decision to focus on newspaper coverage reflected the primacy of newspapers among the nation's media during the Kennedy years. Until September 1963, when the leading television evening news programs were expanded from fifteen to thirty minutes, they offered almost no detailed analysis of foreign policy issues. And news magazines, though influential as lively and widely read summaries of major developments, lacked the day-to-day impact of leading newspapers. "The higher one goes in the formal and informal structures of foreign policy-making in the United States," Bernard C. Cohen wrote in 1963, summarizing numerous studies of media usage, "the more time and attention one finds being paid to the newspaper rather than to radio and television as the important source of foreign affairs news and comment."*

The authors represent two academic disciplines, political science and history, each with its own methodology and approach to knowledge. Political scientists tend to be interested in testing generalizations and contributing to theory, whereas historians generally seek to answer the questions they address to the past within a basically chronological framework. Overall, we believe we have succeeded as political scientists in developing a methodology for studying influences on press coverage that should permit comparative research on other presidencies; and as historians in remaining faithful to the particular circumstances of the Kennedy years.

Collaboration between the two disciplines on a project of this type is rare—regrettably so, in our view. Although many of our conclusions about the press-presidential relationship during foreign policy crises might well be valid for other presidencies, our research, focused on the Kennedy years, does not permit us to claim that they are universally applicable. Having offered these caveats, we still hope that this book will be of value to journalists, historians of the Kennedy years, and political scientists specializing in the press and in presidential power.

Finally, because it obviously was impossible for us to interview Kennedy and because many important documents from his era remain closed to scholars, this study focuses more fully on the various influences on press coverage than on newspapers' influence on presidential decision making. Our theoretical contribution thus is not in the area of crisis decision making, which Graham T. Allison analyzed for the Cuban missile crisis, but rather toward an understanding of the conditions under which the press can apply pressure on a president and, conversely, the influence that he can have on press coverage.

We wish to thank the many people who have helped us with this book. The assistance of Frederick Holborn, who rendered valuable advice to Montague Kern, is especially appreciated. Joan M. Nelson also offered important support, and Leon V. Sigal and Herbert Dinerstein gave her worthwhile critiques. The contributions of Porter Dawson, Evan Farber, Charles E. Kern II, Dewey W. Grantham, Gary R. Hess, Riordan Roett, Robert Lystad, Michael C. Hudson, William C. Adams, W. Russell Neuman, Samuel and Miriam Levering, Merry Levering, Wilton and Carol Lindsey, Betsy and David Morgan, Irene B. Webb, and Phil and Marilyn Wellons are also recognized. A grant from the National Endowment for the Humanities enabled Ralph and Patricia Levering to begin their work on this project during 1976–77; they received additional support from Western Maryland College and Earlham College.

*Bernard C. Cohen, *The Press and Foreign Policy* (Princeton: Princeton University Press, 1963), p. 8.

We also wish to thank the many journalists and officials of the Kennedy period who granted us interviews; their names are listed in the Bibliography. Three journalists—Robert Estabrook, Charles Gould, and Chalmers Roberts—gave us access to valuable primary source materials. Special thanks also go to Ruth Ames, curator of the Arthom Collection of newspaper files at Wake Forest University, and to librarians and archivists at the Library of Congress, the National Archives, and the John F. Kennedy Library. Mark Steinwinter's assistance in the computer analysis of the data is also appreciated, as is Rhonda Kiler's, Mildred Harllee's, and Mary Maloney's conscientious typing.

Part One

Introduction

Chapter 1

The Kennedy
Administration
and the Press

A Case Study

Shortly before President John F. Kennedy was to deliver a major foreign policy address at the University of North Carolina in October 1961, presidential aide Theodore Sorensen asked Joseph Alsop, Walter Lippmann, and several other journalists for their suggestions on how to counter increasing Republican charges of appeasement. What is especially significant in this episode is not that they gave long and thoughtful replies, parts of which were incorporated into the speech, but rather that the president was putting these prominent columnists in a position where it would be more difficult to criticize his policies. By asking them for their assistance, he in effect was working to keep his Republican opponents from obtaining favorable press coverage.[1]

During the Cuban missile crisis a year later, Kennedy used a nationwide, prime-time television address to make his demand that the Soviet Union remove its missiles from Cuba. Having successfully pressured leading publishers to withhold information on the issue until after he delivered his ultimatum, he and other administration officials systematically controlled the flow of information to the press (and hence to the American public) during the tense days that followed. When the Defense Department's ranking information officer, Arthur Sylvester, asserted soon afterward that the government's domination of the news during the crisis had been entirely proper because the media was "part of the weaponry" for waging the cold war, several journalists denounced the administration's persistent "news management" and warned that America's tradition of a free and independent press was seriously endangered. Although Sylvester's comment appeared to sanction lying to the press for cold war purposes, James Reston, the highly respected *New York Times*'s Washington bureau chief and columnist, offered a vigorous defense of the administration's press policies: "When Cain slew Abel and the Lord asked him where the victim was, Cain asked: 'Am I my brother's keeper?' This was the first 'technical' denial and the Bible and governments have been doing it ever since." [2]

During the time between Soviet Premier Nikita Khrushchev's capitulation on 29 October 1962 and the mid-term congressional elections nine days later, Kennedy combined a stated policy of seeing no reporters and allowing no members of the Executive Committee (EXCOM), which had managed the crisis, to talk to the press with an actual policy of allowing selected members like McGeorge Bundy to see selected reporters. The result was a series of approving "now-it-can-be-told" articles in favored large-circulation magazines and newspapers. Kennedy himself was soon on the phone talking with journalists about Cuba and politics, as New Bedford, Massachusetts, editor C. J. Lewin noted on 5 November:

> About 8:50 tonight, my telephone rang and I answered. It was a call from Boston.
> A masculine voice said, "Mr. Lewin? The President wants to speak to you."
> I waited for a few moments, said "Hello" and the voice said the President was on another line but would be on in a minute.
> The President came on the line and said, "Hello, Charlie. How are you?"
> I said, "Fine, Mr. President, and how are you?"
> Mr. Kennedy responded that he was well and then said, "I want to compliment you on that excellent editorial you published on the Cuban situation."
> I said, "Thank you, it was an accurate and complete presentation of the facts, Mr. President."
> He said, "I thought it was the best article I have seen on the subject. I sent it around to the State Department and the agencies and asked them why I had not been able to get something like that from them, that a newspaper down in New Bedford had given the most concise statement made on the situation."
> . . . Then he went on to say, "I want to thank you for the fine job you have been doing for Teddy" [the president's brother, Edward Kennedy, who in 1962 was running for the Senate for the first time]. [3]

The incidents are examples of the numerous press strategies Kennedy and other presidents have used to maximize favorable coverage of their policies.

Despite an extremely small White House staff concerned with press relations as well as sporadic coordination that during his first two years occurred primarily in preparation for press conferences, Kennedy worked hard to obtain favorable press coverage for his administration. His careful preparation for news conferences and facility in using them to publicize administration policies; his extensive personal contact with leading editors, publishers, and reporters; his practice of rewarding journalists who wrote favorable stories with more inside news and punishing those who criticized the administration by withholding scoops from them; his luncheons on a state-by-state basis for editors of papers whose circulations were 25,000 or less—these and other carefully conceived strategies contributed both to his apparent success in receiving largely favorable coverage and to the resentment that some journalists and Republican politicians felt about the administration's methods. William Shannon of the *New York Post* commented in November 1962 that Kennedy "devotes such a considerable portion of his attention to leaking news, planting rumors, and playing off one reporter against another, that it sometimes seems that his dream job is not being Chief Executive of the nation but Managing Editor of a hypothetical newspaper."[4]

Part of the reaction of some of Kennedy's critics may well have stemmed from envy, for his wit and charm could captivate even political adversaries. After attending one of the luncheons, Charles Schneider, editor of the *Memphis Press-Scimitar*, remarked in a typical comment, "He charmed the birds out of the trees."[5]

Kennedy's personal characteristics helped him with the press in other ways. A Harvard alumnus at a time when Ivy League graduates were sprinkled throughout the highest levels of journalism and other professions, he felt fully at home in the sophisticated northeastern political culture represented by columnists like Lippmann and papers like the *Times*. He was also admired for his success as a "wordsmith" in a profession that valued facility with words.[6]

Kennedy knew the Washington press well from his service in Congress from 1947 to 1960, during which time he courted journalists assiduously. Preferring to socialize with them rather than with fellow congressmen, by 1960 he had developed close friendships with well-known journalists like Alsop, Benjamin Bradlee, and Charles Bartlett. Kennedy also had the advantage of his generation, of sharing involvement in foreign policy issues with the press during a self-confident epoch before the shattering results of the nation's Vietnam policies inaugurated a process that altered public attitudes toward presidential authority.[7]

McGeorge Bundy, the national security adviser who worked as closely as anyone with Kennedy on a day-to-day basis, summed up the significance of the press to him as follows: "I think the press was of special interest to him because he knew a lot of people. He knew how they worked, and he knew that what the press said would have an effect on what people thought. He thought of it more as: What are they saying about us? Is it helping or hurting? . . . But don't make it too linear. The press is never more than one element [in the policymaking process]."[8]

Although it is true, as Bundy suggests, that the press was only one of many factors affecting presidential decision making, it is also true that the president was only one of the factors influencing press coverage of foreign affairs.

Given the complexity of the issue, journalists and government officials not surprisingly have tended to disagree sharply on the nature of the press-presidential relationship in modern America. Scholars likewise have presented differing opinions. But for many of these commentators, impressed by Kennedy's performance in his numerous televised news conferences and in situations like the Cuban missile crisis, the Kennedy period represented a high point in presidential effectiveness with the press.[9]

In books published in 1959 and 1967, journalists Douglas Cater and James Reston stressed the growth of presidential power during the cold war and limits on the influence of the press. Alsop—like Reston an important columnist during the Kennedy years—commented in 1975 that "lots of newspapermen think they have influence because they are applauded by people who agree with them." Perhaps partly because it would be imprudent to claim as much power as elected officials, journalists generally have denied that they have much impact on either government policy or public opinion.[10]

To put it mildly, high officials have often thought otherwise. Franklin Roosevelt repeatedly lectured reporters at press conferences on how he thought stories should have been written; Harry Truman reserved some of his choicest profanities for the press; Kennedy angrily canceled all White House subscriptions to the *New York Herald-Tribune*; and Richard Nixon and Henry Kissinger wiretapped reporters' home phones and sought in other ways to clip the wings of newspapers like the *New York Times* and the *Washington Post*. Because the press is "the principal source of the interpretation of events," Kennedy administration official Roger Hilsman has noted, it "is one of the main architects of whatever debate takes place on the policy that the United States should pursue in dealing with those events." While acknowledging that ambassadors and others both within and outside the government contribute to policy debates, Hilsman argued that because "the press is there every day, day after day, with its interpretations makes it the principal competitor of all the others in interpreting events."[11]

Considering the importance of the issues both in terms of democratic theory and in terms of the acrimony that frequently has developed, it is surprising that, at least until recently, the press-governmental relationship has never been a major focus of research either in the social sciences or in history. Recent research on the Carter administration stresses the limits of presidential power in ensuring favorable press coverage, but most other scholars emphasize presidential dominance. Studies focusing on press coverage of foreign policy issues, particularly crisis issues, have even more strongly suggested presidential dominance. Until the issue is studied systematically for several presidencies and for the electronic media as well as for newspapers, journalists and officials may feel justified in following their own instincts and pointing the finger at each other.[12]

Because of the interest of officials, journalists, and some academics, the broad concerns of this book are not new. To what extent is a president (in this case Kennedy) able to influence press coverage on major foreign policy issues? Does the president dominate the relationship, or does the press? It is only when the second question is stated more precisely that the special focus of this study becomes clear: Can other claimants for public attention—foreign leaders, politicians outside the administration, interest groups, widely read columnists, or others—effectively challenge a president's policies in the press? This question is the linchpin of the detailed analyses of four key foreign policy crises of the Kennedy years that form the body of this book.

In order to present as convincing a portrait of the press-presidential relationship as possible, this quantitative case study differs from much of the previous writing on the subject in several important ways. First, there has been a tendency toward overgeneralization, partially because supporting evidence frequently has been drawn from several administrations without detailed primary research on any of them. On the basis of examples like the beginning of the Korean War in 1950 or the Cuban missile crisis, it has often been asserted that the president dominates the press in times of crisis. Often the "crisis" is defined as lasting only a week or so, which in our judgment is a much shorter period than the crisis actually lasted, thus wrenching the press-presidential relationship out of context. To correct this kind of error, we focus on one administration and establish an ample time frame for analyzing each crisis.[13]

Second, whereas much previous writing looks at the press-presidential relationship in isolation, we examine it in the context of other influences. These may be divided into five categories: foreign sources, domestic politicians, interest groups, the general public, and sources within the press.[14] These nonofficial sources are examined more closely as influences on the press—that is, as frequent competitors of the administration in providing definitive interpretations of policy issues in the press—than as influences on presidential decision making. Indeed, unless a president explicitly acknowledges that press coverage had a direct influence on particular decisions, it is almost impossible to demonstrate with certainty that the press triggered a change in policy.[15]

Although it is not possible to prove causation between press coverage and Kennedy's policy decisions, criticism in the press definitely affected him. He read newspapers assiduously and, as Bundy noted, "It [the press] might stir him up. You can't tell. He might make it [a decision in favor of a speech on some subject after Reston had suggested that he needed such a speech] because he had it in the works. Or it might be, 'O.K., if Scotty's going to give us the shaft this week, we'll fool him next week.'" It is possible, however, to delve deeply into pressures on the president that built up in the press and into the motives and viewpoints of the press as well as the president. It is also possible to relate these pressures to the timing and content of key decisions.[16]

Third, much of the previous writing suggests that there is a nearly homogeneous entity—"the press"—whose relationship to the government can be analyzed as a whole. Although we frequently use "the press" as a shorthand designation for the newspapers being analyzed, we do not make this assumption. The literature recognizes differences in depth of coverage of national and international issues, but generally asserts that the press functions as a homogeneous entity due to the common patterns of issue coverage across a broad spectrum of the press: national, regional, and popular.

Two influential theories have been advanced to explain this alleged homogeneity. The first of these is organizational theory, which suggests that press coverage of foreign policy issues derives from organizational requirements within newspapers—for example, where beats are located. The second closely related theory is that of "pack journalism," which suggests that there is little divergence in the coverage of the major national media whose reporters are covering similar beats; and that there also is a filter-down effect from the national press to the lower reaches of the totem pole.[17]

In relation to foreign policy coverage, Bernard Cohen supports the pack journalism theory and suggests primary influence for the *New York Times*, the wire services, and the leading regional papers, while suggesting little independent interest in foreign policy issues on the part of most reporters and editors. But Cohen also suggests that other factors influence press coverage: editors' and reporters' individual perceptions or biases, for example, and those of the papers' readership. Although finding a general internationalism in most leading papers in the early 1960s, he nevertheless tended to discount the effects of such factors on news coverage.[18]

This study combines both a content analysis of press coverage of foreign policy issues and extensive interviewing of the editors, publishers, and reporters who were responsible for that coverage, along with the policymakers who sought to influence it. It also explores in depth the nature and effectiveness of other forces in the society that were attempting to influence both press and president. The results lend support to a theory of press coverage for the Kennedy years far more complex than homogeneity theories would suggest.

Substantial differences in coverage existed not only between the electronic and the print media, but also among the newspapers that provide the focus in this book. Selection of what is printed is affected not only by editors' and reporters' individual perceptions or biases, but also by their perceptions of the views of their readership, which differs from paper to paper. J. R. Wiggins, editor of the *Post* during the early 1960s, gave this explanation of the greater emphasis on human interest stories in the *Post* than in the *Times*: "The *Washington Post* was a newspaper read by everyone. That's the big difference between it and the *Times*, which only circulated to 10 percent of the population in the New York area and appealed mostly to intellectuals and professionals. There aren't sufficient numbers in any other place to support a paper like the

Times. We circulate to more like 50 percent of the homes in our area."[19]
Newspapers vary in three constituency-related dimensions:

1) *The level of intellectual sophistication of the readership.* Some papers, often called the *elite* press, assume a more educated readership than others. Examples in this study are the *Times* and, to a lesser extent, the *Post*; other examples in the early 1960s would be the *Christian Science Monitor* and the *Wall Street Journal*.

2) *The nature of reader interests.* In *popular* newspapers, it is assumed that most readers have little interest in detailed knowledge of national and international issues. Thus lengthy, intellectually demanding articles are avoided. Examples of popular newspapers in this book are the *Chicago Tribune* and the *San Francisco Examiner*.

3) *The location of the newspapers.* A *Washington-oriented* newspaper, located in or close to the seat of government and having a government-oriented readership, develops a pattern of coverage quite different from that of an *outlying* newspaper. In this study the *Post* and the *Times* are Washington-oriented; the *Tribune*, the *Examiner*, and the *St. Louis Post-Dispatch* are outlying.

Fourth, newspapers have differing degrees of contact with and access to the administration and the other categories of influence. These differences result from such factors as the size of the Washington and overseas bureaus, political compatibility with the administration in power, and the newspaper's perceived importance. Other studies generally have not taken this unequal access into account. They have dealt more with the relationship between the president, the White House press corps, and the elite press, on the assumption that it is possible in this way to understand how the press as a whole functions. Popular and outlying papers like the *Tribune* and the *Post-Dispatch* generally cannot expect to obtain exclusive information from high officials as frequently as can reporters from the *Times* and *Post*. As the result of such differences between newspapers, there is substantial variation in coverage of policy issues and in the relative emphases that various papers place on the different categories of source usage.[20]

Fifth, the previous writing that has looked seriously at the press-government relationship has concentrated on news coverage. We also analyze editorials and columns because the views of publishers and editors must be considered if presidential influence on newspapers is to be put in perspective in relation to other competing factors. Because these individuals determine both editorial policy and the types of articles of news and opinion selected for publication, the president's relationship with them and their general opinion of his administration are important. In addition to being widely read and discussed in Washington and New York, columnists played a key role in foreign policy issues in the popular and outlying press, which relied on them for news of what was going on in Washington as well as for opinion. Columnists like Alsop, Reston, and Lippmann were quite important both in official Washington and among other Americans interested in foreign affairs in the early 1960s, and their views will receive close attention in this book; it has been argued that columnists in the early 1960s had an importance similar to that of the major television anchormen of today.[21]

Finally, this study differs from much previous writing in its analysis of the press-presidential relationship in a policy context—in this case, "crisis" foreign policy issues, ones in which the threat of war or at least dramatic confrontations were involved. If a president is most powerful in relation to the press in such situations, as many scholars believe, press influence on the administration at the height of the cold war "imperial presidency" should be negligible. But, if substantial pressure was exerted through the press on a popular president like Kennedy, it seems certain that such pressures would affect other presidencies as well.[22]

This study thus examines the interaction between the president and the press with respect to major foreign policy issues and compares his influence under varying conditions with that of alternative or supplementary sources of news and opinion. In establishing a framework for analysis, we judged that three sets of factors would affect his ability to influence press coverage: differences in the orientation and characteristics of the various newspapers; differences in the context of specific issues; and differences in the way in which he and his entourage managed press relations on these issues.

The first set of factors, which relate to the *newspapers themselves*, include such variables as location and constituency (journalists' conceptions of their readership), editorial tendencies, interests of the publishers, and size and staffing. Newspapers closer to an administration ideologically and in terms of constituency may be expected to favor administration news sources and support the president's policies editorially, whereas newspapers distant from the administration in those dimensions are likely to present more opposing points of view. To the extent these expectations prevailed, press coverage of foreign affairs during this period was in part the result of a political interplay involving journalists and publishers on the one hand, and an administration and its supporters and opponents on the other.

The second set of factors relate to the circumstances in which an issue occurs. These factors, which affect a president's ability to influence the press but which are largely beyond his control, have been termed *external conditions*. They include the degree to which presidential policy conforms with generalized public opinion in the nation as a whole or with an existing consensus among foreign policy activists, as well as the degree of concern and involvement on the part of politicians, interest groups, and the general public.

As in the Laotian issue, a president may become involved in a relative political vacuum, in which neither opposing politicians nor the public are interested in or knowledgeable about the subject. Other things being equal, an administration's efforts to influence press coverage at such a time will be more successful than in a situation involving more substantial domestic involvement. Conversely, greater journalistic independence occurs—as on the Cuban issue—when there is more congressional or partisan promotion of views opposing the president's policies.

When an administration takes office, a popular consensus or climate of opinion on some aspects of foreign policy already exists. On issues that relate directly to this consensus—such as the perceived Russian threat during the cold war—a president's effectiveness in the press depends largely on his ability to compete successfully with other forces that will also seek, on an issue of such grave public concern, to give definitive interpretation to developments in this area.[23]

The third set of factors are called *internal conditions* because they can be controlled within an administration or by the president alone. They include news-generating presidential activity in response to a foreign policy situation: high-level meetings and announcements of troop movements; the quality of presidential activity directed toward the press; his overall press strategy; his news conferences, special messages, backgrounders, and leaks; and the extent of policy review and disagreement within an administration.

In general, two basic press strategies occurred during the Kennedy crises; these we have called "low profile" and "high visibility." Low-profile press strategies involved primarily backgrounders along with an occasional press conference. High-visibility strategies embraced preparations for special television messages, an increased level of press conferences, high-level meetings, and other news-generating activities.

In regard to policy review and internal divisions, Kennedy was relatively blessed. Divisions did not run as deep as they were to during the Carter administration, for example, when institutional conflict existed not only between the State Department and the White House, but also among different levels within the State Department that included factions more loyal to an important senator in a resurgent Congress than to the president. Under such conditions it is quite possible that presidential attempts to control the effects of intraadministration debate would have little effect. During the crises analyzed in this book, internal divisions were noticeable primarily during the periods of policy review. This may have been partly because the president frequently called errant officials who expressed what he did not consider to be his views after a policy was in effect. But it also occurred because, prior to the Vietnam issue of 1963, divisions did not run as deep as they did during some presidencies.

The interplay among these factors under varying conditions will emerge in parts 2 through 5 of this book, which treat the four crises in detail and establish, we believe, a significant new approach to analyzing the press-presidential relationship. Although the overall effects of the second and third sets of factors should become quite clear within those parts, some background is required on the first grouping: differences among the five newspapers that form the basis of this study and each one's general orientation toward the Kennedy administration and toward foreign policy coverage. These concerns provide the focus for chapter 2.

Chapter 2

The Newspapers

General Characteristics

The five newspapers that were analyzed for this study are the *New York Times*, *Washington Post*, *Chicago Tribune*, *St. Louis Post-Dispatch*, and *San Francisco Examiner*. The first three choices were virtually automatic: the *Times* and *Tribune* were the leading papers in the nation's two largest cities, and the *Post* by the early 1960s was the most influential paper in the capital. In choosing the other two, we decided to balance the conservative *Tribune* with a nationally known liberal newspaper, the *Post-Dispatch*, and to add the major West Coast representative of the large Hearst chain, the *Examiner*. All except the *Examiner* were among the ten best American newspapers of the time, both in the opinion of journalism professors polled in 1961 by the *Saturday Review* and in the opinion of newspaper publishers polled in another survey the same year. Moreover, of the ten metropolitan areas whose populations were more than two million in 1960—none of which was located in the South—five are included in this study. The goal, in brief, was not to select a "representative sample" of all the nation's daily newspapers, but rather to choose politically significant papers that had substantial national or at least regional impact.[1]

The two 1961 polls confirmed what Americans interested in foreign affairs already knew: the *New York Times* was the most prestigious newspaper of the day. It was known for its detailed, authoritative news stories, especially of news originating in Washington and abroad. Its Washington bureau, composed of twenty-two reporters, was by far the largest of any out-of-town newspaper and included such leading journalists as James Reston, E. W. Kenworthy, Wallace Carroll, Tad Szulc, and Tom Wicker. The *Times* also had forty-five foreign reporters, approximately four times as many as the second-ranking *Christian Science Monitor* (twelve) and third-ranking *Chicago Tribune* (eleven). The *Times*'s foreign coverage was thus much more comprehensive than that of any other American newspaper.[2]

The *Times*'s superiority in foreign news was reflected in the fact that of all its sources for the four crises, 1,945 (56 percent) were foreign. In contrast, the *Post* had only 1,064 (51 percent) foreign sources, and the three outlying papers had even fewer. Table 1—derived by adding the totals of "front page and inside combined" for the four crises—lists the overall totals in all categories of sources for the five newspapers.

One reason why the *Times* regularly received scoops was because the most important foreign policy readership—both in America and abroad—could be reached through its pages. Because officials used the paper to communicate with each other, at least the front page and the daily news summary were virtually required reading in the capital—whether in the White House, the executive agencies, the Congress, or the embassies. The *Times* was also read and discussed in places like the Brookings Institution in Washington and the Council of Foreign Relations in New York, both of which had close ties to the government, and in newsrooms, editorial offices, and academic departments across the country. The *Times* international edition was frequently read by American officials and foreign policy elites overseas as a guide to administration policy. In short, the *Times*'s elite constituency was a primary source of its power.

The *Times* was an establishment, internationalist paper. In an interview in 1978 Tom Wicker commented perceptively on whom it represented and what its basic orientation was in the late 1950s and early 1960s:

> [It was] the whole foreign policy establishment, basically. The Council on Foreign Relations and Harvard and Yale. You know, Dick Rovere wrote that piece on the establishment in the late 1950s. He said that the president of the establishment was Arthur Hays Sulzberger [the *Times*'s publisher]. And I think that's right. The *Times* did not at that time represent so much the community of New York as it perhaps does now. It represented the Atlantic, postwar, eastern, internationalist, liberal approach.[3]

A problem for a paper like the *Times* was that, in relying so heavily on high officials for the inside information which is the paper's hallmark, the reporters and editors could become too closely identified with official viewpoints. Further complicating the relationship was the fact that *Times*men[4] were frequently offered jobs in government. During the Kennedy administration, for example, William Jorden, the *Times*'s leading expert in Washington on Southeast Asian affairs, accepted a position in the State Department. Tad Szulc, the newspaper's authority on Latin America, also spoke with Kennedy about a possible job in the administration. During that interview, the president, exemplifying his frequent willingness to discuss highly sensitive matters with *Times*men, asked whether Szulc thought Castro should be assassinated.[5]

The Washington bureau was aware of the danger of loss of independence if relations became too close. Before the inauguration, Reston and Carroll agreed that *Times*men should maintain their social distance and not worry about friction with top administration figures. This view was easier to maintain in theory than in practice, for the *Times* wanted the scoops that became

Table 1. Front-Page and Inside-Page Sources, All Crises

	Washington-oriented Papers				Outlying Papers					
	NYT*	%	WP*	%	SLPD*	%	CT*	%	SFEX*	%
Foreign	1,945	(56.0)	1,064	(51.4)	1,047	(48.1)	799	(48.7)	784	(41.6)
U.S. Official	925	(26.6)	646	(31.2)	704	(32.3)	457	(27.9)	652	(34.6)
Domes. polit.	335	(9.6)	254	(12.3)	322	(14.9)	251	(15.3)	282	(15.0)
Interest grps.	145	(4.2)	41	(2.0)	48	(2.2)	74	(4.5)	67	(3.6)
Pub. opinion	88	(2.5)	23	(1.1)	26	(1.2)	33	(2.0)	33	(1.8)
Press	34	(1.0)	44	(2.1)	31	(1.4)	26	(1.6)	66	(3.5)
Nonofficial Domestic	602	(17.3)	362	(17.5)	427	(19.6)	384	(23.4)	448	(23.8)
Total	3,472	(99.9)	2,072	(100.1)	2,178	(100.1)	1,640	(100.0)	1,884	(100.1)

*NYT—*New York Times*
WP—*Washington Post*
SLPD—*St. Louis Post-Dispatch*
CT—*Chicago Tribune*
SFEX—*San Francisco Examiner*

available through close personal contacts. Indeed, Reston became angry at Kenworthy when the latter, soon after becoming White House correspondent and obtaining a private interview with Kennedy, refused to write up his notes for publication because, Kenworthy recalled telling Reston, "I want to be my own man and independent." "I'm damned," Kenworthy remembered Reston telling him. "All right, you're covering the beat, you do it your way." Although Kenworthy was never able to engage in a private conversation with Kennedy after that, the *Times* still received its share of the scoops, often through Reston himself, and Kenworthy soon left the White House beat. Given the *Times*'s position in Washington and elsewhere at the time, it was unthinkable to both the administration and the "newspaper of record" that important inside news might not appear in the *Times*.[6]

If independence from the administration in power was a dilemma for the *Times*, it was doubly so for the second Washington-oriented paper, the *Post*. Lacking the *Times*'s international reputation, reporters at the *Post* could not assume, as reporters at the *Times* frequently did, that officials would continue to give them stories even if they disliked what had been written about them yesterday. Moreover, *Times*men could tell unhappy officials (often with justification) that their stories had been altered by editors in New York, whereas writers and editorialists at the *Post*, a much smaller organization, had nowhere to hide. "The *New York Times* was more independent," Karl Meyer, an editorial writer for the *Post*, recalled. "They're in New York and don't have the White House right next to them. They're not in constant social contact with government officials and don't have to sit down next to the guy they're criticizing."[7]

Reflective of this closeness to the government were the frequent luncheons at the *Post* in which high officials like Charles Bohlen would talk off-the-record with editors and leading reporters and alert them to the issues the administration considered most important. After such a briefing, editorial page editor Robert Estabrook recalled, "suddenly all sorts of stories blossomed about the Berlin blockade or something." Competing with the *Times* in official Washington both for scoops and for readers, the *Post* dared not risk being cut off by the high-level sources who contributed so substantially to its success. Given its closeness to government, it is not surprising that the *Post* used the highest percentage of U.S. official (administration) sources of the five papers on page one (see table 2).[8]

Other factors contributed to the *Post*'s closeness to the government. Unlike the *Times*, it did not circulate widely on the East Coast. Its constituency thus was Washington: political leaders, government workers, and institutions and individuals doing business with the federal government. On the whole, the constituency was sympathetic to the concept of an activist, involved government associated with the party of Roosevelt, Truman, and now Kennedy. And so were most of the paper's editors and reporters.[9]

Table 2. Front-Page Sources, All Crises
(front-page totals)

	Washington-oriented Papers				Outlying Papers					
	NYT	%	WP	%	SLPD	%	CT	%	SFEX	%
Foreign	581	(47.8)	273	(41.4)	552	(40.6)	209	(42.8)	242	(36.7)
U.S. Official	469	(38.6)	300	(45.5)	451	(37.6)	169	(34.6)	277	(42.0)
Domes. polit.	124	(10.2)	58	(8.8)	157	(13.1)	78	(16.0)	90	(13.7)
Interest grps.	34	(2.8)	14	(2.1)	19	(1.6)	20	(4.1)	22	(3.3)
Pub. opinion	3	(.2)	1	(.2)	5	(.4)	5	(1.0)	8	(1.2)
Press	5	(.4)	14	(2.1)	15	(1.3)	7	(1.4)	20	(3.0)
Nonofficial Domestic	166	(13.7)	87	(13.1)	196	(16.3)	110	(22.5)	140	(21.2)
Total	1,216	(100.0)	660	(100.0)	1,199	(100.0)	488	(99.9)	659	(99.9)

The publisher, Philip Graham, shared this orientation. A close friend of Lyndon Johnson and relatively close to Kennedy as well, Graham, in the words of a *Times* reporter, "was involved in politics as no publisher ever should be." He had attended the Democratic convention in 1960 and suggested Johnson as Kennedy's running mate. After the inauguration, he was a frequent visitor at the White House, and his paper was a staunch supporter of Kennedy's programs. Graham also played an active role in managing the *Post*. His daily diary and interviews with several reporters and editors suggest that, unlike many other publishers, he was heavily involved in issues of story selection and editorial direction. When asked whether the editors believed that his close relationship with leading figures in the administration threatened the *Post*'s independence, managing editor Alfred Friendly responded that "all of us did—in theory. On the other hand, we rejoiced in it, because we got a lot of news. And besides, Phil was such a marvelously magnetic personality that it was hard to fault him on anything." [10]

Like that of the *Times*, the *Post*'s foreign policy orientation was cold war internationalist. "We were Marshall Plan even before Marshall," Friendly commented. "His [Kennedy's] general philosophy—'we will take every step, etc.'—could have been the *Washington Post*'s." Unlike the *Times*, however, the *Post* faced definite financial constraints, resulting, for example, in a small overseas staff. In contrast with its ample financial resources by the 1970s, in the early 1960s it was reluctant to spend the $50,000 or more annually that was required to maintain each overseas bureau, and its foreign coverage suffered as a consequence. In cooperation with the *Los Angeles Times*, the *Post* had only seven full-time foreign correspondents in 1963, and in 1961 and 1962 it had even fewer. [11]

Because of its location in the capital, its capable staff covering developments in Washington, and the presence on its editorial pages of leading columnists like Lippmann and Alsop, the *Post* (like the *Times*) was read by Washington-based reporters, officials, and foreign diplomats. Like the *Times*, the *Post* was a Washington-oriented newspaper because it depended on official sources and because its publisher, editors, and reporters shared the official wisdom on foreign policy issues. Unlike the *Times*, however, it had few resources abroad and no base apart from Washington. It thus was the most Washington-oriented of all the papers in this study.

Among the outlying papers, the *St. Louis Post-Dispatch* was known to journalists as one of the journals developed in the late nineteenth century by Joseph Pulitzer, whose belief that the press should be "drastically independent" and progressive in its approach to public issues led to the current highly prized awards that bear his name. A competitor of William Randolph Hearst in the circulation wars at the turn of the century, Pulitzer's papers became known for their liberalism and internationalism, while Hearst's acquired a reputation for conservatism and chauvinism.

Aided by strong-minded publishers and editors, the *Post-Dispatch*'s tradition of liberalism and independence remained strong in the early 1960s. In editorials and in stories by its Washington- and United Nations-based reporters, it challenged some of the tenets of the cold war consensus of the period. Giving emphasis to the work of the United Nations and to nonmilitary solutions to cold war problems, the paper sought to understand the Soviet viewpoint and to move toward slowing the pace of the cold war. Skeptical of American aid to dictatorships in the Third World, the *Post-Dispatch* won the Pulitzer Prize in the mid-1960s for its editorials opposing America's military buildup in Vietnam. Its strong editorial page and independent reporting gave it a readership that included editors at the *Washington Post* and Secretary of State Dean Rusk.[12]

Although the outlying *Post-Dispatch* was clearly more liberal than the Washington-oriented *Times* and *Post* in its overall approach to foreign affairs, there remains the question of how much independence of government, public opinion, and a leading newspaper such as the *Times* was in fact possible. Lacking the population base to support a comprehensive paper comparable to the *Times*, the *Post-Dispatch* lacked the resources to hire a staff of foreign correspondents, and it did not even have a foreign editor.[13] Richard Dudman and other members of the Washington bureau did make trips abroad, filing hard-hitting stories in the muckraking tradition. But the paper had to rely for follow-up coverage on the wire services or the *Times*. Dudman described the problem: "We were covering something hammer and tongs, and then the guy'd go on vacation, or something else, and then there'd be a big gap when a lot of important things were going on and we wouldn't cover it at all. And the wire services are inadequate for coverage of something like this." [14]

Although arguing that limited resources affected their ability to develop independent positions on foreign policy issues, *Post-Dispatch* editors did not feel constrained by public opinion in the St. Louis area. Marquis Childs, who was both a well-known syndicated columnist and Washington bureau chief during the Kennedy years, viewed the *Post-Dispatch* as a liberal paper in a conservative Catholic area, a factor that had concerned him only when he had written from Spain during the Spanish Civil War. Robert Lasch, the editorial page editor, felt the paper was accepted locally and enjoyed a "long-standing reputation as a liberal newspaper." Its readership, according to him, was concentrated in prosperous, middle-class suburban areas. Those who took an active interest in foreign affairs were "chapters of the national groups, some bankers, some university groups—largely university groups." There thus was an adequate constituency in the St. Louis area to sustain the paper's independent liberalism.[15]

The fact that most Washington officials and politicians, including President Kennedy, did not read the *Post-Dispatch* daily gave it greater latitude than the *Times* and *Post*. "We didn't have people calling us up," Lasch noted. On the other hand, the paper's location nine hundred miles from Washington meant that it did not obtain the important scoops. Its news disadvantage is reflected in the story of one *Post-Dispatch* reporter's interview with McGeorge Bundy, a key source for the *Times* and *Post*. "When James Deakin went over and talked to Bundy," Childs recalled, "after about fifteen minutes Bundy said, 'I'm sorry, Mr. Deakin, this bores me.'" Although Childs, as a leading columnist, sometimes received preferential treatment and had White House sources—notably presidential aide Arthur Schlesinger, Jr., and military aide Chester Clifton—the paper normally could not expect special favors from the president or his inner circle.[16]

Although the *Post-Dispatch* at that time would have been likely to back a liberal Democratic president, Kennedy did not take its support entirely for granted. He visited the offices in St. Louis during the 1960 campaign, and made a favorable impression on the publisher, Joseph Pulitzer III. This link was renewed in Washington on such occasions as a luncheon for Missouri publishers that Pulitzer attended. Even though the paper prided itself on its independent tradition, therefore, it could be expected to rally to the administration's defense if conservative Republicans attacked Kennedy's policies.[17]

The *Chicago Tribune* was queen of the Midwest. The largest paper in the area, it operated its own news service, which reached twenty to thirty papers. Circulation was much larger than that of any other Chicago daily. It had bought out the afternoon Hearst paper, and on a Sunday run in 1962 it produced a 234-page paper full of the profitable advertising that led *Time* magazine to call it "one of the country's best-run newspapers."[18]

The *Tribune* used some of this money to maintain a sizable operation in Washington; bureaus in London, Paris, Bonn or Frankfurt, Rome, and Moscow; and an Asia-based correspondent in Tokyo. It had more foreign correspondents than its chief competitor, the *Chicago Daily News*, which had greater standing in the East because of its incisive foreign coverage, but less circulation in Chicago, where it was geared more to the liberal and white-collar market. The *Tribune*, in contrast, appealed to a general, popular constituency. Laurence Burd, White House correspondent during the Kennedy years, remarked: "I would write for the seventh or eighth grader. Walter Trohan [the *Tribune*'s Washington bureau chief] used to say that the best stories were written when you didn't understand something."[19]

The *Tribune* was built into a thriving institution by Colonel Robert McCormick, the ardently Republican, isolationist opponent of the New Deal who died in the 1950s but whose influence remained strong. "McCormick endorsed all Republicans, even the bums," Trohan remarked. The tradition continued in the sixties under editor W. D. Maxwell, who was responsible, along with editorial page editor George Morgenstern, for the paper's endorsement of Republicans on the national level.[20]

Tribune Republicanism was definitely of the midwestern conservative variety. There was no affinity between the *Chicago Tribune* and the *New York Herald-Tribune*, the eastern Republican paper edited by John Hay Whitney and known for its investigative reporting. *Tribune* writers believed that the *Herald-Tribune* had accepted all of the precepts of the eastern liberal establishment, including acceptance of big government and partnership with Great Britain. The British "made us do a lot of things he [the Colonel] didn't like," Morgenstern commented. "They have taken us in the backdoor to war. . . . American foreign policy served the maintenance of the British empire." The *Tribune*'s dislike of Britain was matched by admiration for West Germany, whose free enterprise system it considered one of the most successful in the world.[21]

Like the other papers in this study except the *Post-Dispatch*, the *Tribune* was strongly anti-Soviet. But the *Tribune*'s Russophobia took an inward direction. Trohan, for example, responded to Kennedy's first press conference by questioning the president's motives in muzzling generals and negotiating with the Russians. The following quote from Trohan's column catches the flavor of many of the *Tribune*'s editorials and columns on Soviet-American relations under Kennedy: "The White House made no secret of the fact that it has ordered generals and admirals not to make 'tough' speeches against the Russians. Senators Styles Bridges [R.-New Hampshire] and Barry Goldwater [R.-Arizona] and other members of Congress wonder whether the soft peddling of criticism of Russia is a down payment on the ransom of the flyers, with a summit meeting as the second payment and concessions favorable to the Reds as the third."[22]

Burd saw this approach as "probably political. This was a way of jabbing at the president." Adversarial it certainly was, strongly based only in the Midwest and West among people who labeled themselves "conservatives," and not the sort of journalism that thrived during this period in Washington. In fact, mounting losses had forced the *Tribune* to sell its Washington paper, the *Times-Herald*, in the mid-fifties. But as Washington correspondent Robert Young said: "They loved it out there."[23]

In addition to conservative Republicans, the people who loved the *Tribune* often belonged to the Polish and other Eastern European ethnic groups that were strong in Chicago. These Chicagoans were largely Democratic, but not because of that party's liberal tradition. Their party identification stemmed largely from labor-union membership and the efficiency of Mayor Richard Daley's political machine. On the national level, these Democrats might well support Illinois's conservative Republican senator, Everett Dirksen. Like them, the *Tribune*, although nationally Republican, was locally pro-Daley.[24]

As a result of its circulation and resources, the *Tribune* was the leading opposition newspaper during the Kennedy administration, a role it had held under Truman and Roosevelt as well. In this position, its reporters had little access to the administration. The result was occasional dissimulation as, for example, when a reporter pretended to be from the *Times* in order to obtain a color photograph of Defense Secretary Robert McNamara. Trohan kept his distance and relied on his sources among conservative Republicans and Democrats on Capitol Hill, in the Federal Bureau of Investigation (FBI), and in the military and Central Intelligence Agency (CIA). When the administration gave stories to more sympathetic papers, he cast doubt on the reliability of the information "leaked to the eastern-internationalist-establishment press." [25]

This lack of access, combined with the *Tribune*'s hostility toward the Kennedy administration, was reflected in the fact that it used a lower percentage of U.S. official sources on page one than any other paper. By contrast, it used the highest percentage of nonofficial domestic sources, including domestic political ones (see table 2).

In addition to withholding inside news, the Kennedy administration tried to undermine the *Tribune* with a tactic Roosevelt had used earlier: building up the opposition. Although *Tribune* reporters apparently received no private interviews with Kennedy, the administration repeatedly made such arrangements for *Daily News* correspondents. The administration almost certainly was correct in its tacit conclusion that it could not win the *Tribune*'s support. But neither could it ignore the determined opposition of the most important paper in the Midwest. [26]

Whereas the *Tribune* was known outside Chicago primarily as an advocate of conservative Republican views, the *San Francisco Examiner* enjoyed a reputation as a leading representative of the Hearst chain, which in the early 1960s had by far the largest combined circulation of any chain in the nation. Although the Hearst empire had declined somewhat since the halcyon days earlier in the century under William Randolph Hearst, Sr., it still had popular papers in major cities across the country. The current leader, William Randolph Hearst, Jr., was thus an important figure in American journalism.

As with Pulitzer at the *Post-Dispatch* and McCormick at the *Tribune*, the elder Hearst's influence remained strong at the *Examiner*. "I think the public demands in a newspaper both information and entertainment," Hearst had written, and the entertainment "should largely be found in the news." In the early 1960s, the *Examiner* and other Hearst papers were, first and foremost, popular newspapers oriented, like the *Tribune*, largely toward people who did not want to spend their time reading lengthy analyses of public issues. [27]

The *Examiner* also continued the tradition of the elder Hearst in its emphasis on a strong national defense and other conservative values as well as in its special interest in Latin America. According to Charles L. Gould, the *Examiner*'s publisher during the Kennedy years, the paper was "historically a law-and-order newspaper that believed in a military strong enough to defend the nation against all aggressors. . . . It was against wasteful spending at all levels of government and deplored the burgeoning bureaucracy." The slogan

"America First" still appeared on the masthead, but the paper no longer shared the *Tribune*'s hostility toward all international commitments. Under the leadership of the younger Hearst, the chain had largely adopted the cold war internationalism of the Eisenhower wing of the Republican party. Although Hearst remained committed to "seizing the propaganda initiative" and combating communism, he had been impressed during trips to Russia in the 1950s by Premier Nikita Khrushchev's apparent pragmatism and sense of humor. But, like his father, who had demanded military action against Spain in Cuba in 1898, the younger Hearst considered Russian involvement in Cuba in the early 1960s an unacceptable affront to American honor.[28]

Both the Hearst organization, whose headquarters was in New York, and its San Francisco constituency affected the *Examiner*'s coverage of foreign affairs. Although the paper relied heavily on the wire services for routine news stories, the national office distributed editorials, columns, and stories written by Hearst reporters in Washington and overseas. Leading Hearst reporters and columnists like Serge Fliegers and Bob Considine tended to file stories characterized by a highly conservative, cold war orientation, and Marianne Means (one of only three Hearst reporters in Washington) emphasized human interest stories because she found that they were printed more readily than serious news analyses. According to Tom Eastham, the editorial page editor, San Francisco's diverse, cosmopolitan, and largely Democratic population may have moderated the *Examiner*'s conservatism somewhat; but the paper remained opposed throughout the 1960s to those in the Bay Area who, in Gould's words, "were for peace at any price and willing to burn draft cards and/or bras." [29]

In the absence of extensive foreign or Washington coverage,[30] the *Examiner* tended to rely on Washington columnists selected by chain headquarters both for the news items that appeared in its columns and for interpretation. The paper is especially valuable for this study because its use of columnists differed from that of the Washington-oriented press. At least in the case of Cuba, its selection of them was believed by an administration press analyst to be representative of the popular press as a whole. The *Examiner*'s internationalist, Henry Cabot Lodge Republicanism was valued by a president who had narrowly beaten an internationalist Republican in 1960.

In sum, the five newspapers differed substantially from each other not only in location and constituencies, but also in editorial direction, resources, and relationship to government. As parts 2 through 5 of this book show more fully, these differences profoundly affected the news coverage in the five papers. The single most important generalization emerging from the quantitative analysis for the three major categories of influence is that the two Washington-oriented papers gave more page-one emphasis to U.S. official and foreign sources, whereas the three outlying papers had higher percentages of domestic political sources (including members of Congress) and interest group sources. At the extremes in news coverage were the *Post* and the *Tribune*, which were mirror opposites as well in regard to such other factors as constituency and editorial direction. Whereas the *Post* used the highest percentage of U.S. official sources and the lowest percentage of domestic political and interest group sources, the *Tribune* used the lowest percentage of U.S. official sources and the highest percentage of the other two.

Within the U.S. official category, there was also a pattern of coverage that differentiated the Washington-oriented from the outlying papers. The *Post* and the *Times* source usage was strikingly similar in all categories, but quite different from the outlying papers, notably the *Tribune*. Reflecting its greater distance from the administration, it quoted close to 20 percent fewer unidentified officials and a markedly higher percentage of official spokesmen. The two popular outlying papers also quoted markedly greater percentages of military spokesmen (see appendix III). Analysis of source usage thus demonstrates that the papers differed not only in such obvious areas as editorial policy and choice of columnists, but also on the momentous issue of whose views were considered news.[31]

Part Two

The Laotian Crisis of 1961

The Laotian crisis of 1961 was the Kennedy administration's first major challenge. When Kennedy came into office, he found a civil war in progress. Throughout the Eisenhower period, the United States had maintained that the Laotian government had to be thoroughly anticommunist and pro-American. This policy was conceived in the State Department, and pursued by that agency's Far East desk and the CIA during the years when the Dulles brothers ran the foreign policy establishment. During the ambassadorship of J. Graham Parsons, this policy had led to the withdrawal of support, at a critical juncture, for the neutralist government of Prince Souvanna Phouma. Although supported by the British and the French as well as by a broad political spectrum of Laotians, the prince was suspect because his brother, Prince Souvannouvoung, was a communist who became, in time, head of the political wing of the Pathet Lao. And the Pathet Lao was suspect because it received support from communist North Vietnam.

After the Americans forced Souvanna Phouma out of power in 1958, the situation went from bad to worse. Pro-American governments relied primarily on the support of the military, which was paid by the United States. And the military was more interested in receiving paychecks than in combating the Pathet Lao, which gained in power as those who had formerly been gathered under Souvanna Phouma's neutralist wing fled into the northern provinces and joined forces with the communists.

The pro-American government in Laos sought in early January 1961 to provoke full-scale American military intervention on its behalf by crying the "wolf-wolf" of Chinese or North Vietnamese military intervention. Although there turned out not to be any North Vietnamese border crossers, the government of Premier Boun Oum, which was also called the Phoumist government of General Phoumi Nosavan, was in real trouble. Responding to his plight, the general launched an ill-fated offensive against the neutralist and communist forces to the north.

As Kennedy took office, pleas came from the U.S. embassy in Vietnam to support Souvanna Phouma, who was seeking by means of an international conference to end the fighting and set up a coalition government. This recommendation encountered stiff opposition in the State Department, where Parsons now was serving as Assistant Secretary of State for Far Eastern Affairs. Communist governments would be included in the conference, and communists probably would be included in the resulting neutralist coalition government headed again by Souvanna Phouma. Hard-liners in the State Department, the Defense Department, and the CIA did not find this alternative acceptable.

For purposes of this analysis, the Laotian crisis of 1961 has been divided into three periods. The first period began with Kennedy's inauguration, covered the early period of policy review, and ended 15 March with the United States threatening military action if the communists did not halt their advance against the retreating Phoumist forces. During the second period (16–31 March), the administration escalated the confrontation into one between America and Russia, sent U.S. warships into the seas off Southeast Asia, and tried to bluff Russia into convincing the advancing neutralists and communists to halt. The third period (1–15 April) was a tension-easing phase during which the administration backed off from this position and encountered the first interest in the issue on the part of domestic politicians.

During each period, different forces were at work that affected the relationship between the president and the press. These will be examined in detail. One primary condition, however, affected press coverage of the crisis as a whole: few Americans cared or knew anything about Laos, even to the extent of being able to locate it on a map. Southeast Asian studies had just begun in a few major universities. No one had fought with Laotian allies or had relatives there. No one had emigrated to the United States from there. Thus there was no domestic lobby on the Laotian issue. Throughout the Laotian crisis of 1961, expression of public sentiment in the press about the situation was virtually absent, either by individuals or by interest groups (see appendix I).

Chapter 3

The Press Puts Pressure on the President

22 January–15 March

The president on 22 January 1961 was altogether green on the Laotian issue. Quite a few people in the government knew more about Laos than he did. He was a newly elected president who had campaign debts to pay, a foreign policy bureaucracy to become acquainted with, and a policy to review. This was not a time for him to influence the press on Laotian issues, and it is not surprising that his first public reference to Laos was inconclusive. At his 25 January news conference, he called Laos "uncommitted," a term that could have had explosive repercussions had it been developed but that he did not define. Nor did anyone in the press ask him what the term meant. Kennedy, organizing a Laos Task Force and recalling his ambassador, inaugurated a period of policy review. But the president's role in relation to the press was not well defined. In the absence of public concern, no politicians dealt with the issue publicly. There were those in Washington and New York who did care about Laos, and a civil war *was* going on. Although the pattern varied by newspaper, this was to be a time of primary impact for nonpresidential forces.[1]

The Columnist Who Cared

Joseph Alsop was the member of the Washington press corps who felt strongly about Laos. Indeed, he felt so strongly about it that he wrote a "Dear Jack" letter to Kennedy prior to the inauguration informing the president-elect that he did not feel he could support the selection of Chester Bowles as undersecretary of state unless the president or at least Dean Rusk personally paid attention to Laos and the Congo:

I wonder if you've had time, among all your other pressing preoccupa-
tions, to keep in really close touch with the developing crises in Laos
and the Congo? . . . I feel I must ask the question because I have been
so shocked by the outlines of these two problems that I got from Dick
Bissell [of the CIA] today. Laos can quite easily become utterly unman-
ageable by January 20; the Congo is at least likely to become much less
manageable. . . .

I feel this all the more strongly because I have also gathered (though
not from Dick) that the campaign-paid liaison with Chester Bowles remains a significant channel of communication. All the Bowles sensitive
spots—India, the United Nations, what is called world opinion, and so
on and on—will be wrongly sensitized by the Laos and Congo crises. I
can't be happy about your verdict, therefore, unless you, or at least
Dean Rusk, have found time to study the fairly appalling relevant data
in person.[2]

It is clear that Alsop was performing a press agenda-setting function in a
rather direct way. Indeed, it would appear he believed the president owed him
something. Alsop intended either to collect the debt—that is, be assured that
Kennedy was giving top-level consideration to stopping Soviet inroads in
Laos and the Congo—or make difficulties in the press for the president on
another sensitive issue. The CIA had persuaded Alsop that the Boun Oum
government was in trouble and in need of further support from the new administration—a view he was quite willing to press on the president.[3]

The president did owe Alsop something: support throughout the campaign.
Kennedy had courted him assiduously during his time in the Senate because
he knew Alsop was an important columnist and he needed his help. Alsop was
one of the important press figures with whom the president would deal as he
now moved into a more powerful position in relation to the press. Once the
dependent campaigner, he was now the president, the dispenser of favored
information. In addition, he would deal with Alsop by means of what might
be termed subtle flattery. Kennedy could influence many journalists by using
the power of the presidency for this purpose. It worked especially well in this
case because Alsop was a part of the president's generation and a person with
whom he shared many values and views. Kennedy made Alsop feel that he
was present when critical issues were being raised and discussed.[4]

Alsop's view of this relationship is best summed up by the comment that he
saw the president "as much as anyone without daily official responsibility in
Washington." As he recalled in 1978:

Ours was the only private house in Washington that he used to come to
regularly until he died. Partly because I had the sense to call him Mr. President instead of trying to behave as though nothing had changed when

he became president, which is the most vulgar and second-rate thing a man can do; and partly because I had the sense to remember that when you are with the president of the United States . . . , you don't have anyone except what will give him pleasure. You don't have your rich aunt or editor of your paper or someone else who's going to benefit you. When you see someone privately, you don't turn the dinner party into a press conference, no matter how useful the person might appear to be. . . . The least thing you learn is what the mood is and how people stand, that sort of thing. . . . The other problem is remembering. They had the best wine at the White House that I've ever had at any house in Washington. It was very, very hard not to have an extra glass or so. You could forget almost the whole conversation.[5]

His contact with the highest levels of official Washington gave Alsop tremendous prestige. His articles reverberated with information provided by his high-level Defense, CIA, and White House contacts. He and Walter Lippmann were the ranking columnists of the period. He was valued by editors who favored a columnist liberal on civil liberties but military-conservative on foreign policy. His column was replacing in the popular press people like George Sokolsky and George Dixon, who had passed their prime or proved excessively conservative for the sixties. He was an important figure at the *Post*, as part of the social set that included Phil Graham and the president. His columns in the *Post* were, along with Sokolsky's, the major ones on Laos. His columns even appeared frequently in the nonmilitary oriented *Post-Dispatch*. His brilliant writing style and dramatic philosophy ("There is no such thing as a choice between good and evil. There is a choice between evil and more evil.") produced exciting newspaper fare. At the beginning of the Kennedy era, Alsop was, in Marquis Childs's phrase, "as hot as George Will is today."[6]

On Laos, Alsop was especially notable in the popular press. He was the only syndicated columnist concerned about Laos carried by the *Examiner*, which liked his hard-line approach to foreign policy issues. Alsop was also important on Laos with the press that carried Walter Lippmann, because Lippmann, his opposite number, carried less weight on Indochinese issues. He had not been there, he did not write many columns about the area during this period, and he tended to confine himself to occasional derogatory remarks about "paper pacts" in an area that the government was beginning to take seriously.

The president apparently satisfied Alsop that he was sufficiently concerned with Laos and the Congo during the early period of the Laotian issue. Indeed, according to Theodore Sorensen, Kennedy spent more time on Laos than on any other issue during his first one hundred days.[7]

The Popular Press Ignores the Issue

The *Examiner* during this early period allowed forty-five days to go by with almost no coverage of the events and opinions revolving about the country whose fate, President Kennedy contended on 23 March, "will tell us something about what kind of future our world is going to have." His diplomatic initiatives before 15 March rated two inside-page stories. Only when leaks started to appear suggesting that the United States might become involved in the area militarily, did the *Examiner* take notice. On 12 March its first page-one story reported a "Red" victory, the flight of the U.S.-backed government troops, and a Washington report that "President Kennedy has strongly urged Soviet Premier Khrushchev to halt shipment of Soviet arms to the rebels before the United States decides it is compelled to launch a counter-buildup of government forces." Greater emphasis that day, however, was given to seven-year-old Bobby Kennedy, Jr., who presented Shadrach the Salamander to the president.[8]

Why was there so little interest in Laos in a popular paper such as the *Examiner*? "Hell, no one was in the least interested," editorial page editor Richard Pearce noted later. "The public was not at all aware of Laos, and that includes me. We were not thinking in terms of little countries—just in terms of big power rivalries."[9]

The lack of public interest undoubtedly had its effect on the editors. That the *Examiner*'s first major interest in Laos was a response to leaks of American military moves was also not surprising. Hearst editors were interested in military issues, and the public was interested in the possibility of great power confrontation. In the absence of public interest, the low-profile activity surrounding policy discussion within the administration generated practically no news coverage (see appendix II).

The *Tribune* also ran few articles about Laos during this early period, again apparently because of lack of public interest. But *Tribune* reporters and editors had a firm conviction that they brought to this issue: no land war in Asia. Two weeks before Kennedy took office, Percy Wood, who had covered the fighting in Indochina and Korea in the late 1940s and early 1950s, wrote a lengthy article that presented the Douglas MacArthur view advising against such a war—especially in Laos, which was landlocked, lacking in airports, and far from American supply lines. Such articles, written from the experience of a reporter who had actually seen prior fighting in Asia, were rare in all five papers. This one corresponded to the views of the editors, who were reluctant to fight in Southeast Asia.[10]

On 27 January an article on the admission of lying by the American-backed Boun Oum government made Laos a front-page story in the *Tribune*. This embarrassing news received more attention than did the president's diplomatic initiatives, which rated only a page-eight article, and that was about Secretary of State Rusk rather than Kennedy. Clearly, the fact that the president was involved did not impress the *Tribune*. Even the presidentially inspired activity during early March appeared in the *Tribune* with no front-page and only two inside-page sources. Although the activity itself received little news coverage, it did provoke the paper's first editorials on Laos on 6 and 12 March. The 6 March editorial criticized the State Department while avoiding the issue of what the president was doing: "The State Department has left one important question unanswered. Why are we now threatening to use force in Laos, halfway around the world, to block Communist aggression while refraining from comparable threats toward a Communist-dominated Cuba, less than one hundred miles off our own Florida coast? To say this is not to say that our patience with Cuba is wrong, but that our declarations regarding Laos entail risks greatly disproportionate to anything we are likely to gain there." [11]

In short, in the absence of active public interest, the *Tribune* gave little coverage to the Laotian issue before 15 March. The nuances of policymaking in Washington were of little news value for this paper, which catered to a popular midwestern readership. The administration's diplomatic efforts did generate a few editorials that were generally negative, implying presidential weakness. [12]

The *New York Times* Takes the Lead

It was the *Times* that kept the issue alive during this period. Source and story counts alike indicate that the *Times*, because of its foreign policy orientation and sophisticated readership, had much more coverage of the issue than the other papers. Although the views of no interest groups were covered during the whole period of the Laotian crisis under consideration, some academic and foreign policy groups in New York, such as the Council on Foreign Relations, had an interest in Laos. Thus support existed for the *Times*'s coverage of faraway places, especially those where there was past or proposed American involvement. Indeed, this was the age at that paper of what James Reston later called "Afghanistanism": "If it's far away, it's news, but if it's close to home, it's sociology." [13]

Thus the *Times* was interested in Laos, and, alone among newspapers during this period, it had a reporter, Jacques Nevard, stationed in Vientiane. This gave the *Times* a semimonopoly on Laotian news. Public interest was not sufficient to support permanent Vientiane correspondents for other newspapers, which were satisfied to rely on the stories from news service reporters who were there along with Nevard. This put the *Times* in a position of potential power in relation to the president. It was to other newspapers what Alsop was to other columnists. Both were operating in a vacuum and consequently in a position to exert major influence on Indochinese questions.

During this period, the *Times* was primarily concerned with faithfully reflecting the views of the State Department and the CIA as debate swirled over the head of the president. The *Times* had two reporters on the story. One of these, State Department correspondent William Jorden, consistently reflected the views of the Far East desk. In this view, no sympathy was extended to Souvanna Phouma's desire to establish a neutralist government. In a page-one story on 4 February, Jorden argued that the formation of a government "claiming loyalty to former Premier Souvanna Phouma . . . in the area of Laos controlled by pro-Communist rebel troops" was "a discouraging sign concerning Communist intentions in Laos." [14]

Nevard was similarly oriented toward the State Department-CIA viewpoint. His approach varied, however, because his coverage originated from Vientiane. The American ambassador there, Winthrop Brown, was at the center of a challenge to the CIA-Far East Department perspective. He thought that U.S. support for the Phoumist government was a mistake. Its leader, General Phoumi, was overrated; he was both a poor general and a poor politician. Brown favored returning to Souvanna Phouma and the neutralists whom the United States had "emasculated," and Brown hoped that Kennedy might move in this direction. [15]

Although Nevard in his news coverage did not favor Brown's advocacy of a policy change, his reports did reflect something of the climate in the Vientiane embassy. In contrast to Jorden in Washington, for example, he reported favorably the formation of a Souvanna Phouma cabinet that included four pro-communists. "Experienced observers and well-informed persons here deduced that the move could mean that the Leftists were thinking in terms of negotiations," Nevard reported on 5 February. "These observers feel that the pro-communists have nothing to gain from setting up a regime except bargaining power in eventual talks." [16]

The *Times*'s editors were listening to the hard-liners in Washington; indeed, three of the five precipitators of editorials before 15 March were government officials (see appendix IV). Not long after Brown arrived in the capital, delighted with the opportunity to present pro-Souvanna Phouma views personally to Kennedy, the *Times* editorialized that "the creation of such a puppet regime is standard procedure whenever the communists attempt to take over a country." The United States, the paper argued, is willing to go along with any "promising proposals for a peaceful solution of the Laotian crisis. But as stated in its White Paper last month, it has called on non-communist nations to render any aid required by the legal Government of Premier Boun Oum appointed by the King and confirmed by a unanimous vote of Parliament." [17]

E. W. Kenworthy's comment "We were all hardliners then" is apt. *Times-*

men shared cold war attitudes with their constituency both in and out of government and with much of the public as well. They believed that, though action was required, Souvanna Phouma was suspect and that a Phoumist government might accept communist Chinese aid.

In fairness to the *Times*, it must be noted that the press generally treated Souvanna Phouma poorly. The *Times* at least quoted him, even occasionally at length. AP and UPI were the only other primary sources of stories about Laos for most of the press, and the shorthand they used in their stories left readers unclear about Souvanna Phouma's positions. One AP story, for example, explained his efforts to build international support for a peace conference as a "world tour . . . to sell a Communist-backed plan for a fourteen-nation conference." Such a conference actually was supported by France as well.[18]

The hard-line view prevailing in Washington also dominated the editorial pages of the *Times*, the only newspaper under study except the *Post-Dispatch* that was editorially concerned with Laos before March. Three out of five events-precipitating editorials were inspired by government officials—and the only criticism was of communist China (see appendix IV).

In the absence of domestic political interest in Laos during this early period, the president was quietly considering his options. In such a period, did the newspaper that was most concerned with the issue turn to foreign governments for different ideas on the news pages? The *Times* did not. The views of British officials were cited only three times, and French views only once. The *Times*'s main concern was the sober-sided business of keeping track of the communist threat. This took the form of an ongoing effort to determine whether the neutralist and Pathet Lao "rebels" were receiving communist aid.

This effort paid off at the beginning of March as reporter James Wilde visited Phong Savan in northern Laos and located a "massive Communist arms build-up," including the latest artillery and armor and communist leadership of the Pathet Lao. This lead article was accompanied the same day, 3 March, by an editorial which concluded that the buildup "can leave no doubt that the Russians plan to take over the area in the near future."[19]

Wilde's article had impact: it almost certainly contributed to the announcement of a stepped-up level of National Security Council meetings and a flurry of presidential activity designed to warn the Russians and the Chinese of American resolve. The president was not yet ready to make a public announcement of policy, but at least the issue was now out in the open.[20]

Although the precise influence of the *Times* on Kennedy's thinking cannot be determined, the president appeared to follow it in two ways during this period of the Laotian crisis. First, the news coverage and editorials gave support to the State Department and the CIA in the policy review that was underway during the period before the "threat" was discovered. The president came down on their side—and that of Joseph Alsop—rather than on the side of Ambassador Brown. Secondly, during the period after the *Times* located the threat, announcements of the National Security Council meetings on Laos and hints of military action began to appear.

The *Post* and *Post-Dispatch* Follow
the Administration Line

The most important writer in the *Post* on Laos was Alsop, and on 6 March he followed up on the agenda-setting activity of the *Times* by publishing a hard-line column on the subject. Kennedy had to act now, Alsop warned. The choice was either to surrender Laos to effective communist control, perhaps under cover of negotiations to "neutralize Laos," or to "escalate . . . by sponsoring intervention by the Thai army, by intervening ourselves, or in some other manner." Laos, Alsop argued, was "close to becoming another Korea . . . the price of surrender is the same as that faced by Truman had he ducked the Communist challenge." [21]

The *Post*'s only alternative voice on Laos was Keyes Beech, the veteran Asia reporter for the *Chicago Daily News* whose material appeared occasionally in the *Post*. From his base in Tokyo, he made periodic trips to Laos, resulting in some of the most graphic coverage of the situation in American newspapers. After accompanying the Phoumist forces into the field, he concluded that America was wasting its money and effort because the Laotian army was unwilling to fight. The soldiers were deliberately shooting over the enemy's heads and exploding their U.S.-supplied hand grenades in pools of clear water to catch fish. In an article published on 22 January, Beech criticized the American "decision to overthrow the neutralist regime of Souvanna Phouma," and reported that "a good many people, including the American embassy, would like to have Souvanna Phouma back in Vientiane." It is significant that Beech's article criticizing U.S. policy appeared during the period before the administration settled into a fixed position and in conjunction with the policy debate emanating from the embassy in Vientiane. [22]

Other than the Beech article, almost no coverage of alternative foreign views occurred in the period from late January until 15 March. Great Britain and Souvanna Phouma received only one source reference apiece, and the French viewpoint was not covered at all. As usual (see chapter 4), *Post* coverage of Laos was more strongly dependent on official sources than that of any of the other papers. It had virtually no reporters abroad, and its judgments on whether to use a Beech article or an AP story or nothing at all were based largely on its contacts with those in Washington who were experts, primarily government ones. The view the *Post* heard and printed was largely the hard-line official position.

Robert Estabrook, the *Post*'s editorial page editor during the Laotian crisis, recalled that his paper's "sources of information were very filtered through the government. Now I have no reason to believe that the desk officers at the State Department with whom I talked were talking a party line. I think they were giving it as they saw it." Estabrook also observed that not having a reporter stationed in Laos further isolated the *Post* from different viewpoints: "You know, you could come in on a week's visit, or something, but there was nobody stationed there. . . . I think there was a vacuum. I think it's really a great tragedy of American journalism because more accurate reporting might have opened our eyes. I can't be sure of that, because when we get in a jingoistic mood, we don't want to listen to anybody who's smarter." [23]

From the perspective of officials in Washington, even British and French views were suspect. Estabrook explained, "Well, of course there was the feeling that the British were really a little bit soft on Communism, and the French had their own purposes—they were trying to get back in. Only we had the word of the Lord about it." [24]

The lack of French coverage might also have resulted partly from a reluctance on the part of the French in Washington to promote their views. Estabrook, who at the time attended two or three embassy functions a week, reported, "I've never been in the French Embassy. I've never been invited, for some reason." Lacking any countervailing influences either in its constituency or among the politicians, the hard-line official point of view encountered little competition either in the news or editorial pages of the *Post*.[25]

Unlike the *Post*, the *Post-Dispatch* had been opposed to American involvement in Indochina ever since Dienbienphu, when Vice-President Richard Nixon called on the United States to intervene to save the French. During the Eisenhower years, *Post-Dispatch* editors were suspicious of American policy, which seemed to them to be evading the 1954 Geneva conference's call for elections. The leadership at the *Post-Dispatch* did not want to be drawn into another Asian land war as the result of American commitments to governments that did not represent the people.

In the fall of 1959 a communist Chinese "invasion scare" developed, promoted by the State Department and the CIA-supported Laotian government of Prince Phoui Sonanikone. Alsop wrote a column reporting that the Chinese were crossing the border to assist the opposition neutralists, and the specter of another Korea arose. *Post-Dispatch* managing editor Raymond Crowley decided to send a reporter to Laos. Richard Dudman, who says he barely knew where Laos was at the time, took off immediately. "It was principally some stories by Joe Alsop that got the managing editor all excited," Dudman recalled. "He [Crowley] decided that this was so important that we ought to get out there and either prove it or disprove it. And I disproved it." Dudman flew to the scene of the battle in a Laotian government-supplied plane, with "an Italian newspaperman and there might have been a Frenchman." They unearthed no Chinese. This experience confirmed the *Post-Dispatch* in its suspicion of unrepresentative governments in Laos supported by the CIA and the State Department.[26]

The *Post-Dispatch*'s news coverage, however, was severely limited by lack of resources. Like the *Post*, it had to rely on AP, UPI, and the *Times*. In the absence of public interest in the issue, it did not independently cover Laos as it had during late 1959 when its managing editor perceived a war threat. Dudman, on what may have been the one foreign trip that the newspaper could afford during the period, was in Peru exposing book scandals in the American aid program.[27]

The *Post-Dispatch*'s meager news coverage was confined to articles based on official and foreign sources. On the front page official views predominated. Despite unexceptional news coverage, frequent editorials kept readers abreast of the *Post-Dispatch*'s views. On 24 January, for example, an editorial argued that Kennedy needed to remember that there was much merit in Souvanna Phouma's position, and that American discouragement of his neutralist regime was responsible for the civil war that had brought the communists in the first place. The United States, the *Post-Dispatch* contended, needed to join Britain in seeking an international approach to the problem.[28]

By late February the administration was presenting a proposal for Laos based on what it called "true neutrality." The key administration concession to the neutralists was a proposal favoring the appointment of a three-nation commission that would oversee U.S. weapons shipments to the area—if the communists would agree to the same conditions. From the perspective of Souvanna Phouma and the Laotian neutralists, the proposal offered little, and its sterility was apparent when, almost at the time of its announcement, two of the neutral nations that the administration hoped would serve on the commission declined. The *Post-Dispatch*, however, welcomed this proposal as a "solution all sides can accept with honor." Its former concern for the neutralists, whose interests were being completely ignored in a neutrality plan that insisted on legality only to the Boun Oum government, was abandoned.[29]

Similarly, in early March after the *Times* had discovered Russian aid to the neutralists, the *Post-Dispatch* again supported the American position, placing the blame for the difficulties in Laos squarely on the Soviets. "Kennedy has sent a message reported earlier to Khrushchev [by British sources] that he wants a united, independent and neutral Laos. If the Soviet Union wants the same thing the means are at hand." Again, the *Post-Dispatch* did not raise the basic issue of how the president defined "independence" and "neutrality" and uncritically accepted the American position. When asked why the paper switched from support for Souvanna Phouma to support for administration policy, Robert Lasch, editorial page editor at the time, responded: "We weren't very darned familiar with Laos. We had no strong convictions. We were taken in by the president."[30]

Lasch's comment provides at least a partial explanation of why Kennedy was able to obtain the support of the *Post-Dispatch* editors for essentially the same policy that they had rejected under President Eisenhower. But other factors almost certainly were involved: public apathy, which contributed to its failure to send its own reporters to Laos; the failure of members of Congress or interest groups to develop alternative viewpoints; confusion over the meaning of the policy of "true neutrality"; and, under these conditions, the influence of the *Times*, whose resources were far greater both in Washington and overseas. Not as influenced in its news coverage by hard-line official sources as the *Times* and *Post*, the *Post-Dispatch* nevertheless proved unable to maintain its independent position on Laotian policy.

Conclusion

From this early period of the Laotian crisis, several generalizations emerge about the relationship between the press and the president. The primary external condition of this period, as of the Laotian crisis as a whole, was public apathy. The primary internal conditions were policy review on the part of a new president and a low-profile White House press strategy. To put it mildly, these conditions were not conducive to heavy press coverage of the issue.

Under these conditions, the differences were great between the way the popular press related to the president and the way the Washington and establishment-oriented press related to him. Only newspapers and columnists whose interest in foreign affairs was strong took much interest in Kennedy's Laotian policy during this period. A proadministration, Washington paper like the *Post*, which devoted few independent resources to foreign reporting, faithfully reflected dominant executive branch thinking. For a newspaper with the greatest resources and a constituency that required it to keep up with areas of U.S. involvement, like the *Times*, such a situation of public apathy and policy change improved its chances to serve the media's agenda-setting role. By giving heavy play to a highly interpretive news story concerning an issue the public and other media would consider a threat, the *Times* helped to shape public perception of the issues and thus put pressure on Kennedy to act. A newspaper having a semimonopoly on foreign news was at its most powerful in relation to the president in such a situation. Finally, a columnist like Alsop, who was well connected in the executive branch and enjoyed a semimonopoly position in relation to the popular press, also had substantial impact. He was able to exchange ideas with people in government who were advocating action and use his importance in the press to put pressure on the president.

The same forces at work on Kennedy were also influencing the rest of the press. In the absence of competing influences, the *Times* had substantial impact on the *Post-Dispatch*, whose meager resources prevented it from providing independent coverage of Laos in the absence of a war threat. Lack of resources and a supportive foreign policy-oriented constituency thus weakened the ability of relatively independent editors to challenge a president—especially a charismatic one who had the publisher's political support and the skill to formulate his policies in a way that was, in appearance at least, congruent with the editors' own views.

Chapter 4

The High-Visibility Hard Line

16–31 March

During the period from the middle to the end of March, changes occurred both in Laos and in the president's press strategy. On 11 March the neutralists captured Sala Phou Khoun, a key link between the two major Western-backed Laotian cities, and many of the Phoumist forces of the Boun Oum government fled to the mountains. Facing a bleak military situation, the president switched tactics. Beginning with prepared remarks on Laos at his news conference on 15 March, he adopted an activist press strategy: a White House-orchestrated public relations campaign designed to lend credibility to his tough stance. During the following week, he met with his advisers to discuss escalatory steps. This activity produced high-level backgrounders, leaks of a military alert, the decision to order fleet movements in the seas off Indochina, and the president's full-scale television challenge to the Russians on 23 March. It also produced more page-one and editorial coverage of the Laotian issue in the last two weeks of March than had appeared during the entire period from 22 January to 15 March. Aided by an overwhelmingly supportive press, the president told the Russians in effect that they must either act to halt the neutralist and procommunist advance in Laos or face the possibility of direct and massive Western intervention.

This saber-rattling was a bluff, for the president did not intend to go to war over Laos. "I don't remember any time when there was a decision to engage in military intervention in Laos—discounting what the undercover boys did," McGeorge Bundy recalled. "I have a vague recollection of an intense discussion in the National Security Council in which the president noticed that the only military people who were strongly in favor of intervention in Laos were the Navy people, and just where they were going to land wasn't clear." [1]

The press was not aware of these limitations on top-level thinking. Nor were the Russians, the Chinese, or the North Vietnamese whom the president was trying to impress, though they must have guessed what a serious predicament he faced in backing an army that did not want to fight on difficult terrain.

The range of options was limited because the administration was restricted to a choice among full-scale intervention in a rugged mountainous area that was not favorable for American troop movements, withdrawal, or trying to convince the neutralists to halt their advance while keeping them occupied with negotiations. The administration's first priority was a cease-fire. By the end of this period, the administration had learned that the attainment of this objective would require offering a "carrot" and talk of a coalition government. But at the National Security Council meetings on 20 and 21 March the administration decided to try bluffing first. The press was used as an instrument for this purpose.

Kennedy's public warnings about the communist threat in Laos led to increased public interest in the issue, but only on the level of generalized public opinion. The absence of alternative explanations continued; almost no politicians or interest groups formulated an interpretation of the Laotian issue that countered Kennedy's. Because the full resources of the government were now mobilized behind the president, the forces that previously had competed with the administration's definition of the threat in Laos—notably the *Times* and Alsop—could scarcely compete, even if they had wanted to. Under these conditions, the bluff worked.

Anatomy of a Bluff

On 21 March the *Times* published a page-one article declaring that the United States is "now prepared to take whatever steps are necessary to save Laos from Communist domination and to accept whatever risks are involved in such a policy." E. W. Kenworthy recalled how this story developed:

> I remember I was over in the State Department. . . . It was about 7 o'clock at night . . . and I didn't have a story. Suddenly I got a tip that there was a meeting going on in the White House. The Secretary had gone over and the Assistant Secretary for Far Eastern Affairs and the Undersecretary were all over there . . . I called up Wally Carroll . . . I said, "Wally, I haven't got a damned thing else but that." He said, "All right. We'll run back to the office and do a kind of hold-the-fort piece just to get some space. Here's a short story that will hold it meanwhile." So while I wrote that piece, Wally Carroll from home called that fraud Walt Rostow. Rostow told him, and I can remember with considerable accuracy: "We are resolved on a test of wills with the Soviet Union in Laos."
>
> What bushwah, but anyway he got Wally all excited . . . he jumped into his car and rushed pellmell to the office all the way from the District just over in Maryland . . . he took over the story leading with "We

are resolved on a test" and he's regretted it ever since. But Rostow would do this sort of thing. I can't remember a thing about Laos but that, and Wally is chagrined to this day about how he bit.[2]

Carroll was not the only one who bit. In a front-page story based on unidentified official sources on the day of the president's television challenge to the Soviets, the *Times*'s State Department correspondent William Jorden wrote: "The Western powers will present a new peace plan on Laos to the USSR tomorrow. It is viewed here as probably the final test of Moscow's willingness to work out a peaceful settlement of the Laotian struggle. . . . Officials feel time is running out."[3]

The same line of reasoning appeared in a Chalmers Roberts op ed story in the *Post* 18 March: "The most important development is the American military buildup both within and without Laos, backed by a determination by President Kennedy that there will be no backdown if a crisis develops. Those who should know say that Mr. Kennedy is in no mood for flinching."[4]

To hawkish Joseph Alsop, Armageddon was at hand. His 22 March column insisted that the forthcoming Rusk-Gromyko talks were a last-chance meeting. If they failed, he concluded, then the choice between "decisive surrender in Laos or a series of grimly risky moves" was unavoidable.[5]

Only the *Post-Dispatch*'s Marquis Childs initially took a different line. Consulting his sources and concluding that military intervention in Laos would not be justified, on 20 March he observed: "Since a fighting force . . . is not visible and supplying that force over a distance of many thousands of miles is hardly practicable, the alternative to allowing a rebel takeover is a threat of general war." He added, "Such a threat over Laos seems to some policymakers here slightly disproportionate."[6]

After the president's 23 March television speech, the Laotian issue assumed even larger proportions. By increasing the level of presidential activity and defining the Laotian situation as a crisis on nationwide television, Kennedy increased the volume of news coverage. In the case of the Hearst papers, it was the administration's bluff that alone moved the quiescent *Examiner* to action. From almost no coverage of Laos before 15 March, it shifted abruptly and gave the issue frequent front-page play. Not having developed foreign viewpoints previously, the *Examiner* was now heavily dependent on official sources as the crisis reached its climax.[7]

Favorable Editorial Reactions—Except for the *Tribune*

The president's public involvement also stimulated the Laotian issue's period of greatest editorial activity (see appendix IV). All the newspapers responded editorially to administration initiatives and to a Southeast Asia Treaty Organization (SEATO) conference that the United States called and that was making headline news. In addition, the Russians, the Pathet Lao, and, once in the case of the *Post*, the French precipitated editorial activity.

All the papers except the *Tribune* were directing their criticisms at the same culprit: the Soviet Union. The administration, the *New York Times*, and Joseph Alsop all agreed it was responsible for the difficulties in Laos. The *Post-Dispatch* was impressed that the president again mentioned the term "neutrality" and seemed to be using the threat of force to achieve a worthwhile objective. As before, it did not raise the issue of what he meant by neutrality or how he meant to achieve it by the threat of force. The other papers, which were more hard-line, were delighted to see him standing up to the Russians.[8]

In the area of columnist opinion, the president's speech impressed even *Times* military analyst Hanson Baldwin, who previously had thought that a Western defeat in Laos would not be a "loss" to anybody, so inchoate was the nation, so logistically open to subversion and lacking in strategic resources. On 26 March, however, he concluded that Laos had great strategic importance for the United States. It was geographically a buffer state whose fall would facilitate the "guerilla campaign now underway in South Vietnam and would expose Thailand and Cambodia to the same type of nibbling aggression."[9]

The *Tribune* stood alone in criticizing the administration. After the president's 23 March television address, it noted his warning to "the Russians and all other Communists . . . to cease their machinations in Laos." Otherwise "the United States certainly, and its allies insofar as Mr. Kennedy can commit them, intend to employ military force." The *Tribune* found those sentiments justifiable on the basis of actions taken by former President Eisenhower. The problem was that it was easier to make pronouncements "than to demonstrate that the United States has enough to gain to warrant the risk he [Kennedy] is taking that the Communists will not come to accept his terms." The *Tribune* further hoped that the Democrats would now cease their talk of "brinksmanship" because Eisenhower and Dulles had never played the game with quite the same careless abandon. And it put the final touches on its argument by observing that Nixon's famous statement—if the French quit the war in Indochina, the Americans should take over the fight—had "now been accepted as the wise course by the Democratic administration."[10]

In taking this critical stance, the *Tribune* was out ahead of most Republican leaders, who, led by Eisenhower, were congratulating the president for his strong stand. An exception was Barry Goldwater, who tempered his expression of support for the president with the concern that he lacked the "courage to follow through." It is not surprising that both the *Tribune* and Goldwater expressed doubts about Kennedy's Laotian policy, for both of these conservative Republican voices were already critical of almost everything the liberal Democratic president did.[11]

Editorial page editor George Morgenstern believed the *Tribune* took this questioning attitude primarily because President Kennedy "didn't provide any leadership." Morgenstern also recalled that General MacArthur's idea of "no-land-war in Asia" might have affected the formerly isolationist *Tribune*'s thinking. No commercial pollsters asked in early 1961 whether or not Americans were willing to fight for Laos, but the *Tribune* conducted a straw poll in downtown Chicago immediately after the president's television speech. Only one out of twenty-four persons responded unequivocally "yes" to the question "Should the United States go to war because of Communist penetration of Laos?" In addition to the political issue, the *Tribune* may thus have been reflecting the sentiment of at least part of its Chicago constituency in questioning the president's threat of war.[12]

Using the *Times* to Escalate the Bluff

Following the president's 23 March speech, the next major news story concerned British Prime Minister Harold Macmillan's meeting with Kennedy at Key West on 26 March. The British were concerned about Kennedy's saber-rattling, which to them was reminiscent of Dulles's talk of massive retaliation and Admiral Arthur Radford's plan, pressed hard on London at the time, for Allied intervention to save Dienbienphu, including the use of atomic bombs. The president, for his part, wanted a show of support on the part of the British. In this way, his threat to the Russians to either cease their intervention in Laos or face dire consequences from the West could be made more credible. Although the Kennedy-Macmillan meeting produced mixed results from the administration's viewpoint, its ambiguity was not apparent to the pro-administration press at the time. The *Times*, for example, gave the strong impression that the president had achieved his goal of gaining full British support for a hard-line policy.[13]

The relevant story was a page-one spread by the *Times*'s William H. Lawrence which reported that between the United States and Britain there was " 'absolute agreement' today on all aspects of a common policy to preserve a neutral Laos against threats of Communist aggression." This conclusion could not have been drawn logically from the communiqué resulting from the meeting, which only said that the two heads of government "agree that the situation in Laos cannot be allowed to deteriorate." What the two nations had agreed to do was left unsaid. Lawrence recognized this vagueness but drew his own conclusions from foreign reports about possible actions: "Mr. Kennedy and Mr. Macmillan did not say what their countries would do if the Soviet response [to the president's speech of 23 March and the Western request conveyed through the British for a cease-fire] was negative. Reports from Bangkok, Thailand, said that the United States would urge its Allies, including Britain, in the eight-nation Southeast Asian Treaty Organization, to agree to military intervention, if necessary, to preserve a free, neutral Laos." [14]

Another observation by Lawrence added to the impression that Kennedy had been successful in regaining firm British support for American policy in Laos. "It was said that Mr. Macmillan was impressed by the coolness and calmness his host displayed, and his careful consideration of the problem discussed," Lawrence wrote. "This impression was important in assuring the British that the president would not act precipitately." Although the phrasing is vague, it is possible to conclude from the story that Kennedy had raised the issue of military support for American policies, which is what was known to have prompted the meeting, and that the British had not demurred if the overall result of the meeting was "absolute agreement." [15]

British press spokesman Harold Evans was the only official in Key West quoted for attribution in the story. But at least the part of Lawrence's story dealing with Macmillan's impression of Kennedy came from a backgrounder in Key West with State Department official Charles Bohlen. Pierre Salinger selected favored members of the Washington press corps, including Lawrence, for the briefing with Bohlen. *Tribune* White House reporter Laurence Burd had flown with the presidential party to Key West, but was not included in this briefing. Neither were the reporters for the *Washington Star*, the *Baltimore Sun*, and the *New York Daily News*. Salinger told one of the reporters the meeting had not taken place, and he told Burd "that he was just doing what the British do, or something of the sort." Neither the *Post* nor the *Times*, which were included in the briefing, reported the exclusion of the other reporters. These proadministration papers may not have wanted to jeopardize their privileged relationship with government sources by drawing attention to this incident. [16]

The *Tribune*'s report did not echo the *Times*'s conclusion that the meeting had been successful. Instead, the major *Tribune* response to the Key West meeting was a scathing attack by Trohan on both Bohlen and the background news conference. Trohan called backgrounders "one of the most insidious avenues for implanting dubious and even deceiving information on an unsuspecting public." Such briefings, he contended, allowed both Democratic and Republican administrations to "peddle propaganda for which officials will not hold still for quotations." He also refuted the idea that the meeting had achieved the results suggested by the administration backgrounder: "Although none of those participating would authorize a quote on this fact, briefed reporters were induced to tell their readers, on their own responsibility, that the conference considered stronger action seriously." As Trohan implied, the conference did not necessarily decide in favor of stronger action. [17]

Among the papers covered in this study, the *Tribune* was alone in questioning the administration's line on the Key West meeting. As shown in its handling of the meeting, the administration had learned by this time to use the powerful *Times* to help to create favorable news coverage on Laos. In excluding Burd, the administration was operating on the assumption that the *Tribune*'s opposition would have little effect. The coverage in the other papers confirmed the validity of this assumption.

For most newspapers, therefore, the president's press policies were eminently successful during this period of heightened presidential visibility. Increased administration activity resulted in a dramatic increase of news and editorial coverage. The proadministration press positively helped the administration put the best face on its policies. The press that was less concerned about foreign policy issues, such as the *Examiner*, featured the administration's views almost exclusively in the absence of other groups in the society speaking out on the Laotian issue. Indeed, the coverage in all of the papers except the *Tribune* supports the view that lack of public interest greatly augments the president's powers in relation to the press in the foreign policy area.

While Kennedy was dominating the news about Laos originating in the United States, pro-American sources continued to predominate in the news printed under foreign datelines.[18] As the *Examiner*'s Richard Pearce recalled, interest in the small nations was slight, especially if they were halfway around the world and had little connection with the U.S. experience. In such a situation, the reports and views of American-supported foreign governments, strong-minded columnists, and the U.S. government itself carried the day.

Conclusion

Another set of generalizations about the relationship between the press and the president evolves from analysis of this two-week period. This period was characterized by a president who had brought his policies into conformity with the few, but dominant, forces in the administration and the press that had developed a position on the issue in the absence of public interest. In these conditions, Kennedy sought to use the press to help achieve a specific policy result.

In such a situation, where high visibility was desirable, the president's news-making resources far outstripped those of a leading columnist or, for that matter, of any other force within the society. Kennedy was able to define a foreign policy threat and focus on the administration's news-making activities. The threats and troop movements that only he was capable of inaugurating became the top news stories of the day. Because his actions were within the framework of acceptable public opinion on the issue and because no other forces in the society were giving specific definition to policy alternatives,

Kennedy was able to increase greatly the volume of government-oriented news coverage and favorable editorials. He was even able to bluff the most sophisticated newspaper, albeit a proadministration one, and use it to advance his version of a story with the rest of the press.

The exception to this pattern of press responsiveness to presidential influence was the *Tribune*, which combined resources, a conservative Republican and ethnic constituency at some distance from the administration, and strong editorial views developed during past periods of policy development. Conversely, a popular newspaper such as the *Examiner*—which lacked constituency as well as editorial interest in the issue and which consequently did not cover it prior to White House leaks defining it in a way certain to generate public interest—was most susceptible to presidential influence.

A high-visibility situation in which Kennedy used all the resources at his command to generate news was thus a time of major presidential influence. Lack of public and congressional involvement clearly enhanced the president's effectiveness during this phase of the Laotian crisis.

Chapter 5

The Politicians Discover Laos

1–15 April

By the end of March, it was clear that the administration's policy of bluffing and threatening the Russians was not halting the neutralist and procommunist advance in Laos. The administration would need to consider adopting the "carrot" approach in order to achieve a cease-fire there. A coalition government might need to be set up that would include Souvanna Phouma and some procommunists. The British favored this course when Kennedy met again with Macmillan at Key West on 4 April. Roving Ambassador Averell Harriman, who was trying to mediate the problem, also advocated it.

The president was aware of the potential unpopularity of a change in policy that might involve "concessions" to the communists. Consequently, he did not come out in favor of it. Its public espousal was left to Senator Mike Mansfield (D.-Montana), who noted on 29 March that Laos in the past had had a government in which communist sympathizers had participated and that communists had not taken over. It was also left to Prime Minister Macmillan who, following the Key West meeting, appeared before Congress to promote the coalition viewpoint. After Harriman also publicly supported a coalition government on 2 April, Senator Hubert Humphrey (D.-Minnesota) immediately denied that any "responsible Democrat" had advocated a coalition regime.[1]

Humphrey was responding to the Republican criticism that began to appear as soon as the possibility of a coalition government was broached. On 30 March the *Washington Post* reported that Senator Everett Dirksen and Representative Charles Halleck, the leading Republicans in Congress, had emerged from their weekly party congressional meeting saying that they hoped the United States would not agree to a coalition government in Laos that included communists.[2]

The comments of Democratic and Republican leaders marked the first appearance in the press of substantial domestic political commentary on Laos. It appeared after the *Times* and the president had sensitized the public to the issue of a Soviet threat there and the desirability of a strong American response. When the public is interested, politicians are never very far behind. The Republicans were now ready to hold the administration to its hard-line stance. Most of them did not agree with liberal Senator George Aiken (R.-Vermont) that Laos was the "worst place in the world to force a show-down with Soviet Russia." Republican criticism occurred amid stories from Laos of the crumbling U.S.-backed forces. From the diplomatic front came stories of communist delay. The administration's bluff had not worked: the Soviets were either unwilling or unable to press the neutralists and procommunists to accept the Western cease-fire proposal.[3]

Kennedy Weathers the Apparent Shift in Policy

The president faced a difficult situation. Anti-Souvanna Phouma views that were strong within the administration had been passed on to the press even up until 1 April. General Lyman Lemnitzer, chairman of the Joint Chiefs of Staff, opposed Souvanna Phouma at a 29 March briefing at the Max Freedman-Robert Estabrook Background Dinner Club. Charles Bohlen two days previously had told journalists that a coalition might theoretically work if cohesion existed on the noncommunist side, but that it did not now.[4]

Kennedy now had to both bring his administration into line and persuade press and public alike that a coalition was a feasible option. The answers are not yet available on how the first task was accomplished because of the still unopened record of debate within the administration. Arthur M. Schlesinger, Jr., has argued that Kennedy's tough line in Vietnam represented "a de facto deal with the national security establishment: if it went along with neutralization in Laos, he would do something for resistance in South Vietnam."[5]

It must also be remembered that the coalition government was not intended to be the sole answer to the Laotian problem. Covert assistance continued to sustain a pro-American entity in an ostensibly neutral country. Ambassador Brown, who participated in the negotiating process during April 1961, later said of this coalition government: "Of course it didn't work. It wasn't intended to work. The way Mr. Harriman put it to me on a number of occasions was, 'we must never face the president with the choice of abandoning Laos or sending in troops. This is our job, to keep him from having to make that choice.'" What in effect happened, Brown continued, was a de facto partition of the country that could never have been negotiated.[6]

In such a delicate situation, it is thus not surprising that the president and his advisers approached the press primarily through the background briefing. And, despite switching to a more conciliatory position at a time when cold war feelings ran high, Kennedy's tactics vis-à-vis the press worked: the president was able to switch policies after trumpeting the communist threat with very little criticism. The only major criticism came from the opposition *Tri-*

bune. "In Laos after much bluster the President has enunciated the terms of a deal which will find favor with the Communists," the *Tribune* editorialized on 8 April. "The history of similar coalitions suggests that the Communists inevitably take over; so the Kennedy formula is little better than a preparation for surrender." [7]

Kennedy had been damned for threatening the Russians. Now he was damned for not threatening them. This *Tribune* response suggests how quickly a president can get into hot water over a foreign policy issue. It also illustrates the ironic intensity of feeling of the conservative political opposition, which wanted the United States to "win" the cold war, but at no cost.

The *Examiner* and the *Post* were the only other newspapers that were editorially critical of the administration as this policy switch began to occur. The *Examiner*'s criticism did not amount to much. In its only editorial focusing primarily on Laos in the first half of April, on 6 April it lamented the fact that "Laos is a Communist victory" and "more than $300 million is going down the drain," but it did not criticize Kennedy directly.[8]

The *Post*'s editorial position and that of its major foreign policy analyst shifted as a result of direct presidential intervention. The story of how this happened demonstrates a president's ability to influence a leading newspaper by means of an interview. Estabrook wrote the two strong editorials that preceded the presidential intervention. "Dallying on Laos," written on the day following the 27 March Bohlen backgrounder, followed Bohlen's lead and saw disadvantages in a coalition government. It concluded that "in the last analysis the thrust must be met in Laos if the free countries are to retain any credence and bargaining ability." On 6 April the *Post* ran a second Estabrook editorial entitled "Where is the Victory?" suggesting that the administration should acknowledge a substantial setback. Estabrook, a hard-liner at the time, recalled his views: "I had seen in Vietnam the Viet Cong's effort to disrupt what the AID mission was doing and I knew about the Pathet Lao and some of the difficulties." [9]

On 28 March, the day "Dallying on Laos" appeared, Chalmers Roberts wrote a front-page news analysis that was both early in detecting the switch in policy and inferentially critical. He suggested that the "solution" that was now in sight, "a coalition government which will almost certainly contain Communist leaders," would be independent "unless and until the Communists subvert the government and take it over completely." "The United States," Roberts concluded, "has all but accepted the Soviet terms of last year for a Laotian 'solution.'" [10]

On 6 April Kennedy invited Roberts to a backgrounder at the State Department that was primarily for radio-television editors and commentators. The president spoke of his difficulties with the Laotian army and about the possibility of North Vietnamese and possibly Chinese intervention if the government collapsed and the United States intervened. The geography of Laos was difficult, he noted. After all, the French had had 400,000 men in Indochina and could not hold it. Kennedy nevertheless reaffirmed his determination not to let an insurgent group win in Laos.[11]

On the following day, Roberts was granted an interview with the president. As Roberts explained,

> . . . in discussing Laos with me, Kennedy said that he felt that an article of mine and a *Post* editorial had been too hard on the administration—not inaccurate but too hard. Three other articles in the *Post* from Laos by Warren Unna he praised effusively as showing the kind of situation with which he had to deal. His argument was that the situation was so unfavorable that to get a coalition government would not be a bad outcome. After all, he said, there had been Pathet Lao in the government before and you, the press, ought to point that out.

Nevertheless, Roberts recalled, the president stated that, if force proved necessary, he would put in enough troops to hold the line regardless of Republican charges of "Democratic wars." He clearly was irritated by the criticisms of his Laotian policy by Dirksen and Halleck, Roberts noted. Kennedy proceeded to remark "that a quotation of Walter Bedell Smith's that I had recently reprinted was exactly apt. JFK told me he had given it to someone on *Time* magazine, and asked if I had seen, as I had, that *Time* had just used it as a favorite Kennedy quote. Smith, then Under Secretary of State, had commented on his return from the 1954 Geneva Conference on Indochina, 'It is well to remember that diplomacy has rarely been able to gain at the conference table what cannot be gained or held on the battlefield.'"[12]

This interview illustrates two of Kennedy's traits that worked to his advantage in dealing with the press. The first was the use of his extensive knowledge of press coverage. In talking with reporters, he could comment on specific editorials and news stories. Secondly, he made effective use of subtle flattery, as when he let Roberts know that he had been so impressed with his knowledge that he had passed one of Roberts's insights on to *Time* magazine as his own. If a president indicates that he admires and approves of a journalist's work, his criticisms are likely to be more acceptable and influential. Few journalists could resist presidential charm under such conditions.

Following this talk with Kennedy, no more unfavorable editorials on Laos appeared in the *Post*. One on 13 April contended that there was no need for all the "groans" over the possibility of a growing relationship with Souvanna Phouma. And a favorable editorial on 20 April noted: "He has faced ugly reality in Laos. His willingness to accept a genuinely neutral government plus his determination to intervene militarily if necessary are essential to a stabilization."[13]

Roberts's tone also changed. In a half-page news analysis for the Sunday section on 9 April, he noted that Kennedy did not think that the Laotian problem "would consume so many of his waking hours." Although the United States had sought and was continuing to seek to contain communism, "the West is overextended in attempting to hold a free world position in Laos." But Kennedy, Roberts averred, could not cut the West's losses and get out; the domino theory then indeed might turn out to be valid. Instead, Roberts wrote approvingly, the president had "attempted to find a common Allied position, to accept the idea of a neutralist government for Laos and once again to contain the communist advance." [14]

A final factor needs to be mentioned that may have contributed to the president's success. Like at least parts of the national security bureaucracy, the hard-line press was reconciled to the president's new diplomatic policy on Laos by the "discovery" of Vietnam. Having gone to Bangkok because of a high-level tip-off amid rumors of military action just prior to the president's 23 March television address, Joseph Alsop stayed to observe the SEATO conference and to consult with Thailand's Marshal Sarit. By 11 April he was in Vietnam observing elections and in Ben Tre in Ken Hoa Province. He went into the field with Colonel Hung to observe communist troops trying "to take over the province." With the brave South Vietnamese troops he "found an area of the world which positively inspires hope." It is not clear how he became diverted from the urgent Laotian issue onto Vietnam, but diverted he was just as the administration itself was turning its attention to Vietnam and to the imminent Bay of Pigs invasion. South Vietnam was the endangered part of Southeast Asia that had soldiers willing to fight and a coastline and airports where the United States could land the men and supplies that were soon to be committed there. [15]

If Vietnam seemed a way out of the Laotian dilemma for Alsop, it must be remembered that others were also arguing the importance of Vietnam at the time. Senator J. William Fulbright (D.-Arkansas) sent a memo to Kennedy on 24 March suggesting that "the extent to which you might be willing to go in defending Laos could possibly be influenced by the stability of Vietnam. It would be embarrassing, to say the least, to have Vietnam collapse just as we are extended in Laos." Fulbright may have been trying to dampen the fires over Laos stirred up by journalists like Alsop. But the convergence on the area from opposite poles in the Washington spectrum is striking. The people who did not have any opinions about Vietnam were the American public, who knew no more about Vietnam than they had about Laos at this critical stage in the development of American involvement in Southeast Asia. [16]

What the Sources Show

It is clear that the Republicans faced a formidable opponent. What success then did they have in getting their views across?

Analysis of domestic political sources for the period 1–15 April shows they had precious little. If both front and inside pages are considered, the coverage of the politicians was greater when they were responding to Kennedy's initiatives during 16–31 March than was the case during 1–15 April when the Republicans made Laos a political issue. In the first half of April, only seven domestic political sources made page one—and five of these were in one newspaper, the *Post-Dispatch*. Laos was not even a page-one story in the *Tribune*, which might have been expected to make this a major political issue if any newspaper did.[17]

Republican views were found more frequently on inside pages, where they were quoted by all papers a total of ten times. Republicans received the least coverage in the *Times* and the *Examiner*, both of which quoted them only once on the front page and not at all on inside pages; they received the most coverage—still only five page-one sources—in the *Post-Dispatch*. Coverage of Democratic sources was even more sparse. Whereas on page one the balance was fairly close between coverage of Democrats (46 percent of the total) and Republicans (50 percent of the total), on the inside pages the Republican sources were utilized three times as frequently as the Democratic, though the total figure is small (see figure 1).[18]

Thus, in terms of making Laos an issue by generating news coverage, the Republicans did not achieve much success. Hubert Humphrey's characterization of the sporadic criticism as "guerilla warfare" was apt. An *Examiner* story entitled "Laos Deal Critics Still Sound Off" epitomized the general disparagement of the criticism.[19]

U.S. officials clearly were the group being listened to in early April. Despite Kennedy's decreased visibility, total U.S. official source usage remained almost as high as during the previous period. Only one major change occurred within this source category. As figure 2 shows, an increase in unidentified official sources on the inside pages compensated for a loss of military sources as compared to late March. This reduction occurred as the top-level, saber-rattling ceased and the issue became more diplomatic and political. The increase in unidentified official sources—especially in the *Post*—confirms the impression of increased reliance by the press on backgrounders by the president and other administration officials.

Did foreign sources present a challenge to the administration's position at the height of the Laotian crisis? Judged by percentages alone, they should have: they comprised 50 percent of all page-one sources and 57 percent of all inside-page sources during 16–31 March, and 53 percent of all page-one sources and 70 percent of all inside-page sources during 1–15 April. But, as figure 3 shows, the foreign sources were dispersed into a large number of fairly evenly divided categories, led by U.S.-backed Laotian, pro-Western Asian, Great Britain, and Russia. Thus, whereas the administration publicly was united in its policy in late March and early April, newspaper readers were

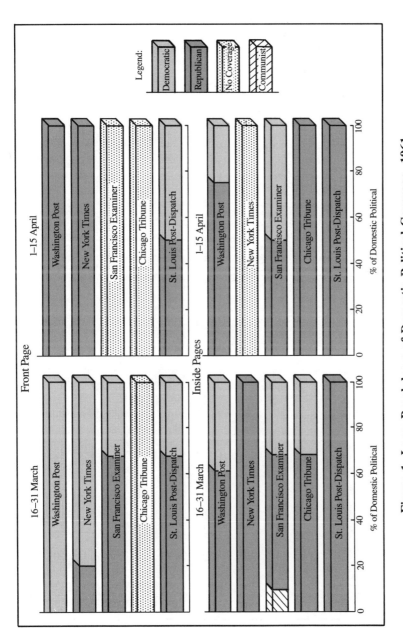

Figure 1. Laos: Breakdown of Domestic Political Coverage, 1961

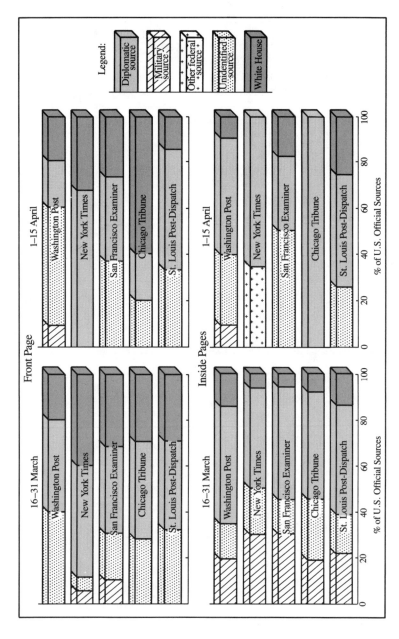

Figure 2. Laos: Breakdown of U.S. Official Coverage, 1961

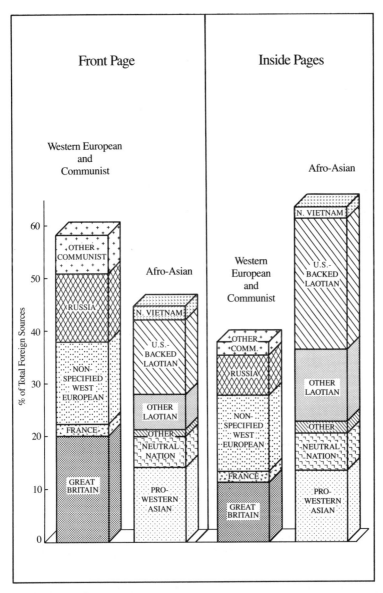

**Figure 3. Laos: Breakdown of Foreign Sources, 16 March–15 April 1961
(Total for All Papers)**

confronted with a cacophony of foreign viewpoints that limited the impact of any one of them.[20]

The administration was aided by the prominence accorded U.S.-backed Laotian and other pro-western Asian sources on both the front and inside pages. Asian neutralist and other Laotian sources (which includes Souvanna Phouma and the Pathet Lao) received very little coverage by comparison. North Vietnam, whose actions over time proved to be critical to any resolution of the dispute in Laos as in South Vietnam, had only a 2 percent source figure. Although the Russians received considerably greater coverage, their opinions and those of other communists—especially the mainland Chinese—tended to be discounted in advance.

The administration created news coverage for pro-Western leaders by sending high-level missions to Allied nations or by publicizing conferences of their leaders. Secretary of State Rusk, for example, flew to the Far East at the end of March to attend a SEATO conference, where he urged the Allies to take military action if the Soviets did not respond to an American appeal for a cease-fire. The major Far Eastern-based reports in the press were on the U.S. position and support of it by the prime ministers of Thailand, Pakistan, and other Allied nations, who responded warmly to the American call for action against the communists.

Other reasons account for this emphasis on pro-Western sources, some relating to the cold war legacy of mutual distrust. Reporters were often not welcome in neutralist and procommunist countries, whereas American reporters tended to be welcome in countries that received U.S. aid. These factors made it harder for them to obtain the views of neutralists and procommunist Asians. And, because of a State Department prohibition in 1957, American reporters were not permitted to travel to mainland China. For whatever reason, this tendency of the press to look to pro-Western Asian nations, including the Boun Oum government in Laos, reinforced the official view.

The second major foreign source category during the Laotian crisis was Western European. Britain ranked high within this category because of its repeated efforts to achieve a peaceful settlement. The news that did appear about the British generally consisted of routine, nonprobing reports of diplomatic activity. Although at the time disagreement existed in British circles about the results of Dulles's Laotian diplomacy, American newspapers did not report it. The British also tried to conceal these views at the top level insofar as possible because a new president was on the scene who offered the possibility of a change in policy.

France received only 2 percent of the source coverage on both front and inside pages. The French supported the neutralists and were viewed by many officials with suspicion. Something of the official attitude appears in Estabrook's notes about Bohlen's remarks at a background luncheon: "The French have been a problem all through the history of recent problems in Laos. They have a 'dog in the manger' attitude about the Indochina peninsula. They think we're wrong and they're right. De Gaulle has just released an interchange of letters with Norodom Sihanouk in which de Gaulle says that Sihanouk has been right throughout. The French did very little to train the Laos army under the genie of an armistice and what they did 'wasn't worth a damn.' "

Administration officials clearly were pushing an anti-French point of view. In the absence of pro-French countervailing forces among the politicians, in the public, or among interest groups, the official viewpoint prevailed.[21]

One final factor contributed to the failure of the British and the French to advance their points of view: they had no support on Laos among the leading columnists. Indeed, Joseph Alsop actively worked to discredit the British and French points of view. On 13 March he commented on the growing "get tough" mood within the administration and described the British position as "politely concealed surrender." He was recently asked why he felt the British were wrong in their thinking about Laos: "They didn't think much about it, and they happened to be represented by fools on the spot who took their line from the French. And the French were exactly like dogs in the manger. They didn't want anyone else to pull off what they had been unable to pull off, and they had this ludicrous vision of a sort of 'mission civilatrice' of their own." William Jorden of the *Times* asserted that British vacillation had been responsible for Dien Bien Phu.[22]

The newspapers differed in their foreign source usage. The *Times*'s largest category by far was "unspecified Western officials." This has been counted as a European category, though it may also include some U.S. officials. Reflecting greater depth of coverage, the *Times*'s total European source figure was 56 percent, nineteen points higher than average (see figure 4). As in the U.S. official category, the *Times* had greater access to high-ranking sources who did not want to be quoted. The *Times* also quoted Laotian sources more than the average, on both front and inside pages.

All the other papers in this study, which used primarily wire service material, were more reliant on American-backed Laotian sources than was the *Times*. The *Post* was especially dependent on this source category both on the front and inside pages. The *Post-Dispatch*, whose foreign source usage was high, used primarily British and pro-Western Laotian sources on the front page. This reliance on pro-Western sources occurred despite whatever reservations the *Post-Dispatch* editors may have continued to have about the Boun Oum government. Significantly, however, in view of its editorial attempts at international understanding, on the inside pages it gave more than average coverage to the neutrals.

None of these differences in foreign source usage, however, altered the reality of domination by U.S. officials of the news coverage in all five papers in

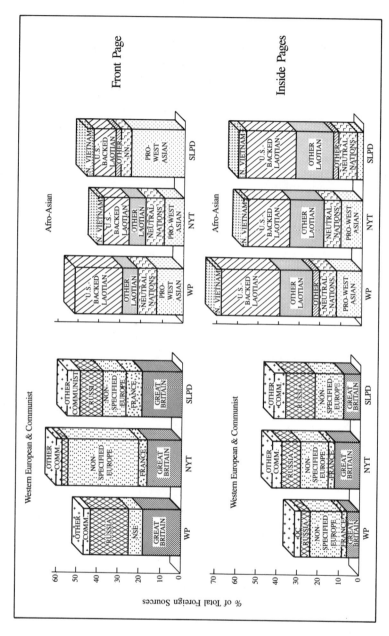

Figure 4. Laos: Foreign Sources, A Comparison of Three Newspapers, 16 March–15 April 1961

Table 3. Laos: Comparison of Official and Nonofficial Sources, 1961
(front-page totals for all newspapers)

	United States Official	Domestic Political	Foreign	Interest Groups	Total Domestic Political and Foreign	Percentage U.S. Official Represents of This Total
22–31 Jan.	11 (58%)	0	8 (42%)	0	8	138%
February	12 (56%)	0	9 (43%)	0	9	133%
1–15 March	5 (31%)	1 (6%)	10 (63%)	0	11	45%
16–31 March	93 (43%)	16 (7%)	109 (50%)	0	125	74%
1–15 April	50 (41%)	7 (6%)	65 (53%)	0	72	69%

the 16 March–15 April period. Just as no political figure in Congress or elsewhere effectively challenged the president's shifting position, so no foreign leader stimulated any of the editors to question administration policy as it evolved in late March and early April.

Conclusion

The 1–15 April period of the Laotian crisis makes possible the generalization that under conditions of public apathy a president could use a much less visible press strategy to achieve a similar result to that achieved during a high-visibility period. During late March, Kennedy had proved his cold war credentials to the small segment of the public that had been sensitized to the issue as well as to interested persons both in the press and in the administration. He had met the requirements of the influential forces at work on the issue partly by taking a hard-line public position and partly by switching interested journalists and officials off onto another issue—Vietnam—that was mutually agreed upon as being important.

When sources are analyzed for the crisis as a whole, it is clear that the only difficulty the administration experienced came during the early part of March (see table 3). This is because the initiative that has been discussed in terms of the dominant *Times* coverage shifted abroad. With the administration's high-visibility, hard-line policies during late March, the president clearly regained the initiative and remained in control during early April, despite the increased difficulties stemming from a potentially embarrassing policy change toward neutrality and the emergence of a political opposition. This was accomplished by means of a changed press policy that involved the use of unidentified officials giving backgrounders. In the absence of both public interest and an effective challenge in the press from abroad, this policy worked as well for Kennedy as had the high-level television address. No newspaper made Laos a political issue in its news coverage. Except for the *Tribune*, an opposition newspaper, no editorial criticism was able to withstand the president's techniques of persuasion. Given conformity of his policies with the main lines of domestic opinion as expressed in the press and given the continued use of effective press strategies, he was able to weather a policy switch with little difficulty.

Difficulties for the president on the Laotian issue came only after the failure of American policy at the Bay of Pigs became known about 20 April. Then the public was aroused, and the opposition could cite Laos as "another failure." Khrushchev was also encouraged, both by Laos and by the Bay of Pigs, to step up his pressure on Kennedy. But that is another story.[23]

Part Three

The Berlin Crisis
of 1961

From its inception, the Berlin issue involved a direct confrontation between the superpowers. During the summer of 1961, the issue was whether Soviet Premier Nikita Khrushchev could change the status of East Berlin, which technically was governed by the four powers under an agreement negotiated after Germany's defeat in World War II. The four powers were the United States, Russia, France, and Britain. The East Germans were not pleased with this arrangement because it left an enclave of free enterprise and propaganda right in the middle of their territory.

It had not been intended that a peace treaty would never be signed ending this postwar arrangement, the Soviets and East Germans argued. But the West Germans strongly opposed the signing of such a treaty, for their policy called for the reunification of Germany. The United States had worked to build West Germany into an anchor of the Western alliance and supported the West Germans: there should be no peace treaty because it would involve acceptance of the communist government and negotiations on such issues as access rights with East Germany. The United States and the West Germans led the Allied effort after World War II to maintain the status quo, backed by the similarly hard-line French. The British, uncertain about the consequences of a reunited Germany, wavered, but supported their more hard-line Allies on critical issues. The East Germans were in a quandary. For them, a free city in West Berlin meant the loss of their citizens in increasing numbers through the open borders into West Berlin and along the access routes into West Germany. By the late fifties, they were suffering a considerable population loss among their most talented citizens, thus exacerbating their growing economic difficulties.

Khrushchev had raised the issue of a peace treaty with Eisenhower. Indeed, he had presented him with an ultimatum on the issue in 1958. The president had met with Khrushchev and discussions had begun, but these were aborted as a result of the U-2 incident of 1960. The Berlin issue was also complicated because for years there had been an emotional defense of the status quo on the part of U.S. politicians and government officials. It was also complicated by the fact that Soviet efforts to support the East Germans had taken a form that Americans and West Germans had interpreted as a Soviet threat. The Berlin airlift of 1948, for example, was hallowed in memory as a heroic American effort to keep the brave West Berliners from being sucked into the yawning jaws of the communist monolith. Russia's suppression of freedom in its satellite countries in Eastern Europe had enhanced this impression. Applying the "lesson" of Munich that any evidence of weakness could invite miscalculation or conquest, the U.S. foreign policy establishment proudly had defended the status quo in Berlin since the end of World War II.

The American public was also deeply involved with the Berlin issue. There was general knowledge of where Berlin was and a strong consensus had formed that the United States should keep its troops there, that no concessions should be made to the Soviets, and that America should go to war if either the Soviets or the East Germans attempted to cut off the access routes.

Support was greater for a policy of going to war to maintain the status quo in regard to East Berlin in the West and the Midwest than in the South and East. This feeling reflected the conservatism that included a "liberation" emphasis and was stronger in the Midwest, where ethnic groups that had emigrated from Germany and Eastern Europe were strongly involved emotionally with the issue. But Germany and Eastern European issues had a constituency throughout the United States. Two world wars had been fought there. America's security was tied to Europe's. The sons of ordinary Americans were still based there. "People could identify with the issue," Richard Pearce, the *Examiner*'s editorial page editor, recalled. "At that time we had 200,000 to 300,000 troops there. Berlin touched most families." In late June, George Gallup found that 76 percent of his sample had already "heard or read" about the Berlin crisis; by late August, after Kennedy's dramatic television address and the building of the Berlin Wall, the figure had risen to 90 percent, an unusually high percentage for a foreign policy issue.[1]

This greater American involvement with Berlin went beyond generalized public opinion to an involvement on the part of domestic interest groups, especially patriotic groups like the American Legion and the Veterans of Foreign Wars (see appendix I). During June the commander of the American Legion, William R. Burke, toured the country giving speeches and press conferences. Before Kennedy's speech of 25 July few interest groups were pushing either the press or the president toward negotiations on the issue.[2]

Partly as a result of this public interest, the need for covering news of Berlin was recognized, and all the newspapers in this study either had correspondents there or could send them easily from their European bases. No one newspaper nor any one columnist could have the impact either on the press or the president of the *Times* and Joseph Alsop during the Laotian crisis. A number of journalists knew a good deal about Germany and had been expecting a crisis in Berlin. The young president who went to meet Khrushchev at Vienna on 3 and 4 June did not recognize the difficulty of the terrain.

Chapter 6

The President Experiences a Setback

1–23 June

In early June 1961, Kennedy stepped waist deep into hot water. The inexperienced young president, hoping to redeem his prestige in the wake of the Bay of Pigs fiasco, accepted an invitation from Khrushchev to meet at Vienna. At this summit, Khrushchev insisted that if the Western Allies were not interested in entering into negotiations leading to the signing of a peace treaty with East Germany, the Soviet Union would go ahead and do so on its own. The treaty would establish a free city in Berlin and automatically terminate Western occupation rights. The Russians would not interfere in the internal affairs of the West Berliners, but they would need to negotiate new road and railway rights for goods and people crossing the territory of the henceforth sovereign German Democratic Republic. In the memorandum that Khrushchev delivered to the president, he further insisted that he would sign the peace treaty within six months.

The possibility of such an ultimatum could well have been anticipated. But Kennedy was psychologically unprepared for it, was overpowered in the encounter with Khrushchev, and emerged considerably shaken. It was impossible to hide this fact from Prime Minister Macmillan, whom the president visited immediately thereafter in London. Macmillan advised him that the important thing was not to drive Khrushchev into a corner where he might feel trapped and react with violence.[1]

Macmillan's advice differed from that of de Gaulle and Adenauer, who subsequently categorically refused to enter into any talks. Khrushchev, they argued, would certainly exploit any such admission of weakness. Thus, when the president returned home, he had a war threat on his hands, a divided alliance, and no strategy for dealing with Khrushchev other than his retort at Vienna: "Then it will be a very cold winter." He also knew that, given the lack of planning during the Eisenhower years for limited conventional wars, any war with the Soviets could quickly escalate into nuclear war.

Kennedy went to Vienna hoping for new prestige as a result of a top-level summit meeting, and, possibly, a new policy breakthrough to demonstrate his success as a statesman. He emerged with a policy setback and no clear direction on how to proceed with an issue of great public concern. The Vienna summit thus inaugurated a period of difficulties in relation to the press that were compounded by a muddled press policy. His press operation was so bad that it prompted a German correspondent traveling on the continent to inquire whether "the Republicans had not infiltrated the operation to discredit the Democratic President." [2]

Attempted Cover-up or Just Plain Inept Press Policies?

The press was alerted to the Kennedy-Khrushchev differences over Germany by James Reston, whom Kennedy granted an exclusive interview after the Vienna meeting while Charles Bohlen briefed the rest of the working press on the "amiable nature" of the meetings. Pierre Salinger also presented the Bohlen line to some of the "important byliners." Reston divulged the results of his interview in a spread-top, page-one exclusive on 5 June that mentioned the president's "somber" assessment of the German situation as a result of the meeting, but gave no word of the ultimatum. Joseph Alsop also acquired an insider's view of the situation when he encountered a visibly shaken president in London. Alsop recently described the scene at the reception following the christening of one of Kennedy's nieces:

> In comes the president looking very gray. I happened to be standing near the door. The president hadn't seen me in Vienna. I really didn't know what had happened in Vienna. Scotty Reston did, but naturally it horrified him so that he didn't write about it properly. The president backed me against the wall and said, "I just want you to know, Joe, I don't care what happens, I won't give way, I won't give up, and I'll do whatever's necessary." It was a little chilling among the duchesses and the champagne. I hadn't the vaguest idea that there was anything to give way or to give up about. I knew there was pressure on Berlin, but I didn't know there had been an ultimatum.

Alsop did not publish his impressions of this encounter. [3]

After returning to Washington, Kennedy briefed congressional leaders and made a 6 June television report to the nation that stressed the seriousness of the Berlin issue but did not mention the ultimatum. It was thus through leaks that the press obtained the rest of the story. AP correspondent Jack L. Bell described how he learned more about it:

> Well, at Vienna they had the usual communique. They didn't say any-
> thing really . . . "informative, amiable meetings" and so forth. So
> after he got back, Kennedy had the Congressional leaders down to the
> White House to tell them what Khrushchev had said. So I made the
> rounds of these people to see who would tell me something. Three or
> four refused to tell me anything. It was a state secret and all that stuff.
> Finally, I called Hubert Humphrey out. . . . Hubert told me what
> Khrushchev had said, in great detail. Not only on Germany, but the
> bone in the throat, Berlin. . . . The only time he [Khrushchev] raised
> his voice was about Berlin. . . . I was amazed at the detail Humphrey
> recalled. . . . I don't think he [Kennedy] had ever run into a buzz saw
> like this before . . . words didn't mean the same thing.[4]

But the Bell story did not mention the ultimatum. In fact, he wrote that Khrushchev had "fixed no date" for signing a separate peace treaty, which he described as an unchanged Russian "position of more than two years stand-ing." Bell even mentioned that the bone-in-the-throat phrase "has been em-ployed before." The "so what else is new" quality of the story, whether deriv-ing from Bell, Humphrey, or misleading comments by Kennedy to the congressional leaders, rated it space on page fourteen of the *Post*.[5]

Something of the seriousness of the Berlin situation leaked through Senator Dirksen to the *Tribune*—though again the ultimatum was not mentioned. Thus, when news of it reached the West as a result of the publication by the Soviet news agency *Tass* of Khrushchev's Vienna memorandum, it was page-one news. Khrushchev thought that Kennedy was suppressing the news and decided to release it himself. But, although to the *Post* and the *Times* the Rus-sian announcement was a relatively routine news story, to the *Tribune* it was a revelation of something the president had withheld.[6]

Because a Soviet threat was involved, the president's fumbling of the Vi-enna story fed the fears of conservative Republicans. Kennedy's first diffi-culties came in the Midwest, which was particularly sensitive to the Berlin issue. On 16 June at O'Hare Airport, Senator Barry Goldwater charged the president with a weak response to Khrushchev. Goldwater was on his way to a $50-a-plate political luncheon in Rockford, Illinois. The *Tribune* rushed to report his remarks. And the *Tribune*—suspicious of summit meetings since the time of Roosevelt—soon itself raised the issue of presidential giveaway, if only by analogy to the Teheran conference of 1943.[7]

The *Post* was also upset about not learning the full story at Vienna—but for professional reasons. Its leading foreign affairs reporters, Chalmers Roberts and Murray Marder, had accompanied the president to Europe, where they wrote widely read reports from Paris and Vienna. Roberts related what happened on their return: "I complained to Phil, I guess. It was very embarrassing to get scooped by Reston." [8]

On the weekend following Kennedy's return from Vienna, Phil Graham spent the weekend at the president's Virginia farm with Alsop and two of the State Department's leading Berlin experts, Bohlen and Llewellyn Thompson. Graham presumably obtained a good deal of the story then. That same weekend, Roberts recovered sufficiently from his embarrassment to write a *Post* op ed piece that put the best light on Kennedy's trip. The president's point of view had a way of reaching the *Post*:

> There is now a lot of criticism about town that the administration does not seem to have a coherent plan and that the President is not evangelizing the American public to do what it must—indeed, that he has not told the public what to do.
>
> This is not quite fair. . . . The President's trip to Europe demonstrated how much the Western Allies look to him for leadership. His own remarks show how well he understands the problems of the free world. Perhaps this weekend of reflection will help him to sort out his thoughts on how to mobilize the nation. [9]

The president did not seek to mobilize the nation, at least not for the next eighteen days. For he was ill with his back ailment for several days after returning from Vienna. And, for a whole month, until 28 June, he did not hold a press conference, partially because he did not want to appear on crutches, but apparently also because he did not know what to say about Berlin.

Rusk largely took over coordination of policy as well as press relations on the Berlin issue. He told Khrushchev that the United States would respond in writing after consulting its allies. He also commented publicly on the issue on 22 June, saying that the Soviet ultimatum would not change Allied policies but also leaving open the possibility of negotiations. [10]

An Interagency Task Force was charged with contingency planning and the president awaited the recommendations of a panel chaired by Dean Acheson. The process of seeking an Allied position on the Berlin issue was also begun. This was a difficult process that continued until 18 July. The fact that policy review took place at this initial stage, when an undecided president was making no public statements on the issue while gathering Allied views on a Soviet threat, strongly affected the character of the news and opinion during June.

The Initiative from Abroad

During June the news initiative shifted abroad. This shift was reflected in the source figures for the 1–23 June period, which showed that foreign views on

Berlin had their greatest influence on the American press, with the sole exception of the Berlin Wall period during August (see appendix II). It was also reflected in the fact that the major columnists during the period devoted a great deal of their attention to promoting or discrediting foreign views. During Laos the columnists' discussion had responded primarily to differences within the administration. Now, because it was clear that American policy was to be formulated in reference to Allied views, Allied governments competed to have their views heard by the U.S. press and president alike.[11]

The Russians and the East Germans took and retained the initiative as far as foreign source coverage was concerned. What they said was perceived as threatening, and, perhaps because the adversarial is news, what the Russians and East Germans said came to dominate the news. Collectively, they received top billing. Individually, each ranked second only to the views of the West Germans who, aided by their interest to the American public for historic and economic reasons, were quick to project their views during the entire crisis (see figure 5).

The *Times* on 14 June published a story from West Germany that embarrassed the American government. It reported that the United States was moving toward negotiations with Khrushchev on the German issue. Upon whose information this story was based is unclear, for only "diplomats and officials in Bonn" were cited. It is well to recall, however, a comment by E. W. Kenworthy that in such a situation one might "look to see who's angry." Certain West German officials were upset about Kennedy's weakness at Vienna and were concerned that he might in his weakness negotiate away too much on Berlin. And, if the sources were not West German officials, the story could only add to West German worries and American discomfort.[12]

If the *Times* could print a story from West Germany that put the United States in an unfavorable light, the more conservative popular press could favor West Germany editorially. During this period, *Tribune* editors, who believed that West Germany's free-enterprise system was superior to America's, supported the West German position on Berlin. The trip abroad of editor-in-chief William Randolph Hearst and his Hearst Task Force, which started at Vienna and continued with European interviews, demonstrates how West Germany influenced the news and gained the editorial advantage in a paper like Hearst's *Examiner*. Significantly, in view of the forthcoming battle between the unhappy British and the more hard-line governments of Germany and France, the task force selected only hard-line officials to interview: West German Chancellor Konrad Adenauer, Berlin Mayor Willy Brandt, and French Premier Michel Debre. In addition, Hearst obtained written interviews with East German communist leader Walter Ulbricht, Francisco Franco of Spain, and Antonio de Oliveira Salazar of Portugal. Before presenting Ulbricht's written remarks, Pierre Huss, a Hearst correspondent and a member of the task force, summarized them by saying that the "goat-bearded" Ul-

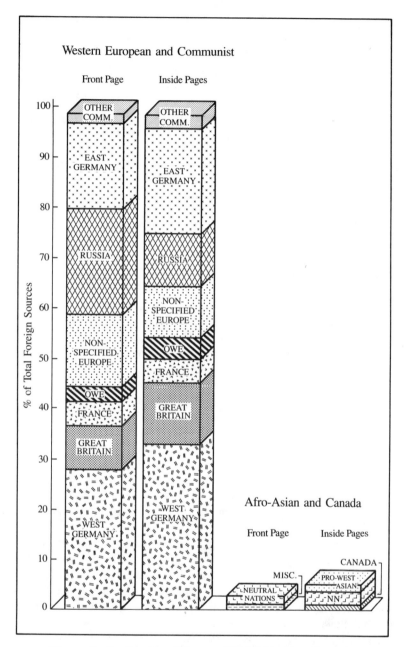

**Figure 5. Berlin: Breakdown of Total Foreign Sources
for All Papers and Periods Combined**

OWE = Other West European

bricht "outlined today the kind of Germany he has been ordered by Soviet Premier Khrushchev to bring about by hook or by crook." [13]

These comments grossly misrepresented the impetus behind the move in Berlin. It was Ulbricht who pushed Khrushchev to raise at Vienna the issue of a peace treaty; it was Ulbricht who precipitated the Berlin crisis because his country was losing skilled workers. The *Post-Dispatch* recognized his responsibility, as did Flora Lewis of the *Post* and some of the German-based writers for the *Times*. But the Hearst view was more typical. By viewing Khrushchev as a dangerous revolutionary and responding primarily to the Soviet threat, Hearst and his colleagues were easily swept up by the emotionalism present in Germany. "We can 'appease' our way out of the developing crisis," Hearst editorialized on his return, "but let's face it: The world will recognize that we have backed down in the face of Communist pressure and our national prestige may be compromised for all time." [14]

As figure 5 also shows, the British, who were in a quandary on the Berlin issue, experienced much more difficulty getting their views into the press throughout the entire crisis, especially on page one. The British were committed to a strong defense of Berlin. But British public opinion did not want to see Germany reunited, fifty million strong, and consequently become a powerful rival. There was also concern in Britain that German nationalism was on the march—its symbol being Franz Joseph Strauss, who, as Marquis Childs of the dovish *Post-Dispatch* commented, "with his zeal to get nuclear weapons . . . seems to foreshadow a new drive for ascendancy that will let nothing get in the way." Many Britishers believed that negotiations were necessary on the Berlin issue and sympathized with Khrushchev's view that the postwar agreements had been intended to be temporary. [15]

Before the British government could formulate a public position and while the president was still flat on his back, Alsop—who was again almost the only op ed commentator on the issue in the *Examiner* and important at the *Washington Post* as well—opened with a salvo designed to wipe the British off the face of the map. The root of the problem, he contended, lay in past American failures to respond to Soviet threats with military measures and in the "open British willingness to compromise at Berlin and the constant British refusal to make hard commitments about Berlin defense." After discussing stepped-up U.S. military planning on Berlin, Alsop concluded with a final slap at the British: "Serious consideration is also being given to seeking sole Franco-German-American agreement on a tripartite approach to British Prime Minister Macmillan, with the hard question: 'Are you with us, or do you mean to stand aside?' " [16]

The British reportedly were "stung" by this attack. On 15 June the *Post's* Robert E. Baker reported the semiofficial British response that their position was as strong as any in the West. Although British leaders were prepared to go to war to preserve Allied rights in Berlin, he reported, they believed that, contrary to the West German view, negotiations were not synonymous with concessions and that world opinion would insist on negotiations as the crisis intensified. As for Mr. Alsop's hard question, British authorities pointed out that President Kennedy and Prime Minister Macmillan had recently stated that they had reached "full agreement" to defend Berlin, Baker concluded.[17]

Two days later, Lord Home, Britain's Foreign Secretary, appeared at a luncheon in Chicago to "counter the rumourmongers who are starting up their presses again over Berlin." Britain, he said, might not "always choose to express our opposition to Communism in the military context," and balance-of-payments problems might force a cutback of British troops in Germany, "but we stand with the United States of America in the front line against aggressive, expanding Communism." The *Tribune*, which had been leading the "rumourmongers" in Chicago, was briefly satisfied.[18]

The matter did not end then for the *Tribune*, however, for, toward the end of June, unidentified sources in the authoritative *Times* of London proposed negotiations as the middle ground between the Gaullist position of paying no attention whatever to the Russians and the other extreme of stepping up military preparations to convince Khrushchev of the seriousness of the situation. The *Tribune* seized upon this proposal as well as suggestions in British newspapers that East Germany should be recognized as evidence of a common source for all weakness on the Berlin issue: "the British government itself." A Foreign Office spokesman expressed surprise about this charge, and Prime Minister Macmillan the same day publicly took a firm position.[19]

The intensity of the British government's feelings about its treatment in the American press—particularly by Alsop, who was believed to be reflecting White House views—was summed up in a memo that Prime Minister Macmillan sent to Queen Elizabeth in August when he thought the long ordeal was over:

> On the question of Berlin, . . . Your Majesty will have seen from recent telegrams that the Americans are, as I expected, getting off their high horse. They would, of course, like to put the blame for this upon us, but I think the Foreign Secretary has with great skill protected himself and our country from this accusation. In spite of the efforts of journalists known to be very close to the White House, the vigour of the attack upon us has much decreased, and I think they will find it difficult to pretend that the President's desire for negotiation is due to the weakness of the Allies.[20]

Marguerite Higgins was another influential hard-line columnist on Berlin. She had won fame for her reporting from Germany in the early postwar years, and she had developed an emotional investment in the West German leadership. In addition to helping to "discover" Adenauer at the end of the war, she had worked for Axel Springer, publisher of Germany's largest newspaper chain. One of the few highly successful female American journalists, she had made her way by means of charm, grim determination, and occasional ruthlessness.[21] A staunch Cold Warrior, she was a friend of Robert Kennedy and her ties were close with Vice-President Lyndon B. Johnson and the military. Higgins, who had no qualms about marching in and talking with Robert Kennedy or his brother, the president, experienced no trouble obtaining a hearing in an administration that was as sensitive about press coverage as Kennedy's was.

The effect of Higgins's writing during this period of presidential indecision was to provide important support for the hard-line West German viewpoint. In a column on 19 June, for example, she emphasized the doubts German leaders would not express in public about America's willingness to defend Berlin. "Why do we doubt?" an unidentified high German official asked. "Not because of anything that President Kennedy has said or done about Germany. . . . But elsewhere, in Laos for instance, the president has said something was the last straw, then retreated."[22]

The only influential defender of the British was Walter Lippmann, Alsop's arch-rival on Berlin and other issues. Lippmann was held in high regard, especially by liberals, for his broad knowledge of contemporary issues, and many would have agreed with *Look* magazine's assessment that he was "America's foremost political philosopher and commentator." But he was not as close to Kennedy personally as were Alsop and some other reporters. In fact, when Lippmann criticized Kennedy for not being a "good teacher" on public issues in a television broadcast in late May, the White House virtually cut him off. "They never protested to me," Lippmann recalled, "but after that, it was over."[23]

The views of the seventy-one-year-old gray eminence seemed to smack of defeatism to many of the new generation then making their way in Washington. A May 1961 letter to Arthur Schlesinger from Henry A. Kissinger, who, ironically, was later to build a foreign policy based on many of Lippmann's premises, illustrates both the need to react to Lippmann that was felt among those who sought to advise the president and the nature of some of the reactions: "I was outraged by Lippmann's column on Tuesday. I thought the personal comments very low. In addition it is really disingenuous for someone who is opposed to the defense of Quemoy and Matsu, as well as Berlin, to argue that we should not get involved in Southeast Asia lest we weaken the defenses in Quemoy, Matsu and Berlin."[24]

Although Kennedy respected Lippmann and read his columns regularly, he blamed some of his problems in dealing with Khrushchev on him. Peter Lisagor, the *Chicago Daily News* Washington bureau chief, recalled a visit he and chief European correspondent William Stoneman had with Kennedy:

Bill [Stoneman] was a real kind of a militant patriot abroad. Kennedy actually had spoken awhile about how he viewed the German problem, the Berlin problem and a few others. Bill was pleased, and he said, "Why that's wonderful, Mr. President. That's exactly what I think ought to be done." Or something like that. And Kennedy then shrugged and said, "You know what our policy is but the Russians read Walter Lippmann. They read Walter Lippmann and Khrushchev reads him. I know Khrushchev reads him, and he thinks that Walter Lippmann is representing American policy. Now how do I get over that problem? It's a problem that's been in this town for many years, of course."

A bit of patriotic hewing of the hard line was expected of "responsible" journalists. The president conveyed this view to the press that summer, but Lippmann did not follow the rules.[25]

Lippmann's views on Germany paralleled those of the British. His first reaction after Vienna was to urge negotiation. He believed conditions had changed since the signing of the postwar agreements that called for German unification and divided Berlin into sectors administered by the four powers. The decision to make West Germany an armed member of the North Atlantic Treaty Organization (NATO) had integrated the Federal Republic into the West, thereby rendering reunification impractical. Many violations of the four-power agreements on the status of Berlin had been tacitly accepted. Therefore it was important, Lippmann argued, to renegotiate the legal status of the area in keeping with the power changes that had already taken place.[26]

At the end of the month, Lippmann criticized both West German Ambassador Wilhelm Grewe and Kennedy. Lippmann countered the ambassador's conclusion that "West Berlin cannot, in the long run, be held if its population must come to the conclusion that the West has in fact accepted the division of Germany." Lippmann also remarked that the current crisis derived not from Khrushchev but from Kennedy's failure to offer proposals on the Berlin issue, which had allowed the initiative to be lost to Khrushchev. Lippmann might have added that the initiative had been lost to the West Germans and their supporters in the press as well. For, as Kennedy began to take a position in late June and July, it was clear that he was rejecting Lippmann's suggestions and moving toward acceptance of the hard-line position.[27]

The Newspapers Also Choose Sides

During this period of presidential weakness, the columnists thus selected their favored foreign power and championed its cause on the op ed pages. The same sort of partisanship occurred on the editorial pages of almost all the newspapers, as editors also developed positions. In some cases, columnists were included because they supported the editors' position or neutralized each other. Partisanship was also evident in sources utilized as the different newspapers followed widely varied patterns of source usage that in some cases corresponded to their editorial positions. This partisanship was evident in the use of foreign and government sources.

During this period when foreign sources were having their major impact, the *Times* and *Post* gave relatively greater play to official sources than the other three papers. In fact, alone among the newspapers, the *Post* had more page-one official sources than foreign sources during the 1–23 June period (see appendix II). But in both papers the effect of the front-page news coverage was to lend support to the government and ease the pressure from abroad.

These two papers were also editorially most supportive of the president during the period. The *Post* criticized the government only once during the whole Berlin crisis, in August (see appendix IV). The *Post*'s only criticisms during June and July were of the Soviets, the East Germans, and once each for the West and the Republicans. Over the period of the whole crisis, it more single-mindedly directed its criticisms at the Russians and the East Germans than did any other paper except the *Times*.

In the *Tribune* and the *Examiner*, in contrast, criticism of the Russians and the East Germans was implicit. They directed their overt barbs at the administration. During this period of the Berlin crisis, these two conservative popular papers launched a strong editorial challenge to the administration. This was in fact their period of greatest editorial criticism of it.

The *Post*'s way of dealing with the British viewpoint was to ignore it editorially. During this early period, as throughout the crisis, British actions precipitated no editorials—nor did the *Post* criticize the British. The Germans were also ignored editorially during June. It was on the op ed page that the lively debate occurred over the Berlin issue. Alsop and Lippmann slugged it out with three columns apiece, and Childs joined them with three columns, one of which presented the British view and defended Senate liberals, such as Mansfield, who were trying to make their voices heard. From London, Robert Baker also backed the British. Roscoe Drummond took the opposite position.[28]

Although the *Times* on its news pages used a greater percentage of British sources during this period than did any of the other papers, its editorial position did not soften. The editors again followed the hard-line stance in the administration which paralleled that of West Germany and called for a tough response to the Soviet Union. During this period, the hard-liners felt that the United States should counter the Soviets with an immediate military response. An early expression of this view was floated by Alsop, who called for a speedup of United States contingency planning—again, no doubt, seeking to put pressure on the administration. The *Times*'s editors picked up this theme immediately. They also called for reaffirmation of "greater Berlin" and the use of the German-backed idea of reunification as the starting point for any Western response.[29]

Unlike the attitude at the *Times* toward Laos, there was substantial diversity of viewpoint on Berlin. Germany was an area of major European concern, the *Times* and the constituency it served had long been involved there, and different forces abroad affected the paper in varied ways. No united pro-German constituency could be found in New York. Indeed, one German expert who was in the administration at the time and the *Times*'s assistant foreign editor both believe that the *Times* had an anti-German bias that stemmed from the World War II experience. Whether or not this view is valid, it is clear that different forces—domestic, foreign, and governmental—were at work on the newspaper.[30]

Among the columnists, C. L. Sulzberger, writing from Paris and London, took the perspective of one familiar with liberal thinking in those countries. He contended that reunification was not possible and argued that some agreements with the Russians in regard to Berlin would be in the interest of both sides. He urged Americans to "shed the idea that no negotiation is possible, and that the status quo must be kept precisely as it is."[31]

Krock raised the unmentionable issue as far as the Germans were concerned: why had not access to Berlin been legally specified in the four-power agreements? Reston made no mention of "greater Berlin" or "reunification" and took an unperturbed attitude toward Khrushchev, whom he believed was not interested in war. Reston sided with the soft-liners who, deep in the innermost councils of the administration, were considering an economic response should the access routes be cut off. Reston noted that Khrushchev was probably most concerned about the refugees and concluded: "A dangerous mood has developed that we can do nothing except get ready for a fight; that Khrushchev is working on a military and not on a nonmilitary strategy. Chances are he is doing nothing of the kind. Having tried persuasion in Vienna and failed, he is now trying intimidation. The problem is to see that this fails too without getting in a panic about his angry threats." The only writer who truly represented the hard-line position on the op ed pages was *Times* Soviet expert Harry Schwartz.[32]

For the *Post-Dispatch*, the initiative in news coverage was coming from abroad. A major characteristic of its source coverage was the high level of West German sources used on page one (see appendix III). This was clear evidence of the success of the West German effort to have their views presented in the American press. But editorially the *Post-Dispatch* found no appeal in the West German viewpoint. The paper accepted the view that Khrushchev had precipitated the crisis. Its first reaction to Khrushchev's fireside speech, however, was to call for negotiations that "would guarantee the West's safety in West Berlin and Russia's safety to the East." It approved

Rusk's statement of 22 June, which it interpreted as proving the administration's willingness to talk. The *Post-Dispatch* in fact criticized no one during this period, and simply hoped for the best as far as negotiations were concerned (see appendix IV).[33]

On the op ed page it was clear that the editors favored the flexible European position. During July they began reprinting editorials from British newspapers calling for negotiations and columns by C. L. Sulzberger offering bargaining points on Berlin. One of his columns promoted a French suggestion as his own: "How about exchanging recognition of Latvia, Estonia and Lithuania and the Oder-Neisse line on Soviet terms in exchange for reaffirmed guarantees of West Berlin's freedom until Germany is reunified?" The *Post-Dispatch* also printed three columns by Reston, but did not print any by such hard-line columnists as Alsop and Higgins.[34]

Unlike the *Post* and *Times*, therefore, the *Post-Dispatch* presented a consistently soft-line viewpoint in its editorial and op ed coverage. But the pressures on the president to adopt a hard-line policy were reflected in its news coverage, and they were reflected even more strongly in the news and editorial coverage of the other four papers.

The Conservative Republican Challenge

The partisanship that appeared in June in all the papers and that challenged the president resulted not only from foreign and intragovernmental influences; it also came from growing Republican criticism of Democratic "softness" in dealing with Russia. Although this criticism was much less intense than it was to be during the Cuban missile crisis fifteen months later, it was considerably stronger than it had been on Laos, and it remained a concern of the president up until the 1962 elections. In June 1961 the Republicans (and their journalistic supporters, the *Tribune* and the *Examiner*) felt more knowledgeable on the Berlin issue than on Laos, and the Bay of Pigs fiasco in April had ended the honeymoon period of limited criticism of the new president's foreign policy. Kennedy's silence and confused press strategy, combined with an impolitic speech by Senate Majority Leader Mike Mansfield, during a period when the administration was in fact considering negotiations, opened the gates for the Republican attack.

Like the British and Lippmann, Mansfield believed that the West should take the initiative because Khrushchev was a political leader with whom one could deal. In a Senate speech on 14 June, Mansfield proposed that the West negotiate to make Berlin, both East and West, into a free city, a proposal that would have involved renegotiating the postwar agreements. Although Mansfield consulted neither with Kennedy nor with other Senate Democrats before presenting his proposal, leading Republicans quickly jumped on it as proof of

Democratic confusion and weakness in foreign policy. The *Tribune*, which did not run as a news story the speech in which Mansfield made the proposal, did publish an editorial the next day suggesting that the proposal was a trial balloon signifying administration weakness.[35]

On 21 June Richard Nixon provided a widely publicized commentary on the Mansfield proposal. In Laos, Nixon commented, Kennedy "talked big and backed down when the chips were down." At the Bay of Pigs, "we committed our prestige and failed at the critical moment to commit our power." And now the "Administration's top leader in the Senate" had "seen fit to suggest weakness rather than strength of will about Berlin by recasting one of Khrushchev's own proposals for making Berlin a 'free city.' "[36]

In the sharp three-day Senate debate that erupted over the issue, Republicans repeatedly criticized the Mansfield proposal and questioned the administration's firmness in foreign affairs. Senator Goldwater, who led the charge, was on the cover of *Time* the week after his initial attack on Kennedy's policies and during the period of the Senate debate. He was quoted as urging greater strength vis-à-vis the Russians and was not only termed "the political phenomenon of 1961" but was also mentioned by GOP Chairman William Miller as a favored presidential candidate for 1964. This was a blow to the president, who valued *Time*'s mass audience, read every issue, and took particular pains to use all his powers of personal persuasion to influence its coverage. Under Miller's leadership, the national committee also lashed out at the president's policies. Even liberal Senator Jacob Javits (R.-New York) called the Mansfield proposal "inopportune."[37]

Both in editorials and in news, the Republicans were getting the best of the coverage. Only the *Post-Dispatch* commented favorably on Mansfield's proposal, and both the *Tribune* and *Examiner* published editorials sharply critical of the administration. The *Times*'s page-one story emphasized that Mansfield delivered the speech before an empty house, thus implying that the idea was totally lacking in support. Editorially, the Republicans were criticized only in the strongly proadministration *Post* (see appendix IV).[38]

Analysis of news sources for the period shows that 67 percent of all domestic political sources on page one and 64 percent on inside pages were Republican. The Republican challenge was most pronounced in the *Tribune*, which quoted only Republican viewpoints in early June, and in the *Examiner*. Conversely, the two papers that most strongly disagreed editorially with the Republican position—the *Post-Dispatch* and the *Post*—had the smallest percentages of Republican sources. Except for the *Times*, editorial positions on Berlin and the papers' general pro- or anti-administration stance clearly appear to have affected the selection of domestic political sources during this period.[39]

Although partisanship of a specifically Republican-Democratic dimension did not continue to influence news coverage after this period, ideological par-

Table 4. Berlin: Comparison of Official and Nonofficial Sources, 1961
(front-page totals for all newspapers)

	United States Official	Domestic Political	Foreign	Interest Groups	Total Domestic Pol., Foreign, and Int. Grps.	Percentage U.S. Official Represents of This Total
1–23 June	56 (36%)	27 (17%)	74 (47%)	0	101	55%
24–30 June	23 (40%)	5 (9%)	29 (51%)	0	34	68%
July	170 (44%)	113 (29%)	104 (27%)	0	217	78%
August	213 (34%)	20 (3%)	397 (63%)	0	417	51%
September	109 (42%)	12 (5%)	141 (54%)	0	153	65%
1–6 October	24 (42%)	2 (4%)	31 (54%)	0	33	73%

tisanship did. Over the remainder of the two crises involving the greatest level of domestic political involvement—Berlin and Cuba—clear tilting occurred in the case of the *Tribune*, which favored conservative sources on these issues, and the *Post*, which favored liberal sources (see appendix V).

Conclusion

Thus presidential weakness—in this case in both the areas of decision making and press strategy—unleashed forces that challenged Kennedy's ability to influence press coverage. As table 4 demonstrates, one result of this weakness was a relatively low percentage of official U.S. sources during the period 1–23 June compared with the total sources in two other major categories, domestic political and foreign. Only during August, when coverage was heavy of foreign reactions to the building of the Berlin Wall, was the relative page-one coverage of American officials lower. And the absolute page-one coverage of official sources—only fifty-six sources in twenty-three days in the five papers—was never again nearly so low during the remainder of the crisis.

During the 1–23 June period, in short, neither the external factors outside a president's control nor the internal factors subject to his direct influence worked to Kennedy's advantage in his relationship with the press. Externally, he faced a highly interested public and strong involvement on the part of domestic politicians and foreign leaders; internally, he generated little news as the policy review within the government began. Under such conditions, the power of the presidency in relation to the press was at a low ebb.

Chapter 7

Kennedy Regains the Initiative

24 June–31 July

The president's first move after recovery from a "viral infection" that had caused him to cancel the previous day's appointments was a highly publicized meeting with his military advisers at Hyannis Port on 23 June. This gave him his first headlines since his report to the nation after Vienna.[1]

On 28 June, at his first press conference since Vienna, Kennedy declared that the Soviets had "manufactured" the crisis and intended to expel the West from Berlin. He pressed the hard-line German view favoring reunification and indicated that a decision favoring a military buildup in Western Europe might soon follow. But he left a tag line for the soft-liners—foreign and domestic—by referring to "unfinished business" with respect to Germany. He indicated a willingness to discuss the settlement of the German problem based on the principle of self-determination—a precondition Khrushchev could not possibly accept—but which became for those who favored negotiations an "offer to talk."[2]

In fact, the president was inclined to keep the idea of negotiations alive. The Allies were still involved in the question of a response to Khrushchev, which did not come until 17 July. While the Allied position was being worked out, unattributed reports appeared in the press about the possibility of negotiations over who should stamp the papers governing the access routes and how. Despite these evidences of presidential interest in negotiations, this idea had to take a back burner. The president was under heavy pressure—from within his own government and from all of the newspapers except the *Post-Dispatch*—to demonstrate military strength first. Only after all concerned were aware of American and Allied strength could negotiations even be considered.[3]

The White House was concerned that Kennedy's difficulties over the Berlin issue had led to an impression of presidential weakness in the public at large. A Trendex poll taken in early July asked this question of the people of New York. The results were telegraphed to Salinger at the White House the following day. They confirmed the view that the public wanted a hard-line response to the Soviets and showed that 58 percent of the sample agreed that their estimation of Kennedy's ability had either remained the same or decreased since the inauguration.[4]

The president was a politician before he was a statesman, and there was no doubt about which way the adrenalin was flowing. Little support existed for soft-line policies—or for policies that might involve U.S. adjustment to the needs of the East Germans and Soviets. The *Times*, for example, printed a lead, two-column editorial on 25 June warning that "each day we draw nearer to the hour of maximum danger," and calling for an immediate military buildup to demonstrate Western resolve not to negotiate "under duress." The story of late June and July was that of a president bringing his policies into conformity with the hard-liners whose views, favoring military rather than political solutions, were predominant in the press; and then skillfully using presidential powers to gain the support of both the more extreme hard-liners and the less numerous soft-liners as well.[5]

Hard-line Leaks and Hard-line Policies

It was in the context of White House concern about the president's image that an extraordinary journalistic event occurred which linked Kennedy with the most fulsome of hard-line positions without any statement on his part. A story in the 3 July issue of *Newsweek* revealed a number of measures that the Joint Chiefs of Staff were to recommend to the president the following week regardless of possible diplomatic developments. These included reinforcing the five American divisions and their supporting units in West Germany; evacuating U.S. dependents from exposed positions in West Germany and France; declaring a limited emergency; calling up National Guard divisions and reservists; and demonstrating America's intention to employ nuclear weapons in the event of war, perhaps by resuming atmospheric testing or by moving nuclear weapons from NATO stockpiles to advanced "ready" positions. The article concluded that Kennedy was aware of the "value" of these measures "and was convinced he would have to implement at least some of them in the near future."[6]

These leaks received far more publicity than they otherwise would have because of an administration decision to call in the FBI to investigate them. The administration claimed that the contingency plans were leaked before the president had had a chance to see them. A suspicious reporter from the *Herald-Tribune* suspected that they were in fact leaked by the White House and then investigated to generate additional publicity. Angered by the FBI investigation, Pentagon officials told reporters that the published material had been discussed before a large audience at a State Department briefing. Deputy

Secretary of Defense Roswell Gilpatric confirmed on 11 July that the administration was seriously considering some of these military measures.[7]

David Klein, a staff member of the Interagency Task Force that was responsible for contingency planning, recently concluded that the leak probably was "authorized from the Pentagon or the White House. If it was unauthorized, somebody would have caught it, and I don't remember that happening. After all, it is more potent to threaten to drop the bomb than to do it."[8]

The leaking continued after Kennedy met with the National Security Council on 8 July and was formally presented with the hard-line Acheson plan, which included the idea that the United States should mobilize, dispatch additional troops to Germany, and send two full tank divisions up the autobahn if the Soviet Union tested the access routes.[9]

As Kennedy reviewed military plans during the following two weeks, the leaking became so pervasive that Senator Mansfield sent a memo to the president about the recent

> press reports which suggest that the Administration is planning to ask up to $6 or $8 billions of increase in defense spending because of Berlin. . . . If the reports stem from authorized "leaks," I would have to question them on the grounds that the uncertainty which such reports, as distinct from acts, stimulate among our own people is probably more damaging than any gain from the consternation which they may produce among our adversaries. If the reports stem from unauthorized "leaks" then they are not only inexcusable, they portend great difficulties for us if the Berlin situation grows more delicate.[10]

The president rejected the more extreme of these proposals. Instead, as the long days of July wore on, he accepted the advice of General Maxwell Taylor and Defense Secretary Robert McNamara to announce a defense buildup of $3.2 billion, which included a strengthening of conventional forces in Europe that strategists hoped might reduce the necessity of nuclear war if a head-on confrontation with Khrushchev ensued. This military preparedness, combined with an announcement of a major civil defense program, was indeed a hard-line response long in the making and finally presented in a major television address on 25 July. But, in comparison with the leaks, the president's proposals seemed restrained. From a public relations standpoint, Kennedy thus had the advantage of appearing both firm and conciliatory depending on the point of view.

Selling this program to the hard-liners did not prove difficult. Alsop learned early of the administration's decision and helped to explain the buildup. It was necessary, he contended, because of the "purblind years of complacency [which had] reduced the Pentagon to what can only be described as a state of nuclear frivolity." The tough, pro-German Higgins was also satisfied, for the call to the colors was expected to match the level of the Korean War. She was also informed early. Her friend, Axel Springer, the hard-line German press magnate, was convinced of Kennedy's toughness. The Germans made no comment about the administration's failure to mention "greater Berlin" in the speech. They were, at least publicly, satisfied by the tough talk; the new military programs; and the Allied response to Khrushchev on 17 July, which reaffirmed the previous Western interest in reunification and acceptance of self-determination as a precondition for negotiations.[11]

James O'Donnell, Higgins's friend, who had also spent long years in Germany as a journalist and now worked for the State Department, made a rare protest. In a luncheon meeting with Sorensen just before the speech, he commented on the president's failure to make any commitment to defend all of Berlin—both East and West. Like most other observers, the *Times*, which during the June period had advocated "greater Berlin," failed to note the omission.[12]

The Press Responds

During July the administration was able to satisfy practically everybody. During the 24–30 June and July periods, official sources dominated the front pages of all papers except the *Tribune*. In contrast, the *Examiner* provides a dramatic example of how the administration's efforts to regain the initiative succeeded in a newspaper that during early June had been more attuned to foreign sources. Because of the hard-line leaks and reports of the growing possibility of military measures, U.S. official sources came to exert more influence during July in the *Examiner* than in any of the other newspapers. Foreign-based articles largely left the front pages (see appendix II).

Only five page-one articles were published in the *Examiner* between 20 June and 23 July based on foreign sources. All these depicted either Russia or East Germany as threatening and were based either on West German or Soviet sources. Only one article, based on West German sources, was critical of Kennedy. This was a page-one interpretive piece by Higgins, whose conclusions conformed to one of Hearst's major editorial positions: the solution to the German problem was reunification. She argued that American policy was discouraging a revolt in East Germany. According to the hard-line German approach, only by encouraging dissent in East Germany would Khrushchev realize that his position was untenable and would he support reunification.[13]

These articles point to the importance of the *Herald Tribune* News Service for an outlying paper like the *Examiner*. Its writers, such as Higgins, Gaston Coblentz, and Warren Rogers, received more front-page space than those of the Hearst Headline Service during this period. Alsop dominated the op ed page: nine of thirteen Berlin op ed articles between 24 June and the end of July were his columns. His support for and prodding of the president, plus his interpretation of the issue as requiring a military response, thus again was of special importance for the popular press.[14]

In the case of Berlin, however, Hearst had his own viewpoint, which drew inspiration not only from the West Germans, but also from moderate Republicans, such as Henry Cabot Lodge. Firmness, self-determination, and above all "seizing the propaganda initiative" were favored. Hearst was not at all certain any propaganda experts were left in Washington, and he helped to organize a campaign to pressure the president to find some. He gave his readers the name of a group to write to and reported on the status of its efforts to see Kennedy. The Hearst critique was nevertheless relatively mild, for he retained kind feelings toward "the young President." Despite his youth, Kennedy was sage enough to appoint Lodge, whom Hearst had since the election been promoting for higher office, as chief of a blue-ribbon panel that would assist the president with propaganda activities. The president's efforts with Hearst undoubtedly were also assisted by the fact that moderate Republican Richard Nixon was convinced by Kennedy's 28 June news conference to support his policies.[15]

Whereas occasional doubts about the president's firmness in supporting the West German position surfaced in the *Examiner*, the president gained clear and unalloyed initiative at the *Post*. According to Phil Graham's diary, he had extensive contact with administration officials over the weekend preceding this period.

Friday, June 16
—dinner dance at Paul Mellon's place, Upperville, Spring Oaks
Saturday, June 17
—evening at Bob Kennedy's in McLean
Sunday, June 18
—lunch with Jean Monnet; dinner, 8:00 p.m. at Glen Ora, President Kennedy's Virginia estate
Monday, June 19
—meeting between 11:15 and 1:15 at night with Chip Bohlen and Tommy Thompson at Bohlen's house
Tuesday, June 20
—arrived at the office at 10:00 a.m. with Benjamin Bradlee
—met with Roberts, Marder, Friendly, Wiggins and Bradlee
1:00 p.m.
—staff luncheon with Rostow, Marder, Unna, Wiggins, Truitt, Friendly, Foisie [who was running the editorial page], Herblock, Joe Paul and Fishbine[16]

According to Roberts, the purpose of the morning meeting with the staff on 20 June was to allow Graham to share with the *Post* staff the "fallout" from his weekend. The result was the "Beleaguered Bastion" series of front-page articles that began in late June and continued into July. By focusing attention in Washington on the alleged seriousness of the Berlin issue, they aided the administration in moving toward enunciating a hard-line policy. They also represent an excellent example of a government-oriented paper working in partnership with officials in setting the national agenda.[17]

Unlike the situation in other papers in this study, the *Post*'s use of government sources on page one had not lagged behind foreign or domestic political sources during the 1–23 June period. Even so, its official U.S. source percentage increased dramatically during July, from 43 percent during the earlier period to 60 percent. Its editorials likewise strongly supported the president and criticized Russia and East Germany (see appendixes II and IV).

The *Times*'s government source figure also increased dramatically in July, and its editorial page was very supportive. But the op ed page continued to show considerable diversity, generated by Europe-oriented C. L. Sulzberger abroad and doubting Arthur Krock at home. Reston, who on 23 June had decried the tendency to believe "that we can do nothing except get ready for a fight," expressed doubts as the military speculation increased but remained basically supportive of Kennedy.[18]

Three weakened centers of opposition to the president's policies remained. The first of these was conservative Republicans who were not afraid to appear partisan. They did not want to let Kennedy off the hook despite his emerging hard line. Their major reservation—that Kennedy still was not firm enough—was expressed by Republican congressional leaders Dirksen and Halleck after the president's 28 June press conference. House Republican leaders continued to entertain doubts about Kennedy's policies, as did Senator Alexander Wiley (R.-Wisconsin), though this position became very difficult to maintain as July progressed.[19]

The doubters appeared mainly in the *Tribune*, whose source pattern differed from that of the other newspapers. It followed the general pattern in that its front-page foreign source coverage declined drastically. But, unlike the other papers, it turned primarily to domestic political sources rather than to official ones. Unusual news stories also appeared in the *Tribune*, such as an exclusive report from Hyannis Port that the president had deliberately dropped a conciliatory passage from the press announcement of a 4 July message to Khrushchev in order to hide the first glimmering of a possible concession. Walter Trohan later commented that the information on which this story was based came from a dissident in the State Department.[20]

Editorially, the *Tribune* became slightly less critical of the administration than it had been in June, but its policy of criticizing Britain and praising West Germany continued (see appendix IV). Its news coverage recognized a growing split between Adenauer and Brandt in Germany, and its editorial preference for Adenauer carried over into its news coverage. Editorial criticism of his arch-rivals, the British, also affected the selection of news, in this case material from British newspapers embarrassing either to Kennedy or British officials.[21]

In addition to conservative dissent, two pockets of liberal opposition affected news coverage: policy debate within the administration itself that continued until the president's speech of 25 July announcing a policy decision; and minor variation within the liberal wing of the Democratic party. Some of the *Times*'s columnists were affected by this debate. But, because the challenge to the growing hard-line policy direction during the period preceding the president's 25 July speech was faint, the *Post-Dispatch* was the only paper in this study seriously affected by liberal Democratic and soft-line intra-administration dissidence. The *Post-Dispatch* picked up and featured these faint voices in its editorial section because of its concern about the growing hard-line consensus.

Because Lippmann was on vacation, Marquis Childs, the *Post-Dispatch*'s Washington bureau chief and syndicated columnist, was at the center of this challenge to the hard-line position; Alsop was his primary antagonist. Alsop's columns in late June reverberated with talk of partial mobilization and emergency efforts to build the nation's civil defense system. He even suggested the desirability of nuclear war with Russia under certain conditions. But an evening with Kennedy at his retreat at Glen Ora, in which the president expressed his concern about possible losses in a nuclear war, moderated Alsop's thinking. In a private message to Kennedy following this meeting, Alsop told him that "no man who has not got the responsibility [to make a decision for war] can really know what he would do if the responsibility were his," and promised the president that "I'm ready to follow your lead" on this issue. This meeting and Alsop's response not only demonstrate Kennedy's concern about the possibility of nuclear war, but also provide an example of direct presidential influence on the press.[22]

In mid-June, Childs had praised Mansfield even though he did not agree with the idea of the free city. In early July, Arthur Schlesinger, Jr., of the White House staff, and State Department legal adviser Abram Chayes confided something of their position to Childs as they tried to head off the hard-line mobilizers' meeting with the president at Hyannis Port. Childs also went to talk to Senator Fulbright, who was then saying little publicly about the Berlin issue. His chief of staff on the Foreign Relations Committee, Carl Marcy, described what probably happened at the meeting: "Mark Childs and Fulbright respected each other. One day Childs probably came around and said, 'are you having any influence?' Fulbright probably thought no, but I can have some influence with the press and gave him the story of his memo to the President at the time of the Bay of Pigs and of his Berlin memo."[23]

The result was an article by Childs on 9 July describing Fulbright as "one of the major figures on the international scene" and concluding that a memo on Berlin he had sent Kennedy could "be an important factor in whatever decision is taken. On one side is the Acheson plan providing for the callup of at least two National Guard divisions to be sent to Europe to buttress American forces in Germany. . . . On the other side, some of the executive branch are convinced that the U.S. must come up with constructive alternative plans for Berlin to protect the status of the city while possibly opening the way to negotiation." [24]

Childs also publicized the views of Senator Humphrey, who visited Germany during July and returned with a proposal to the Soviets espoused by Berlin mayor Willy Brandt. Brandt thought a four-power foreign ministers' conference should be called. If the Soviets declined or it proved fruitless, then a peace conference involving all fifty-two nations that had fought in World War II should be proposed. [25]

The Brandt-Humphrey ideas did not receive much serious attention. The "war psychosis" was being inflamed, as Childs noted, by Soviet statements and hard-line Allied responses. Childs ultimately came to fear that Kennedy's policies, which were based on careerists who have "come up with the same old plans," might lead to war, "that last desperate suicidal course." "Turn to your old friends in Congress, Senators Humphrey and Cooper," Childs pleaded on the day before Kennedy's speech as talk of a national emergency continued. On that same day, Higgins and Alsop reported that Kennedy had decided in favor of a military buildup. [26]

Some of Childs's fears may have grown out of conversations with Schlesinger. Childs was asked why his article expressed fear that Kennedy might still come up with a plan that would include mobilization or the declaration of a national emergency:

A. Well, [why Childs was afraid] it might have been Schlesinger.
Q. Was he afraid of that?
A. He was afraid of it. He was afraid that the whole Acheson hard-line crowd would push him [Kennedy] over in that direction.

Concerning the president's decision, Childs said: "I think he was under tremendous stress. His brother was in favor of a much more hard-line approach than he was, and his brother was very influential. Of course, you always have to remember that the Bay of Pigs background was so damaging to his credibility." [27]

It is not clear who talked to Childs after his alarmist column of 24 July. But it may well have been Kennedy or one of his closest advisers, such as Maxwell Taylor, whom Childs had gotten to know, who helped to convince him that a military buildup was necessary. [28]

The president was well aware of Childs's significance as a leading liberal columnist of the day. He was a friend of the much neglected but politically important Adlai Stevenson, who was also a window to the Democratic left. Kennedy certainly hoped to bring as much of this left wing of the party along with him as possible, even as he put the country on a war footing with the funds for the military buildup requested in his 25 July speech. These were the authorizations that enabled the president to move into Vietnam and this speech was, as Childs correctly noted, the "most important speech since his [Kennedy's] inauguration." Childs later ruefully commented: "Kennedy . . . was almost too clever for his own good. I was a great admirer of Kennedy, but I'm afraid I failed to see the flaws in his character. And this cleverness: that owed a lot, I guess, to his character." [29]

In any event, for his column on 25 July, the morning of the pivotal speech, Childs had consulted "authoritative sources" and was satisfied. The cost of the buildup would be "closer to $3 billion than to $4 billion." Kennedy had rejected the advice of "those who would respond to the immediate crisis of Berlin with measures for mobilization or the declaration of a national emergency." The Allies had been informed that the message would be calm in tone. "The reaction in London, where there was widespread concern over reports of a call-up of 1,000,000 men, is certain to be one of relief." No questions were asked. [30]

The speech and the buildup thus were accepted without a murmur by Childs, as well as by the *Post-Dispatch* editors who had long questioned military spending and solutions. By comparison with what had been expected, the buildup seemed mild. The term "mobilization" was not used to describe what Kennedy was in fact proposing. The *Post-Dispatch* was also pleased that the president mentioned at "one point in the speech that he was willing to consider 'an arrangement or treaty' consistent with freedom for the people of Berlin." Forgotten after the speech was the editor's request of only six days before that Kennedy talk in terms of realities such as the division of Germany—and that he stop expressing shock at Russia's professed intention to sign a peace treaty with East Germany. [31]

Although the administration had succeeded in gaining the support of the *Post-Dispatch*, the process had been much more difficult than in the Washington-oriented *Times* and *Post* and in the hard-line *Examiner*. The *Post-Dispatch*'s source usage also differed from the other three, especially in its lesser reliance on U.S. official sources on page one. Also, unlike these three papers, which tended to limit their editorial criticism to Russia and East Germany, the *Post-Dispatch* variously criticized the administration, Russia, West Germany, and the West in general (see appendix IV).

Editorial page editor Lasch was asked why the *Post-Dispatch* ended up supporting the president's decision. Lasch believed several influences were involved: fear of the even more hard-line position, the support of respected liberals in the administration, and Childs's influence with the publisher. But the dominant factor, Lasch felt, was that Joseph Pulitzer III was "enamored with Jack Kennedy" and "wanted us to stand by [the president] in a national emergency." [32]

Conclusion

The period from late June through late July provides both an example of the successful use of the powers of the presidency to influence the press during a period of policy change as well as an example of the more subtle kinds of pressures the press can bring to bear on the president. Whereas in early June he was on the defensive because the press was emphasizing the views of others on Berlin, in the subsequent period the balance shifted in his favor, as his own initiatives and other official sources began to dominate the news. But, partly because of his weakness during the previous period, the president was under substantial pressure from important segments of the press to formulate hard-line policies on Berlin during July.

Kennedy did in fact react to the dominant forces that were reflected in the press. The talk of negotiations, which Rusk stated was Kennedy's policy as of 22 June, was replaced by leaks and eventually also policies based on military solutions. The president's policy, which was finally announced in a major television address on 25 July, was not as hard-line as that suggested by advisers such as Dean Acheson. It was nevertheless a response involving primarily a military buildup and increased civil defense measures, presaged by the president's pro-German comments in late June. Both the West Germans and Richard Nixon were satisfied.

The president was successful by the time of his major policy decision not only with the important hard-liners in the press like the editors of the *Times* and the *Examiner*, but also with the soft-liners like the *Post-Dispatch*. His success with this segment occurred in large measure because no real soft-line impetus existed among the public or politicians to which a paper like the *Post-Dispatch* could respond. No consistent critique depicted Kennedy as "hawkish," nothing, as Tom Wicker has noted, that was forceful enough to make him back up politically. Like the president, the press responds to pressure centers, and the soft-liners in Congress quickly fizzled because of institutional limitations and lack of support from other politicians or from the public.

As the president formulated his policies according to dominant forces reflected in the press, the way was open for him—using sophisticated high-visibility press policies combined with well-placed leaks—to dominate the news and editorial coverage of all but the editorially independent conservative newspaper in this study. Kennedy was able to establish his primacy on the Berlin issue and hence set the stage for overwhelming press and public approval of the military buildup that he confidently requested Congress to ratify.

Chapter 8

The Berlin Wall Crisis

Weathering the Storm, 1–31 August

Early in August an Allied foreign ministers' conference reiterated the Western position that cutting off the access routes to Berlin would be a causus belli. This was followed by a Warsaw Pact meeting, at which Khrushchev reassured the West that the Soviets would not permit a cutting off of the routes. He was also quoted as warning that in the event of war hundreds of millions of people would lose their lives. But the most significant topic discussed at that meeting was not then reported. The Warsaw Pact powers were preparing a move to halt the daily increasing refugee flow, a move designed to take the West by surprise.

In the early morning hours of Sunday, 13 August, the East Germans, backed by Soviet troops, began to build a wall between the eastern and western sectors in Berlin. This move caught the United States totally unprepared. American officials were uncertain about what to do. Despite all the publicity derived from the efforts of the contingency planners, no plan for this contingency was known to the ranking American official in Berlin.

The importance of what the Russians and East Germans were doing was not conveyed to Washington in the first critical hours, and no diplomatic or military effort was made to stop the Wall at the outset. A little before noon on the 13th, Rusk called Kennedy at his weekend retreat in Hyannis Port, informed him of the situation, and said that there was no evidence of the signing of a peace treaty or any threat to the access routes. It was agreed that the president should continue his vacation. After Kennedy authorized a mild statement protesting the illegality of the Wall under the four-power agreements, Rusk left the State Department to attend an afternoon ball game. No crisis task force was set up in the White House. As Willy Brandt later noted, nothing was done for three days that might have prompted the Soviets to reconsider their decision.[1]

First Reactions: The West Germans Take the Lead

The reports from West Germany began on Sunday and first appeared in the press on Monday morning. Thousands were assembling on both sides of the Wall, which was snaking its way through the city, and Brandt was urging the United States, Britain, and France to take energetic action. Germans have the right of access, he said. They should be able to travel and work anywhere in the city.[2]

From Washington a report based on "western diplomats" linked the president with the possibility of retaliation by the Allied bloc. The AP's John Hightower reported that a ban on travel from West to East Germany was one step being considered. Front-page stories in the *Times* on 14 and 15 August stressed West German concern and Adenauer's certainty that the Allies would react. A troubled Adenauer warned that the Western powers would institute a total trade embargo of the Communist bloc "if the problems with the Soviet Union cannot be brought to order." Breathless headlines in the *Examiner* played the Berlin story as if the United States were preparing for imminent action, which was not the case.[3]

The press was excited by the West German reactions that inspired the first headlines. But the administration was more interested in calming the situation down than in heating it up. There was fear of a revolt in East Germany—a possibility that conservatives such as the *Tribune* and Marguerite Higgins welcomed—but that the administration feared might bring a head-on confrontation with the USSR.[4]

From the administration's viewpoint, the situation had to be quieted. After the Wall, with the two Germanys divided and the flow of refugees virtually halted, tensions eased. "What we in Berlin regarded as a cruel blow may almost have come as a relief to others," Brandt noted later. "The separate peace treaty with the GDR, so often threatened, had not been concluded nor had the presence of the Allied garrisons been called in question. Above all, war did not seem imminent." Thus Kennedy remained quiet, and the only action following the administration's initial response was a written protest by the Allied commandants in Berlin that was delivered to the Soviet commandant after the Wall had been built.[5]

To the West Germans, this response was scarcely adequate, especially because those same commandants had reaffirmed just a few weeks before that the principle of freedom of movement was basic to the agreement regarding Berlin. The administration's emphasis on building American military strength was not enough.[6]

Given its policy, the administration's task was to convince the press that it should do nothing gracefully, West German opinion notwithstanding. Chester Bowles appeared at the National Press Club and said that the situation was not all bad because it epitomized the repressive character of the East German regime. McGeorge Bundy briefed Max Frankel of the *Times* to the same effect. The United States could now exploit the propaganda advantage inherent in the communist admission that they "cannot hold the allegiance of the people," Frankel wrote after his talk with Bundy. Only by extreme countermeasures that probably would lead to war could the West undo the communist action. On balance, Frankel reported, it "is probably a good thing that East Germany will not be entirely depopulated of citizens who oppose Communist rule." The administration viewed the new development as "a mere extension of what it has been willing to accept throughout the last decade" and demonstrated interest "in diplomatic explorations to determine whether the latest Soviet move might not contain the seeds of a solution." [7]

Of all the papers in this study, the *Post* was the least receptive to the West German viewpoint. Emphasizing the administration's position, it ran a lead article on the 15th similar to Frankel's that was based on "authoritative sources" in Washington. The *Post*'s two articles that day expressing the West German view were on the inside pages while, in addition to the lead article by Murray Marder, Chalmers Roberts contributed a page-one story about the administration's crisis news operations center. In fact, the *Post* did not give the Germans page-one coverage until Brandt took to the streets on 16 August with 300,000 West Berliners and publicized a letter to Kennedy requesting action, not words. Editorially, the *Post* supported the administration by depicting the building of the Wall as "inevitable." [8]

The *Times*'s editors, believing that the Wall might be the first step to signing a peace treaty and cutting off the access routes, initially called on the United States to do something besides sending "oral and written protests as the Soviet Union unilaterally violates past solemn commitments." But, the day after the Frankel article, they accepted the wisdom of the administration's course and remarked with more fervor than originality that Soviet rule of Eastern Europe rested on "brute force." [9]

Alsop's comments could not have been more supportive as he sought to forestall Republican charges of weakness. No responsible leader, he said, including the "bolder ones like Presidents Eisenhower and Kennedy," had suggested war to prevent Khrushchev from signing a peace treaty; the key issue was the access routes. [10]

In view of its often reiterated concern for German self-determination, the *Examiner* might have been expected to demand firm steps to counter this ultimate infringement of that right. Hearst's initial bow to the Adenauer position was deeper than most and favored the cutoff of Western trade with East Germany. But this stance was quickly abandoned as the administration's position solidified. On 18 August the editors protested Brandt's speech and letter to the administration. Brandt was an admirable man, but in the future his criticisms should be sent through regular diplomatic channels. The *Examiner*'s only columnists on this issue were Alsop and White, both of whom supported the administration.[11]

The *Tribune* was not moved to call for immediate assistance to the Germans. Its page-one response was to publish Washington stories dealing with both military movements and appeals from West Germany. Its immediate editorial reaction was to term Khrushchev worse than Attila the Hun and Adolf Hitler. Only ten days after the Wall had gone up and it was clear that nothing could be done did it criticize the administration.[12]

This criticism came a week after the first Republicans had begun theirs. The first attempts were feeble: they tried to blame the administration for Khrushchev's decision to build the Wall. Kennedy after all was a Democrat, as was Senator Fulbright, who had been in Germany a few days before the Wall and remarked that he would not be surprised if the East shut the border to halt the refugee flow. Dirksen and Halleck suggested that this comment had been an invitation that Khrushchev could not pass up. This innuendo was followed by a more serious criticism from hard-line Senator Thomas Dodd (D.-Connecticut), which was given full play in the *Tribune*. Dodd, who was in Berlin when the Wall was built, remarked on his return: "our protest was so weak . . . so completely incommensurate with the crime that had been committed, it was nothing short of toothless."[13]

The *Tribune*, however, allowed the blame to be spread around. Its cartoon "Quandary at the Gate" expressed the situation well. Khrushchev is sitting on the porch in an undershirt reading the paper while the Allies scratch their heads. Adenauer says: "Why don't you do something?" Macmillan says, "Maybe it will go away." De Gaulle says, "Not while there's growling." A dog named "Berlin Threat" peers through the gate. The *Tribune* during August made fewer editorial criticisms of the administration than before, and its attack on the Soviets was so much greater that the administration's failures seemed mild by comparison. Despite its emphasis on stories from abroad during the period, West German feelings were not going to induce the *Tribune* to urge the administration to risk war over Berlin (see appendix IV).[14]

Higgins Makes a Suggestion

Marguerite Higgins was the journalist most moved by the German predicament. Upon hearing on 13 August that the Wall had been erected, she contacted her friend James O'Donnell of the United States Information Agency (USIA), whom she knew would be trying to stir up some active response by the State Department. Finding that Foggy Bottom was taking its usual "appeasing" position, they decided that Higgins should get in touch with another of her friends, General Lucius Clay, hero of the Berlin blockade, who, like

Higgins, was vacationing on Cape Cod. When they met, Higgins and her husband, General William E. Hall, who had been with Clay in Berlin, suggested that Clay should go there to reassure the West Berliners. He agreed with the idea, and, after consultation with O'Donnell, it was decided that Higgins, a friend of Robert Kennedy, should broach the idea to him as the best route to his brother. When approached, the attorney general agreed to explain the idea to the president, but he indicated that Clay could not go alone because he was a Republican. Even at the height of crises, the Kennedy administration never overlooked the domestic context of foreign policy.[15]

As the German protests grew and rumors flew in West Berlin about the reasons for the West's inaction, the president accepted Higgins's idea. Added to the mission, however, was Vice-President Lyndon Johnson, who was informed of his involvement while dining with Higgins and Speaker of the House Sam Rayburn. The mission, scheduled for 20 and 21 August, was to link up dramatically with an American military convoy that was to proceed to Berlin on the autobahn and reinforce the garrison there.

The next morning, Friday, 18 August, the president met with Higgins and told her what she already knew. That evening, she flew to Germany along with the Johnson and Clay retinues and columnist Max Freedman, who was associated with the *Post* and was helping Johnson write speeches for the occasion.[16]

From the public relations standpoint, the trip was a tremendous success. Americans concerned about Berliners' feelings saw West Germans pouring into the streets in apparent appreciation of the Johnson-Clay visit. Brandt and the vice-president were photographed together. The administration could no longer be accused of inaction. It was back on the front page and praised by all the papers except the *Tribune* and the *Post-Dispatch*. The *Tribune* editorially ignored the trip, and the *Post-Dispatch* editors reverted to the criticism of the administration they had emphasized in July. They praised the British and thanked them for American restraint. The editors had been suspicious of the administration since Rusk had "rushed" into print the previous Sunday with a proclamation that the border closing had "directly violated East-West agreements." Now the administration was trying to compensate for its failure to "back with action the loud noises we made at the outset." In the continuing dialogue with the publisher over the question of maintaining independence on the administration's Berlin policy, the editors were again having their say.[17]

Reflecting their relative editorial independence, the *Post-Dispatch* and the *Tribune* used the smallest percentage of government sources on the front pages during August. These two papers contrasted sharply with the *Examiner*, which was dominated by government sources, and indeed quoted the highest percentage of all the newspapers during the period (see appendix II). The Johnson-Clay mission appealed to the *Examiner*: "President Kennedy clearly scored a ten-strike," its editors declared.[18]

Higgins's efforts thus greatly benefited the administration. Moreover, during this period she expressed in her columns none of the sharp criticism based on German feelings that had been the hallmark of her coverage during June. On the day after the Wall was first visible, she confined herself to combating those individuals, particularly in the State Department, who might argue that world opinion should keep the United States from aiding the East Germans if a revolt ensued. Her next article, written in Berlin during the Clay trip, praised the president for taking the "political offensive" against those who might call him weak.[19]

Nor was there any mention in Higgins's or Alsop's writings of a criticism that angered the president. This was a contention by J. V. Murphy that contingency plans for Berlin existed but the administration had overlooked them. The president suspected this leak had come from Allen Dulles at the CIA because Murphy had good access to him. The major newspaper repetition of this charge was in a David Wise article in the *Herald-Tribune*. This piece was not published in the *Examiner*, which used the *Herald-Tribune* News Service. The critique would have received further circulation if important users of the news service had published it and if the major columnists had picked it up.[20]

Why the West Germans Failed

The real challenge for the president during August and partially on into September, when the foreign sources in newspapers remained high, was the West Germans. Why did the West German position fail in this period to elicit the same preponderance of source coverage and exert the same impact on editors and columnists that it had during the June period of presidential weakness? There were several reasons.

First, the West Germans stood alone among the Allies in demanding an immediate response. Kennedy decided immediately not to follow the German position—in contrast to the indecision and lingering discussion among the British, French, and Americans that had characterized the June period. Furthermore, the administration quickly conveyed the rationale for its thinking to leading columnists and journalists. And no alternative centers of news and opinion presented themselves because the president—holding regular and successful news conferences, announcing aspects of the continuing military buildup, and sending Johnson and Clay to Berlin—was clearly in control.

Second, the administration's rationale for not responding to the West German position was in keeping with its July stance—that war would come only over the access routes—though it remained officially committed to reunification and self-determination. No desire for war over East Berlin was expressed even in the most conservative of journalistic circles. The West Germans did not press the real failure of the administration—its negligence in planning for a Wall contingency—which meant that the administration was off the hook in relation to the hard-liners in the American press who responded to the German criticisms.

Third, the president's policy was in keeping with public opinion, which did not as strongly support a policy of going to war over East Berlin as it backed a policy of going to war over the access routes combined with a general display of strength. According to a Gallup poll taken as Kennedy was making his decision in July, only 58 percent of the public was in favor of a United States obligation to East Berlin . . . even if it meant "going to war." Americans were, however, strongly (78 percent) in favor of keeping troops in West Berlin in order to "give hope" to the people of Eastern Europe. They similarly favored (67 percent) fighting if necessary over the issue of the access routes. "Liberation" and "going to war over East Berlin" sentiment was higher by from 2 to 6 percent in the Midwest and West, where the *Examiner* and the *Tribune* were located. This greater public sentiment in their areas, however, was not enough to induce these two papers to advocate "liberation" or going to war over East Berlin when the possibility was at hand. The fact that the president's policy coincided with public opinion undoubtedly contributed to its success with the press.[21]

Finally, the Republicans did not lend their support to the West German position during the critical first few days after 13 August. Like administration officials, opposition politicians are usually not very far ahead of public opinion. The Republicans did not demand immediate action to support the West Germans at the risk of war. Had they done so, the *Tribune* and the *Examiner*, which responded to Republican initiatives and functioned in the West and Midwest, where hard-line opinion was stronger on the German issue, might have been encouraged to join the criticism. Scattered comments about American "weakness" by Republican leaders like Richard Nixon and William Miller after the Johnson-Clay trip were too little and too late. And when huge headlines on 31 August announced the resumption of Soviet atmospheric nuclear testing, a move that prompted fervent and repeated denunciations of Russia by politicians and journalists, the Berlin issue receded from the public prominence of the past three months.[22]

Thus the building of the Berlin Wall, which was widely viewed as a crisis in West Berlin and West Germany, did not turn out to be a crisis for the Kennedy administration. In the absence of Republican criticism immediately after it was built, opposition in the conservative and popular press was muted and hard-line columnists largely supported the administration. And the lack of a critique of the president's policies from within the administration contributed to the absence of criticism in the Washington-oriented press. The president's decision to oppose the West German position but to send Johnson and Clay to

Berlin to reaffirm Western resolve also aided the administration in maintaining a favorable image in the press. Having established his toughness in his 25 July speech, the president smoothly traversed August's potentially perilous terrain.

Conclusion

A number of overall generalizations can be made about the press-presidential relationship as a result of this analysis of the Berlin issue of 1961. As during the Laotian crisis, differences among newspapers relating to constituencies and editorial directions were able to influence both editorial and news coverage on foreign policy issues quite independently of the president's best efforts. Although Kennedy influenced newspapers by making policy changes and formulating press strategies, newspapers were more likely to consider independently an issue—like Berlin—in which there was constituency interest.

Another factor affecting Kennedy's ability to influence the press was his need to articulate policies in a way that was responsive to public opinion. Failure to do so created difficulties for him because domestic forces were then able to offer competing interpretations of the issue. If critical forces do gain momentum in the press, as occurred in June 1961, two conditions are certain to compound a president's difficulties: indecisiveness while engaged in the incipient stages of a policy review process; and failure to utilize available press strategies, thus generating little foreign policy news.

If a policy review involves Allied governments whose views critically affect American policy, new forces will be released in the press as competition begins to define the nature of a decision. The views and decisions of such governments become important in the press and are leaked in the same way as are those of the U.S. government. During June, the views of foreign governments that were familiar to the public and had constituencies in the United States received special attention, though just how they were covered varied by newspaper. The news and views of governments perceived as threatening also received special attention. The overall effect was to put pressure on and challenge Kennedy.

Under these conditions, the flow of influence tended to proceed from press to president. Kennedy faced a difficult political situation in which critical political forces were reflected and magnified in both the elite and popular press. At this time, in McGeorge Bundy's phrase, Kennedy was "hurt by what they are saying about him." [23]

If a president does formulate his policies according to dominant forces that are reflected in the press, as he did in late June and July, the way is open for him to dominate the news and editorial coverage of all but the editorially independent liberal and conservative papers. Through the use of leaks and careful speech and press conference formulations—which offer some basis for the belief that the president's policies were in conformity with their own—Kennedy was able to gain support from even these newspapers. Defining an issue as a crisis requiring emergency measures also contributed to bringing most dissident elements into line.

In short, the Berlin crisis suggests that the president has considerable power to put his policies in the best light by means of the press strategies available to him. Given conformity of his policies with the main lines of domestic opinion as expressed in the press and given the continued use of effective press strategies, Kennedy was able to weather policy failures and foreign criticism with little difficulty. As coverage in the wake of the Berlin Wall demonstrated, he was in the driver's seat well before the end of the Berlin crisis of 1961.

1. *Joseph Alsop at Sam Neua airport awaiting a Vientiane flight, 2 September 1959 (Wide World Photos)*

2. *President Kennedy talks with reporters at the State Department after a conference with government advisers on the Laos crisis, 15 April 1961 (Wide World Photos)*

3. Premier Nikita Khrushchev and President Kennedy meet in Vienna, 3 June 1961 (Wide World Photos)

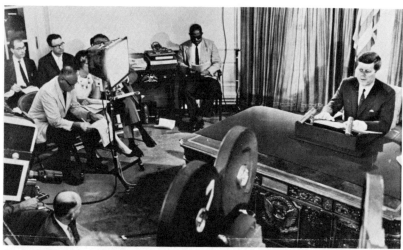

4. President Kennedy announces a major military build-up related to Berlin in a television appearance at the White House. Journalists listening off camera are (left to right, front row) Jack Sutherland, U.S. News and World Report; *Mary McGrory,* Washington Star; *Ed Morgan, ABC; (second row) Tom Wicker,* New York Times; *Anthony Goodman, Reuters; Vladimir Vashodchenko,* Tass; *at center is Assistant Press Secretary Andrew Hatcher, 25 July 1961 (Wide World Photos)*

5. *This sign at a West Berlin protest rally refers to a call for action against the Communists by the United States and the western allies, 16 August 1961 (Wide World Photos)*

6. *President Kennedy answers a question during a news conference devoted to the Cuban situation, 13 September 1962 (Wide World Photos)*

7. *Six Cubans, described as raiders, who sank a Cuban patrol boat, aboard the Coast Guard vessel that brought them to Key West from the British island of Cay Sal where they had sought refuge, 15 October 1962 (Wide World Photos)*

8. *President Kennedy speaks to the nation on television concerning the United States' naval blockade against Cuba, 22 October 1962 (Wide World Photos)*

9. *Missile site under construction in the San Cristóbal area in Cuba, 22 October 1962 (Wide World Photos)*

10. *United Press International photographer James Atherton shows a news conference from President Kennedy's point of view, 17 July 1963 (United Press International Photo)*

11. Philip L. Graham, president and chief executive officer of the Washington Post Company, 3 August 1963 (Wide World Photos)

12. Malcolm W. Browne, Associated Press reporter in Saigon, wins the World Press photo contest with his famous picture of the burning monk, 14 December 1963 (Wide World Photos)

Part Four

The Cuban Crisis
of 1962

The Cuban issue of 1962 resulted from increasing Soviet involvement with Cuba's Premier Fidel Castro, who had emerged as an avowed Marxist by the end of 1961. President Kennedy had tried in April of that year to overthrow him through a CIA-sponsored operation at the Bay of Pigs that failed. Kennedy's decision against the use of extensive American air cover or the deployment of U.S. troops gave rise to Republican charges of weakness. As the midterm elections of 1962 approached, the Republicans stepped up their attacks.

The issue was complicated because the Russian-Cuban embrace tightened after the Bay of Pigs operation. This process was facilitated by America's refusal to negotiate or to accept the possibility o. peaceful coexistence with Cuba, even when its leaders in August 1961 privately offered the possibility of an agreement neither to ally with the Soviet Union nor to subvert other Latin American countries. The adamant American position during 1961 and 1962 reinforced Castro's fear of the United States. This position—taken primarily for domestic political reasons—gave Castro, in Herbert S. Dinerstein's words, "good grounds for procuring more powerful weapons. A better-armed Cuba would serve to dampen American ardor for a new trial by arms." From the Soviet standpoint, having missiles in Cuba would help to reduce the pronounced strategic superiority of the United States and enhance Russian prestige.[1]

In this context of American hostility, Cuban insecurity, and Soviet strategic inferiority, the Russians and Cubans decided in early 1962 to increase shipments of Soviet military supplies and personnel—including camouflaged missile parts. U.S. intelligence sources apparently did not find out about the ground-to-air missiles included in these shipments until early September, though the ground-to-ground missiles—which Kennedy declared on 4 September were "offensive weapons" whose discovery would necessitate a firm American response—were not discovered until 14 October. But, because substantial Soviet military activity was apparent during the summer of 1962, the issue of a direct Russian threat to the United States had emerged by late August.

The Republicans played up this threat while administration officials tried to tone it down, arguing that Castro was having difficulties as a result of an American and Organization of American States (OAS) boycott and would fall of his own weight. Meanwhile, the administration had continued to conduct covert CIA operations intended to insure his overthrow. But its inability to publicize its hard-line covert activities, combined with its relatively mild public stance, put it in a difficult position as the election approached.

The issue was further complicated when Senator Kenneth Keating (R.-New York) charged that the Soviets were shipping missiles to Cuba, and he and other Republicans refused to accept the administration view of the Russian military personnel as "technicians." They were convinced these were regulars in the Red Army and that Cuba was rapidly becoming a Soviet base.

The administration was acutely aware of the Cuban issue and had kept track of it through polls ever since the Bay of Pigs in the knowledge that Cuba was, in Theodore Sorensen's apt phrase, President Kennedy's "Achilles heel." The polls that the administration solicited and picked up from newspapers showed the same thing: a public acutely aware of Cuba and eager for the government to "do something" about it. Louis Harris, who studied attitudes on the Cuban issue in Florida for the administration in December 1961, concluded that "the vast bulk of public opinion favors doing everything possible short of armed intervention." A poll clipped from the *San Francisco Chronicle* and sent to Sorensen in early 1962 indicated that on Cuba, alone among foreign policy issues, the administration received a 62 percent negative rating. By September 1962 many Americans clearly were in an angry mood: a Gallup poll of 18 September reported that 71 percent of those having opinions wanted action against Cuba and that many respondents used words like "bomb," "invade," or "starve them out." Compared with a poll taken three months earlier, this one also showed a large rise in public concern about the Soviet threat.[2]

Cuba's close economic, historic, and geographic ties to the United States heightened public awareness of what was happening there. Russian support of Cuba violated the Monroe Doctrine, which Americans had been taught to revere as school children: no European government should be allowed to establish a foothold or acquire territory in the Western Hemisphere beyond that already established prior to 1823. The United States consistently had upheld this doctrine, many Americans believed. How could it possibly allow a foreign government—especially Russia—to gain a foothold in the Western Hemisphere now? If the United States could not cope with Castro, ninety miles from Key West, how could it possibly hope to deal with the communist challenge elsewhere?

As a result of these historic and geographic considerations, Americans as a whole were more concerned about Cuba than they had been about Berlin. Apart from the general public opinion consensus, public interest was indicated by the greater numbers and variety of organized interest groups taking a position on Cuban issues published in the press. Interest groups ran across a broad political spectrum and were included on both page one and inside pages. One category of interest groups stood out for its impact on the news coverage: the Cuban exiles represented nearly half of the total interest group sources covered on page one and a similarly high percentage of sources cited on inside pages as well during the period before 22 October. The major page-one competition was from the Cuban Families Committee, a semiofficial organization supporting freedom for Bay of Pigs prisoners. Business groups and trade unions were also involved with Cuban issues, however, and were quoted on issues relating to an expanded economic boycott of Cuba.

In combination with the Republicans, the refugees were to cause the administration a good deal of trouble. This is because they helped the Republicans define the nature of the Soviet-Cuban threat, an issue of popular concern frequently bordering on hysteria. Because of this public concern and the lack of other issues, Cuba became the Republicans' number one campaign issue. Caught in the contradictions of its policies and the strength of public emotions, an otherwise popular administration sought to contain this challenge. In addition to his popularity, the main thing Kennedy had going for him was the closing of the ranks within his administration and with the liberal wing of the Democratic party during the election period. In the atmosphere of heightened public awareness regarding Cuba that characterized late August 1962, the initiative belonged not to the president, but to the Republicans and the Cuban exiles.

Chapter 9

Republicans and Refugees Define the Issues

25 August–30 September

The late August period illustrates the administration's dilemma. On 24 August a "refugee" group, the Directorate of the Student Revolution in Miami, raided a hotel housing Soviet technicians in downtown Havana. The story appeared the next day on page one in all five newspapers, though it received more play in the non-Washington oriented newspapers. It ran with a State Department denial of American involvement, the comment that "U.S. officials were surprised," and official speculation that the raid might have been undertaken by dissident members of the Cuban navy itself. Again the next day the story had front-page play, and again the State Department denied it.[1]

The Cuban exiles thus had sufficient power or potential for conflict to warrant significant attention by the press. Furthermore, the existing virulent anti-Cuba atmosphere meant that press response to them often was favorable. The raids, which were violations of the Neutrality Acts, were criticized by only two papers, the *Tribune* and *Post-Dispatch* (see appendix IV). *Tribune* editors thought that the refugees might well be "thrown out of the country." But the front page included an interview with a "student" who had piloted one of the boats. The author, Jules Dubois, was a *Tribune* Latin American correspondent and former Castro supporter who felt the "betrayal" personally, for he had helped to arrange a Washington luncheon for Castro in 1960. Dubois was now in Miami interviewing refugees. He reported that one of them "told me that in the 49 trips he has made to the Cuban waterfront he had never met artillery fire."[2]

Such stories redounded against the administration for seemingly not doing anything, even though the smiling "students" on the front pages of all the papers but the *Post* and the *Times* may well have made the raids in boats and with explosives and techniques supplied by the CIA. This support of the exiles was part of an administration plan to overthrow Castro, designed to culminate in October 1962, the month before the elections. This was the administration's form of "doing something." But it could not be publicized and it was not proving successful in furthering the overthrow of Castro before the election.[3]

Instead of being appreciative and working for the success of the American plan, however, the "students" were doing a lot of talking and being altogether unruly in public. Internal rivalries between left and right and the striving for administration backing may have had something to do with this reaction, though the full story remains to be told and it is not clear which groups were receiving American support. Part of the refugee critique of the administration may have been cover. But, for whatever reason, a statement by José Miro-Cardona, president of the Cuban Revolutionary Council, appeared on page one of the *Tribune* on 6 September, two days after Kennedy sought to make the definitive public statement on the military situation in Cuba. Miro-Cardona said that missile bases and electronic equipment for "warlike operations" and the detection of and interference with "launchings from Cape Canaveral" were being installed on the northern coast of Cuba. Another refugee leader appeared on a TV interview program on 2 September requesting administration support for the "students." On the same day, Senators Strom Thurmond (D.-South Carolina) and George Smathers (D.-Florida), encouraged by the attention the refugees were receiving, demanded military intervention.[4]

Why could the government not emulate the refugees, who were only "students" but nevertheless made it into Cuba with so little resistance? The argument that Castro was on the verge of collapse was the administration's basic position over the course of the summer, in press conferences and leaks, and again at Kennedy's 29 August press conference. If so, then why could the administration not help with the final push?[5]

The *Examiner* criticized the State Department, source of the denials of U.S. involvement, and praised the "students" for the raid:

> How do they know it did not inspire anti-Castro forces in the same fashion as Allied air attacks in World War II put fresh heart into the European underground?
>
> And just what is this heavy armament of Cuba for, anyway? To shoot at Cuban freedom fighters in and out of Cuba? To light the torch of Communism elsewhere in Latin America? To establish a Soviet base 90 miles from Key West? These are the matters the administration's State Department should be addressing itself to, not to the deflation of an heroic and desperate gesture.[6]

The *Examiner* fully supported the raids, which continued into October. The students were doing a good job and should receive CIA support, the paper argued. Indeed, because they reportedly were in such desperate straits, the address of the group was given so that readers could send checks. The editors believed the administration was dilatory on the matter and that the public should act on its own. During September the brave seaborne exiles received more support from Hearst than did the now flaccid former commander of PT-109 (see appendix IV).[7]

The *Post* did not carry things that far. In late August it editorially defended the administration, as it continued to do throughout the entire Cuban period. But it let its support of the exile raids be known: "This country isn't neutral," the editors declared.[8]

The *Times* criticized no one on the raids. Nor did it or the *Post* raise the types of questions that could have been raised even after exiles with machine guns raided a British ship. The British charged that the refugees came from American soil, and probably had the support of the U.S. government. This charge could have produced an inquiry on the issue of whether or not the United States was encouraging an armed assault on another country. None was forthcoming. Instead, in the *Post* story a State Department denial was given the lead. The British view was subordinated, as was a story by *Post* reporter Dan Kurzman from Miami supporting the British view. There was no follow-up. It can only be concluded that the *Post* editors did not want to investigate the issue of responsibility for the raids. The administration was committed to Castro's removal, and so was the *Post*. Editorial judgment, not lack of manpower, halted further investigation by the paper of the issue.[9]

In addition to Kurzman, whose talents in this area obviously were not exploited, both the *Post* and the *Times* had reporters whose links to the exiles made them adept at uncovering exile secrets. Tad Szulc of the *Times* was the reporter who had learned the details of the Bay of Pigs invasion. He was invaluable to the paper because of his links with the "crazies." These undercover sources had told him just before the Bay of Pigs fiasco took place that the CIA was sponsoring an imminent invasion; but the *Times* editors, under government pressure, excised the crucial details from his story. He spoke of the extent of his knowledge in 1961 and 1962:

> Let's divide this into parts. Journalists knew afterward, and I did, that there was a continuing CIA activity in the Cuban area after the Bay of Pigs invasion. You know, raids . . . and we wrote about this. . . . On the part of assassinations you get into . . . the Mafia area, and I confess we had no clue. . . .
>
> It's one thing to be in an area like Miami and be able to track a paid, major movement such as an invasion brigade, because people depart, families hear things, Cubans talk too much. . . . When you deal with a very, very deep cover situation, then it's obviously much harder because knowledge then is confined to a very small group. Maybe a small

group such as the Kennedys or the Max Taylors, or the president or one or two people in the CIA.[10]

Szulc did not write about American involvement with the raids in the *Times* during the period under review. His articles, the major ones in the paper about Cuba, were concerned with United States economic and diplomatic activities and foreign reactions to these initiatives. "My stories presumably reflect what the government here was trying to accomplish," Szulc recalled.[11]

The *Post* had a counterpart to Szulc on its editorial staff, Karl E. Meyer. He also had links to the exiles and had obtained a good deal of the Bay of Pigs story. Because there was no possibility of its publication in the *Post*, he sent it to the *New Republic*, whose editor, Gilbert Harrison, accepted it and then at the last minute, after a call to Schlesinger, decided to hold the story.[12]

Meyer did not believe that the Monroe Doctrine applied to the current situation, and said that he disagreed on this issue with Managing Editor Russell Wiggins, who had assumed responsibility for the editorial page. But Meyer did favor an uprising against Castro and CIA support for it, provided that the intended beneficiaries were Cuban liberals. On 29 September Meyer wrote a *Post* editorial encouraging American support for an anti-Castro uprising within Cuba. He explained how he had come to write the piece: "I was under the influence of Ernesto Betancourt, a liberal exile. I probably wrote this to get the paper away from the idea of invading Cuba, but instead to give discreet aid to the Cuban liberal underground. I'm still not sure how I feel about this. I'm against dirty tricks, but maybe it's okay to help democratic resistance movements."[13]

The liberal press thus was just as actively supporting liberal refugee efforts to overthrow Castro as Hearst was promoting the conservatives. In their insistence that Castro be overthrown, journalists may well have been affected by public attitudes. In the case of the *Times* and the *Post*, anti-Castro journalists were also influenced by the fact that they shared attitudes with high administration officials whose activities they were assigned to report.

These shared attitudes did not solve the administration's problems in the press during this election period, however. For, as we have seen, the main element of the administration's effort to "do something" about Cuba—for which the politicians were clamoring—could not be talked about, not even by any proadministration journalists or newspapers that might have known about the undercover operation. The policy of the administration thus contributed to its failure to influence the popular and conservative newspapers and columnists concerning the validity of its policies. It did undertake a high-visibility press effort, involving press conferences and presidential policy statements, but it became clear that this also had limited effect during this preelection period. During late August and September, the president stayed one step behind the Republicans.

The Republicans Define the Issue

At his late August press conference, Kennedy said the administration had no information on the Soviet "technicians" and opposed an invasion, but it did support the Monroe Doctrine. These words did not satisfy the popular press. Marguerite Higgins, for example, gave favorable play to a campaign speech by the Republican senator from Indiana, Homer E. Capehart, that occurred shortly after Kennedy's news conference:

> He [Capehart] therefore put himself on the side of the many Cuban refugees, some of them knowledgeable, who have insisted that the degree of Communist military intervention in Cuba has been underestimated by the administration.
> Said Senator Capehart: "How long will the president examine the situation?" From the standpoint of international law, the U.S. has every right to land troops, take possession of Havana and occupy the country, unless the Cuban government answers satisfactorily the request of the United States government that all Soviet military personnel be sent home.[14]

Senator Keating also received big play in the press for his 31 August Senate speech claiming that there were twelve hundred Russian troops (not "technicians") there and "concave metal structures supported by tubing" that appeared to be designed for rocket installation. He warned that the Soviets might be constructing a missile base.

Kennedy responded with a 4 September statement that new U-2 evidence of 29 August had located "Soviet anti-aircraft defense missiles with a slant range of twenty-five miles . . . along with Soviet-made torpedo boats carrying ship-to-ship guided missiles having a range of fifteen miles." The number of Soviet "technicians" was put at 3,500. This statement came exactly four days too late. The president had not revealed information on the Soviet military buildup until after the Republicans had demanded it.

Kennedy tried to retrieve the situation by doing the same thing he had done during the Berlin crisis. On 6 September he asked Congress for authority to call up 150,000 troops. He followed this move with a high-visibility presidential press conference on 13 September in which he spelled out his position in greater detail. Both in a prepared statement and in response to questions, he returned to his theme of earlier in the summer that it was Castro who was "in trouble." The Soviet military buildup was a continuation of one that had been going on since 1958—that is, since the administration of his Republican predecessor. He blurred over the fact that there had been a sharp increase in the buildup since July and promised that America would take action if offensive missiles—which the president had on 4 September defined as ground-to-ground missiles—were discovered. Surface-to-air missiles and torpedo boats were not offensive weapons, he contended. Furthermore, the Republicans were helping Castro by their "loose talk" of an invasion, which gave a "thin color of legitimacy" to his claim of self-defense.[15]

These press and policy initiatives did not halt the Republican offensive. On the same day that Kennedy held his news conference, the Senate decided to hold hearings before a joint session of the Foreign Relations and Armed Services committees. Senator Fulbright's Latin American expert on the Foreign Relations Committee, Pat Holt, remembered why these hearings were called: "Keating kept making these charges and everybody got excited as hell about it. The main object of the Joint Hearings, as I recall, was to try to find a formula which would satisfy Keating and the hard liners without doing too much violence to the principle of nonintervention. . . . It was a question of degree, of how tough you got. The question was easy for Keating, Capehart and Goldwater."[16]

A number of Republicans and conservative Democrats wanted tough language demanding immediate action to remove Castro. After hearing administration witnesses, they were brought around to acceptance of a joint resolution that Holt described as "a sort of post-dated declaration of war." As had the military reserves bill a week earlier, the resolution passed the Senate on 21 September with overwhelming support.[17]

To the administration's dismay, passage of the resolution did not end the matter. Many Republicans supported the bill but insisted that it did not go far enough. Senator Prouty of Vermont, for example, continued to argue for a blockade, as did Goldwater and Nixon. A conservative Democrat, Congressman Paul Kitchen of North Carolina, opened an investigation of maritime trade with Cuba. And Castro's 24 September announcement that Russia and Cuba were building a port for the Soviet fishing fleet further exacerbated the situation.

The Editorial Critics: The *Examiner* and the *Tribune*

Editorially, the administration did poorly on the Cuban issue during this period. The *Examiner* had been a swing paper that went the president's way on Laos and that was turned around on Berlin as he used the full resources of the presidency and offered a military-oriented policy. During this late August and September period, the *Examiner* offered its strongest critique of the administration. It carried more editorials than any of the other papers during September, and a higher percentage of them than of those in other papers were critical of the administration (see appendix IV).[18]

Hearst did not accept the official view that the Soviet weapons were defensive. Instead, he viewed them as a real threat to American security and consequently supported the active military response—including a blockade—favored by hard-line Republicans. Following the president's 13 September press conference, Hearst commented: "The press boys bobbled their lines. . . . They neglected to ask the question . . . 'Why not blockade?' Then they missed the cue to follow up when the president (pointedly it seemed to this listener) ignored the question about how he interprets the Monroe Doctrine." Hearst concluded: "I have been informed that the president reads this column fairly regularly. If he finds time to read this one, I end it with a question which he might consider answering at his next press conference. It is, Mr. President, IF THE SUPPLY OF SOVIET WAR MATERIEL AND PERSONNEL CONTINUE, AS SEEMS CERTAIN, AT WHAT POINT, IF ANY, WOULD YOU INVOKE THE MONROE DOCTRINE?" [19]

September was also the time of greatest editorial criticism in the *Tribune*. As with the *Examiner*, its criticism was greater than during its previous high point during the Berlin crisis. None of the president's actions elicited a favorable response. Neither did the bipartisan resolution, which was not considered to be strong enough in dealing with the Soviet military buildup. Nevertheless, the *Tribune* did not favor "precipitate action." America, the editors commented in a unique rationale, already had "a war on our hands in Vietnam and a beleaguered garrison in Berlin to say nothing of Berlin's civilian population to protect." If the United States invaded and drove Castro out, "the real trouble would begin. Cubans have a penchant for bad government. So if we set up a good one it wouldn't be supported, and we would get the blame if it were a bad one." Despite this conclusion, the *Tribune* took an interest in Keating's charges and questioned the administration's intelligence on the strategic issue. Walter Trohan also gave the Keating charges play in his column. [20]

The Popular Columnists Are Critical

In the *Examiner*, no columnist during the entire month of September had a good thing to say about the president's policies. Goldwater, who now appeared regularly in the paper as a syndicated columnist, led with seven columns on Cuba. He provided the *Examiner*'s first commentary by a columnist following the president's 13 September news conference. Conservative David Lawrence, one of the leading columnists of his day in terms of circulation, appeared with four columns urging action beyond that which the administration was willing to take. Early in the month, he declared that the Soviets were defying the Monroe Doctrine with the "technicians"; if they were not removed, the least the administration could do was to break relations with the Soviet Union and institute an economic blockade of Cuba. By the end of the month, he was pointedly invoking the Munich analogy. [21]

William S. White was also a popular columnist who appeared in the *Examiner*. A self-styled independent, he tended toward the Republican viewpoint, though at times he could be lavishly laudatory about Kennedy and the "burdens" of his office. Although the administration often was able to win White's support on key foreign policy issues, in September 1962 he was unhappy about its Cuban policies, which seemed too oriented toward the Allies and the OAS. The last straw for him was the defection of former President Eisenhower in mid-October, which White blamed on Kennedy's alleged partisanship.[22]

Joseph Alsop, who believed that Berlin and Vietnam were more important issues than Cuba, supported the administration's position, but he was not focusing on Cuba in September. His silence left the president virtually without supporters among the popular columnists. The administration was aware of the few columnists who backed it. One was Henry Wriston, who was not a regular columnist, but was drawn into service by the *Washington Post*, which could not find other supportive columnists. According to an administration press analyst, William F. Buckley, Jr., David Lawrence and Robert Murphy, a former diplomat who was acting as a columnist, favored a "flat showdown right now." This left Drew Pearson as the lone pro-Kennedy popular columnist in September.[23]

Krock Supports the Republicans

Arthur Krock of the *Times* agreed with the Republicans and popular columnists in August and September that a crisis was at hand. He was an example of the rougher side of Kennedy's press policies—of the tendency at the White House to cut off journalists who were not favorable to the administration. Krock became a leading Washington correspondent of the *Times* in 1932. During the Roosevelt and Truman years, he was on the receiving end of presidential patronage. Exclusive interviews with Roosevelt in 1937 and Truman in 1950 had caused press flurries at a time when exclusives had been less frequent than they were to be under Kennedy.[24]

Krock had been a family friend of the Kennedys—particularly of Joseph Kennedy, Sr., with whom he shared many conservative views. But Krock's relationship with the Kennedys began to turn sour during the election of 1960 and by 1962 he was an outsider who could not expect the inside tips from high officials that columnists rely on. "Krock felt they had stabbed him in the back," Wicker commented. "He had been very helpful to that family from the old man down. . . . Then when Jack got into the White House he cut him off." Another reason for the estrangement related to questions of generation and style. According to Holborn, "Kennedy just wearied of Krock. He decided he was basically unreadable. At this stage of his life Krock had a thin skin and an elevated view of his role. Kennedy respected him, but he didn't like him. . . . Kennedy thought of him as a valuable period piece, evocative of another age." [25]

Such factors, combined with the now consistent critique involving interest groups, Republicans, and popular columnists, brought Krock to his period of strongest opposition to the administration. He criticized the president's 29 August press conference. Kennedy had criticized those who favored invading the island, Krock said, "but he never gave his views about a naval patrol which is the most effective means of keeping Cuba from acquiring Communist missiles and other offensive war weaponry, and does not involve military invasion at all." [26]

Although in opposition, Krock was still from the *Times*, and this column brought an immediate dispatch to the newspaper of word that the administration did have a "naval patrol." In his next column, he termed this patrol "a very cautious operation" that was only checking what the Soviets were doing. He then criticized Kennedy for not providing "official confirmation" of Russian forces and supplies on Cuba that appeared to have "as much potential for offensive as for defensive military activity." That very day, 4 September, the president countered with his version of the Soviet buildup. Kennedy's early initiatives did not satisfy Krock, who thought that the administration's call-up of the reserves was a political move. [27]

Although Krock was impressed by the president's 13 September press conference, even that did not silence his criticism. In his column the following day, he accused the president of surreptitiously turning the Monroe Doctrine into a "Kennedy Doctrine." Under the Kennedy Doctrine, the president would take action only if a foreign power is "endangering our peace and safety," not just because a foreign power had a military presence in the Western Hemisphere. Krock also noted that Kennedy's response to the Monroe Doctrine question at his 13 September press conference was not to the point. [28]

From Krock in September, Kennedy received the kind of consistent criticism that had been absent in the *Times* during his earlier crises. His 13 September news conference obviously had failed to satisfy many swing and conservative columnists and editors, and he held no more news conferences for two months. Because so many forces in the society were stirred up over Castro and the Soviet threat, they had proved ineffective in dealing with such a sensitive issue during an election period.

The Favorable Press Becomes More Favorable

In the summer of 1962, *Post* editorial writer Alan Barth wrote an article on the press-government relationship. The press, he argued, was exercising a "patriotic" self-restraint that was an abdication of its First Amendment role as governmental watchdog. Whatever muckraking existed was being done not by newspapers but by someone like Senator John J. Williams of Delaware. The editorial page had turned into "a mere vestigial appendage—an adornment perpetuated long after its purpose has been forgotten. . . . This is especially true today, it seems to me, in foreign affairs. The most remarkable thing about American editorial comment on the U-2 incident, on the Cuban invasion, on the impasse at Berlin, on Laos and Vietnam and the Congo is its essential uniformity. . . . There is no real debate on the matters that mean life or death to the nation."[29]

Barth exemplified precisely what he was describing. He wrote liberal editorials on civil rights and civil liberties—concerns of the *Post*'s publisher. But he was not considered to be an "expert" on foreign policy issues and was reduced to airing his views in the *Progressive*.[30]

The *Post*'s editorial page in September was again devoted to defending the president's position. An editorial by Wiggins after Kennedy's 13 September press conference consumed three-fourths of the space for editorials. It accurately noted that the real importance of the president's statement was the projected American response in the event of discovery of weapons in Cuba that he defined as offensive. The *Post* concurred and urged that in such an eventuality "the military response of this country must be prompt, decisive, and overwhelming." The congressional resolution was seen as support for the president rather than as the political maneuver it also was. Another editorial supported a call by Rusk for an OAS parley on Cuba that came several days after an unnoticed suggestion by Keating for just such a meeting.[31]

The *Post*'s main response was to play the Cuban issue in a restrained fashion, just as the administration was doing. Few of the events that precipitated editorial activity in the other papers—such as the exile activities or Republican charges—stirred the *Post* editors to comment (see appendix IV). During the Berlin crisis, there had been a hint of impatience as the criticism came from abroad. There was none now. Republican opposition only increased the *Post*'s support for the president.

As in other situations, an important factor in the *Post*'s stance on Cuba was the close connection between high officials and the paper's leadership. "By September 1962 the paper reflected more and more the government's position on Cuba," Karl Meyer recalled. "Phil Bonsal, former Ambassador to Havana, who was a friend of Kay's [Katharine Graham] and Adolph Berle, who had an extreme anti-Castro feeling, were forces to be reckoned with."[32]

The *Times* also provided editorial support for the president during September without the impatience evident during the Berlin crisis. Its primary editorial criticisms again were directed at Russia, Congress, and Republicans (see appendix IV). The editors assumed that Kennedy had better information than Keating and feared that a move in Cuba could provoke a countermove in

Berlin or Southeast Asia. Very little editorial comment was inspired by Congress, then in its most active period on the Cuban question.[33]

Sokolsky and Drummond criticized Kennedy on the op ed pages of the *Post*, but—except for Krock—most of the *Times*'s columnists were not accepting the idea of a Cuban crisis as propounded by the Republicans. The foreign perspective found a rare expression in the paper. Max Frankel wrote about how the European allies viewed Cuba, and Hanson Baldwin saw Cuba as one among many issues. The Republican charges irritated Reston; his only column on Cuba during September was entitled "How About a Blockade on Nonsense?" The rhetoric surrounding the Soviet presence in Cuba that stirred people in Peoria had little appeal for the *Times*'s European-oriented constituency.[34]

Opposition to the Republicans moved the *Post-Dispatch* to support the administration. As usual, it came to the Cuban problem from a different perspective. During the summer of 1962, the paper ran a series of interpretive pieces by its UN correspondent Donald Grant, who gained permission to visit Cuba at a time when other American reporters were excluded. His series touched on such issues as the normalization of relations and British Foreign Secretary Alec Douglas Home's opposition to isolating Cuba. Grant even interviewed Jacobo Arbenz Guzman, the leftist former Guatemalan president residing in Cuba, whose government was overthrown with CIA assistance in 1954. The publication of this series showed a concern about improving relations with Cuba rare in American journalism during this period.[35]

In presenting stories raising the issue of possible parallels between the situation in Cuba and Guatemala eight years before, the *Post-Dispatch* was also making an unusual effort to explain continuities in U.S. policy toward Latin America. Many Cubans believed that the Bay of Pigs invasion had been an effort to replicate the Guatemalan experience and that the United States continued to represent a grave threat, thus justifying large-scale Soviet aid. Like much of the American public, most of the press was so preoccupied with the threat to the nation that few could see or care about the threat that it constituted to leftist governments in Latin America.[36]

Editorially, the *Post-Dispatch* supported the president and focused all its criticism on the Republicans in its 9 September editorial. Its critique of the Republicans was undiluted by the derogatory statements about the Cubans and the Russians that marked the editorials in the other liberal papers. The *Post-Dispatch* editors had been pleased by Kennedy's 4 September statement, which in their view constituted a warning both to Fidel Castro and to the war hawks in Congress. The editors were especially critical of the Republicans for trying to use the Cuban issue to make a fast buck in the political marketplace instead of responding to it in unemotional and thoughtful tones. "Political exploitation of the Cuba problem is all the more reprehensible because it comes so easy," the *Post-Dispatch* editorialized on 9 September. "Senator Dirksen and Representative Halleck are mining this rich lode of public sentiment with all the recklessness of politicians who know they do not have to be responsible for the consequences." [37]

The *Post-Dispatch* was thus more flexible toward Castro than the other papers in this study, and it was also more conciliatory than the president. During this election period, however, it concentrated on criticizing the Republicans. This position paralleled that of Senator Fulbright, who likewise avoided innovative positions on Latin America at a time when he was focusing his attention on his reelection campaign in Arkansas. "In such a situation any first rule would be, 'Don't Rock the Boat,'" congressional aide Pat Holt observed. "The same was the situation for many of the other Democrats who were running for re-election." Thus no weighty contestants entered the lists to challenge the president's position from the left. Not wishing to see conservative Republican gains in Congress, the *Post-Dispatch* and most liberal Democrats swallowed their doubts and praised Kennedy for his relative restraint on Cuba. [38]

Conclusion

The press-presidential relationship during the Cuban missile crisis is often cited as a sterling example of presidential dominance of the press because of press coverage during the crisis week beginning on 22 October. But the issue of Soviet missiles in Cuba had begun two months earlier, in late August and early September. And much of this early coverage was harmful to Kennedy, illustrating the difficulties that can arise for a president when his political opposition exploits a popular issue during an election campaign.

Kennedy enjoyed many advantages in relation to the press. One of these was partisanship, which resulted, for example, in continued greater *Post* usage of the liberal sources who were inclined to support his policies (see appendix V). Largely because of their partisan support of the administration and opposition to the Republican critics, the *Post*, the *Times*, and the *Post-Dispatch* also backed the president editorially on Cuba during September. Still, the Cuban exiles and the Republicans clearly held the initiative on the issue. Their hard-line stance was reflected not only in the editorials and columns in the popular and conservative press but, more importantly, in the news stories in all the papers that trumpeted the Russian "threat" and the administration's "weakness." Thus, as it entered the election period, the administration did not have public opinion behind it on the Cuban issue, and it was not able to use policy pronouncements and a high-visibility press policy to turn the issue around. The fact was that the administration had no visible policy that responded to concrete public concerns.

Table 5. Cuba: Comparison of Official and Nonofficial Sources, 1962
(front-page totals for all newspapers)

	United States Official	Domestic Political	Foreign	Interest Groups	Total Domestic Pol., Foreign, and Int. Grps.	Percentage U.S. Official Represents of This Total
25–31 Aug.	24 (43%)	0	17 (30%)	15 (27%)	32	75%
September	157 (36%)	160 (36%)	105 (24%)	20 (5%)	285	55%
1–19 Oct.	75 (38%)	42 (21%)	51 (26%)	31 (16%)	124	60%
20–22 Oct.	16 (67%)	3 (13%)	4 (17%)	1 (4%)	8	200%
23–29 Oct.	258 (43%)	37 (6%)	264 (44%)	30 (5%)	331	78%

The source figures attest to the administration's difficulties (see table 5). The September period was for all the newspapers in this study the single period in the four crises of greatest influence for the politicians. It was also the lowest point, except for early August of the Vietnam crisis, of official impact on page-one coverage. On page one in the *Post*, the *Tribune*, and the *Post-Dispatch*, the politicians took the lead during September; in the *Examiner* and the *Times* they were the second category behind administration officials.

Thus, the impact of domestic political sources for all newspapers was pronounced during this period and greater than during any of the other three crises. The politicians remained a critical element until Kennedy's somber announcement on 22 October that there was indeed a crisis in Cuba and that the United States was indeed "doing something."

Chapter 10

Some Successful Policy Diversions

1–19 October

Partly by accident and partly by design, the administration achieved some lessening of the pressures on its Cuban policy during the early part of October. In both cases, the success occurred as the result of policy diversions that seized the headlines. The first unplanned diversion was the violent climax of the federal government's efforts to ensure that James Meredith would be able to become the first black student at the University of Mississippi. The second was the reemergence of the Berlin issue in a way that allowed the president to look very presidential.

A planned third diversion was Secretary Rusk's convening of an OAS conference in Washington, at which measures to further cripple the Cuban economy were discussed. This conference preempted the news in the more internationalist-oriented press, raising the level of U.S. official and foreign source usage at the expense of domestic political sources in the *Post* and the *Times* (see appendix II).[1]

At the same time, the administration unilaterally announced a policy of denying the use of American ports to ships bound for Cuba. The *Times*'s editors lauded this action, but more importantly it won for the administration the support of the other side in foreign affairs, the unilateralists like William Randolph Hearst, Jr. He thought the embargo was the blockade he had been advocating, and shouted "Hallelujah!" on the front page. His joy was short-lived as the embargo turned out not to be a blockade, but the administration's initiative scored some points with hard-liners.[2]

Surfacing as a factor in the administration's public relations strategy during October was an emphasis on the importance of Berlin as a way of diverting attention from Cuba. Louis Harris, the president's pollster and political adviser, was traveling around the country and wrote Kennedy on 4 October:

> Some of the edge has been taken off the Cuban issue by Mississippi, but tensions are still high on foreign policy. Majorities ranging from 70–80 percent are with you on Berlin. On Cuba, however, the balance

is still 38–62 percent negative. In Michigan, within the past week, a majority of 82–18 percent wanted a blockade on Cuba, although a majority of 68–32 percent oppose going to war there.

It is my belief that you are more in control of this election than ever before, provided in the last three weeks you put the issue in a perspective on which the people can vote Democratic. This is that perspective: (a) You may say that matters such as the Mississippi crisis, Cuban policy and Berlin are not partisan political issues. You would never seek to exploit them for partisan purposes. . . .

(b) But you have been shocked and dismayed by the extreme partisanship of Republicans on many of these matters in this campaign. . . . On Cuba they have been shooting from the hip and in the process have gone a long way toward undermining abroad the notion that we Americans are united in our firm and steadfast stand against Communism and Communist imperialism. By their recklessness in Cuba, they have cast doubt on our position in Berlin. You can then state that if it came to it, we would stand by the freedom of West Berlin, even if we had to do it alone. And in Cuba let it be understood that this government will settle for no less than the obliteration of all vestiges of Communism in this hemisphere.

The Republicans know full well that this is the policy of this government. But they would deliberately shoot craps with the destiny of this nation, would play petty politics with the national security, whether in Mississippi, Cuba or Berlin to try to gain votes this fall.

The American people will not be fooled by this political chicanery.[3]

The strategy, in short, was to accuse the Republicans of playing politics with difficult and sensitive issues while conveying the impression that the administration would never dream of doing such a thing. Berlin, for which it was now receiving highly favorable ratings, was to be stressed as the primary issue. The Republican preoccupation with Cuba, the president should say, was damaging his efforts to resolve this long-standing issue.

The Political Uses of Berlin

One element of the strategy was to emphasize the seriousness of the Berlin issue. About the time of the first anniversary of the Wall in August, tension had occurred involving the East German shooting of a refugee and a riot in West Berlin. At the beginning of September, the initiative came from the Western side: an Allied demand that the Russians stop bringing armored cars into West Berlin. Soviet harassment of American planes followed. All these moves were what Joseph Alsop, visiting Berlin in mid-September, called "thrust and parry again." But these, along with intelligence leaks of an increase in the East German military budget, and, in Alsop's words, "the placing of Soviet rockets where they can threaten the Western corridor," were used by the administration to justify the remobilization in mid-September that many thought was connected with the Cuban problem.[4]

In late September and early October, top officials stepped up their assessment of the seriousness of the crisis. The president briefed congressional leaders to the effect that Khrushchev had revived the Berlin issue, and leading journalists were also given the story. "The Kennedy Administration is in a 'batten down the hatches' mood over Berlin in expectation of a major crisis once the November 6 election is over," Chalmers Roberts wrote on 9 October, citing "aides of both Rusk and Kennedy." But lower-level officials whom he asked to corroborate the story told him that "there is no evidence that Khrushchev is going to precipitate another crisis." Roberts's colleague, Murray Marder, reported on 12 October that "this especially strong alert by publicly anonymous administration sources" was based on a Soviet statement of 11 September which implied that Khrushchev would "step up pressure on West Berlin" after the election.[5]

In fact, as the American ambassador in Moscow, Foy Kohler, and others have pointed out, the comment on the German issue in the 11 September statement did not constitute a threat against Berlin requiring the president's undivided attention. It was a weak reed upon which to hang a crisis. Even Roberts, generally proadministration, accepted the idea of a forthcoming Berlin crisis only on 18 October when the administration began its high-level meetings on what turned out to be the Cuban missile crisis. "The truth is that the president and his associates do believe a Berlin crisis is ahead and that the public ought to be forewarned," Roberts wrote. He was clearly deceived by administration cover stories designed to protect the secrecy of its deliberations on Cuba.[6]

Much of the Washington-oriented press bought the Berlin issue before Roberts did. This included the editors of the *Times*, who were always attuned to Berlin, and Walter Lippmann, who wrote much about that city but practically nothing about Cuba during the period.

The case of Alsop is particularly instructive. At the time, he was on the campaign trail with Louis Harris. He did write about Cuba, but he tied that issue to Berlin in much the same way Harris had suggested to Kennedy in his memo. Alsop's writings on Cuba looked primarily at its political aspect. On 8 October he declared that, because of public sentiment for strong measures against Cuba, "President Kennedy could stir the country to its depth, and lift it partly from the doldrums, by the simple act of ordering a blockade." But, instead of advocating a hard-line course, as he had done during the two previous crises, Alsop used the administration's line on Berlin to urge restraint: ". . . although few people realize it, Berlin ties the President's hands in the

Cuban situation, at least for the present. As the President himself told the Congressional leaders at a briefing a few days ago, the delicate and dangerous task of meeting the unexpected challenge at Berlin must not be complicated by the Cuban problem . . . the Berlin corner must be rounded before the final choice is made on tackling the Cuban problem." [7] Alsop then extolled the administration's efforts at the time to negotiate the ransom of the Bay of Pigs prisoners, but warned that it would require taking "time off from preparing for the Berlin climax" to free the prisoners.

When asked why he downplayed Cuba and emphasized Berlin in his articles in September and early October, Alsop responded that he was "deceived by the same . . . bad [CIA] intelligence that the president had been deceived by." Rusk and others in the government, Alsop recalled, "were afraid that the Soviets would countermove at Berlin if we were unduly risky about Cuba." He also downplayed Cuba because "Bob McNamara in the government—everyone I respected in the government—thought that Keating was crazy. I believed that and I was wrong, and so were they." [8]

The Domestic Political Challenge Declines

Republican charges in regard to Cuba in early October lacked the freshness and the newsworthiness they had enjoyed a month before. Thus, even though Keating was making even more serious allegations than in September—including the assertion on 9 October that construction had started on "at least a half-dozen launching sites for intermediate range tactical missiles"—the papers were much less likely in October to give them page-one coverage or favorable treatment in editorials and columns. [9]

In his only column on Cuba during early October, Reston criticized Keating sharply: "No longer do Senators check their private reports of secret military information with officials of their own government, but publish them on their own and 'confirm' them on their own responsibility." His reason for discounting Keating was similar to that of Alsop. According to E. W. Kenworthy, "Somebody told Scotty he [Keating] was off his nut. Later, after the crisis, he said, 'I'm sorry, Ken, you were right. My informants either were wrong or misled me.'" [10]

Reston concluded his article with an approving assessment of the real nature of the American effort in Cuba. He commented on an "Alpha 66" raid that had just killed twenty defenders at the Cuban port of Isabela de Sagua, including some Russians, and then summarized current U.S. policy:

> What is going on is something quite different from the black and white picture of the Cuban controversy presented from the political plat-

forms. In those angry talks it appears that the issue of American Cuban policy is between those who want to invade or at least blockade Cuba on the one hand, and those who want to "do nothing" on the other.

This is not, however, the actual situation. There is a missing element in the debate which distorts the whole argument. This is the element of subversion, which is going on all the time in that island and which can be increased substantially if necessary. . . .

In present circumstances, there will be no invasion, and no blockade, and no acquiescence in Soviet control of Cuba. But there will be total surveillance of Cuba and there will be more turmoil in Cuba than Castro has yet experienced or imagined.

In thus presenting official thinking, Reston was coming as close as he dared to explaining that the administration was "in control" as well as "doing something" and that the political debate was just muddying the water.[11]

The government's view that there were no ground-to-ground missiles in Cuba by this time was taking effect even with many who had earlier paid attention to Keating. Robert J. Donovan, Washington bureau chief of the Republican *New York Herald-Tribune*, recalled, for example, that his paper was less interested in Keating's charges in October than it had been in September. Thus the charges lost credibility at least in liberal sections of the Republican press.[12]

The relative decline in the importance of the domestic political challenge was also reflected in source usage. As table 5 shows, the percentage of page-one domestic political sources declined from 36 percent in September to 21 percent in early October. Whereas there had actually been more domestic political than official U.S. sources on Cuba in September (160 to 157), in the 1–19 October period the number had dropped to little more than half as many (42 to 75). Initiatives like the OAS meeting and the strengthened embargo were paying off for the administration.

In the case of the *Examiner*, the page-one foreign sources did not increase as a result of the diplomatic efforts, but the administration sources did. Although its page-one domestic political sources remained dangerously higher than in the *Post* and the *Times* during early October, they experienced some decline over what they had been in September (see appendix II). The administration found some relief, but it was not out of hot water yet.

Some relief was also evident on the editorial pages. The number of editorials critical of Kennedy declined in the *Tribune*. That paper devoted itself instead to a critique of the administration on grounds that it violated the civil liberties of right-wing General Edwin Walker, who led a racist demonstration at the University of Mississippi. The number of *Examiner* editorials on Cuba dropped, and its criticism of the administration on the issue was not so intense (see appendix IV). Criticisms by columnists also declined: Krock, for example, paid tribute to former President Eisenhower's bipartisan spirit and went on vacation.[13]

Despite the administration's improved position in the press in early October, the Cuban issue still would not go away. The *Post* reported on 18 October that 344 editors and 208 members of Congress considered it the primary campaign issue.[14]

Conclusion

During September the president clearly had been on the defensive on the Cuban issue. During the first part of October, there were administration charges and countercharges, planned and accidental diversions, and a newly developed political strategy emphasizing Berlin and the irresponsibility of Republican charges on Cuba. What generalizations can be made about the relationship between a president and the press as a result of the experience of the seven weeks before the actual missile crisis?

It is clear that differences between opposition and proadministration newspapers and journalists were accentuated during an election campaign on a disputed foreign policy issue. Newspapers may well give greater support to an administration or intensify their opposition to it as a result of a heightened level of domestic political concern about an issue. A paper like the *Examiner*, which had supported Republican presidential candidates and which tended to favor the use of military power in cold war confrontations, could be expected to provide emphasis quite different from that of a paper like the *Post-Dispatch*.

Public concern and conservative viewpoints also put constraints on Kennedy's ability to influence newspapers on the Cuban issue. A high-visibility press strategy worked poorly in September, but a low-visibility one worked somewhat more effectively in early October. Proadministration journalists and newspapers, such as the *Times*, had little influence with other segments of the press, such as popular columnists and newspapers, which reflected other forces in the society, notably conservative politicians and interest groups.

Despite constraints on Kennedy, he was not powerless. He still had newsmaking potential as a result of his ability to stage events and enunciate new positions. The fact that journalists report and speculate about what is new also worked to his advantage, for he had the power to create new issues like Berlin simply by indicating his concern about them. Although this form of presidential influence may have diminished as the result of the emergence of alternate power centers in the foreign policy area, it certainly held true at the height of the cold war "imperial presidency."

Chapter 11

The Cuban
Missile Crisis

The Administration Dominates
the Press, 20–29 October

On 14 October the administration discovered by means of a U-2 flight that Keating's information had been correct. The Soviets were placing missiles in Cuba. The president, who had just returned from a campaign trip, was not told about this new development until the next morning, after he had had a good night's rest. Immediate high-level meetings were held and it was decided that no diplomatic overtures should be made to force the removal of the weapons. Instead, the choice was narrowed to either a "surgical strike," which the military believed would need to be followed by an invasion, or a blockade—just the measures the Republicans had been proposing. A decision was made to keep suspicious journalists off the track. The Defense Department denied the presence of the missiles after they had been discovered and described military preparations in the Caribbean as "maneuvers." The president went back to campaigning until he had to return from a Chicago campaign trip with a "cold" on Saturday, 20 October, when the administration was ready to make its final decision to confront the Soviets.[1]

Later, this secrecy was termed a vital factor in putting Khrushchev on the defensive and forcing him to back down. It also put an immediate halt to domestic debate—and the publication of dissident foreign views. Because of the secrecy, which the press helped to protect, the president's nationwide television and radio message on 22 October announcing the blockade was a "memorable address" and doubly effective. From this, the first confrontation with Russia involving nuclear weapons, the president emerged a national hero: at last, he had really "done something."[2]

During the week before the television address and the six days of the publicized crisis, the administration sought to use the press as an instrument of national policy. It was asked to keep the secret until Kennedy could dramatically announce his policy, and it was expected thereafter to embrace the administration's interpretation of the issue. With very few exceptions, reporters, editors, and columnists accepted this strategy. Lacking alternative explanations from Congress, dissidents within the administration, or Allied foreign powers, the press allowed Kennedy, McNamara, and other officials to disseminate their views without challenge, and thus contributed during the missile crisis to a significant expansion of presidential power.

The Press Keeps the Secret

Although the president took personal charge of keeping the news secret, his abrupt cancellation of campaign appearances raised suspicion that something serious was brewing. Even more suspicion arose as journalists noticed that important officials were strangely absent from their Saturday dinner parties. In his book *With Kennedy*, Pierre Salinger recalled the difficulty of keeping the news away from the press. He reported that at 10:08 P.M. Saturday

> [A] call came from Eddie Folliard of the *Washington Post*. He informs me that columnist Walter Lippmann has just told *Post* editor Al Friendly at a party that we're on the brink of war. I called the President back. He's angry. "This town is a sieve." Then, after a pause, "Pierre, how much longer do you think this thing can hold?"
>
> "Whatever the story," I reply, "too many good reporters are chasing it for it to last much longer. I would say through tonight and maybe tomorrow." [3]

Salinger described the situation on Sunday as getting worse: "I called the president four times to alert him that security was crumbling. Certain reporters had the entire story except for the actual time the quarantine would take effect." Kennedy then interceded with the publishers of the *Times* and the *Post* to halt publication. In the case of the *Times*, he did so before the newspaper actually had the story. E. W. Kenworthy described what happened:

> On Saturday night my wife and I had just got back from our vacation in West Virginia. . . . We went over [to Reston's house for supper] and just before we left I heard on the TV that Kennedy, who had just gone out to Chicago had suddenly turned around and come back because he had a bad cold. [The two agreed this was suspicious.] Scotty said, "What do you think it is?" I hadn't the faintest damned idea what it was. I said it might be something to do with another Berlin crisis. He said, "I'll tell you what." So we left our wives and he took the phone in one study and I took the phone in the bedroom or vice versa. Then we started calling up, with the reporter's standard trick. You call the State Department and say, "What the hell is this about Berlin?" as if you knew all about it. Or you say, "Is there something boiling up with

Castro?" We didn't have the faintest idea. But the minute you start doing that the flags all start going up.

We hadn't been on the phone more than an hour and a half, calling everybody we knew and blustering and so on. We didn't have the faintest clue, the honest truth is. We weren't getting much either. But the State Department and the White House got alarmed. It may have been Dean Rusk, but I think it was Kennedy who called the publisher in New York and asked us not to print. But we didn't know a damned thing.

Well, now, you know something is up when they ask you not to print. That was Saturday night, and by midnight or the next morning we knew. . . . Tad Szulc, who had awfully good sources, had picked up something. I think Scotty also got a real grasp on the thing, certainly by Sunday noon. Then, of course, we honored the agreement not to publish because Kennedy was going to have this speech on Monday.

Kenworthy explained why the *Times* did not print the story: "We didn't publish a word simply because you don't dare to take the risk if negotiations are really going on back and forth from Washington to Moscow. This was a very risky situation. Don't forget, Kennedy was terribly nervous having been beaten to a pulp on the Bay of Pigs and then having all that trouble with Khrushchev in Vienna."[4]

For Joseph Alsop, the missile crisis began earlier than for most:

It effectively started in my house, you know. The President was dining with me the night that he got the news. It was, I think, the 15th. I was giving a dinner for Chip Bohlen. . . . It was a very small dinner—just the great friends, and the Bohlens, and ourselves. And the President and Jackie, and two other people whom I've forgotten. It was about as difficult an evening as we ever had, because Susan Mary, my wife, was a wonderful, wonderful person but never could quite get it through her head that what the President really wanted to do with women was gossip. . . .

It was perfectly impossible that night because he was in a thick brown study, and if you have the President of the United States at the table in a thick brown study, no matter how good the food is, it tends to cast a pall. I had no idea—no notion—of what was happening, but before dinner and after dinner he was constantly taking Chip off into corners. He wanted Chip to stay here, instead of going to Paris the next day. Chip was saying, "I mustn't do that, because the Soviets would know that we know about this. If I stay, they'll smell a rat."

After dinner, when the ladies and gents still separated in those days, we went into the room where the men always sat—the garden room— and Chip got an argument going about historical chances. The Presi-

dent was always interested in that sort of thing, and it caught his attention. And he came out of the brown study to remark that if you just
calculated the historical chances on a mathematical basis, the chances
of a nuclear war within ten years were at least even. This was also
[about] Bob McNamara, because Bob had this complicated business
about if China gets the bomb, more than two persons, it goes up to
quadruple sizes. A lot of garbage: it doesn't go up like that at all. But
the President had been given this information by McNamara, and
hadn't really thought about it, and was just repeating it.

It was a little chilling, if I do say so. . . . [It was] two days later, I
guess, that I learned that something was really very badly wrong. . . .
I don't remember when I learned. I guess when everybody else did, or
just a little before. I probably learned a little before. If so, I didn't say
anything about it.[5]

The result was that, despite a few veiled suggestions in the press that something was happening with Cuba, the story was held in an atmosphere of
heightened expectation as the press awaited the president's word. Although
total quoted sources between 20 and 22 October were few (see table 5), the
administration dominated the sources during this period of expectation as
never before.[6]

On the evening of 22 October, Kennedy spoke to the nation. He explained
the change that had taken place in Cuba that now made it a "definitive threat
to the peace" because of the emplacement of "large, long-range and clearly
offensive weapons of sudden mass destruction." The United States had to respond. The president announced that the "initial" action of a quarantine to
halt the Soviet buildup had begun and insisted that all missiles be removed.
Otherwise "further action" might be necessary. The president concluded:
"My fellow citizens: let no one doubt that this is a difficult and dangerous
effort on which we have set out. No one can foresee precisely what course it
will take or what costs or casualties will be incurred. Many months of sacri-
fice and self-discipline lie ahead."[7]

The country was electrified. Richard Neustadt, the Harvard expert on
presidential power whom Kennedy admired and with whom he kept in contact, wrote Sorensen a memorandum a few days after the president's address.
He described the significance of the speech and of the fear it generated:

The reaction among students here to the President's speech of Monday
last was *qualitatively* different from anything I've ever witnessed before in moments of foreign crisis since I started to teach nine years ago;
this time these kids were literally scared for their lives and were as-
tonished, somehow, that their lives could be risked by an *American*
initiative. . . .

More people see and feel our Cuban action more intensely, as a real-life happening with immediate personal meaning for them, than has been the case with any event, foreign or domestic, in many years.

In consequence, there'll be a lot of "learning" done in these next days and weeks. These worried people will absorb lots of impressions about JFK; about our power, and its limits, about the cold war and its prospects. . . . And so long as they're watching intently they'll be listening, above all, to the President. Their worries could well give *him* more *direct attention* from a bigger share of the mass audience than he has ever had . . . here's a chance to do the kind of "teaching" Scotty Reston's always yakking about. . . . You can nail down the no-win nonsense, and at the same time hold down easy optimism, jingoism (which might later box you in).

Neustadt correctly described the apprehension that Kennedy's speech generated. He also noted the opportunity for the expansion of power this situation afforded the president—and of which he was to avail himself.[8]

Journalists were exposed to other immediate doses of the Communist threat. One was in the White House press office of Pierre Salinger, whom the president made responsible for all releases from the White House, and in the State and Defense department press offices as well. Immediately after the president's speech, Salinger had his largest-ever number of correspondents in attendance. Kennedy personally briefed him on what to say. Salinger believed that "every word that came out of the White House would play a fateful role in determining the course of events" because the press was a critical means of communicating with Khrushchev. Following this official briefing, Salinger took aside the Washington reporters who were to go with the president to Virginia caves in case of war. Adding to the somberness of the situation, he informed them that they were never to be more than fifteen minutes from the White House and must report all changes of location. The next day, he briefed the leaders of television, radio, and the wire services, telling them that the United States was "locked in a crisis that could lead to nuclear war." Voluntary press censorship guidelines were passed out.[9]

The McNamara Backgrounder

In a not-for-attribution backgrounder immediately after Kennedy's speech, Defense Secretary McNamara emphasized the extreme danger of the situation because of the possibility of Soviet-Cuban use of the nuclear weapons in Cuba. This approach was used to silence most questions in an area of primary administration weakness, the distinction between "offensive" and "defensive" weapons. The United States had missiles of the same nature ringing the Soviet Union and targeted on its cities. The U.S. government had previously called these missiles "defensive." How could it argue that comparable Soviet missiles in Cuba were "offensive"? Sorensen had been aware of this problem while preparing the president's speech, noting that "the Soviets will probably be able to point to one or more U.S. statements in the past that our base structure, including missile bases, was clearly defensive in purpose." Instead of addressing this issue directly in his speech, Kennedy called the weapons "clearly offensive." [10]

In his backgrounder, McNamara talked about how the Soviet missiles in Cuba might hit virtually every population center in the continental United States. In fact, the administration did not know that any actual Intermediate Range Ballistic Missiles (IRBMs) were in Cuba at the time that might have had this capability, and McNamara withheld information on numbers of missiles and sites. He produced only one picture of "scars" in the ground that he called a rudimentary IRBM site. In response to a question about how far the missiles could reach, he pointed to a chart: "The inner ring just happens to cover Washington at this point, most of Central America. The outer ring covers for all practical purposes all of the United States except a small slice of Washington and the northern part of the Pacific Coast. The outer ring covers much of the northern part of South America." [11]

McNamara also did not name the types of missiles the Soviets had in Cuba. The absence of details raised no problems with most reporters, who simply accepted his version of the weapons and the threat. An exception was the *Times*'s Hanson Baldwin, who reviewed the types of missiles the Soviets were known to have and concluded that neither the known Soviet Medium Range Ballistic Missiles (MRBMs) nor its IRBMs had the range that McNamara described. Baldwin charged the administration with creating "confusion." [12]

McNamara used the threat of an attack by Cuba on the United States to deflect another approach to the issue of whether the Soviet weapons were "defensive." The difference lay, he said, in the intended use of the missiles. United States missiles were placed in Europe because of the threat of Soviet attack. Cuba was not "under the threat of nuclear attack or attack from this country." [13]

The administration's argument clinching the threat to the United States was that the Soviets had brought their weapons in "surreptitiously," whereas the North Atlantic Treaty Organization (NATO) countries had acted publicly. And, when this had not been the case, as in the "emplacement of American missiles in the United Kingdom," it was "not a comparable case since Britain was and is an atomic power in its own right." [14]

The validity of this distinction was not challenged in the press. Nor was there any question of whether Britain's possession of atomic power when the United States secretly introduced "nuclear weapons" really made a difference. The administration had an advantage in that it could leak or not leak the classified information that might clarify such issues. During the crisis week, it leaked material supporting its argument about deliberate Soviet deception. The *Times*'s Max Frankel, for example, was permitted to take verbatim notes from the classified transcript of the Kennedy-Gromyko meeting of 18 October in which the Soviet foreign minister stated that no offensive weapons had been placed in Cuba.[15]

Based on its previous coverage, the *Post-Dispatch* was the paper most likely to raise questions about issues such as the "secrecy" and "offensive weapons" arguments. Instead, the editors based their support of the administration on both. "In such a serious crisis it was impossible to stand up to the president," Robert Lasch recalled. Media opinion-makers thus accepted the official view of Soviet and Cuban motivation and left debate about these issues to future historians.[16]

Lippmann vs. Reston

The one important journalist who raised issues about the president's action was Walter Lippmann. He questioned the resort to direct confrontation without any diplomatic overtures. Like Dean Acheson, the administration's adviser and a primary, though quiet, critic of the blockade, Lippmann believed that it could halt the shipment of missiles, but that it left no way to get the missiles out of Cuba short of war. This interpretation had led Acheson to the conclusion that the United States must immediately bomb or invade Cuba to attain this end. It led Lippmann in the opposite direction. In his 25 October column, he advocated trading the Cuban missiles for those in Turkey, a proposal that was explored at the United Nations and finally espoused by the Soviets.[17]

Lippmann's column, apparently read and considered by the Soviets to be somewhat official, was discussed in a secret meeting between ABC's John Scali, who was acting as an administration negotiator with the Russian embassy in Washington, and State Security Committee (KGB) operative Alexander Fomin. In explaining the unacceptability of this Lippmann idea, Scali informed Fomin that "everything Mr. Lippmann writes does not come straight from the White House, and if the Soviets were going to seek to judge administration intentions by following the words of reporters, they should . . . listen to different reporters than the ones they have been following." Again, Lippmann's international readership had proved him influential.[18]

Lippmann was one of the journalists concerning whom Chester Clifton, a White House military aide, had inquired: "Is there a plan to brief and brainwash key press within twelve hours or so?" Others of the "key press" included the *New York Times*, Childs, Alsop, and leading bureau chiefs. For the president, Henry Luce also was "key press," for he met with him on 24 October despite the rigors of the crisis week.[19]

Someone also spoke to Reston, who emerged on 24 October with a scoop designed to indicate the prudence of the administration's action. He reported that the inclination of the politicians Kennedy had briefed at the White House before his 22 October address was to invade or bomb Cuba. But members of both parties now supported the administration's more cautious response.[20]

Reston's columns of 26 and 28 October were devoted to countering Lippmann's viewpoint. Khrushchev probably had emplaced the missiles in Cuba for the very purpose of arranging a deal on the Turkish missiles, Reston argued, or perhaps even to remove the ones defending Berlin. Khrushchev already had achieved part of his objective by stimulating "half the world [to clamor] for negotiations which would gain him the European missile trade." It was not possible to trade the bases of U.S. allies. For one thing, he argued, it would encourage President de Gaulle to take independent action. Reston clearly was listening to U.S. officials concerned about the political consequences of a change in the strategic balance rather than to French ones. In fact, a reason for de Gaulle's decision after the missile crisis to proceed with an independent French nuclear force was the fact that, like congressional leaders in the United States, he had been informed but not consulted about the administration's decision.[21]

For Reston, President Kennedy had come of age. Faced with a "power play," he had "reduced the dangers of miscalculation in Moscow by demonstrating his willingness to fight for the vital interests of the United States." And, after Khrushchev capitulated on 28 October, Reston praised the president for displaying all the virtues of a modest victor.[22]

Waiting for the White House Line

That the administration was questioned little during the crisis week is hardly surprising. Few Washington reporters failed to be impressed with the seriousness of the situation. Even the business of gathering news changed. Hearst White House reporter Marianne Means described the routine for most reporters. From 6:00 A.M. to 10:00 P.M. she would sit at the White House doing "donkey work." "We took what they gave us," she recalled. She was on the list of people to be taken to the underground caves—though low down on the list, she discovered later to her chagrin. She approved the control that the administration exercised over the news. "The stakes were high," she said later. "We had told them that we would bomb them if they didn't comply." She accepted the fact that the *Times* and *Post* obtained better stories: "The Russians read the *New York Times*; it's important that the story be accurate in a crisis. They don't read the *San Antonio Light*."[23]

From the perspective of those who were presenting the line, the crisis was also a shaky business, for press releases were being used first to keep pressure on the Soviets and second to keep negotiations progressing. "Certainly the statements I put out at the White House on three occasions during that fateful week, pointing out that the Soviets were continuing to work on their missile sites," Salinger observed, "were as important in keeping the pressure on the Soviet Union as the movement of troops into position for a possible invasion." [24]

By Thursday, 25 October, the administration was in the box that Acheson and Lippmann feared. The Soviets had halted their shipments, but the administration was having difficulty in having the missiles removed. Responding to American pressure, Khrushchev suggested in a private letter on 26 October that he would trade removal of the missiles for a noninvasion pledge. But on the following day the administration received a letter from him returning to the Turkish missile deal. That same day, a stray U-2 overflew Russia, and in this delicate situation word was received that a U-2 was also missing over Cuba. The president had said in his 22 October speech that the shooting down of an American plane would produce an immediate military response. In the Saturday afternoon EXCOM deliberations, the military pressed for immediate action and sentiment for this course was strong. Instead, at the suggestion of Robert Kennedy, the administration's response was to propose a counter-letter responding only to Khrushchev's first one. The attorney general also informed the Russians in Washington that the administration would act within a few days if the Soviets did not remove the missiles. Both U-2 incidents were officially ignored and information was withheld from the press. [25]

In regard to the U-2 intrusion into Russian territory, Salinger later explained that announcement of the incident would further reduce Soviet options in a situation in which Khrushchev already had very few. In withholding the information, the president again was using a press weapon to achieve a diplomatic result. [26]

The reason for withholding information about the U-2 lost over Cuba has not been as fully clarified. This information may have been withheld to avoid reducing the president's options. He was under pressure from within the administration to take further action, and an announcement could have led to public demands that he fulfill his 22 October pledge. Given the delicacy of the situation, it is probably fortunate that nothing leaked and that the press on that Saturday [27 October] continued to wait for the White House line. [27]

One reason the president remained in control of the situation clearly was the reporters' acceptance at the time of the idea that the administration had the right to control information during a situation defined as a national emergency. Elie Abel of NBC noted later that Rusk and Stanley Grogan of the CIA were particularly helpful to reporters. Warren Unna of the *Post*, who was often skeptical of official reasoning, expressed high praise for Rusk and for his press assistants, Robert Manning and James Greenfield:

We'd go to see them [Manning and Greenfield], trying to flush it out. They said, "Just take our word for it, it is terribly serious," and they kept us on tenterhooks for a couple of days as this thing grew and grew.

I remember the interplay. More than I've ever remembered, I've had some feeling, "Look, you've got to be a responsible reporter because the national security is involved." And because I knew these people, I believed it. And it was true.

And then, at the end, they did something that I thought was very good: Rusk and a couple of them came and talked to us at the State Department, explaining what it was all about. And they did it in a very clear way. And I thought they had showed good faith with the press. They held them off, because there was a reason for holding them off, and then they said, "Here's what happened."

And I remember the next day I saw Mrs. Rusk and I said, "It was magnificent." And she said, "From what I read about it that you wrote in the paper, I agree with you!" That was a strong example of the press and the Kennedy administration.[28]

Official and Foreign Sources Prevail

The front-page sources reflected the change that took place during this period. The virtual elimination of domestic political sources from the front pages of both the *Tribune* and the *Post-Dispatch* was indicative of the changed situation. Administration sources scored gains in all papers except the *Examiner* over the September and early October periods. U.S. official sources were at a slightly higher level in relation to other sources than in previous crises (see appendix II).[29]

Among U.S. official sources the greatest change in late October was the rise of military sources (see figure 6). This was dramatic in all papers both on the front and inside pages. It was especially pronounced in the popular papers, the *Examiner* and the *Tribune*. Diplomatic and unidentified officials were quoted less often. This trend held in all papers, but less so for unidentified sources in the *Post* and for both categories in the *Times*. The two papers having the best contacts in the administration continued in their semiofficial press role on both front and inside pages. The *Tribune*, which had no unidentified sources on the front page during September, added some during this latter period—a fact that suggests a bit more acceptance of the administration line than usual.

Another characteristic of the official sources during late October was journalists' use of sources in the categories "other federal" and "other local" officials, including civil defense officials and mayors asked about contingency planning at the community level. The newsworthiness of these sources during the crisis is another indication of its seriousness.

The only competition for coverage was from foreign sources, which experienced a rise in all papers during this period to their highest level on the Cuban issue (see appendix II). Throughout the crisis, from late August until the end of October, foreign views received less front-page attention on Cuba than on any of the other crises. Among Western European and communist nations during September, only Russia received much attention. Britain was a distant second. As figure 7 shows, this pattern continued during the latter part of October.

Among Latin American nations, during September, only Cuba received much attention. With a few exceptions, other Latin American nations were ignored. The failure of the newspapers to turn to other Latin Americans for views on the subject requires some explanation. The best is that the press was affected by the public's provincialism, epitomized in Reston's quip that Americans would do anything for Latin America except read about it. Gunboat diplomacy and condescending stereotypes loomed large in popular thinking. The fact that West Germany received more front-page source coverage during September on Cuba than all other Latin American countries combined reflected the European bias of the American press. As figure 7 indicates, the tendency was greater for the papers to include more Latin American views after the president made his surprise announcement on 22 October. But Latin American sources were still less influential than Britain and France combined.[30]

Although European-centered like the other newspapers, the *Times*, because of its emphasis on comprehensive foreign reporting, gave more coverage to Latin American sources than did the *Tribune* and the *Examiner* (see figure 8). Among Latin American governments, Cuba, which was perceived as threatening, received a lesser percentage of the source coverage in the *Times* than in the more popular *Tribune* and *Examiner*. Of these three papers, the *Examiner* devoted the fewest independent resources—overseas correspondents, bureaus, etc.—to Latin America. Concerned almost exclusively with the foreign threat, the paper used very few Latin American sources outside of Cuba. This pattern paralleled more extensive reliance on Russian sources in the European arena as compared with the broader coverage of the *Tribune* and the *Times*.

The *Tribune* did have correspondents stationed in Latin America and did provide some coverage of other Latin American views, though it too was a popular paper and relied primarily on Cuban views among Latin American sources. Figure 8 shows that the threatening sources dominated the front pages of the popular papers. The percentage of threatening sources—both Russian and Cuban—in the *Times* was not so great as it was in the more popular papers, but it was still quite high. Concern about the Cuban and Soviet

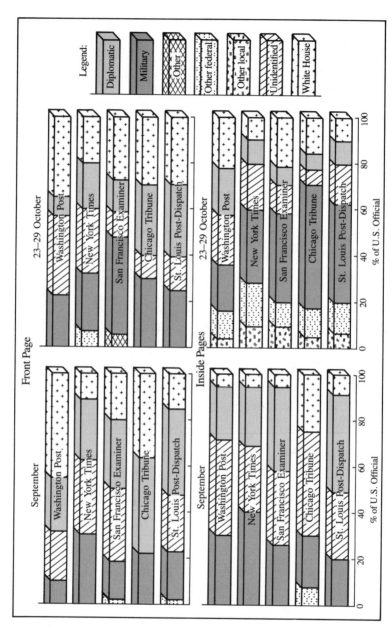

Figure 6. Cuba: Breakdown of U.S. Official Sources Used by Each Paper, 1962

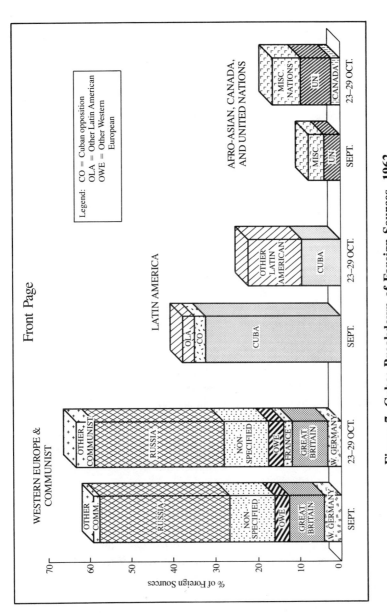

Figure 7. Cuba: Breakdown of Foreign Sources, 1962

threats may have been less urgent to the *Times*'s more elite editors and readers, but it was still quite important.

Figures 7 and 8 also show what happened to front-page coverage of United Nations officials who were engaged in an effort to mediate the dispute. The United Nations received approximately half the source coverage of Great Britain during the 23–29 October crisis period. The United Nations received more page-one coverage in the *Times* and the *Examiner* than it did in the *Tribune*, where it received none at all. The *Tribune*'s skepticism about international institutions thus continued to affect its news coverage.

In short, because the public was preoccupied with the foreign threat, the contest among sources for news space concerned who could best interpret what could be done about it. During September and early October, the Republicans made great headway. During the missile crisis, the president succeeded in turning a popular issue to his advantage.

Success with the Editors and Popular Columnists—But a Few Reservations Remain

The government's rise in terms of sources was matched by its enhanced editorial status: it was praised repeatedly by all newspapers, including the Republican ones. Indeed, praise was so steadfast and single-minded in papers like the *Times* and the *Post* that there is no need to analyze their editorials in detail. During the 23–29 October period, criticisms in all the papers went elsewhere, primarily to the Soviets, but also to Republicans in the case of the *Post* and the *Post-Dispatch*; to the United Nations in the case of the *Times* and the *Tribune*; and to the press in the case of the *Examiner* (see appendix IV).

The *Examiner* could not resist the opportunity to accuse the rival *San Francisco Chronicle* of "yahooing through life." It will be recalled that the *Examiner* had argued all along that a blockade was necessary. "Such thinking awakens painful memories in the American mind," the *Chronicle* had commented earlier. "It suggests that a younger Hearst is adopting the fateful words of an older Hearst to fit today's Cuban crisis." Now the *Examiner* was vindicated. The editors were especially pleased when the administration intensified the pressure on Khrushchev toward the end of the week. "The armed forces, as the president noted in his declaration, are prepared for 'any eventualities,'" it editorialized on 27 October. "All of us should be too." In its final editorials, the *Examiner* again lauded both itself and the president. Kennedy, Hearst wrote on 28 October, "repudiated those among his advisors who have sold their 'soft' line until it brought the United States to the brink of nuclear disaster. . . . Any time [as in September] we feel it necessary to differ with official policy for the sake of the country, the Hearst newspapers will

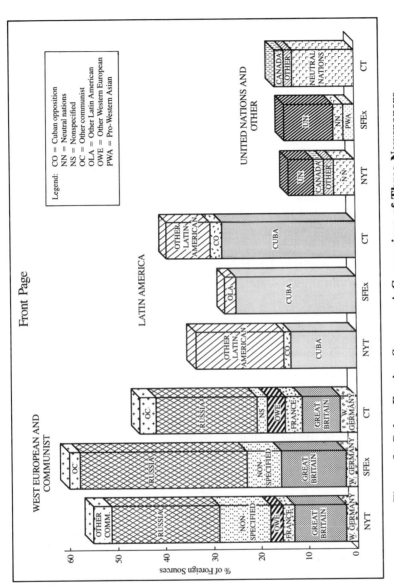

Figure 8. Cuba: Foreign Sources, A Comparison of Three Newspapers

gladly let apostles of appeasement call us 'warmongers' or anything worse they can dream up." [31]

After Khrushchev capitulated, the *Examiner* rejoiced that Kennedy's firmness "should restore our proper prestige everywhere. . . . The only reservation we have of a job superbly done is that if we had acted sooner the brink might have been avoided." Having reached a conservative apogee in September, the paper now offered the president high—if mitigated—praise. [32]

For columnist William S. White, the issue was "manhood." The "proclamation of the Kennedy Doctrine means that the United States will retreat no more," White exulted in his column on 23 October. Failure to have confronted Russia "would have been an unmanly betrayal of this nation." Arguing that Chester Bowles should be replaced immediately by a Republican, White called for a "government of national unity free of the symbols of past weakness." [33]

David Lawrence was also favorable in his first column after the president's speech. But then he raised the issue of why Kennedy had waited so long. "Americans," he said, "can only hope that the delay has not been irreparable and that within the next several days the Soviet missile pads in Cuba will be wiped out by force if necessary," a point he repeated in his next column. Lawrence and White later shared the general view that the president's success in forcing removal of the missiles was a major triumph. [34]

In the case of the *Tribune*, the success of the administration was particularly striking. At the pinnacles of the two previous crises, it had been unable to prevent the paper from criticizing both the administration and the Democrats. Now, one week before the 1962 election, the *Tribune* offered unprecedented praise (see appendix IV). "For the first time in twenty years," Trohan commented, "Americans can carry their head high because the president of the United States has stood up to the premier of Russia and made him back down." The *Tribune* gave front-page play to a *Times* article dealing with some issues that had troubled the Republicans: why the administration had denied Keating's charges; why the Defense Department had denied the existence of the missiles after they had been discovered; and why the administration had lied about the "cold." The *Times* concluded that the reason for all this was the need for secrecy, which had "forced the administration down the path of deception . . . and of deliberately giving misinformation to reporters." The *Tribune*'s editors let it be known that they would disclaim any Republicans who might try to deem the president's move political. "We do not believe that anyone as indebted to the American people as is Mr. Kennedy would ever expose them to the dangers of an atomic war for so mean an end," the *Tribune* editorialized on 23 October, and added with obvious satisfaction: "once again [Kennedy] established the Monroe Doctrine as a basis for U.S. policy." [35]

Some Criticism of the Administration's
Press Policies

The greatest criticism during the crisis week resulted from official unwillingness to allow reporters to travel to the scene of the blockade. The issue
emerged dramatically after the news of the first U.S. boarding of a Soviet vessel on 25 October reached the press through a Republican, Representative
James E. Van Zandt of Pennsylvania, who had learned of the event at a State
Department briefing. Reporters were upset because journalists had been allowed to accompany U.S. warships during World War II but not now. Salinger
later described the press briefing following this incident as emotionally
charged and admitted that his explanation that the boarding was to be announced publicly by the Defense Department forty-five minutes later did not
convince the reporters. Jittery about the flow of news during the crisis, Kennedy was upset because such information had been given to congressmen by
the State Department.[36]

It is remarkable that more difficulties did not arise involving leaks in the
naval area, for the Secretary of the Navy and Secretary of Defense McNamara
were at loggerheads over how to conduct the blockade. Some of McNamara's
aides suspected that even he had not been told the truth about the number and
location of Soviet ships.[37]

Because so much momentous news was flowing from the Caribbean, the
United Nations, and elsewhere, this friction between reporters and officials in
Washington did not receive sustained coverage in any of the papers, and it
certainly did not induce any of them to withdraw complete editorial support
for the president's course. On Friday, 27 October, the administration did attempt to tighten up considerably on the traditional freedom of interchange between officials and reporters. Officials at the White House, the State Department, and the Defense Department were requested to report any contacts with
reporters, along with the questions asked and the responses given, to the press
office where they worked.

After the missile crisis, when Defense press official Arthur Sylvester brash-
ly proclaimed that the government had the right to deceive the press in the
interest of national security, a furor developed over the administration's "news
management" during the missile crisis and at other times. But that charge,
advanced mainly by critics like Krock and Goldwater, did little to detract from
the reality that, during the missile crisis itself, Kennedy gained immeasurably
in public esteem and emerged from the ordeal a national hero. The press, by
giving full credence to the administration's interpretation of events, had
played a major role in his multifaceted triumph.[38]

Conclusion

What final generalizations about the press-presidential relationship emerge from the Cuban experience? The vulnerability of a president in relation to newspapers that reflect and transform domestic concerns into an election critique is clear. Press strategies and the advantage that Kennedy enjoyed with proadministration papers did not assure the successful communication of his views by the press. The primary external characteristic of an issue such as Cuba—a high level of domestic interest and involvement—worked to his disadvantage with the press as long as his foreign policy direction was not in conformity with public concern. Thus, a president who is at a disadvantage in relation to domestic forces in the competition for authoritative interpretation of a popular foreign policy issue may well need to produce new information or a new policy if he wishes to transform the issue to his advantage.

If a president is in conformity with generalized public expectations and adopts the policies of his critics, such a condition of high domestic interest may work to his advantage. The period after Kennedy's announcement of a national emergency, of a virtual war footing for the nation, produced press compliance and an utter lack of questioning of the facts he made available and his interpretations of them by even the opposition press. A president who announces a national emergency consistent with public opinion eliminates all the centers of strength in the society and in the press itself that counterbalance his influence in relation to the greater part of the press. Foreign views, which exert little influence on the press under normal circumstances in any but their most primitive form, scarcely represent a challenge to an administration's powers of news-making and authoritative interpretation under such conditions. Domestic dissent is negligible, and few journalists will pick up on the glimmerings of dissent that may appear.

Under such conditions, the normal tendency of a politician to maximize power may well come into play. As politicians first and foremost, presidents—at least at the height of the cold war—realized that a national emergency had great potential for the expansion of presidential power. Under such circumstances, the same qualities of the press that make it a reflective institution—its need for news, its weakness before authoritative sources with news-making power, and its firm rooting in domestic opinion—make it an instrument to be exploited in the hands of a strong president.

Part Five

The Vietnam Crisis of 1963

The Kennedy administration's first major crisis had concerned Laos; two-and-a-half years later, the president's final foreign policy crisis involved neighboring South Vietnam. As in Laos, a civil war was in progress in Vietnam when Kennedy took office: the Vietcong guerillas, backed by North Vietnam, were challenging Ngo Dinh Diem's South Vietnamese government, supported since its establishment in 1954 by the United States. But, unlike the attitude of top officials toward Laos, they were not inclined to seek negotiations on Vietnam. A military victory over the Vietcong was the clear goal, though some skeptics within the administration doubted that this was achievable. During 1962, when American forces in Vietnam grew from less than a thousand to more than ten thousand, substantial progress in the war against the Vietcong appeared to be occurring; but, by early 1963, after South Vietnamese military defeats characterized by poor leadership and reluctance to fight, it was clear to most Americans in Vietnam—including the resident American reporters there— that the official optimism about the progress of the war was unwarranted.[1]

Whereas the most important influence on press coverage during the early stages of the Cuban crisis had been criticisms by opposition politicians, the most important one during the Buddhist crisis was division within the administration on policy toward the Diem regime. As Theodore Sorensen has noted, this division ran deeper on Vietnam than on any other foreign policy issue of the Kennedy years. On one side were those who believed, even before the Buddhist crisis, that the Diem regime was so unpopular and corrupt that the war could not be won as long as it remained in power. In Washington, this viewpoint was strongest among Southeast Asian specialists in the State Department, especially Roger Hilsman and Paul Kattenburg, who were ably assisted in propagating this view in National Security Council meetings by high-ranking State Department officials like Averell Harriman and George Ball. In Vietnam, anti-Diem feelings pervaded the lower levels of all the American missions: the embassy, the CIA, the military, and others. Among the many criticisms of the ruling Diem family was the charge that appointments to military and civilian positions were made on the basis of loyalty to Diem and his brother, Ngo Dinh Nhu, rather than on the basis of competence, thus undermining the possibility of progress in the political and military struggle against the Vietcong.[2]

On the other side were those who believed that Diem was no more corrupt or unpopular than many other leaders the United States supported, that Diem represented stability and a commitment to anticommunism, and that progress was being made in the war against the Vietcong. In Washington, this view was the official wisdom at the Pentagon, at the highest levels of the CIA, and among some hard-liners at the State Department. In Saigon, the anti-Diem viewpoint was stronger than pro-Diem feeling in the American mission as a whole, but the three top American officials there at the beginning of the Buddhist crisis—Ambassador Frederick Nolting, General Paul Harkins, and CIA chief John Richardson—were all strongly pro-Diem. A key to understanding Kennedy's policy during the Buddhist crisis is to note that Nolting was replaced by the anti-Diem Henry Cabot Lodge in late August, and that Lodge then secured Richardson's recall in early October and successfully bypassed Harkins in pursuing anti-Diem policies before the coup against Diem on 1 November.

Although the journalistic ideal is for reporters to be recorders and interpreters of events rather than partisans for one viewpoint or another, it was almost impossible, given the cleavage within the administration, to interpret events in Vietnam in 1963 without having as a point of reference either a pro-Diem or an anti-Diem perspective. For a variety of reasons, the three resident American newspaper reporters in Vietnam at the beginning of the Buddhist crisis— David Halberstam of the *New York Times*, Neil Sheehan of UPI, and Malcolm Browne of AP—reported from an anti-Diem perspective, as did the few resident correspondents for magazines and television.

In brief, these anti-Diem reporters believed that the regime was hopelessly corrupt and inefficient, that it unfairly harassed foreign correspondents who reported any unfavorable information about it, and that pro-Diem American officials repeatedly lied about Diem's popularity and the progress of the war. "What we were reflecting was reality as seen by American and Vietnamese officers who were fighting the war," Halberstam recalled. "Our conflict was not with officers who were there; our conflict was with people who were in Saigon at the official level who reflected not what was happening in the field, but what they wanted to happen in the field."[3] As subsequent events in Vietnam and the *Pentagon Papers* affirmed, the resident reporters' pessimistic assessment of the progress of the war turned out to be accurate.[4]

Not surprisingly, the pro-Diem officials also had their journalistic supporters, though not among the resident reporters who daily influenced news coverage of the issue. Hard-liners like Alsop, Higgins, and Frank Conniff of the Hearst newspapers were highly critical of the resident reporters, as were others like Keyes Beech, who considered them inexperienced and overly emotional. Most of the resident reporters in 1963 were in their twenties or early thirties, and this was their first war. Sheehan sees this as an advantage:

> We were young and we were inexperienced, and I think this was a good thing, because we didn't have a lot of mental baggage to interfere with reporting the story. Unlike the World War II generation of correspondents like Keyes Beech—and I like Keyes personally—we weren't viewing Vietnam in the light of World War II. We weren't seeing the same images, and while we were very anti-communist, and supported American policy—that is, we wanted to see the United States win a war in Vietnam—we didn't feel the necessity to say we were winning it when it didn't look like we were.[5]

Beech, a close friend of the hawkish Higgins and a longtime admirer of Diem, still sees things differently:

> Halberstam and Sheehan were getting a lot of information from the Buddhists, of course, who'd call them up during the day and tell them they were going to have an immolation. They'd call me, too, and I'd go out to the immolation. . . .
>
> I'd been through the Pacific War and seen a lot of dead people; I'd been through the Korean War and seen a lot of dead people. So I didn't react in horror as much as they did to the immolation. I thought it was a coldly cynical thing that the Buddhists were doing. . . .
>
> Neil Sheehan and Halberstam would say, "Don't you see that Diem's got to go? We'll never win the war with a guy like him as president." And I said, "I would remind you of only one thing: I was writing nasty stories about Ngo Dinh Diem when you guys were still in Harvard. Secondly, I have no illusions about Diem, but if I've learned anything in these misspent years in Asia, it is that you don't go around overthrowing governments unless you're reasonably sure that you have something better in the wings."[6]

American officials tended to divide in their view of the resident reporters according to whether or not they agreed with their analysis of the unpopularity of the Diem regime. Rusk recalled later, for example, that "it was not the reporters' function to say whether Diem should fall or not," and Salinger doubted that "the destruction of a government is within the legitimate framework of journalistic enterprise." Others, like Ball, were more sympathetic to the Halberstam-Sheehan approach. "Personally, I had a great deal more sympathy with it than the President did. I suspected that Halberstam was just about right."[7]

From the time he began making major decisions about Vietnam in May 1961 until September 1963, Kennedy's press strategy consistently was to play down the issue. Although urged by advisers to do so, he did not give any television addresses concerning it. Nor did he discuss it in any detail at press conferences or, apparently, in backgrounders with journalists. Salinger has noted that the president was "particularly sensitive" about articles on the military involvement in Vietnam, which began appearing fairly regularly in early 1962, and that he "pushed hard for us to tighten the rules there under which correspondents could observe field operations in person." Kennedy's desire to keep Vietnam out of the newspapers was reflected in efforts by the State and Defense departments to restrict reporters' access to information in Vietnam, efforts that were more successful in generating ill feelings than in achieving their goals.[8]

The president was also irritated by articles, especially those by Halberstam in the *Times*, pointing out weaknesses in the South Vietnamese army and hence in the optimistic premises undergirding American policy. "I heard criticism, and I heard about criticism in high places," James Thomson, Jr., a State Department official at the time, recalled. "I heard that Kennedy was furious; I heard that Mac Bundy had told Kennedy that he'd known Halberstam when Mac was dean at Harvard and Halberstam was the *Crimson* managing editor, and Kennedy should not take college journalists too seriously."[9]

Despite the substantial military buildup and friction between American reporters and officials in Vietnam, Kennedy was largely successful until June 1963 in keeping the topic off the front pages of the newspapers. In addition to the administration's careful avoidance of labeling Vietnam a major foreign policy issue, this relative neglect resulted from the same factors that had limited coverage of Laos: public apathy, lack of congressional involvement in the issue, and a paucity of reporters on the scene in the absence of constituency interest. But the president's strategy collapsed on 11 June 1963 when the dramatic self-immolation of the Buddhist monk Thich Quang Duc in downtown Saigon brought the Buddhist opposition to the Diem regime to worldwide attention. Browne's AP wirephoto of the monk sitting erect and in flames was printed and reprinted all over the world, dramatically drawing attention to Vietnam and suggesting that all was not well with America's ally. Tipped off in advance like Browne that something was going to happen, Halberstam also attended the immolation, "too shocked to cry, too confused to take notes or ask questions, too bewildered to even think." Away from Saigon on a military operation that morning, Sheehan missed the immolation. "I was in trouble with my boss in Tokyo for two months," Sheehan recalled. "He was going wild because I didn't have that photograph."[10]

One result of this immolation and the other aspects of the Buddhist-Diem clash surrounding it, therefore, was that Sheehan and the other resident reporters tended to stay in Saigon to cover the developing Buddhist crisis rather than risk missing another key event. The Buddhist-Diem clash thus became the number-one story from Vietnam, relegating the war against the Vietcong to an inferior position until after the coup in November. Achieving regular page-one coverage for the first time, the hardworking, anti-Diem reporters in Saigon were pleased to provide material now that the Buddhist crisis offered the opportunity to discuss opposition to the regime. Another consequence was that the Kennedy administration, faced with increased news coverage and concerned as always about its image both at home and abroad, put pressure on Diem to adopt a conciliatory stance toward the Buddhists, including the announcement on 27 June that Henry Cabot Lodge would replace Ambassador William Nolting later in the summer. As Rusk remarked to Nolting after additional immolations occurred in early August, "We cannot stand any more burnings." [11]

Although public and congressional interest in the Buddhist crisis in Vietnam was not as great as it had been during Berlin and especially during Cuba, it was, as Rusk's remark suggests, much greater than during Laos. Source analysis bears out this observation: whereas only 74 domestic political sources were quoted in all newspapers during the Laotian crisis, 181 were quoted during the Buddhist crisis. Berlin's 521 domestic political sources and Cuba's 708 reflect the much greater partisan interest in these issues. Similarly, interest group and public opinion sources were much more numerous for Vietnam than for Laos; indeed, they were more numerous than for Berlin but not for Cuba, where public and partisan interest was most pronounced (see appendix I).

The general public was alerted to the issue by the Buddhists' skillful use of immolations, demonstrations, and public statements of their grievances to generate heavy, favorable press coverage for their cause. Liberals were incensed by the Diem regime's "repression" and by impolitic, well-publicized statements by Diem's brother and chief adviser, Ngo Dinh Nhu, and by his influential and outspoken wife, Madame Nhu, who ridiculed the immolations as "barbecues." Conservatives were concerned about the possible effects of the turmoil on the war against the Vietcong, and many Catholics were torn between continuing their support for the Catholic Diem regime and sympathizing with Buddhist grievances. Because of the variety of conflicting viewpoints, Kennedy risked losing significant political support if he embraced any clear-cut policy for dealing with the issue. But, as Diem's position deteriorated, the president also risked serious criticism of his leadership—and, quite possibly, a congressional cutoff of aid to Vietnam and an end to support for the war effort—if he appeared to be doing nothing to ameliorate the situation.

During the early months of the Buddhist crisis (roughly from May through July), the main issue was the conflict between the Diem regime and its Buddhist and other noncommunist opponents within South Vietnam. But, beginning in August and continuing through Diem's assassination on 1 November, the crucial issue was the relationship between the regime and the United States. Managing this deteriorating relationship with minimal loss of support for the war was the real Vietnam crisis for the Kennedy administration. How the administration and the press interacted from early August through early November on this sensitive issue is the subject of the pages that follow.

Chapter 12

Pressures Build on the President

1 August – 2 September

Like the third act in a Shakespearean tragedy, the events in Saigon and Washington in August 1963 inexorably foreshadowed the demise of the Diem regime. Early in the month, Nhu and Madame Nhu made statements sharply critical of the Buddhists, who in turn responded with a series of immolations and demonstrations that reached a crescendo by mid-month. Then, in the early morning hours of 21 August, Nhu's CIA-trained special forces assaulted the major Buddhist pagodas in Saigon and Hue, where they clubbed and arrested the monks and damaged the pagodas. Believing that Diem had betrayed a promise made a few days earlier to seek reconciliation with the Buddhists, U.S. officials in Saigon and Washington—including the newly arrived Lodge—encouraged equally enraged South Vietnamese generals in their coup plotting against the Diem regime. Uncertain of the coup's chances for success, the dissident generals backed off from an immediate coup attempt at the end of the month, but not from continued planning to ensure a successful one in the future. From a relatively close relationship at the beginning of August, the Kennedy administration and the Diem regime had shifted to thinly disguised hostility.

The onrush of events in Saigon shattered the previous U.S. policy of quiet pressure on Diem for concessions to the Buddhists and precipitated several weeks of often bitter policy review that culminated in September, as the *Pentagon Papers* and numerous memoirs have revealed. More importantly for this study, the events of August finally rendered untenable the president's low-visibility press strategy on Vietnam, though he waited until Labor Day to seek to regain control of the situation in the press. During this entire month of low visibility on the issue, Kennedy and other White House officials were only cited once on the front pages of three of the papers and not at all on the front pages of the other two.[1]

While the president was playing out his largely passive role, impolitic South Vietnamese leaders, anti-Diem South Vietnamese and American officials, and reporters and editors seized the initiative. This made it virtually impossible for Kennedy to adopt a pro-Diem position even if he had been so inclined. On the other side, the ruling family in Vietnam and pro-Diem journalists actively sought to counter the opposing viewpoint. Gaining sympathetic treatment for their views in early August was difficult given the favorable publicity accorded the Buddhists since June, and it was almost impossible after the pagoda raids. Even before the raids, the coverage—especially in Washington-oriented and liberal papers—increasingly involved pressuring the president to "do something" about the regime.

The *Times* Takes the Lead against Diem in Early August

Unfortunately for the Diem regime, the paper that provided the most extensive coverage of the Buddhist crisis was the *Times*. As in its coverage during the Laotian crisis, it was in a perfect position to apply anti-Diem pressures on the president. It had a strong tradition of covering foreign news, the resources and experience in Southeast Asia to report crises there much more authoritatively than any other newspaper, a constituency that appreciated and expected extensive coverage of major foreign policy issues, and a Washington bureau sufficiently large and independent to pick up and report emerging policy preferences within the government.

The *Times*'s comparative advantage over the other newspapers was greater in early August than at any time subsequently in the Buddhist crisis, after the pagoda raids stirred the other papers and columnists to more active involvement in the issue. Indeed, the *Times*'s impact almost certainly was greater than at any other time during the four crises. In August no major columnist competed for influence on policy, as Alsop had on Laos and Lippmann and Childs had on Berlin; and no opposition politicians became involved in the issue, as Nixon had on Berlin and Keating had on Cuba. This lack of domestic political involvement limited the coverage of Vietnam in two papers attuned to public interest and political controversy, the *Tribune* and the *Examiner*. And, although the *Post* and the *Post-Dispatch* showed much more interest than the two conservative papers in covering the crisis, their coverage was also limited and frequently influenced by the *Times*, as had been the case during the Laotian crisis. Lacking a reporter in Vietnam, the *Post* largely used the wire services and gave only sporadic coverage to the debate within the administration on the issue. And, although it was the most anti-Diem editorially of all the papers, the liberal *Post-Dispatch* was unable to provide independent coverage of the issue because the Diem regime, angered by a series of articles on Vietnam by Richard Dudman during the winter of 1963, denied him a visa to return to cover the Buddhist crisis.[2]

Comparison of the number of news stories, editorials and columns on Vietnam during the August period demonstrates the *Times*'s predominance, especially before the pagoda raids of 21 August. As table 6 shows, the *Times* had twelve of the twenty-eight page-one stories (43 percent) and three of the seven editorials (43 percent) in the five papers in early August, whereas the newspaper with the least coverage—the *Tribune*—had only two page-one stories and no editorials. This table also shows that the Washington-oriented *Post* was second only to the *Times* in the total number of news stories, whereas the *Post-Dispatch* was second to the *Times* in editorial interest.

The man of the hour for the *Times* was twenty-nine-year-old David Halberstam, who had arrived at Saigon in the fall of 1962 and who had quickly established a close working relationship with the even more youthful Sheehan. Sheehan's dispatches appeared frequently in the *Post* and *Post-Dispatch*, but only occasionally in the *Examiner* and *Tribune*, which apparently were suspicious of his anti-Diem viewpoint. In a situation in which high-level American and South Vietnamese officials disliked reporters and withheld information from them, Halberstam and Sheehan cultivated a wealth of sources at lower levels who were totally disaffected with the Diem regime and American support for it. Although these two key reporters had, in Halberstam's words, "some damned good Vietnamese sources," they relied more heavily on American sources because "it was harder to get information from the Vietnamese" and "you knew the American chain of command better than you knew the Vietnamese chain of command." While the president remained silent on Vietnam throughout August, Halberstam had fifteen page-one stories and nine inside-page stories printed under his byline in the *Times*. Like Sheehan's numerous stories appearing in other important newspapers, these prominently played stories in the leading newspaper clearly were pressuring the administration to end its support of the Diem regime.[3]

An example of the impact that Halberstam and the *Times* could have was a page-one story on 8 August featuring an interview he had the day before with Madame Nhu, South Vietnam's influential first lady. She used the interview to warn Washington that Lodge's appointment to succeed Nolting as ambassador later that month must not signify a break with the Diem regime. "If he is a good American he will do as well as Nolting," she told Halberstam. But, if any difficulties arose, "we shall publish everything and tell all the differences." She also told Halberstam that she was "absolutely furious" because the American embassy had "threatened and blackmailed" the government in an effort to "shut me up." Agreeing with her husband's recent call for firmness in dealing with the Buddhists, she said that she "would beat the bonzes [Buddhist monks] ten times more."[4]

Like many other stories based on interviews with Madame Nhu that summer and fall, the Halberstam dispatch emphasized confrontation and conflict, journalism's stock in trade. She was clearly granting this interview and most

Table 6. Number of News Stories, Editorials, and Columns on Vietnam, 1 August–2 September 1963

	1–20 August						21 August–2 September					
	p. 1	Inside Pages	Editorials	Columns	Total	Percent	p. 1	Inside Pages	Editorials	Columns	Total	Percent
New York Times	12	35	3	0	50	(30)	25	78	6	4	113	(39)
Washington Post	4	31	2	1	38	(23)	15	46	3	1	65	(22)
St. Louis Post-Dispatch	5	18	2	1	26	(15)	16	15	5	3	39	(13)
Chicago Tribune	2	22	0	1	25	(15)	9	26	1	0	36	(12)
San Francisco Examiner	5	21	0	3	29	(17)	12	22	1	2	37	(13)
TOTAL	28	127	7	6	168	(100)	77	187	16	10	290	(99)

of the others to seek to explain and win sympathy for the official position, as did, for example, Kennedy when he granted interviews to favored reporters on sensitive issues in American foreign policy. But, in writing about Madame Nhu, reporters chose her most controversial phrases—her claim that the U.S. embassy had "threatened and blackmailed" her, for example—and wove them into a story in a way that often distorted their contextual meaning. By singling out the most "newsworthy" phrase, headline writers further distorted her remarks.

The Halberstam story exerted tremendous impact in the press. The interview was a page-one story not only in the *Times*, but also in the *Post-Dispatch*, which was relying heavily on the *Times*'s news service for its Vietnam coverage. The AP office in New York treated the Halberstam dispatch as a news story and rewrote it for the AP wire; the resulting story appeared in the *Examiner* the next day under the overly sensational headline "Let the Buddhists Burn—Mrs. Nhu." Although the *Post* did not print the AP story, it did print a condescending State Department denial of the validity of her "blackmail" charge.[5]

Halberstam's story also led to a *Times* editorial on 9 August that included the strongest attack to date on the Nhus. The paper's line during early August was that Diem needed to separate himself from the Nhus and renounce their hard-line approach to the Buddhists. Although he was "rigid and dictatorial," he did have "some sense of social and political reality and responsibility," qualities "completely lacking in Lucretia Borgia Nhu." Referring to the Halberstam interview and to previous statements by Madame Nhu, the *Post* that same day angrily editorialized that "her vain and hysterical assertions demonstrate an inordinate capacity for malicious mischief."[6] Both the *Post-Dispatch* and the *Tribune* also took their lead on this issue from the *Times*. The *Post-Dispatch* disparaged Madame Nhu's comments, and the *Tribune*, in its only commentary on Vietnam in early August, reprinted the *Times* editorial of 5 August sharply criticizing the Diem regime's treatment of the Buddhists. Although it is not surprising that the *Post* and *Post-Dispatch* agreed editorially with the *Times*, it is remarkable—and indicative of a lack of conservative Republican opposition to Kennedy's policies in Vietnam—that the *Tribune* would permit the administration-oriented *Times* to establish its editorial position in early August.[7]

Halberstam's stories from Vietnam were not only influencing editorial offices, but they were also reverberating in official Washington. In the only public statement by a high-level official in Washington during August, Rusk said at his press conference on the 16th that the United States was "deeply distressed" by the Buddhist crisis and urged the Diem regime to "take a strong lead now" in resolving the dispute. The secretary also stressed what he considered to be the improvement in the military situation during the past year in order, as one reporter noted, "to refute recent reports from Saigon [a Halberstam story on 15 August] that the situation had again taken a turn for the worse, particularly in the Mekong Delta." [8]

The *Times*'s New York office, nervous about being corrected publicly by the secretary of state, cabled Halberstam and asked him to respond to the criticisms. In situations like these, the paper also had Wallace Carroll call Richard Helms, a good source at the CIA. "It's not going well," Helms said, thus confirming Halberstam's pessimistic reports. Rusk and McNamara apparently believed the more optimistic military estimates that General Paul D. Harkins was sending to Washington; for, Rusk recalled, "after Diem's departure we found that Diem had been misrepresenting what had been going on in the countryside." [9]

Although far fewer stories on Vietnam emanated from Washington in early August than from Saigon, partly as a result of the administration's low-visibility press strategy, the *Times* again took the lead in spreading the anti-Diem viewpoint. An excellent example is a page-one story on 8 August by Tad Szulc headlined "Concern Rises on Diem," in which unidentified anti-Diem officials clearly were seeking to put pressure on both Diem and Kennedy. "The Administration believes that South Vietnam's President, Ngo Dinh Diem, may be overthrown by his own military and the civilian bureaucracy if he fails to settle the Buddhist crisis within the next three or four months," Szulc wrote, apparently relying heavily on anti-Diem officials in the State Department. Given the dispute within the administration on Vietnam policy, it is significant that none of the papers in early August printed a story from Washington based on pro-Diem sources. The newspapers that might have been more likely to seek out pro-Diem military sources—the *Tribune* and *Examiner*—simply did not cover the issue in any depth before late August. [10]

Higgins's Pro-Diem Efforts Are Largely Ignored

While the Washington-oriented newspapers and anti-Diem officials were reacting negatively to the ruling family's position in the crisis, the indomitable Marguerite Higgins had journeyed to Vietnam in an effort to shore up support for the Diem regime by presenting the Ngo family in a favorable light and by denigrating the Buddhist position. Angered by what she considered the resident reporters' anti-Diem bias, she argued in numerous articles in the *Herald-Tribune* that, as she later summarized it, "the revolt was political, not religious; that Diem was fighting to save his government, not to persecute anybody; that the activities of some thousands of Buddhists in the city had no effect on the continuing war gains in the countryside; and that the perils of dumping Diem in midwar were greater than the perils of sticking with him." [11]

Considering her views and her close personal relationship with the ruling family, it is not surprising that Diem chose interviews with her as the vehicle for his only two public statements in early August. After a five-hour interview with Diem on 8 August, she wrote a pro-Diem article that strongly implied a lack of discrimination against the Buddhists. Diem was "plainly exasperated at what he felt was the outside world's suspicions that a religious issue has sprung up in Viet-Nam that was somehow his doing," Higgins wrote. On the contrary, "the President took the view that his regime constituted in fact 'the only and true guarantee for the security and freedom' of the Buddhist Association." In another interview on 14 August, Diem told Higgins that conciliation had been his policy toward the Buddhists all along and that this policy was "irreversible." [12]

In contrast with Halberstam's widely publicized interview with Madame Nhu, Higgins's interviews with Diem were largely ignored. Of the five newspapers studied, the stories appeared only in the *Post*; but, even there, the first appeared on page fifteen and the second was tucked away in the food section. Nor did any editorials in the five papers refer to the interviews. In fact, the only paper that showed any appreciation for Higgins's viewpoint was the *Examiner*, which under a page-one AP dispatch on 14 August headlined "Viet Suicide Wave Out of Hand?" noted that a column by Higgins appeared on that day's editorial page. Arguing that the demonstrations and suicides were intended to get rid of Diem and to ensure that Lodge would replace Nolting, Higgins denied the existence of any religious persecution and said that Catholics too would be beaten and jailed if they "took to the streets." [13]

Higgins's column struck a responsive chord in Conniff, who was pleased to learn "that the story is not all one-sided in the Buddhists' favor." In a thinly disguised jab at eastern liberal journalism, he said that Diem was now "under the same kind of attack that a section of the press once mounted against Chiang Kai-shek." Finally, in an implicit comparison of Halberstam with Herbert Matthews, the *Times* correspondent who had praised Castro's overthrow of Batista in 1959, Conniff said that the last time American officials "hearkened to a climate of opinion generated by a newspaper, we caught a character named Fidel Castro." [14]

Because the press had no compelling reasons to pay attention to conservative support of the Diem regime—including the absence of outspoken congressional or interest group sympathy for Diem—Higgins and Conniff had minimal impact on the press during August 1963. Although Higgins worked almost as energetically to build support for Diem as she had to bolster the hard-line West Germans during the Berlin crisis, her efforts were hampered by the fact that South Vietnam's ruling family lacked the potent American constituency that had aided West German officials. There also were serious doubts within both the press and the administration by 1963 about the accuracy and impartiality of her reporting. Finally, the fact that Alsop and other influential conservative columnists were silent on Vietnam during August isolated her and thus hurt her cause. Like most of the press, the administration was responding primarily to the dispatches of the resident reporters and to the increasingly dramatic events in South Vietnam.[15]

The Pagoda Raids Sharply Increase Anti-Diem Pressures

The large-scale raids on the Buddhist pagodas marked a turning point for the Diem regime by undermining the loyalty of important South Vietnamese generals, by increasing international criticism of both the regime and American support for it, and by transforming the Vietnam issue into the leading foreign policy story in American newspapers. Most importantly, the raids resulted in an immediate hardening of U.S. policy toward the regime that Ambassador Lodge, who arrived in Saigon on 22 August, enthusiastically carried out. As Halberstam wrote in a news analysis from there a couple of weeks later, the raids signaled "the end of the Buddhist affair and the beginning of an international crisis." "For better or worse," the authors of the *Pentagon Papers* observed, "the August 21 pagoda raids settled the issue for us."[16]

Such judgments about the importance of the pagoda raids seem largely valid in retrospect. But, at the time, both the plotters in Saigon and the policymakers in Washington were often hesitant and indecisive, and it remained unclear until the actual coup more than two months later that the Diem regime would in fact be overthrown. The plotters in the South Vietnamese army who informed Lodge on 23 August of their interest in ousting the regime and who received encouragement in a hastily drafted cable from Washington on 24 August, informed Lodge and Harkins on 31 August that the coup attempt had been called off. And officials in Washington, lacking firm direction from Kennedy, remained badly split between the pro-Diem and anti-Diem factions. Although a clear U.S. policy was not established until early October, the pagoda raids definitely boosted the anti-Diem position. As CIA official William Colby noted in his memoirs, "they [Diem and the Nhus] made it virtually impossible for their friends in the American government like myself to do anything but go along with the ideas in Washington to force them to change their methods to ones that did not cause the kind of political repercussion in America that the raid on the pagodas and the burning bonzes did."[17]

The president had said very little about Vietnam publicly since the crisis began in May; at his press conference the day before the raids, he was not even asked about the issue. The raids and the press's heavy coverage of them assured that this situation would soon change: although Kennedy was able to avoid questions on Vietnam by limiting his 30 August news conference to the issue Congress was debating at the time, foreign aid, Vietnam came up repeatedly in each of the four press conferences and two television interviews that occurred between 2 September and his assassination in November. After the raids, the president was also unable to prevent heavy leaking, particularly from the anti-Diem perspective, which further pressured him to act decisively against the Diem regime. Maintaining his low-visibility press strategy much longer, Kennedy and his closest aides must have realized, would have invited serious charges that he had lost control of both U.S. policy and the situation in Vietnam, and even demands that the United States withdraw from the war against the Vietcong.

In the continuing absence of presidential initiatives in the press, the most important factor in the press-presidential relationship on Vietnam in late August was the sharply increased coverage of the issue, coverage that was almost certain to increase public and congressional interest in Vietnam. As table 6 shows, the number of page-one stories on the issue in the five papers jumped from twenty-eight in the first twenty days of August to seventy-seven during the thirteen days after the pagoda raids. There also was a substantial increase in the number of inside-page stories, editorials, and columns. For the first time since the American military buildup had begun nearly two years before, the press was treating Vietnam as a big story and hence bringing it to the consciousness of many Americans who heretofore would have had no compelling reason to pay attention to the issue.

As table 6 also shows, the coverage remained substantially greater in the Washington-oriented *Times* and *Post* than in the outlying papers. The *Times* gave much greater coverage than any other newspaper to foreign reactions to the pagoda raids, and both papers covered the story closely in Washington. But, even the *Tribune*, which had the least coverage throughout the entire crisis, had nine page-one stories and twenty-six inside-page stories in the thirteen days after the raids, thus showing its interest in the dramatic events in Saigon despite the absence of Republican criticism of the administration. The *Post-Dispatch*, which wanted the administration to break with Diem, gave the issue page-one emphasis second only to the *Times*, and the *Examiner* played the story mainly for its elements of conflict and drama.

The news coverage in all of the papers in late August was overwhelmingly hostile to the Diem regime. From Saigon the resident reporters, seemingly vindicated by the raids' demonstration of the insensitivity and unpopularity of the ruling family, remained highly critical of the regime. Halberstam, for example, wrote on 25 August that "Vietnamese sources are bluntly warning Americans that the future of the anti-Communist cause is threatened because the Vietnamese public is losing confidence in the United States and is turning against Americans." The only pro-Diem journalists in Saigon in late August were Beech and Higgins, both of whose writings appeared occasionally on the inside pages of the *Post*. Featured on page one only in the conservative *Examiner*, Higgins argued that the Buddhists intended "to keep agitation—and publicity about it—at a high level until Washington finally 'ordered' new Ambassador Henry Cabot Lodge somehow to remove the Diem family from power." [18]

The coverage from Washington was also strongly anti-Diem in late August. In contrast to Saigon, where only the *Times* had full-time reporters, all five papers at least occasionally used their own reporters in Washington to cover the story there. Given their greater resources and readership interest in the issue, it is not surprising that the *Times* and *Post* did so most fully. In fact, because the *Post*'s leading foreign policy reporters, Chalmers Roberts and Murray Marder, were on other assignments until September, the *Times* again took the clear lead in covering the story.

With American-encouraged coup plotting in full swing in Saigon during the last week in August, the page-one stories based on unidentified sources by Szulc described the main features of the anti-Diem policy being debated almost daily in the National Security Council, as revealed in fuller detail in the *Pentagon Papers*. On the 27th Szulc reported that the administration hoped that South Vietnam's military leaders "would force a change in the regime." On the 28th he noted that coup plotting "has been hinted at, but officials are far from assured that it would be feasible." And on the 29th he discussed the belief that "democratic military government or one supported by the military could erase the hatred aroused by the Ngo family's repression." While American officials in Saigon were keeping in touch with the plotters about their plans, anti-Diem officials in Washington clearly were using the front page of the *Times* to signal their encouragement and to commit the administration to an anti-Diem policy. [19]

Warren Unna, a critic of the Diem regime and a close personal friend of the South Vietnamese ambassador to the United States, Tran Van Chuong, covered the Washington side of the story for the *Post* in August. An expert on Asia who made frequent trips to report on developments there, he believed that neutralism offered the best hope for the region's future, and he opposed American military involvement in the area. He went to Vietnam for the *Post* each spring from 1961 to 1963 for approximately ten days. Apparently recognizing the importance of the story, *Post* managing editor Alfred Friendly wanted him to stay longer, Unna recalled, but he refused because "I totally distrust the professional military, and a reporter out there was very dependent on them." [20]

Unna had written a page-one story on 6 August about Tran Van Chuong's angry reaction to the anti-Buddhist remarks of his daughter, Madame Nhu, and on 23 August he wrote the page-one story on Chuong's resignation as ambassador. "There is not one chance of winning the war against the Communists as long as we have this regime," Chuong asserted. In his subsequent news analyses, Unna stressed the effect that the pagoda raids were having on American prestige in "Buddhist Asia." Numerous page-one stories by

Sheehan and other reporters in Saigon also maintained the anti-Diem pressure on the president in the *Post*.[21]

Precisely what Kennedy thought about the leaking of information concerning the coup plotting and the other anti-Diem stories from Washington is unclear. There is no evidence as yet that he either participated in the leaking or sought to stop it before September. But some evidence indicates he was feeling the pressure by the end of August, at least partly because of the heavy, anti-Diem coverage of the pagoda raids. In his book on the Kennedy years, Hilsman recalled that McGeorge Bundy phoned him on 31 August

> to point out that the *New York Times* that morning had put two stories side by side on the front page—one on the Vietnamese Government's repression of the Buddhists and our disapproval, and the death of two more Americans in Vietnam. Diem would have to be made to understand that this could not go on. The foreign aid bill had just suffered the worst cut in its history, and the President felt it was largely due to the sense of disillusionment about the whole effort in Vietnam. There were also reports that an amendment might be put forward to forbid any aid at all to Vietnam unless the regime changed its policies.[22]

In addition to their page-one news stories, the *Times*, the *Post*, and the *Post-Dispatch* each carried several strongly anti-Diem editorials during this period. These papers clearly were more influenced by anti-Diem attitudes within the government and among liberals generally than were the conservative papers, and they also were more upset by evidence of repression in governments America was supporting. On 28 August, at the height of the coup plotting, the *Times* called for "change—either of Government leadership or of Government policies—brought about by the Vietnamese themselves." This editorial foreshadowed—and may well have inspired the phrasing for—Kennedy's own televised call for "changes in policy and . . . personnel" five days later, discussed more fully in the next chapter.[23]

Embodying the liberal idealism of the early 1960s, the *Post-Dispatch* editorialized on 29 August that Americans "must find some way of identifying ourselves with the people and not with their oppressors." "Either the Diem family will have to go, or the United States will have to get out of the Southeast Asian War," the *Post-Dispatch* editorialized on 3 September. In the absence of significant liberal sentiment in Congress or elsewhere to withdraw from Vietnam, the *Post-Dispatch*—like anti-Diem officials and the Washington-oriented press—much preferred the first alternative.[24]

What the Sources Show

Foreign sources and administration officials dominated the coverage in August, as table 7 shows. Because politicians were receiving absolutely no page-one coverage on Vietnam in any of the newspapers, the field was left open for American officials and especially for the South Vietnamese,[25] who comprised 97.4 percent of all page-one foreign sources in early August and 86.3 percent for the entire crisis. No other foreign nation received such heavy coverage in any of the earlier three crises, a fact explained partly by the absence of the Soviet Union and West European nations as important influences on the press during the Buddhist crisis. Moreover, at no time during the three earlier crises had official U.S. sources been so negligible as compared with those of another nation as during early August. As table 7 shows, it was only after Kennedy's televised remarks on Vietnam on 2 September that official U.S. sources exceeded the South Vietnamese. Still, administration sources comprised a significant percentage of the total during August, especially during the period of coup plotting after the pagoda raids.

Because the overwhelming majority of all page-one sources (70 percent) in the period 1–20 August were South Vietnamese and because nearly half (48 percent) continued to be South Vietnamese during the next two weeks, the leading resident reporters in Saigon had an impact on coverage in August far greater than any foreign correspondents had during the earlier three crises—and also more than they themselves would have beginning in September, when a larger percentage of the coverage shifted to Washington (see table 7). This heavy emphasis on news from Saigon was a major reason why these reporters became controversial at the time, especially with pro-Diem officials in Washington and the ruling family in Saigon. Alsop, who was close to the ruling family, recalled that Nhu was obsessed by the *Times*'s coverage and "hardly ever talked of anything else." Diem and Madame Nhu repeatedly made public complaints about the treatment of the crisis in the American media.[26]

Whether or not the resident reporters are viewed as fair-minded chroniclers of the Diem regime's difficulties whom the ruling family and others tried to use as scapegoats, or whether or not their coverage is considered to be unfairly anti-Diem, one fact stands out: the Diem regime was given ample opportunity to state its case. As table 8 shows, all five papers relied heavily on official South Vietnamese sources, especially on the front pages, while the Buddhist opposition was quoted much less frequently. But, although these figures demonstrate that the press followed its usual practice of quoting official sources extensively, they do not answer the more difficult qualitative question of whether or not the Diem regime's views were presented fairly. And, even if they had been, it still would have been quite possible for the interviews and other public statements of South Vietnam's leaders to have made a negative

Table 7. Vietnam: Comparison of Official and Nonofficial Sources, 1963
(front-page totals for all newspapers)

	United States Official	Foreign (South Vietnamese sources in parentheses)	Domestic Political	Interest Groups	Total Domestic Pol., Foreign, and Int. Grps.	Percentage U.S. Official Represents of This Total
1–20 Aug.	15	39 (38)	0	0	39	38%
21 Aug.–2 Sept.	102	146 (123)	0	1	147	69%
3 Sept.–2 Oct.	114	101 (89)	27	2	130	88%
3 Oct.–1 Nov.	85	68 (53)	22	6	96	89%
2–10 Nov.	54	85 (76)	13	1	99	55%

Table 8. South Vietnamese Official and Buddhist Sources as Percentages of All Foreign Sources, 1 August–10 November 1963

| | Front Page | | Inside Pages | |
	South Vietnamese Officials	South Vietnamese Buddhists	South Vietnamese Officials	South Vietnamese Buddhists
New York Times	57.5	10.2	49.0	5.9
Washington Post	62.1	5.9	49.6	8.9
St. Louis Post-Dispatch	65.3	5.9	48.3	9.8
Chicago Tribune	62.0	12.0	54.3	9.7
San Francisco Examiner	72.9	13.6	65.6	6.3

impression in the press, given the fact that these officials were already controversial and on the defensive. Finally, the Diem regime, like most other foreign governments, lacked an influential and vocal constituency in America to insist on more favorable treatment in the press.

The paucity of foreign sources other than South Vietnamese is best explained by the lack of public involvement in the issue by Western European nations with American constituencies, especially Britain and West Germany, and by the continuing assumption that communist leaders had nothing to contribute to the resolution of important disputes. Given the cold war atmosphere, it is not surprising that the National Liberation Front (NLF), the Vietcong's political arm, and the communist nations that supported the "other side" in Vietnam, comprised only 2.2 percent of page-one sources and 2.9 percent of inside-page sources. The Soviet Union, which had played such an important role in the other three crises but which did not want to disturb the developing détente on a peripheral issue like Vietnam, contributed less than 1 percent of the total sources cited on Vietnam. The two main adversaries—the NLF and North Vietnam—together contributed only 1.2 percent of total sources. Having no correspondents in either North Vietnam or mainland China, American newspapers were forced to rely on occasional Reuters dispatches from Peking and on the monitoring of Chinese and North Vietnamese broadcasts in Tokyo and Hong Kong.

Some of the communist sources who were quoted made predictably anti-American statements, such as Mao Tse Tung's comment on 29 August that Diem was a "faithful lackey of U.S. imperialism" whom the Americans would remove if he had "outlived his usefulness." But there also were reports in late August and in early November—which the *Times* and *Post* relegated to the inside pages and the other papers did not carry—that Ho Chi Minh was interested in a negotiated settlement with South Vietnam. The North Vietnamese, these reports indicated, sought two primary objectives: the right to purchase rice from South Vietnam in exchange for other goods; and the desire to limit Chinese influence in North Vietnam, which had increased as the war in the South had escalated. Tad Szulc and M. S. Handler both reported in the *Times* that North Vietnam wanted a "neutralized" Vietnam, partly to avoid excessive Chinese influence and to free North Vietnam from the consequences of being in the middle of the increasingly bitter conflict between Russia and China. As in the Laotian crisis and for essentially the same reasons, the North Vietnamese viewpoint had little impact on news coverage and even less on editorials and columns during the Buddhist crisis.[27]

The only non-South Vietnamese foreign official who received significant page-one and editorial coverage was French President Charles de Gaulle, who issued a statement on 29 August urging the Vietnamese to establish a nation "in independence from external influences, in internal peace and unity, and in concord with its neighbors." The statement was released in the context of diplomatic reports of French contacts with North Vietnamese officials and with Nhu in which both sides were said to look favorably on the idea of neutraliza- tion and eventual reunification. The French newspaper *Il Figaro* explained that the proposal should not be viewed as a slap at the United States, but rather as "the advice of an elder to a newcomer in the field." [28]

De Gaulle's proposal was quickly dismissed by American officials, assisted by the press, which once again showed its susceptibility to official interpreta- tions and its tendency to discount totally foreign views that lacked a constitu- ency within the government or elsewhere in American society. Only the *Tri- bune*, which disliked the administration and had long-standing doubts about the wisdom of American military involvement in Indochina, urged Kennedy not to permit his "irritation with de Gaulle" to "prevent him from seeing and taking advantage of an opportunity to shed part of this burden." When de Gaulle repeated his proposal after the coup in November, the press almost en- tirely ignored it (see appendix IV). [29]

Finally, the total absence of page-one domestic political sources during Au- gust reflected a combination of circumstances, including the simple fact that, as on Laos, few legislators had made the effort to acquire expertise on this issue. Unlike Berlin or Cuba, Vietnam had not stirred much interest in the constituencies to whom members of Congress were accountable. Like Laos, Vietnam was too remote and unfamiliar for the general public to develop much interest at this early stage in the war. Vietnam had also not become a political issue (and hence one that would generate news coverage) because most conservative Republicans strongly supported the American military commitment in Vietnam. Occasional expressions of dissent had come in 1962 and early 1963 from liberal Democrats like Mansfield and Representative Robert Kastenmaier (D.-Wisconsin), but most Democrats were not interested as yet in publicly challenging the president on this issue. [30]

Because politicians were dormant on the matter and the views of most for- eign leaders were discounted, the pressures on the president in the August news coverage to adopt a clear-cut anti-Diem policy were coming primarily from anti-Diem American and South Vietnamese officials, from South Viet- namese Buddhists, and, ironically, from the Diem regime itself. Although the resident reporters and editors seeking dramatic headlines contributed to the negative impact, it was the ruling family that made provocative statements about the Buddhists and the American government. Most importantly, it was the ruling family that ignored American suggestions for conciliation and in- flamed the issue worldwide by ordering the raids on the pagodas.

Conclusion

The president's low-visibility press strategy in August had the advantage of not stirring up domestic opposition on the left or right, which coming down too heavily in favor of either the Diem regime or the Buddhists probably would have done. But this strategy had the important disadvantage of leaving the initiative in the press to others, almost all of whom undermined American support for the Diem regime.

In contrast to the Cuban crisis, in which the conservative, popular papers were the major vehicles for pressure on the administration, these anti-Diem pressures were concentrated in the liberal, Washington-oriented papers, with the *Times* clearly taking the lead. The failure of important hard-line columnists like Alsop to write pro-Diem articles in August further shifted the balance of press coverage in an anti-Diem direction.

Although the need to articulate a new American policy toward Vietnam was much more urgent at the end of August than it had been at the beginning of the month, the immediate pressures on Kennedy should not be exaggerated. Foreign proposals for neutralization could be ignored, and conservative Republicans in Congress and in the press were more interested in trying to defeat the test-ban treaty than in criticizing American policy in Vietnam. Gallup reported in September that, in the wake of the march on Washington in late August and continuing demonstrations and violence in the South, a majority of the public viewed civil rights as the most important problem facing the nation. Several more years would elapse before distant Vietnam became as emotional an issue as nearby Cuba had been in September 1962.

This relative lack of public interest in Vietnam gave the president room to maneuver, as did the fact that the press itself in late August was primarily angry at the provocative Diem regime, not at the publicly cautious administration. Nhu and Madame Nhu—not the administration—seemed to be mocking the American ideals of democracy and fair play and undermining the legitimacy of the substantial American commitment in South Vietnam. Nevertheless, the postponement of the coup, the continuing defiance of the Diem regime, the growing but still private concern in Congress, and, not least, the heavy coverage of the Buddhist crisis in the press virtually forced the president after the end of August to seek to demonstrate his personal leadership on the issue.

Chapter 13

Kennedy's Ambiguous Initiatives Fail

3 September–2 October

Although Kennedy broke his six-week-long silence on Vietnam in early September and sought throughout the month to maintain the initiative on the issue, his efforts yielded only modest success. Through his public comments in two television interviews and a news conference as well as his initiatives, such as the dispatch of Defense Secretary McNamara and General Taylor to Vietnam in late September, the president was able to convey the impression that he was taking at least some steps to deal with the crisis. But this more active press strategy was largely unsuccessful, partly because American policy in Vietnam in the wake of the well-publicized pagoda raids and the relatively unpublicized coup plotting remained ambiguous. Kennedy offered no clear answer, for example, to the question of how long the United States would work with Diem if, as appeared likely, he refused to make significant changes in his government and policies.

The president was in a difficult position. The divisions within the administration were deeper and more bitter after the unsuccessful coup plotting than they had been earlier, for pro-Diem officials naturally questioned the wisdom of the aborted undertaking. Moreover, as long as Diem remained in power, the administration, committed above all to defeating the Vietcong, had little choice but to continue working with him, though it could—and did—adopt in early September a de facto policy of gradually increasing the pressure on his regime. Sorensen argues convincingly that Kennedy at this time "hoped to move the administration away from its total dependence on Diem without causing South Vietnam to fall or his own team to split wide open." Achieving these various objectives simultaneously was virtually impossible. In particular, the president's public efforts to strike a balance between the pro-Diem and anti-Diem viewpoints within the administration failed to clarify U.S. policy and hence left Kennedy open to criticisms from all sides in the press.[1]

The most publicized division within the administration in September was between CIA bureau chief Richardson, who had been closely associated with

Nhu and continued to provide funds for his special forces, and Ambassador Lodge, who clearly opposed the ruling family and supported the anti-Diem reporters in Saigon. In Washington, tensions between pro-Diem military and CIA officials and anti-Diem State Department and White House officials were quite apparent. Harmed by leaking on both sides of the debate within the administration on policy toward Diem, the president's position was further weakened by the fact that, in trying to unify the government, he could not discuss publicly the seriousness of these internal difficulties.

Unlike the major initiatives in the other three crises that had left him in control of the situation in the press, Kennedy's actions in September 1963 thus failed to consolidate his position. Instead, questioning increased about American policy in Congress and in the press, reporting of the bitter split within the administration between supporters and critics of Diem intensified, and the administration was more openly defied by the Diem regime. When on 2 October McNamara and Taylor reported to the president on their trip to Vietnam, no significant changes in South Vietnam's policies or personnel were apparent, the controversial Madame Nhu was en route to the United States, and the Washington-oriented press was much more inclined to criticize official policy than it had been a month before. To a politician like Kennedy, the questioning of American policy amplified in the press could appear to be as serious as the situation in Vietnam itself.

The President Tries to Capture the Initiative

Kennedy took the initiative on Vietnam four times during September: in his interview with Walter Cronkite of CBS on 2 September, in his interview with Chet Huntley and David Brinkley of NBC on 9 September, in his news conference on 12 September, and in the White House announcement of the McNamara-Taylor mission to Vietnam on 21 September. Although often ambiguous and contradictory, Kennedy's responses to the five questions on Vietnam posed by Cronkite, the five raised by Huntley and Brinkley, and the six posed at his news conference offer the best guide available to Kennedy's public position on Vietnam, a subject he frequently had avoided in the past and would do so in the future.

Presidential aides Ted Clifton and Pierre Salinger let reporters know that Kennedy planned to make a major policy statement on Vietnam in his interview with Cronkite. The president's comments were not disappointing. In a remarkably sharp attack on an allied government, he criticized Diem's policies toward the Buddhists as "very unwise," said that the regime had lost "popular support," and called in effect for Nhu's resignation. Although Kennedy told Cronkite that it was "their war," he insisted that American withdrawal would be a "great mistake." [2]

According to Salinger, Kennedy was upset when he saw the Cronkite inter-view on television because it had been cut from about thirty minutes to twelve and only the more critical remarks about Diem had been included. Before agreeing to the interview with NBC, Kennedy therefore insisted on—and re-ceived—the right to give final approval of the footage that was used. Re-sponding to doubts expressed in Congress about the domino theory—which postulated that the fall of one nation to communism would lead to the takeover of others—and about the continuation of aid to Diem, the president said that he believed in the theory because the fall of South Vietnam would "give the impression that the wave of the future in southeast Asia was China and the Communists," and that the United States should not cut aid to Diem "at this time."[3]

Kennedy's use of television news programs to make most of his substantive comments on Vietnam illustrates a more general point about his relationship to the media. During the earlier crises, he had considered it essential in propa-gating his viewpoint to talk with leading print reporters like James Reston of the *Times* and Hugh Sidey of *Time* magazine. But, by 1963, Sidey and others have reported, Kennedy had decided that the evening news programs—which expanded from fifteen to thirty minutes in September 1963—were more im-portant in reaching the public than any newspaper or magazine. Partly as a result of this thinking, Kennedy cut down markedly in 1963 on the number of interviews he granted to print journalists. More specifically, there is no evi-dence that he discussed Vietnam during the Buddhist crisis with any of the reporters or columnists—except Alsop—who wrote for the five important newspapers in this study. In fact, Kennedy's failure to grant background inter-views on Vietnam to important journalists like Reston and Roberts may well have contributed to the unfavorable coverage of his policies in September and early October in the Washington-oriented press.[4]

All five papers gave heavy page-one emphasis to Kennedy's remarks. The Washington-oriented *Times* and *Post* gave similar coverage to all four of Ken-nedy's initiatives; the *Tribune* put three on page one, including banner head-lines for the 2 September comments and the decision to send McNamara and Taylor to Vietnam; and the *Post-Dispatch* and the *Examiner* both featured the Cronkite interview and the McNamara-Taylor mission. For papers like the *Examiner* and the *Tribune*, which carried relatively little page-one coverage of Vietnam in September, the emphasis on Kennedy's initiatives was espe-cially pronounced. As in August, the overall coverage in these two papers pre-sented the least challenge to the administration's ambivalent policy.

The prominent coverage of Kennedy's initiatives contributed to a sharp jump in the percentage of page-one official sources from 38 percent of the combined total of the other categories in early August to 88 percent in Sep-tember (see table 7). The September percentage, in fact, was the highest except for the 3 October–1 November period. But, unfortunately for the president, many of the officials quoted in September were using the press—especially the Washington-oriented papers—to air disagreements on policy, a serious problem for Kennedy that his 12 September plea for unity within the administration failed to discourage. Thus, in this instance, official influence on the press did not contribute to acceptance of Kennedy's middle position between the fervent pro-Diem and anti-Diem factions in his administration.

Discordant Voices Largely Drown Out the President

The president's difficulties in gaining support for his policies in the press are illustrated by the kinds of questions on Vietnam raised in the 12 September news conference as well as the concerns leading to these questions. All six grew out of the apparent failure of American policy in Vietnam as exemplified in the pagoda raids and the continuing turmoil reported in the press, and all six tended to put Kennedy on the defensive. The first questioner on Vietnam asked whether, "in view of the prevailing confusion," it was "possible to state today just what this Government's policy is toward the current government of South Viet-Nam." The second asked whether "any significant changes in the policy of South Viet-Nam can be carried out so long as Ngo Dinh Nhu remains as the President's top advisor." And the third questioner asked Kennedy to respond to critics' charges that "you are operating on the basis of inadequate information." [5]

These questions clearly grew out of published reports that the CIA had failed to provide adequate intelligence about the pagoda raids as well as from the Diem regime's public defiance of Kennedy's call for Nhu's resignation. Two other questions were responses to calls in Congress for the cutoff of aid to the Diem regime and to a resolution by the liberal California Federation of Young Democrats for withdrawal from Vietnam. Given pointed questions like these, it is not surprising that Kennedy chose to announce the McNamara-Taylor mission in a brief White House press release and that the next presidential press conference was not held until 9 October. [6]

If McGeorge Bundy is correct in his recollection that Kennedy read the papers largely to see the view of the world and of his policies others were receiving, the president emphatically would not have liked the coverage of the Vietnam issue in September, especially in the *Times*, *Post*, and *Post-Dispatch*. These three papers had a total of seventy-one page-one stories on Vietnam in September, compared with only twenty-five in the *Tribune* and *Examiner*, and most of these and numerous inside-page stories quoted dissident sources and raised questions about American policy. The most important challenges in the press were coming from the Diem regime and from contentious American officials in Saigon and, to a lesser extent, in Washington. Lesser pressures to act forcefully against the Diem regime were coming from anti-Diem reporters in

Saigon, from Congress, and from nongovernmental groups. Each of these challenges can be illustrated briefly.[7]

The Diem regime made clear in September its refusal to go down without a fight. On 2 September Nhu's mouthpiece, the English-language *Times of Vietnam*, charged under a banner headline that the CIA was financing a coup attempt against the regime. Played as a page-one story in all papers except the *Examiner*, this charge was embarrassing to the administration even though the stories from Saigon and Washington were not written in such a way as to lend credence to the charge. Now that Kennedy had criticized the Diem regime, Nhu and Madame Nhu stepped up their charges. Nhu, whose sanity and judgment were subjects of speculation, asserted that the Voice of America was not the "voice of the Government of America but the voice of a group of capitalists who control it." Madame Nhu commented on 11 September that "President Kennedy is a politician and when he hears a loud opinion speaking, he tries to appease it somehow." These frequent stories based on comments by the Nhus and Diem provided a direct challenge to the administration's position.[8]

More important than the ruling family's attacks in contributing to the appearance of confusion in American policy was the wholesale leaking among American officials in Saigon and Washington, a situation that led Senator Mansfield to demand on 20 September that the administration put its house in order. Although leaking on possible aid cuts was occurring in Washington to reporters like Szulc and Roberts, the leaks that received the biggest headlines were being given to Halberstam and Sheehan in Saigon, who were sharing information much as Bob Woodward and Carl Bernstein of the *Post* were to do during the Watergate crisis a decade later. Halberstam recalled the broad range of officials who were talking to Sheehan and himself who enabled them to obtain the detailed stories in September on the split within the American mission in Saigon:

> We had the ambassador and the hand-picked person below him, on a personal basis. . . . We had the people who had been our sources for a year. And then, as events began to build up, and as the regime began to flaunt itself against American will and began to go down—I mean, quite clearly coming apart, as we later had in Watergate—you had guys who'd once been critical of Woodward and Bernstein or Halberstam and Sheehan cut away and become sources. The moment one of these things collapses, everyone becomes a source, they all begin to talk, and they all change sides.[9]

An example of the kind of story from Saigon that had repercussions within the administration, in Congress, and in editorial offices was a dispatch by Halberstam on the front page of the *Times* on 9 September. He reported that the CIA had "quietly decided" to continue payments to Nhu's special forces, which had been widely condemned for conducting the pagoda raids the previous month. Halberstam noted the "widespread opposition" to the decision within the CIA in Saigon and in other American agencies there. Officials in Washington gave Reston a weak denial that the CIA was still financing the special forces, but the damage to the administration's position had been done.[10]

A few days later, Sheehan and Halberstam each presented detailed accounts of the divisions between U.S. civilian and military officials over whether to continue to support Diem. "Almost all high-ranking American officials here are reliably reported to be opposed to the present U.S. action to retrieve what they believe is a steadily deteriorating situation," Sheehan reported in a dispatch played as the lead story in the *Post* on Sunday, the 15th. "One [American] General is reported to have said he would get a high civilian Embassy official if it was the last thing he did," Halberstam observed.[11]

Once a few stories appeared on CIA financing of the special forces and on civilian disagreement with the military leadership's view that the war was being won under Diem, the leaking tended to become vicious. Richardson was subjected to harsh criticism, which appeared to contribute to his recall in early October. A State Department official in Washington condescendingly told Unna that the McNamara-Taylor mission in late September had served as a "primer" on Vietnam for the previously uninformed McNamara. Responding in kind, a Defense Department source told a reporter from the *Herald-Tribune* that Hilsman had been responsible for the hitherto undisclosed 24 August cable authorizing support for a coup against Diem, and that McNamara was furious because he had not been consulted before it was sent to Lodge. A newspaper reader might well have concluded that leading officials were more interested in attacking each other in the press than in formulating a unified policy toward the Diem regime.[12]

While the Ngo family and American officials in Saigon were reminding officials in Washington and the public that the crisis was continuing, American reporters in Vietnam became more openly hostile to the regime and to American support for it. The pagoda raids had vindicated their conviction that the Diem regime was hopelessly ruthless and unpopular; and, now that Lodge and other officials in Saigon and Washington were equally hostile to it, this conviction could be included more readily in news dispatches. "When a young Vietnamese and a young American get on well together," Halberstam wrote on 3 September, "one thing they have in common is that neither likes his own country's policy." Or, as Browne observed on 8 September, "In the last few months, the United States has lost most of the friends it had in South Vietnam."[13]

The new willingness to criticize openly extended well beyond the established resident reporters. Roy Essoyan of AP, for example, wrote that Nhu, "possibly the most powerful and most hated figure in South Vietnam," was reported to prefer to "make a deal with his country's arch enemy, Communist North Viet-Nam, before he would bow to American pressure." And, when Saigon's elementary and high school students openly protested the regime's policies and received heavy coverage from American reporters, the *Times*'s Robert Trumbull praised them for "developing a tradition of revolt against repression." By September, in short, the story from Saigon was that the regime was evil and its opponents were good. Because the popular newspapers relied primarily on the wire services, which were emphasizing this viewpoint as much as the *Times*, there was little difference in the image of the Diem regime presented by the five newspapers.[14]

Like the reporters, members of Congress of both parties also began to speak openly against the Diem regime in September. After generating considerable coverage in regard to his intention to urge Congress to cut off aid to the regime unless it ceased its repression of the Buddhists, Senator Frank Church of Idaho, a liberal Democrat, introduced a strongly worded resolution to this effect on 12 September. Twenty-one other Senators—eighteen Democrats and three Republicans—joined him in introducing the resolution, which the State Department had helped to draft and which anti-Diem officials favored in order to put pressure on Diem. The number of mostly liberal signers had grown to thirty-three by early October, but it was reported that most Democrats would vote against the resolution if Kennedy opposed its passage and that most Republicans, wanting to win the war at all costs, would also vote against it. The Senate Foreign Relations Committee quietly inserted a watered-down version of the resolution in the foreign aid bill on 15 October.[15]

Because leading figures in Congress like Fulbright and Dirksen failed to support the initiative, Church's resolution could only generate modest pressure through the press for a change in policy. Fulbright, a tacit supporter of the administration, recalled that "we didn't take this too seriously" until the Gulf of Tonkin incident in 1964. Bryce Nelson, a foreign affairs assistant to Church at the time, recalled that "a number of [liberal] Senators were holding back on Vietnam for fear that speaking out would hurt them politically." Even Church himself, who Nelson says believed that the United States should not be involved militarily in Vietnam, carefully directed his criticism at the Diem regime and did not question the premises of American policy. But the sharp criticism of Diem and of official bickering and indecision, unbalanced by any press reports of congressional sympathy for the president's predicament, added to the pressure on the administration to "do something" about Diem.[16]

Finally, indications were growing in the press in September that liberals outside of Washington were becoming increasingly uneasy about American policy in Vietnam. The public as a whole was not involved in the issue—35 percent of Louis Harris's sample in September declined to state an opinion on what American policy toward Diem should be, partly because Vietnam was "too remote"—but liberals, particularly on the east and west coasts, were becoming interested in the issue. Because many liberal organizations were concentrating on passage of the test-ban treaty, the only interest group focusing exclusively on American policy toward Diem was the Ministers' Vietnam Committee. This group had been founded during the summer by Donald S. Harrington, pastor of the Community Church of New York, and included such well-known Protestant leaders as Harry Emerson Fosdick and Reinhold Niebuhr. The committee took out full-page advertisements in the *Times* denouncing the "loss of American lives and billions of dollars to bolster a regime universally regarded as unjust, undemocratic, and unstable," and received coverage of its activities in the *Times*, *Post*, and *Tribune*. "We were all feeling our way at that point," Harrington recalled. "My ideas on Vietnam were not totally formulated." [17]

The California Federation of Young Democrats, whose controversial resolution on 8 September for a cutoff of all aid to the Diem regime and withdrawal of American troops from Vietnam within six months generated considerable coverage and led to the question at Kennedy's news conference, were also still thinking through the issue. Their convention easily passed resolutions favoring recognition of mainland China and improved relations with Cuba and East Germany, but the resolution on Vietnam only passed by the thin margin of 1,527 votes to 1,460 after a heated debate. At the other ideological pole, the national commander of the American Legion, in a wire service story used only by the *Tribune*, admonished the administration on 10 September to be "absolutely certain we are protecting the type of [South Vietnamese] government that we want to protect" in order to ensure military victory. [18]

Taken together, these diverse challenges undercut the president's leadership on Vietnam in September. They demonstrate again that, in a period of uncertainty and policy review, the president's interests and those of even pro-administration newspapers diverge. The president was interested in avoiding harmful publicity and moving gradually to unify the administration and to carry out the policy he had selected, in this case slowly and quietly increasing pressure on the Diem regime. The press as a whole was less interested in protecting his position than in highlighting the conflict and controversy that emerged as the major actors traded accusations. And the newspapers that had become committed to particular outcomes—the *Tribune* and *Examiner* on the Russian role in Cuba in 1962 and the other three on the fate of the Diem regime in 1963—had become involved in pushing the president more rapidly than he might have chosen toward their viewpoint.

Normally Proadministration Editorialists
and Columnists Get Nasty

Whereas in August the editorials and columns on Vietnam had directed almost all their criticism at the Diem regime, in September these attacks became more perfunctory and the cutting edge was directed at the administration. The number of editorial criticisms of official policy increased from five in August to thirteen in September (see appendix IV), and their tone became more sharply antiadministration. September was also the period in which the most columns appeared on Vietnam, and these too contained many pointed criticisms of official policy. Although normally hostile voices like the *Tribune* and Conniff continued to make desultory attacks on State Department officials as well as anti-Diem journalists in Vietnam and the maverick Arthur Krock asked whether America should get out of Vietnam, critiques from such normally friendly quarters as the *Post* and Reston were more harmful to the president's position. For if his leadership on Vietnam were questioned too much, especially in the papers read in Washington, there was a real possibility that more members of Congress might demand a role in the making of policy on Vietnam and in overseeing the operations of the CIA.[19]

The *Post*, which had supported the administration editorially during the previous three crises, led the attack on Vietnam. On 4 September it criticized Kennedy for his failure in his interview with Cronkite to "call a trowel a trowel" and tell Diem that "American opinion is outraged" by his repression of the Buddhists. And on 11 September, responding to the president's remarks in his NBC interview, the *Post* criticized him for suggesting that the United States should remain indefinitely in Vietnam. Arguing that it could be "lost to communism" whether or not the United States remained, the *Post* argued that withdrawal should be considered a viable option that the president "must keep in a state of day-to-day review." "There must be some limit" to the American commitment, the editorial concluded.[20]

The *Post*'s other two editorials on Vietnam in September bear the unmistakable imprint of Russ Wiggins, who firmly believed that the CIA should be brought under close congressional oversight. Responding to Halberstam's and Sheehan's revelation that Nhu's special forces were still on the CIA payroll, the *Post* demanded a "real reorganization of the CIA," which in Wiggins's view should have been effected immediately after the Bay of Pigs. Referring in a subsequent editorial to press accounts critical of Richardson, the *Post* notes that it was "shocking to read that intelligence deputies persist in the bad habit of operating as if the Ambassador were merely a pleasant man sent on a courtesy visit to a foreign capital."[21]

Perhaps because it was more distant than the *Post* from the bureaucratic infighting in Washington over the CIA's role in Vietnam, the *Post-Dispatch* did not stress this issue in its September editorials. Instead, it repeatedly pressured the administration to act "boldly and decisively" to encourage opposition elements in South Vietnam to overthrow the Diem regime. "The time has come for the United States to face the fact that the whole ruling family must go," the *Post-Dispatch* editorialized on 5 September. Arguing on 12 September that it was "too late for Diem to regain the confidence of the Viet Namese people" and on the 22d that no South Vietnamese government could win the war unless it had "overwhelming popular support," the paper persistently challenged the administration to move quickly to encourage a change in regime.[22]

More supportive of the president's cautious policy, the *Times* did not offer its sharpest criticism until after the McNamara-Taylor report in early October. But on the 22d concern was expressed about "the deep split inside the administration on just what policy to pursue." Echoing Mansfield's critique, which had appeared on the front page the day before, the *Times* insisted that "any policy is better than no policy at all or a dozen policies operating at cross-purposes." Like the *Post*, it believed that the "confusion" in American policy would diminish if the CIA's activities in Vietnam were put under Ambassador Lodge's control.[23]

Finally, the administration came under unusually sharp attack from two normally friendly columnists, James Reston and Drew Pearson. On 4 September Reston criticized Kennedy for the "naked diplomacy" in his Cronkite interview and suggested that Vietnam "is a mess recommending silence." On 8 September Reston asked whether, in view of the Sino-Soviet split, it was still necessary to spend billions of dollars each year to bolster the regimes in South Vietnam, South Korea, Iran, and elsewhere on the fringes of the communist bloc. This critique of heavy spending on defense, combined with emphasis on the need for greater attention to pressing domestic problems, was a frequent refrain in Reston's columns in 1963. "President Kennedy has asked the American people to be 'patient' about Vietnam," he wrote on the 11th, "but it would be nice to know what we are being asked to be patient about." Referring to Halberstam's reporting as "brilliant," he argued that Americans could not be fully informed about Vietnam until the administration successfully pressured the Diem regime to lift censorship of dispatches by American reporters.[24]

In his widely syndicated column on the 14th, Pearson reported that Senator Church had given Hilsman a well-deserved tongue-lashing in regard to the administration's continuing support of Diem at a closed-door session earlier in the month. "What are you going to do about this mandarin? There has been nothing like him since the Borgias," Pearson quoted Church as saying. When a normally friendly columnist uses a leak from normally supportive sources to criticize administration policy, a president almost certainly is losing the public relations battle in the press.[25]

Alsop Concludes That Diem Must Go

If Kennedy was going to yield to the pressures building around him and move more decisively against Diem after the McNamara-Taylor factfinding trip to Vietnam in late September, he would need the support of the hard-line journalist who had taken an almost proprietary interest in Southeast Asian issues, Joseph Alsop. In numerous columns on Vietnam in 1961, he had insisted on making a firm commitment to Diem and sending military advisers to assist the South Vietnamese. At a time when no other columnist was visiting the country or taking an interest in the issue, his advice was influential, and Kennedy had even invited him to accompany Taylor and Rostow on their mission to Vietnam in the fall of 1961 that had led to the sending of troops. Because of his stature on this issue with those who supported hard-line policies, the conclusions Alsop reached on his trip to Vietnam in September 1963 would be important in shaping the climate of opinion in which the administration charted its course.

In contrast to the meager use of Higgins's pro-Diem writings from Vietnam in August, six of the seven columns on Vietnam in the *Post* in the last half of September were by Alsop, and the *Post-Dispatch* and *Examiner* each featured four of his columns from Vietnam. This trip—and particularly an interview with Nhu—convinced Alsop that U.S. support for the Diem regime no longer made sense. He recalled the interview with Nhu and his comment to Kennedy upon his return:

> Nhu had gone stark, raving mad; he had raving paranoia. I spent four hours with him. Three quarters of the time he spent denouncing Diem, his brother, as an old fool and no good, or that he had merely to wave a handkerchief and a million men would spring to arms at his back—that he had the biggest following in the country. And at the other extreme he told me that he was independently, without Diem knowing it, I think, negotiating with North Vietnam through the French.
>
> As I saw no feasible way to detach Nhu and Diem—and nobody else had found one—I concluded that the show wasn't viable. And with all the risks involved, I told the president—he called me in when I got back—"well, I don't think this is viable."[26]

Although Alsop was not as blunt in his columns as he apparently was in his private meeting with Kennedy, he made it clear that Diem and Nhu were no longer effective leaders. He wrote on 20 September, for example, that "success in the struggle against the Communists can hardly be expected if the real world of the leaders of that struggle has tragically contracted to the narrow limits of the palace walls. So there are likely to be changes here." He depicted

Nhu as being "beyond normal vanity" and Diem as "another man who has lost his ability to see events or problems in their true proportions." [27]

In addition to changing his mind publicly about Diem and Nhu, Alsop used his columns from Vietnam to praise American soldiers there as "a rather special breed who make you proud of your country"; to criticize Senator Church "and his attendant chorus of experts on guerilla wars who have never seen a guerilla"; and to denounce Halberstam and other "crusaders" in the press who had "helped mightily to transform Diem from a courageous, quite viable national leader, into a man afflicted with galloping persecutionmania." David Klein, an assistant to McGeorge Bundy at the time, recalled that Reston phoned Bundy after Alsop wrote the column criticizing Halberstam and said, "Why don't you call off Alsop?" The quick-witted Bundy replied, "Don't you believe in freedom of the press?" [28]

Alsop's columns from Vietnam and his conversation with Kennedy upon his return did much to clear the way politically for the administration to institute more concrete anti-Diem policies in early October, policies that almost certainly would lead to changes in the Diem regime or, more likely, to its overthrow. From the perspective of the late 1970s, Alsop regretted the coup against Diem and believed that he bore "a good deal of responsibility" for it. Although Alsop's personal role should not be exaggerated, his anti-Diem actions in late September did deal a substantial blow to the remaining pro-Diem elements in the administration and in the press. [29]

Conclusion

The president's position in the press continued to deteriorate in September largely because he was unable to prevent challenges to his cautious, middle-of-the-road policy toward Diem—challenges which, taken together, received considerably more press coverage than Kennedy's own initiatives. Because the views of Vietnam's ruling family tended to be discounted in advance and because leading members of Congress were not interested in pushing the president on this issue, the challenges from the Diem regime and from liberals in Congress were not in themselves sources of substantial pressure on the president. But, added to the heavy leaking by dissidents on both sides within the administration—leaking that led to the most damaging news and editorial coverage—these influences placed Kennedy on the defensive throughout September. As during the early part of the other three crises, the major flow of influence continued to be from the press to the president. When a pro-Kennedy columnist like Reston could chide the president for resorting to diplomacy by television and failing to achieve his objectives, and when a prowar columnist like Alsop could suggest in his dispatches that the Diem regime no longer merited support, Kennedy clearly was under pressure to adopt a more forceful anti-Diem policy.

Like the September period of the Cuban crisis, this period demonstrates that an active press strategy alone will not ensure success for a president in advancing his position in the press. Both the internal conditions within the administration and some of the external conditions that Kennedy faced were too turbulent for his views to become dominant in the press. Moreover, this experience suggests that, when the administration is divided and Congress is restive, public statements and activities may not be sufficient to win the support of the Washington-oriented press. The president may also need to use his personal influence to attempt to sway key reporters and editors from these newspapers, especially when he is granting bounteous favors to their electronic competitors.

Nevertheless, certain external conditions in September enabled the president to maintain some control over the situation. Most significantly, Republicans did not try to turn his difficulties concerning this issue to partisan advantage. Senator Goldwater and others appear to have been waiting quietly for him to make mistakes and then to use them against him in the 1964 election. As long as he did not abandon the goal of military victory or become involved too openly in overthrowing Diem, leading Republicans and the more conservative newspapers withheld criticism. Also aiding the president was the fact that public opinion and interest groups, except for a small segment on the left, were not stirred to action on the Vietnam issue. Finally, he continued to benefit from the fact that papers like the *Times* and *Post-Dispatch* as well as reporters like Halberstam and Sheehan remained more interested in changing the government in Saigon than in criticizing the administration in Washington.

By the end of September, therefore, the president's position on Vietnam had weakened far more than it ever did during the Laotian crisis, but the situation was still considerably more favorable than it had been at the low point during the Cuban crisis twelve months before. But with Nhu still exercising influence in Vietnam, with Congress questioning the value of foreign aid generally and aid to Vietnam specifically, and with papers like the *Post* challenging the assumptions of policy as never before, the situation was highly volatile. His initial public initiatives having failed to stem the growing criticism, the president was under substantially more pressure in the press than he had been at the end of August to resolve the crisis in American policy toward South Vietnam.

Chapter 14

The President's Position Finally Improves

3 October–10 November

The classified McNamara-Taylor report to Kennedy on 2 October was the last key development in American relations with the Diem regime. By accepting Lodge's view that pressures against the Diem regime should be intensified, the two military leaders effectively embraced the anti-Diem viewpoint that had such committed advocates in the State Department, among liberals in Congress, and in the Washington-oriented press. Although reporters in Washington were not given the full story of the McNamara-Taylor recommendations, they could see in such events of the following week as the recall of CIA bureau chief Richardson and reports in Saigon that economic aid had been cut that the administration was tightening the screws on Diem. Because the anti-Diem viewpoint was triumphant, the Washington-oriented papers that had applied the most pressure on the president in August and September ceased attacking the administration on Vietnam by 10 October.[1]

The terse White House press release of 2 October relating to the McNamara-Taylor report was the last presidential initiative before the coup thirty days later. In contrast with the frequent presidential initiatives and the heavy leaking by officials of differing viewpoints in September, the administration successfully pursued a unified, tight-lipped press strategy on Vietnam in October. This public unanimity contributed to a lessening of front-page stories and editorial criticism, especially in the Washington-oriented *Times* and *Post*. Behind the scenes, the administration reverted in October to its late-August policy of encouraging a coup and added unannounced aid cutoffs to its earlier practice of frequent consultations with dissident generals. Because Washington reporters were kept in the dark about coup plotting in Saigon this time and because the only explicit reporting on the subject was deleted in UPI's Tokyo office, there was no open press coverage of the plotting as there had been in late August. But the opposite was true concerning Madame Nhu's visit to the

United States beginning 7 October, a visit that both helped the administration by diverting attention from the continuing crisis in Vietnam and hindered it by stirring up modest domestic divisions on the issue. As with any dramatic event, coverage was strong of the bloody coup in Saigon on 1 November, but the administration escaped with only minor criticisms of its probable involvement and with few publicized suggestions for reevaluating American policy in Vietnam.[2]

Although this period began inauspiciously for the administration with sharp editorial criticism of the White House press release, the president's position improved as October progressed. What did not happen was as helpful as what did. Liberals in Congress did not continue to make an issue of Vietnam policy, Catholic leaders did not rally to the defense of the Diem regime, Madame Nhu did not gain significant public support, and reporters in Saigon and Washington did not expose American involvement in the coup plotting in Vietnam. And, now that leading military officials had accepted the essential features of the anti-Diem position, the embarrassing leaking of disagreements on policy within the government virtually ceased.

The decline of leaking in Saigon and Washington and the tight-lipped public press policy led to a sharp decline in official source usage in the *Times* and *Post*, as table 9 shows. In fact, comparison of two thirty-day periods—3 September–2 October and 3 October–1 November—shows that total page-one source usage declined 71 percent in the paper most attuned to official policy, the *Post*; 44 percent in the *Times*; and 4 percent in the more independent *Post-Dispatch*. Paralleled by a decline in the number of editorials on Vietnam, especially in the *Post*, these figures illustrate the lessening pressure on the president from the Washington-oriented press in October. The increase in page-one sources in the *Tribune* and *Examiner* largely reflected the impact of Madame Nhu's visit, which stirred interest in Vietnam among the public and hence led to increased coverage in the popular press. Because this coverage focused on her as a controversial personality rather than as a national leader, it did not pressure the president to change his policies in either a pro-Diem or an anti-Diem direction.

The McNamara-Taylor Report Unifies the Government but Angers the Press

At 6:05 P.M. on 2 October the National Security Council met and unanimously approved the McNamara-Taylor recommendations on American policy in Vietnam. After the meeting adjourned at 6:30, Pierre Salinger read a brief statement to reporters that contained four general points and one specific one. The general points represented a compromise between the military and civilian viewpoints that had been so bitterly debated in September: the military

**Table 9. Comparison of Front-Page Source Usage,
3 Sept.–2 Oct.–3 Oct.–1 Nov. 1963**

	Official U.S.		Foreign		Dom. Pol.		Other		Total Front-Page Sources		Percent Increase and Decrease
	Sept.	Oct.	Sept.	Oct.	Sept.	Oct.	Sept.	Oct.	Sept.	Oct.	
New York Times	33	19	33	18	9	4	0	1	75	42	(−44%)
Washington Post	25	11	29	3	7	3	2	1	63	18	(−71%)
St. Louis Post-Dispatch	26	26	31	24	8	8	0	4	65	62	(−5%)
Chicago Tribune	11	13	4	5	0	2	1	6	16	26	(+65%)
San Francisco Examiner	19	16	4	18	3	5	3	10	29	49	(+69%)
TOTAL	114	85	101	68	27	22	6	22	248	197	(−21%)

effort had "made progress and is sound in principle," but "the political situation in South Vietnam remains deeply serious." The specific point was that "the major part of the U.S. military task can be completed by the end of 1965." As a step toward achieving this goal, a thousand military personnel were to be removed before the end of 1963.[3]

Realizing that the 1965 objective would make the headlines and that the administration's credibility in Vietnam had been undermined in the past by overly optimistic statements, several officials sought to have the reference to that year deleted from the press release, but to no avail. Ball, who attended the White House meetings that day, recalled that "some of us said it was very foolish at that time." Chester Cooper, who also sought to delete the reference to 1965, has noted that McNamara himself seemed unable to change it when McGeorge Bundy phoned him about it. This led Cooper to conclude that "the sentence may have been worked out privately with Kennedy and therefore embedded in concrete." It is not clear whether the statement's primary purpose was to signal Kennedy's determination to begin to extricate the United States from Vietnam, as Arthur Schlesinger, Jr., has argued, or whether it was, as General Taylor observed later, mainly "a pressure device to get better Vietnamese performance." The only certainty is that it further harmed the administration's position in the press.[4]

In its lead editorial on 4 October, "Candor Needed on Vietnam," the *Times* delivered its sharpest attack of the entire Buddhist crisis on the administration's handling of the situation. "The vital statistics of victory or defeat . . . are still 'classified' in Washington," the editorial complained. "Even the number of helicopters lost to hostile action in South Vietnam are regarded as 'secret.'" Warning that "the support of public opinion in a war of attrition is vital to victory," the paper concluded that the optimistic press release "will never be verified by history if the Government loses the support of an informed public opinion—as, indeed, it appears to be doing."[5]

Except for the defense-oriented *Examiner*, which praised the "stature" of McNamara and Taylor and their "encouraging" prognosis that "the end of the American military aid tunnel to that country plus victory over Communist guerilla forces" was in sight, the other papers also criticized the press release sharply. The *Post* denounced the reference to 1965 as a "groundless prophecy," the *Post-Dispatch* said it did not "share the optimism of General Taylor and Mr. McNamara," and the *Tribune* noted that the McNamara-Taylor mission was "but one of a series which have produced all sorts of guesses, none of which has been realized in the event." Nor did the administration fare better in news stories. When Salinger was asked how many American military personnel were stationed in Vietnam, he replied, "We're not about to answer that question." Carroll Kilpatrick's lead story in the *Post* contained questioning comments like these: "No explanation was given as to how the military leaders arrived at their estimate that the war would be sufficiently won by the end of 1965 to permit the withdrawal of the major part of the American force. Nor did they explain why 1000 troops may be withdrawn at the end of this year, at a time when it is widely believed the political situation has seriously deteriorated and when the two men themselves remarked that it could affect the military situation." [6]

The administration carefully avoided public initiatives after the 2 October press release. Kennedy could not avoid being questioned on Vietnam at his 9 October and 31 October press conferences, but he was able to give platitudinous answers that avoided clarifying American policy. The important decisions actually agreed upon in the 2 October meeting—notably, continuing the cutbacks in economic aid and cutting off support to Nhu's special forces— eventually appeared in the press under Saigon datelines and did not attract the coverage or editorial comment that public initiatives in Washington received. In fact, the *Post* published its last editorial on Vietnam before the coup on 8 October, Washington-oriented columnists like Reston and Krock each wrote their only columns on Vietnam policy on 6 October, and Walter Lippmann did not write any on Vietnam during this period. Aware by the second week of October that intense pressure was being applied on the Diem regime, the *Times* and *Post* could await the fruits of this policy with the knowledge that the administration had effectively adopted the anti-Diem viewpoint. [7]

Madame Nhu's Controversial Visit Takes the Spotlight off the Administration

Between 7 October and the overthrow of the regime on 1 November, Madame Nhu spoke in most major cities and at several leading universities, appeared on television interview programs, and met with prominent publishers and reporters—all to build support for the government led by her brother-in-law and husband. Like de Gaulle and most other foreigners who had attempted to make an impact on American public opinion and policymaking, she failed in her mission. More accurately, the cards were stacked against her from the beginning, and she never really had a chance to succeed.

Both officials and journalists contributed to the failure. Administration officials not only refused to greet Madame Nhu when she came to Washington, but in background briefings they also urged reporters to play down her visit in protest against the censorship of stories and beating of American journalists in Saigon. Members of Congress also expressed irritation that she was being allowed to visit the United States and criticized her viciously. "This lady has been traveling around the world on an expense account provided by American taxpayers," Senator Stephen Young (D.-Ohio) declared the day of her arrival.

"Let her slander us from her native land or from any other country, but not from our own soil." Representative Wayne Hays (D.-Ohio) received attention by calling her a "comic strip dragon lady."[8]

In their coverage of Madame Nhu's visit, reporters and editorialists reflected the view promulgated in the press during the previous months that she was a sinister person representing a dictatorial and unpopular government. But they also had a stake in maintaining her image as a controversial and fascinating woman, whose blunt speech and interest in political power were out of place in the male-dominated world of her time. In his story about one of her speeches in New York, William Fulton of the *Tribune* referred to her "turquoise blue gown, her jet black hair set off by diamond earrings"; when Warren Unna of the *Post* covered a speech in Washington, he wrote of "her long, sharpened red fingernails detracting somewhat from her posture of defenselessness." These are but two examples of the kind of commentary on clothing and grooming that almost never appeared in stories about male political leaders.[9]

Compared with some of her comments earlier, most of Madame Nhu's statements during her visit were models of decorum and tact. She praised U.S. servicemen for their aid in the war and emphasized that she was in America to build support for Diem, not to criticize the administration. But the reporters covering her were looking for stories and they seized upon any poorly phrased or controversial comment to head their dispatches. And editorialists were quick to criticize. The *Post-Dispatch* admonished its readers to listen to her father, Tran Van Chuong, rather than to her, and the *Tribune* criticized "her virulent anti-Americanism." Perhaps heeding the suggestion of Robert Manning of the State Department to play down the visit, the *Post*, alone among the five papers, had no page-one stories and no editorials on the subject. Only the *Examiner*, which contrasted the unwillingness of official Washington to greet the anticommunist Madame Nhu with its warm reception of President Tito of Yugoslavia shortly thereafter, expressed any favorable editorial commentary on her visit. Easily angered during the cold war by any foreign criticism of American policy, the press as a whole found it especially easy to ridicule the female voice of South Vietnam's ruling family.[10]

It was in the San Francisco area, which had both the largest and best organized New Left and a circulation war between the *Examiner* and the *Chronicle*, that the impact of Madame Nhu's visit was the greatest. The *Examiner*, playing the two-day visit to the hilt, gave it four page-one and nineteen inside-page stories. Madame Nhu's speeches to packed houses at the Commonwealth Club and at the University of California at Berkeley, the antiwar activities both in San Francisco and at Berkeley, the concern of Governor Edmund G. Brown and the San Francisco police department about her safety, the reactions of people on the street and students at Berkeley to her visit—all were covered extensively. Acting like a tabloid, the *Examiner* even implied that serious romance was involved in "the friendship between the beautiful teen-age daughter of Madame Ngo Dinh Nhu and the handsome young Texas millionaire Bruce Baxter III." [11]

Although the *Examiner* emphasized human interest aspects of Madame Nhu's visit, the repeated evidence of well-organized and militant antiwar activity was more significant. A group called the Ad Hoc Committee to End the War in Vietnam announced several weeks before she came that it would be holding demonstrations to protest American policy in Vietnam, and it began carrying them out on 21 October. The series of demonstrations culminated on the evening of Madame Nhu's arrival, when four hundred protestors blocked three entrances at the hotel where she was to stay and scuffled with police. "We merely hope that if enough people demonstrate the United States Government will change its policy in Vietnam," Susan Currier, the committee's chairperson, stated. At Berkeley, four policemen seeking to arrest two demonstrators were threatened and jostled by an angry crowd of about two hundred antiwar students. San Francisco's acting mayor denounced the protestors' behavior as "outrageous" and "far beyond the bounds of common courtesy and the right to peacefully protest." [12]

Although the antiwar demonstrators in the Bay Area and in the major eastern cities and university towns served notice to Kennedy that militant opposition to American involvement in Vietnam now existed, their actions received meager nationwide publicity and hence put little pressure on him to reexamine the premises of his policy. And Madame Nhu's well-publicized but discounted activities aided the administration's position—especially in the popular press—by shifting attention away from its openly anti-Diem activities and by serving as an alternative lightning rod for domestic criticism.

Waiting for a Coup in Saigon

Except for the report on 7 October that commercial aid had been halted and the report on the 21st that funds had been eliminated for Nhu's special forces, most of the news from Saigon during this period was less novel than it had been earlier. So what if two more Buddhist monks committed suicide or if Nhu again criticized the CIA? The real story from Saigon—that coup plotting was proceeding more seriously than ever—was not being published by American newspapers. The story that received the most coverage in the press concerned the beating of American reporters by South Vietnamese police, but the most interesting developments relating to the press were the unpublicized removal of Sheehan from South Vietnam about a week before the coup and Kennedy's unsuccessful attempt to see that Halberstam was removed.

The beating of the three journalists—Halberstam and John Sharkey and Grant Wolfkill of NBC—occurred after Wolfkill had shot the only moving picture footage of the immolation on 5 October, the sixth since June. Plain-clothes police apparently were under orders to seize any film of the immola-tion to prevent its showing on American television, and they attacked the three journalists when they refused to surrender the movie camera. The police fi-nally procured the film, thus preventing its showing on the evening news, but the regime's behavior was castigated by Lodge, Rusk, and Mansfield, all of whom used the incident to separate themselves further from Diem and Nhu. "Here's John Sharkey of NBC who was beaten up by the police," Lodge said in introducing him before American television cameras to a group of visiting congressmen. "They had a perfect right to be there and they were beaten up by police." Rusk and Mansfield meanwhile had arranged to have their sharp criticisms made available to reporters in Washington in time for inclusion in the Sunday papers on the 6th.[13] Thus, although the Diem regime was able to keep the immolation from appearing on American television, administration officials used the incident to improve relations with the embattled press corps in Saigon and to publicize their displeasure with the ruling family.

Sheehan's forced vacation in Tokyo just before the coup was a perfect illus-tration of the intergenerational conflict among journalists on the Vietnam is-sue. Like Keyes Beech, Ernest Hoberecht, the UPI managing editor for Asia stationed in Tokyo, had begun his coverage of Asia as a correspondent in World War II and had risen gradually to the top UPI job there. A "drinking buddy" of Beech's, he tended to overlook the fact that the regime was dic-tatorial and believed strongly that Diem would not be overthrown. "When you get these young reporters down there, they get more concerned about sav-ing the world than reporting the news," Hoberecht recalled. "There was a lot to be said for people who knew the country and knew how to run it."[14]

Hoberecht's muzzling of Sheehan was reflected in the greatly reduced use of his stories in the press. Whereas Sheehan's news analyses and detailed dis-cussions of the pagoda raids and the split in the American mission had ap-peared frequently in August and September in all papers except the *Times*, in October only one story under his byline appeared in all of the papers. In re-calling this period, Hoberecht offered the explanation that "you can't send out on the wire every story that is written."[15] But, in preventing much of Shee-han's reporting from appearing in American newspapers—especially in the popular press that relied most heavily on the wire services—UPI's Tokyo of-fice in effect was lessening the pressure on the administration to act.

Unlike Sheehan, Halberstam did not attempt to reveal his knowledge of coup plotting in his dispatches in October, though he did note on 24 October that "restlessness is growing again among South Vietnam's military." "If you write that dissidence is increasing, I think you've done your job," Halberstam recalled. "Your job isn't to tip off one group against another." Moreover, by late October so many rumors of planned coup attempts had circulated in Sai-gon that it was hard to take any one of them very seriously. "We had been alerted," Halberstam observed in reference to the actual coup of 1 November. "But I certainly had other plans for the day if the coup didn't take place." [16]

Still angry about Halberstam's earlier coverage that could be viewed as forcing his hand against Diem, President Kennedy on 21 October took the extraordinary step of seeking to have him removed from Vietnam. In a private meeting with *Times* publisher Arthur H. Sulzberger at the White House that afternoon, Kennedy asked him what he thought of his "young man in Saigon." Sulzberger replied that he thought he was doing a fine job, but Kennedy persisted, suggesting that Halberstam was too involved personally in the story and that he should be transferred to another assignment. When Sulzberger arrived at a nearby club soon thereafter for a dinner with members of the *Times*'s Washington bureau, he immediately told Reston and Hedrick Smith what had happened. Smith, who already had been asked to prepare himself to replace Halberstam in Vietnam because the *Times*'s management, in Smith's words, "thought that David was tired," recalled the discussion: "Punch came in and said, 'The President said he wished like hell we'd take Halberstam out of there,' and Scotty said immediately to Punch, 'Well, obviously we can't do what we were thinking of doing, because if the President says so we can't buckle in to that kind of stuff.' And Punch agreed, and that was that. So the idea of my going over there was put on ice for a while." [17]

This episode demonstrates that Kennedy, for all his customary adroitness in dealing with the press, could also commit serious blunders. The *Times* had a tradition of independence in foreign reporting that even he could not override, especially not by a move so lacking in subtlety. In his book on his experiences in Vietnam, Halberstam praised the *Times* for backing him fully during the difficult months before the coup. As Kennedy apparently realized, it was the *Times*'s foreign reporting, known for its independence and reliability, that had applied the most pressure on him during the early stages of the Buddhist crisis. [18]

The Washington-oriented Papers Accept the Official Euphoria about the Coup

In the early afternoon of 1 November, almost all of South Vietnam's leading generals initiated a coup against the Diem regime and quickly seized all important government installations in Saigon except the presidential palace. By the following morning, the palace had been captured, Diem and Nhu had been taken prisoner and killed, and rejoicing was considerable in Saigon at the news that the unpopular regime had been toppled. Although officials in Washington regretted the deaths, most of them also were quietly pleased by the coup, as were most journalists in Saigon and Washington. Despite some criticism in Congress and in the conservative press, the administration had little difficulty in establishing the view that the shift of power had been a positive development that offered greatly improved prospects for victory over the Vietcong.

Upset by the brutal murders of Diem and Nhu (which the leaders of the coup initially described as suicides) and fearful of charges of American involvement in the coup, no high administration official spoke publicly about the situation until Rusk commented at a news conference on 8 November. Leaving the public handling of the situation almost entirely to the State Department, the president did not comment about Vietnam until he was asked about it at his 14 November news conference, at which time he said he hoped that "the new situation there" would lead to "an increased effort in the war." The only public statement at the time of the coup was one on 1 November by State Department spokesman Richard I. Phillips, who declared, "I can categorically state that the U.S. government was not in any way involved in this coup attempt." [19]

Far from questioning the administration's credibility, leading reporters in Washington presented the views of their unnamed sources sympathetically. "The United States is particularly interested in seeing a restoration of such constitutional processes as free elections so the Vietnamese people . . . will have more reason to want to rid their country of its Communist terrorizers," Unna wrote in a page-one story in the *Post* on 3 November. According to a Dudman article in the *Post-Dispatch*, administration officials "see grounds for optimism in the promises of the new regime for a strong fight against the Communists and a measure of democracy." [20]

Hedrick Smith, who also wrote several stories from Washington that uncritically conveyed official thinking, believes on the basis of his own experience that public affairs officer Robert McCloskey played a key role in facilitating contact between reporters and officials at the State Department and hence contributed substantially to the administration's overall credibility with the press. On the day of the coup, for example, Smith and other reporters were briefed in detail on the events in Vietnam. Another factor that helps to explain the favorable news coverage the administration received was the absence of dissent among the officials who were talking to reporters on the subject; all supported the coup and expected progress in the war to result from it. Washington reporters for the *Tribune* and *Examiner*, who tended to rely more heavily on military sources, were able to write approvingly that officials were now turning their full attention to stepping up the war against the Vietcong. [21]

A final factor contributing to the administration's success in dominating the news from Washington and presenting a unified view of American policy was the playing down of congressional views. Whereas official U.S. comprised 33.3 percent of page-one and 21.9 percent of inside-page sources in the November period, domestic political made up just 8.0 and 8.7 percent, respectively. And, even when members of Congress or other political leaders were quoted, the purpose was usually more to express their reactions to events than to present them as legitimate initiators of policy proposals. Thus the views of senators like Mansfield and Church were reported much less prominently in the aftermath of the coup than they had been in September, and no editorials or columns were precipitated by any statement of a domestic political figure. Because of the change in government in Saigon and the apparent harmony of viewpoint within the administration, Mansfield's call on 1 November for a "reassessment and reappraisal of our policy in South Vietnam" did not make the front pages of any of the five newspapers. The same was true of coverage of his statement on 5 November that there was "no interest of the United States in Viet-Nam which would justify . . . the continuation of the war in that country primarily as an American war to be fought with American lives." [22]

The official U.S. view also dominated in news coverage from Saigon. There, too, Lodge and other high officials were not speaking for the record, but they had no difficulty in conveying their views. In a page-one story on 4 November based on wire service reports, the *Post* noted that "Embassy sources said the Embassy was pleased with the overthrow of the Diem government, and made it clear they thought coup leaders were capable of forming a new government which the United States expects to recognize shortly after it is formed." Roy Essoyan of AP quoted an American military source as saying that the skill with which the coup was executed "shows the Vietnamese can run a pretty good war if political considerations are removed." [23]

Fortunately for the administration, the dispatches from Saigon in early November did not implicate the United States in the coup plotting. In his lengthy account of the events leading up to the coup, published on page one of the *Times* on 6 November, Halberstam stressed the plotting among the generals and devoted only one brief paragraph to their meetings with Americans in October. "All they were reported to have told the Americans was that they wanted no interference," he noted. Whether he or the other reporters knew more of the details of American contacts with the coup leaders and did not report them is unclear; what is certain is that none of the reporting from Saigon in the aftermath of the coup buttressed the claim of Madame Nhu and of a few right-wing groups that the United States had betrayed Diem. [24]

Clearly pleased that the Diem regime had been overthrown, Halberstam wrote on 4 November that "Americans are gratified by a sense of joy that they find in Saigon." He reported that there was now "hope . . . that the repressive political climate that weighed heavily on the population and on the army has been lifted for good" and "hope that the new Government . . . will be able to rally the people and to turn back the Communist threat." Sheehan later recalled that the resident reporters in 1963 "were just as interventionist-minded as Joe Alsop; we didn't share any basic differences with Robert McNamara. It was a question of how do you win the war." In referring to the common goal of victory, Sheehan was justly referring to Halberstam as well as to himself. [25]

Sheehan's comment helps to explain why the coverage from Washington and Saigon in the wake of the coup was so favorable to the administration. For most reporters and for the editors of the Washington-oriented and liberal papers, the coup represented the culmination of the policy that they had been advocating. Now that the long-awaited coup had occurred and an anticommunist government was establishing its authority in Saigon, these journalists reflected in their dispatches their own satisfaction and that of most American officials.

Like the reporters in Washington and Saigon, the editorialists and columnists of the Washington-oriented and liberal papers were not interested in pressing the issue of possible American involvement in the coup. The *Post-Dispatch*, the *Post*, and the *Times* all were pleased and relieved that the coup had taken place, and all three were content to leave the issue of American involvement in it moot. Of the columnists who wrote on Vietnam in these papers in early November, only Reston urged the administration to consider a change of policy in the wake of the coup.[26]

Two of his columns challenged the administration's optimism about winning the war now that Diem was overthrown. Arguing that lack of clarity on war aims had led a decade before to the "disastrous policy of trying to capture and control all Korea," Reston on 3 November implied that a similar emphasis on victory in Vietnam might again lead to disaster for the United States. On 6 November he called for negotiations that might lead to neutralization of Southeast Asia. "The official assumption here is that a negotiated political settlement in Vietnam is impossible and maybe even dishonorable, but how do they know?" he asked. Pointing out that the government had made no effort to contact Ho Chi Minh, he urged that the possibility of negotiations be explored before pursuing "the purely military policy of 'killing Communists,' who in turn have a nasty habit of killing Americans."[27]

The administration was not under pressure to act on Reston's suggestions because no other moderate or liberal voice seconded his argument. Lippmann and Krock did not write about Vietnam during this period, and Childs limited himself to the "prayerful hope" that the coup would "provide a stable government with much wider popular support." Roscoe Drummond and Max Lerner, both of whom were widely syndicated, echoed the official line that the coup had been necessary to strengthen the military and political effort in Vietnam.[28]

Alsop also provided strong support for the administration. In columns on 4 and 6 November, he wrote that the coup was inevitable because "Diem refused to put his house in order" and that the United States could have prevented the coup only "by stultifying itself." And what about the future? Here Alsop's views diverged from those advocated by the editors of the liberal papers, who called for more emphasis on political reforms and the need for popular support of South Vietnam's government. "Creating a workable civil government in Vietnam is simply not feasible in the midst of civil war," Alsop wrote. "Let the war be won first, as it can be won, and let the Vietnamese settle their own political affairs thereafter." [29]

The *Tribune* and *Examiner* Pay Tribute to Diem

Although the more liberal papers and leading columnists were pleased with the coup and turned their attention to the appropriate policy for the future, the *Tribune* and the *Examiner* criticized the administration for its role in encouraging opposition to Diem and paid final tribute to the fallen leader. In a long editorial on 3 November entitled "Who Pulled the Rug?" the *Tribune* blamed the resident reporters in Saigon, the 24 August cable, the president's televised remarks, the liberal senators who supported the Church resolution, and the cutoff of aid for inciting the coup. "If it should turn out that these devious maneuvers have opened the way for a communist take-over, will the Kennedy administration then be disposed, as with Russia, to tide the new Red regime over its troubles with sales of wheat and other help?" the paper asked sarcastically. As in its previous editorials on Vietnam, the *Tribune*, lacking sustained interest in Southeast Asian issues, was more interested in knifing the Democratic administration than in suggesting alternative policies for Vietnam. [30]

The *Examiner* was not so bitter, but in its editorial on 3 November it pointed out the "irony" that the United States had not been able to topple Castro but had succeeded in overthrowing Diem, whom it praised as an "heroic figure" who had "managed to stave off Communist aggression during his rule." Not wishing to belabor the past, the newspaper declared that the "important thing is to get on with the war against the Communist guerillas, in which 100 Americans have been killed and into which we are pouring $1.5 million a day." [31]

Although the *Examiner* carried no subsequent editorials on the subject, it did publish two bitter columns by Conniff, who denounced the *Times* for spreading the "carefully contrived propaganda theme" that the Buddhist-Diem conflict had been a religious controversy and called on Kennedy to "apologize for murder most foul." Because Higgins was not appearing in any of the papers and because Alsop's columns supporting the coup were being played prominently in the *Examiner* as elsewhere, Conniff was isolated as a lone dissenting columnist on the right. [32]

Although the *Tribune* and *Examiner* complained for the record about the American role in the events leading up to the coup, they lacked the open support of leading Republican politicians or of public opinion that might have resulted in an effective challenge to the administration. The president could also have been damaged in the press in October and early November if leading Democrats in Congress had insisted that the United States withdraw from

Vietnam or if feuding and recriminations had occurred within his administration after the coup and made their way into the press. Fortunately for the president, who through Bundy had expressed reservations to Lodge about going ahead with the coup as late as 30 October, none of these scenarios materialized. In the absence of any significant domestic challenge to the president's policies and because the press itself had contributed substantially to the anti-Diem pressures that presaged the coup, it is not surprising that the administration's viewpoint was dominant in the press during the final weeks of the Buddhist crisis.[33]

Conclusion

The most important conclusion about the press-presidential relationship that emerges from the experience of the Buddhist crisis is the focus of the Washington-oriented press on what was transpiring within the administration. Because the administration was divided on policy during August and September, newspapers like the *Times* and *Post* reflected and amplified these divisions in their news and editorial coverage. They also tended to back one policy position within the government or another—in this case the anti-Diem viewpoint—and pressured the president to move toward the position with which they identified. And, once they identified fully with this viewpoint, they did not rally to the support of even a popular president just because he adopted a high-visibility press strategy. Only when Kennedy clearly brought his policy into line with their views and effectively silenced the policy debate within the administration did coverage in the Washington-oriented press become supportive of his position. In a crisis in which the administration is openly divided, therefore, the Washington-oriented press can put very substantial pressure on the president to adopt a preferred policy. But, once this policy has been adopted, these newspapers are likely to reciprocate by backing him fully.

In addition to division within the administration, other factors contributed to this flow of influence from the Washington-oriented press to the president. As it did during the Laotian crisis, the *Times* was in a position to play a key role in interpreting events in Vietnam. Unlike the situation during the Berlin and Cuba crises, the opposition party, to which the conservative press tends to respond, was not challenging Kennedy, and there was relatively little involvement by the general public or by respected allies that could have pressured the president in one direction or another. Given the frequent criticism of the Diem regime by officials and journalists before the crisis, the overwhelming majority of journalists writing on Vietnam were more influenced by the anti-Diem viewpoint within the administration in Washington and the American mission in Saigon than by the pro-Diem viewpoint. Partly because of the dominance of the anti-Diem viewpoint, especially in the papers read in Washington, it seems fair to conclude that the press played a greater role in influencing the policymaking process than in any of the three earlier crises.

Although this conclusion is especially applicable to the Washington-oriented newspapers, it seems valid as well for the outlying papers. The *Post-Dispatch*, reflecting the liberal viewpoint that Diem was totally unworthy of American support, put the most consistent pressure on the president to move against him, though of course it lacked the influence in Washington of the *Times* and *Post*. And the *Tribune* and *Examiner* were important because, lacking conservative political or constituency interest in the issue, they did not mount a strong defense of Diem either in news coverage or on the editorial pages. In the absence of a strong stand against the establishment viewpoint in the conservative and popular press, therefore, the impact of the Washington-oriented press was enhanced.

Like administration officials, the journalists who wrote on Vietnam policy in 1963 differed among themselves over means, not ends. Almost everyone supported the goal of military victory; the debate was over whether the war could be won with Diem. Unna observed that no anti-Diem officials he used as sources in Washington—Harriman, Hilsman, Michael Forrestal, and others—"ever asked what I thought were two basic questions: where does this policy take the people of the area, and where does it take the people of the United States?" Sheehan, whose writing reflected the anti-Diem viewpoint in Saigon, later recalled: "I think the immaturity of our reporting, if there was any, was the fact that we didn't have a very long view of American foreign policy. We didn't see the basic kind of weaknesses in what the United States was trying to do there: that is, what it was trying to do there was going to end badly. But no American had that perspective."[34]

Thus, although leading newspapers put heavy pressure on Kennedy through early October to move firmly against Diem, they did not challenge him to reconsider the basic assumption that a military victory could be won. Yielding to the pressures in the administration and in the press to dump Diem, Kennedy emerged from the crisis with his basic objectives in Vietnam intact. An institution like the press, which consistently reflects and amplifies viewpoints that originate elsewhere, could not have been expected to launch and sustain on its own a challenge to the premises undergirding the U.S. military involvement there. Only when the question of whether the United States should be in Vietnam became controversial years later within the administration, the Congress, and the public did press coverage effectively challenge the American role in Vietnam.

Part Six

Conclusion

Chapter 15

Does the Presidency Dominate or React?

The foregoing analysis has developed the concept of the press as a reflective institution. This is true because reporters, editors, and columnists are affected not only by their professional settings, but also by their political environment. Therefore, the pressure that the press puts on a president reflects questions raised by other forces in the society. The issue thus is not so much whether the press exercises influence or whether the president dominates the relationship, but whether competing political forces are at work on an issue. If the forces are there, then the press is like a prism. It will reflect, focus, and magnify their views. Like sunlight focused through a magnifying glass, political forces reflected in the press lens may be powerful enough to start a fire, to put constraints on a president, or, conversely, to assist him in the elimination of his opposition and the acquisition of power.

If one looks at the press in this way, it becomes clear that the literature asserting that the president dominates the press is valid only under certain conditions. There is no doubt about the ability of the president and the executive branch to obtain high percentages of the source coverage in the news coverage of foreign policy crises. But the administration may obtain a majority news source figure, as in the Cuban crisis of September 1962 and in the Vietnam crisis a year later, and fail to dominate the press. This flow of influence from press to president can be the result of a powerful critique developing in the columnist and editorial coverage during a period of domestic criticism of the president, or it can occur at a time in which the administration is divided. Despite the strong impact of presidential leadership on press treatment of crisis issues, the overall generalization emerges that the president dominates press coverage primarily in situations where competing interpretations of events are not being espoused by others whom journalists consider important.

Although Kennedy was able in the latter stages of each of the four crises to eclipse rival influences and achieve a dominant position in the press, it is possible in analyzing the crises to see why many presidents have come to view the press as an adversary. Early in each of the crises, forces outside Kennedy's control—foreign leaders, opposition politicians, journalists reflecting dissident viewpoints within the administration—challenged official policy. A president understandably might come to the conclusion that the press is forcing his hand, that if opposing viewpoints are not appearing in the press he can continue with the existing policy or make changes more slowly. A president less adept than Kennedy in establishing friendships with key journalists and in turning the situation to his advantage at crucial moments especially might long wistfully for a state-controlled press.

As applied to foreign policy, the American concept of freedom of the press means in practice that strong pressures for changes in policy will arise in some segments of the press at some times and in other segments at other times. The *Tribune* and *Examiner*, for example, took the lead in reflecting conservative opposition to Kennedy's Cuban policy in September 1962, and the other three papers provided a forum for opposition to Diem the following year. As much as a president might like to dominate press coverage of important foreign policy issues, the experience of the Kennedy years suggests that, under certain conditions, an administration may well receive substantial pressure from the press.

This study supports the view that the press plays a major role in defining public issues. Before the major presidential initiative in late March during the Laotian crisis, the issue of whether the administration was doing enough to prevent a communist victory was dominant in the press. By late June during the Berlin crisis, the press was focusing on the issue of whether Kennedy would exhibit firmness and resolve in dealing with Khrushchev. By mid-September 1962 the issue in the press was whether the president was responding adequately to the Soviet threat in Cuba. And in 1963 the press was instrumental in defining the question as whether the United States should actively encourage Diem's overthrow. It seems an understatement to note that Kennedy would not have chosen to have had all of these issues defined in the way they were. And it is significant that he followed the dominant viewpoint reflected in the press in his key policy initiatives during each of the four crises.

Although the press assisted in defining the issues, the crucial distinction that emerges from this study is that the manner in which issues were defined did not originate in the press, but rather stemmed from the politically significant forces at work on the issues. In this vital sense, the press during these years was largely a reflective institution.

The fact that newspapers largely reflected the views of other political actors on foreign policy issues did not make them unimportant. On the contrary, their ability to highlight some views and play down others was extremely significant. Each of the five papers showed quite predictable orientations toward such matters as coverage of Congress and depth of foreign reporting. Of equal importance was the fact that, because journalists emphasized conflict and confrontation among those in positions of political power, the press tended to feature confrontational views in Congress and elsewhere and hence to push the administration toward a hard-line stance in regard to foreign governments. That, at least, was the experience during each of the four "crises" examined in this study.

The Press as a Reflective Institution

During this period, the press was largely a reflective institution for three major reasons. These relate to the timing of issues, partisanship, and the influence of newspaper constituencies.

The timing of issues was not determined by journalists. Rather, an issue developed if there was interest in it either in government, among the domestic politicians, or in the various publics with which journalists interacted. Tom Wicker recently stressed the importance of such factors in the timing of press issues: "We [in the press] did not, on a large scale, question or ignite debate on the crossing of the 38th parallel in Korea in 1950, but we did examine and feed controversy on the bombing across the 17th parallel in Vietnam. Not because we alone decided that one war was more just than another . . . but communities to which we reported were divided on Vietnam in sufficient degree to alter our perspective." [1]

In this study, the question of timing meant that—except for the *St. Louis Post-Dispatch*, a few European-oriented *New York Times* columnists, and Walter Lippmann—improving relations with Russia was not an issue for journalists so long as the subject was of little interest in the administration, among nationally known politicians, or in the public at large. Or consider the Cuban example: opinion leaders in the press certainly had their own views, but it was the Republicans who kept the Cuban issue alive in the press during late August and September 1962. They raised the issue during an election period and were responsible for the intensity of press coverage of it.

There were exceptions to this generalization regarding timing, and the importance of a leading newspaper or columnist having overseas experience in situations in which few other political forces were operative is clear. Which forces were most important in stimulating press coverage of issues also varied according to characteristics of the newspapers. But the overall responsibility of forces outside of the press for determining the timing of issues remained valid.

The press was also a reflective institution because of partisanship, in the broadest sense of the term. Publishers, editors, and columnists often took positions for reasons based not so much on the merits of an issue as on support for a politician, an ideological faction, or a party. The editorial policies of at least four of the five newspapers analyzed in this study reflected the publishers' views. Partisanship also affected the choice of sources. The conservative and frequently Republican-oriented paper in this study turned to conservative sources and a leading Democratic paper to liberal ones.

Partisanship affected access to the White House as well as to other politicians. This study reveals that the conservative Republican press did not have the same access to the president as did the pro-Kennedy press. Similarly, cold war liberal journalists could more easily contact their counterparts in the White House than they could those in the White House whose positions were more hawkish. The conservative press turned to opposition sources in Congress and within the bureaucracy. In general, columnists used sources they agreed with. Not surprisingly, partisanship intensified and became more clearly party oriented during the 1962 election, when the president emerged as a party leader.

Although publishers, editors, and columnists often exhibited partisanship, individual reporters were partisan far less frequently. Indeed, this study generally supports the conclusions of the organizational theorists in at least two areas. Reporters faced the dual task of keeping their superiors happy, so that they could win promotions and prized assignments, and remaining on good terms with their sources, who had the power to supply or withhold news on their beats. They also were expected to operate within the journalistic canon of "objectivity" in the writing of news stories. Nevertheless, the experience of the Kennedy years provided examples of reporters who were "used" by their sources to advance a particular viewpoint and of reporters who chose in their stories to lend more credence to one viewpoint than to another. In situations like Cuba or Vietnam, as has been demonstrated, it was virtually impossible to avoid some form of partisanship.

Finally, the press was a reflective institution because newspapers ordinarily pitched their coverage to their readerships. The process by which journalists absorb and respond to the views and values of their constituencies is in need of substantial additional research. This study has shown, however, that coverage of foreign policy issues in individual newspapers seemed to vary along three readership-oriented dimensions: an elite press that assumed a high level of intellectual sophistication on the part of its readership; a popular press that expected little readership interest in foreign policy issues; and a Washington-oriented press that covered the government more extensively. Faced with the practical need to maintain its reputation and circulation in its community, each of these different segments of the press responded to policy issues in different ways.

Although we have found that newspapers were responding largely to their political environment, two ways in which they were able to enhance their independence of government and other domestic influences on foreign policy coverage were noticeable. Reporters and columnists abroad who were given relatively free run by their editors and publishers were a source of that independence. The dispatches of such overseas correspondents as Sulzberger and

Halberstam, for example, contributed to the *Times*'s independence of government as well as to its influence on other newspapers. The second way newspapers could hope to achieve some independence of their political environment was to follow the precepts of the first Joseph Pulitzer, who argued for "drastic independence" of editors from publishers, as well as from government and the general public. Despite all the difficulties discussed in this study, the *Post-Dispatch* attempted to uphold this standard.

The Press as Reflector and Presidential Influence

How did the fact that the press is a reflective institution affect the president's ability to influence it? Stated succinctly, presidential power varied according to the nature and effectiveness of the other forces that were in competition with him.

Other politicians were Kennedy's principal rivals. Three major factors explain why their influence on the press normally was greater than that of other domestic competitors, including individual members of the public and interest groups. First, the views of politicians were important because they were either supportive possessors of power or they were contenders for power. In either case, their views could have consequences—if not immediately in relation to the formulation and conduct of administration policy, then ultimately in relation to one party or another's electoral chances. Second, politicians stood out among public sources because the expression of their views often involved conflict, a primary news value. And third, politicians opposing the administration's policies often received substantial coverage because reporters and editors believed that "fairness" and "balance" were essential components of responsible journalism; therefore, they sought out the views of leading "conservative" members of Congress to balance the views of "liberal" officials, and vice versa.

Although politicians received far more coverage than such other domestic sources as public opinion and interest groups, they received far less than administration officials. In the Cuban crisis, politicians received 18 percent of page-one coverage; in the Berlin, 11 percent; in the Vietnam, 7 percent; and in the Laotian, 6 percent. The respective percentages for official U.S. were 40, 38, 40, and 42. This much smaller coverage resulted partly from the discounting of the importance of congressional views by some papers, especially the *Post* and *Times*, and partly from the tendency of leading members of Congress, especially liberal Democrats, to fail to present their views forcefully or to avoid giving the appearance of disagreeing sharply with the administration. This study demonstrates that congressional coverage was especially weak in the press on Southeast Asian issues, thus enabling a virtually uncontested administration to slide into an increasingly serious military involvement there.

Except on perennial issues like foreign aid or emotional ones like Cuba, Congress during the Kennedy years was not viewed as a vital factor in the making of American foreign policy.

Interest groups having a similar partisan appeal, or potential for conflict or power, also influence the press, though it occurred in this study only in the case of the Cuban exiles. Interest groups that emphasized resolutions, speeches, and other verbal activities—the American Legion on the right or Americans for Democratic Action on the left, for example—received little coverage on these issues. Greater interest group activity and corresponding reflection of these activities in the press might well appear in a study that focused, for example, on international trade or on the Arab-Israeli dispute.

Officials within a president's own administration can also create difficulties for him in relation to the press during a period of indecisiveness or policy review. Much of the policy debate within the administration during the early stages of the Laotian and Berlin crises made its way into the press. In these two cases, the effect of many of these leaks was to pressure the president to adopt a more hard-line position. During the Buddhist crisis, in contrast, most of the pressure came from those who emphasized the political nature of the struggle in South Vietnam and argued that the United States no longer should support Diem because he had lost his popularity. Whereas the politicians represented the major domestic challenge to the president in the Berlin crisis and especially in the Cuban crisis, officials within the Kennedy administration had greater impact during the Southeast Asian crises.

Although total foreign sources exceeded those in any other source category in this study, foreign opinion, whether governmental or private, rarely represents a challenge to a president. This is because, under most circumstances, foreign views are either ignored or taken into account only on a highly selective basis. Because foreign coverage is focused through a domestic prism, the views of some foreign leaders—Khrushchev, Castro, and de Gaulle, for example—were discounted almost entirely in the cold war atmosphere of the early 1960s. Only in circumstances combining a confused or passive presidential press strategy and policy weakness, such as occurred during the early weeks of the Berlin and Vietnam crises, did foreign views exert an impact that affected the president's ability to influence the press.

The general weakness of Congress in foreign affairs and the persistent discounting of views from abroad made it relatively easy for the president to establish dominant influence in the press as soon as the administration had formulated a clear policy during each crisis. In retrospect, it would appear that Kennedy's task was too easy at times: the press and other forces in the society did not question whether a military buildup was necessary in July 1961, whether a public confrontation with Russia was required in October 1962, or whether the overthrow of the Diem regime in November 1963 actually would improve the chances for a military victory over the Vietcong. A cardinal weakness in American foreign policy in the early 1960s—a weakness the press reflected—clearly was the assumption that no foreign leaders other than those firmly allied with the United States would ever have a point of view on an important issue worth considering. Such an assumption augmented the power of the presidency not only in relation to the press, but also in relation to Congress and other forces in American society.

The Role of Press Strategies

This study suggests that skillful press strategies can enhance a president's ability to influence the press. A high-visibility strategy expands the available news by means of heightened presidential activity. New subjects for speculation can be opened up and leaks made selectively to friendly reporters and columnists. New pronouncements, either at press conferences or in a policy address, take the front pages away from the domestic news competitors. A president can also enhance his effectiveness with the press by having different advisers provide interviews to journalists of varied ideological perspectives.

A high-visibility press strategy—including increased military activity, announcement of new military policies, calling for emergency meetings of the advisers and of the Allies—enhanced presidential influence with the press at the height of the cold war. Some of these same techniques were to be used in 1979 and 1980 in the crises involving Iran and Afghanistan.[2]

Conversely, poor press strategies can reduce presidential effectiveness with the press. For example, the price of total neglect of the press—of no news conferences, of few backgrounders—may well be loss of initiative on a foreign policy issue to competing political forces. What constitutes a "poor" strategy also changes through time as press expectations of a president change. An acceptable policy in the early 1960s could involve lying to the press. A poor policy then was one that involved withholding information on an issue of cardinal importance to the public that could then be revealed by another source. This occurred when Kennedy withheld information about Khrushchev's ultimatum on Germany in June 1961 and when Keating warned of Soviet missiles in Cuba in September 1962.

All the press strategies analyzed in this study occurred in relation to the dynamics of policy development and change. When they are looked at in this perspective, it is clear that they alone did not determine presidential effectiveness with the press. The majority of the high-visibility strategies discussed in this study occurred in combination with a more hawkish foreign policy stance. That press tactics alone did not determine the president's success is indicated by the fact that the high-visibility approach that he employed in September 1962, involving press conferences, policy announcements, and a military buildup, did not turn the press around and away from the Republican critique. Partisanship was a more important factor because the press that was in favor of Kennedy's policies found ways to keep quiet on difficult points and responded favorably to his press conferences, while the Republican-oriented press was not influenced by his press policies. Thus, although an appropriate press strategy can be helpful, it is clear that the critical factor in relation to presidential effectiveness with the press is what forces are at work on an issue.

Three constellations of political forces provoked an effective press challenge to the president. The first occurred during a period of indecision on Berlin, an issue of broad popular concern. Kennedy experienced pressure from within his administration, some questioning from within his party, and a critique from both the moderate-bipartisan and conservative branches of the opposition party as well. In such a situation, all the forces in the press were sensitized to the issue, including those that responded to administration influences and those that responded to the opposition. The result was a domestic critique reflected and magnified across a broad spectrum of the press. The second constellation of forces was more purely partisan and involved the exploitation by the opposition of the popular issue of Cuba during an election, assisted by an interest group with which the public could identify. Finally, the president was challenged, as in August and September during the Vietnam crisis, by a combination of dramatic events highlighting the difficulties of an allied government and a bitter debate within the administration over the policy to pursue toward it.

If intense domestic involvement or open division within the government limited Kennedy's effectiveness with the press, the reverse was also true. The president could dominate the press if there were little domestic political involvement or intraadministration squabbling. In the Laotian crisis, Kennedy had great power of policy definition, limited only by the effects of the muted debate within the government on the Washington-oriented press and by the initiatives that resulted from the efforts of the elite press, which had independent foreign policy resources. When Kennedy was able to neutralize the political opposition and stop harmful leaking from within the administration— as he did, for example, after July 1961 in the Berlin crisis and during the later stage of the Cuban and Vietnam crises—it is clear that he had a great deal of influence on the press. Indeed he could dominate it. And he certainly used the expanded power inherent in such a situation to his political advantage.

Changes Since Kennedy

More than any other president since World War II, Kennedy had the capacity to maximize the benefits from his relationship with the press. He knew many of the key people and shared values with many of Washington journalism's most successful practitioners. He evolved a press strategy that could relate to both the Washington and the out-of-town and foreign press. He functioned when the executive branch was more dominant than it is today in the making of foreign policy and when the tendency was greater to mute criticism of the president because of public support for the cold war. His presidency came before changes began to take place in the United States that affected public attitudes toward government and authority. All these factors helped him in relation to the press on foreign policy issues. Still, as noted repeatedly in this study, he experienced substantial difficulties and constraints.

Presidents since Kennedy have lacked many of these advantages. Changes have occurred in the balance of power between the executive branch and the Congress since the late sixties. The public, through informed individuals and interest groups, may have come to play a greater foreign policy role. Liberal and conservative presidents whose origins are in Texas, California, Michigan, and Georgia have not shared the values of the eastern, Washington-oriented press to the same degree. The post-World War II foreign policy consensus of public opinion has broken down and made it more difficult for a president to know the nature of public opinion. Most important, perhaps, the press itself has changed substantially since the early sixties. For some journalists concerned with the issue of news management, the Cuban missile crisis was a turning point. The subsequent leadership of the *New York Times* and the *Washington Post* in the publication of the Pentagon Papers and in the revelations about Watergate prompted the phrase "adversarial journalism." By the late 1960s and early 1970s, television news had also assumed a much more prominent role.

Studies of television and the presidency have generally stressed presidential dominance. Because the president represents the nation as a whole and his actions affect the entire country, television news producers tend to assume that what he does will be of interest to the medium's intended viewers in "Peoria." Although the presidential beat is thus heavily covered, this may not always be to his advantage, for aggressive television news organizations now compete not only with each other but with leading newspapers in locating stories challenging an administration's position.[3]

It has also been argued that television has become the only other national institution that can compete effectively with the presidency. Whether or not this view is correct, technological advances in the medium—live interviews and improved worldwide coverage of fast-breaking stories—mean that the medium has far more ability now than it had in the early 1960s to influence perceptions of events as they occur. Recent studies of television news suggest that changes in public opinion have followed differences in the nature of television coverage—as, for example, in relation to the Middle East issues that followed Vietnam in the 1970s as the major foreign affairs story covered by the networks. The new technologies have also opened up opportunities for foreign leaders like Anwar Sadat and Menachem Begin to conduct "media diplomacy."[4]

Detailed analysis of television coverage of three issues in the Carter and Reagan administrations indicates that, in the absence of domestic criticism—as in the case of the Afghan crisis of 1979–80—the president clearly dominated television news coverage. But, under conditions of internal policy debate and strong domestic criticism—as in the cases of Carter's proposed Arab-Israeli negotiations at Geneva in the fall of 1977 and Reagan's El Salvador policy in the spring of 1981—a pattern prevailed that was much closer to the experience of the early phases of the Berlin and Cuban crises of the Kennedy years. A separate study of newspaper coverage of Carter's foreign policy initiatives in the fall of 1977, including the SALT and Panama Canal negotiations, found that, in the wake of the Bert Lance affair, these issues were covered as part of the administration's "October malaise." Presidents may well be experiencing more difficulties with the press than during Kennedy's time.[5]

Changes in the nature of the media have indeed occurred. But, before the conclusion is made that these alone are responsible for the increased public relations difficulties that presidents may be experiencing, it is important to consider changes in the society since the Kennedy years, including the fact that different values and forces are now at work. Even in Washington, where newspapers have been most disposed to defend and respond to the government, "Deep Throats" have been judged to contribute to better government. The question of whether press coverage of foreign policy is still as reflective of the major strands of political opinion as it was during the Kennedy era or whether it has moved in the direction of homogeneity or responsiveness to new forces lies beyond the scope of this study.

Appendixes

Appendix I.
Total Sources by Category for Each Crisis

1. Laos (all periods combined)

A. Front Page

	NYT	WP	SLPD	CT	SFEx	TOTAL
Foreign	48	36	61	10	46	201
	(50%)	(45%)	(51%)	(45%)	(56%)	(50%)
Official U.S.	40	40	46	12	33	171
	(42%)	(50%)	(39%)	(55%)	(40%)	(43%)
Domestic pol.	7	3	11	0	3	24
	(7%)	(4%)	(9%)		(4%)	(6%)
Interest group	0	0	0	0	0	0
Public opinion	0	0	0	0	0	0
Press	1	1	1	0	0	3
	(1%)	(1%)	(1%)			(1%)
TOTAL	96	80	119	22	82	399

B. Inside Pages

	NYT	WP	SLPD	CT	SFEx	TOTAL
Foreign	100	84	48	54	36	322
	(76%)	(63%)	(59%)	(62%)	(50%)	(64%)
Official U.S.	29	29	22	20	22	122
	(22%)	(22%)	(27%)	(23%)	(31%)	(24%)
Domestic pol.	2	17	7	12	12	50
	(2%)	(13%)	(9%)	(14%)	(17%)	(10%)
Interest group	0	0	0	0	0	0
Public opinion	0	0	0	1	0	1
				(1%)		(0%)
Press	0	4	4	0	2	10
		(3%)	(5%)		(3%)	(2%)
TOTAL	131	134	81	87	72	505

C. Front and Inside Pages Combined

	NYT	WP	SLPD	CT	SFEx	TOTAL
Foreign	148	120	109	64	82	523
	(65%)	(56%)	(55%)	(59%)	(53%)	(58%)
Official U.S.	69	69	68	32	55	293
	(30%)	(32%)	(34%)	(29%)	(36%)	(32%)
Domestic pol.	9	20	18	12	15	74
	(4%)	(9%)	(9%)	(11%)	(10%)	(8%)
Interest group	0	0	0	0	0	0
Public opinion	0	0	0	1	0	1
				(1%)		(0%)
Press	1	5	5	0	2	13
	(0%)	(2%)	(3%)		(1%)	(1%)
TOTAL	227	214	200	109	154	904

2. Berlin (all periods combined)

A. Front Page

	NYT	WP	SLPD	CT	SFEx	TOTAL
Foreign	237	110	256	93	80	776
	(54%)	(41%)	(55%)	(49%)	(37%)	(49%)
Official U.S.	160	130	150	52	103	595
	(36%)	(49%)	(32%)	(28%)	(48%)	(38%)
Domestic pol.	38	23	52	44	22	179
	(9%)	(9%)	(11%)	(23%)	(10%)	(11%)
Interest group	0	0	2	0	0	2
			(0%)			(0%)
Public opinion	3	0	2	0	0	5
	(1%)		(0%)			(0%)
Press	2	5	7	0	10	24
	(0%)	(2%)	(1%)		(5%)	(2%)
TOTAL	440	268	469	189	215	1581

B. Inside Pages

	NYT	WP	SLPD	CT	SFEx	TOTAL
Foreign	645	314	199	231	266	1655
	(73%)	(64%)	(64%)	(59%)	(55%)	(64%)
Official U.S.	161	85	62	84	131	523
	(18%)	(17%)	(20%)	(22%)	(27%)	(20%)
Domestic pol.	59	71	41	63	68	302
	(7%)	(14%)	(13%)	(16%)	(14%)	(12%)
Interest group	9	5	1	5	3	23
	(1%)	(1%)	(0%)	(1%)	(1%)	(1%)
Public opinion	12	10	7	2	1	32
	(1%)	(2%)	(2%)	(1%)	(0%)	(1%)
Press	2	8	1	4	19	34
	(0%)	(2%)	(0%)	(1%)	(4%)	(1%)
TOTAL	888	493	311	389	488	2569

C. Front and Inside Pages Combined

Foreign	882	424	455	324	346	2431
	(66%)	(56%)	(58%)	(56%)	(49%)	(59%)
Official U.S.	321	215	212	136	234	1118
	(24%)	(28%)	(27%)	(24%)	(33%)	(27%)
Domestic pol.	97	94	93	107	90	481
	(7%)	(12%)	(12%)	(19%)	(13%)	(12%)
Interest group	9	5	3	5	3	25
	(1%)	(1%)	(0%)	(1%)	(0%)	(1%)
Public opinion	15	10	9	2	1	37
	(1%)	(1%)	(1%)	(0%)	(0%)	(1%)
Press	4	13	8	4	29	58
	(0%)	(2%)	(1%)	(1%)	(4%)	(1%)
TOTAL	1328	761	780	578	703	4150

3. Cuba (all periods combined)

A. Front Page

	NYT	WP	SLPD	CT	SFEx	TOTAL
Foreign	169	42	117	56	57	441
	(39%)	(31%)	(31%)	(36%)	(25%)	(33%)
Official U.S.	165	58	163	54	90	530
	(38%)	(42%)	(43%)	(35%)	(40%)	(40%)
Domestic pol.	63	21	76	25	57	242
	(15%)	(15%)	(20%)	(16%)	(25%)	(18%)
Interest group	33	13	17	18	16	97
	(8%)	(9%)	(5%)	(12%)	(7%)	(7%)
Public opinion	0	0	1	0	3	4
			(0%)		(1%)	(0%)
Press	1	3	1	2	3	10
	(0%)	(2%)	(0%)	(1%)	(1%)	(1%)
TOTAL	431	137	375	155	226	1324

B. Inside Pages

	NYT	WP	SLPD	CT	SFEx	TOTAL
Foreign	278	145	105	130	80	738
	(40%)	(42%)	(33%)	(39%)	(24%)	(36%)
Official U.S.	124	91	87	83	107	492
	(18%)	(26%)	(27%)	(25%)	(32%)	(24%)
Domestic pol.	130	85	99	64	88	466
	(19%)	(25%)	(31%)	(19%)	(26%)	(23%)
Interest group	91	13	22	39	34	199
	(13%)	(4%)	(7%)	(12%)	(10%)	(10%)
Public opinion	62	9	7	15	9	102
	(9%)	(3%)	(2%)	(4%)	(3%)	(5%)
Press	16	3	1	6	17	43
	(2%)	(1%)	(0%)	(2%)	(5%)	(2%)
TOTAL	701	346	321	337	335	2040

C. Front and Inside Pages Combined

	NYT	WP	SLPD	CT	SFEx	TOTAL
Foreign	447	187	222	186	137	1179
	(39%)	(39%)	(32%)	(38%)	(24%)	(35%)
Official U.S.	289	149	250	137	197	1022
	(26%)	(31%)	(36%)	(28%)	(35%)	(30%)
Domestic pol.	193	106	175	89	145	708
	(17%)	(22%)	(25%)	(18%)	(26%)	(21%)
Interest group	124	26	39	57	50	296
	(11%)	(5%)	(6%)	(12%)	(9%)	(9%)
Public opinion	62	9	8	15	12	106
	(5%)	(2%)	(1%)	(3%)	(2%)	(3%)
Press	17	6	2	8	20	53
	(2%)	(1%)	(0%)	(2%)	(4%)	(2%)
TOTAL	1132	483	696	492	561	3364

4. Vietnam (all periods combined)

A. Front Page

	NYT	WP	SLPD	CT	SFEx	TOTAL
Foreign	127	85	118	50	59	439
	(51%)	(49%)	(50%)	(41%)	(43%)	(48%)
Official U.S.	104	72	92	51	51	370
	(42%)	(41%)	(39%)	(42%)	(38%)	(40%)
Domestic pol.	16	11	18	9	8	62
	(6%)	(6%)	(8%)	(7%)	(6%)	(7%)
Interest group	1	1	0	2	6	10
	(0%)	(1%)		(1%)	(4%)	(1%)
Public opinion	0	1	2	5	5	13
		(1%)	(1%)	(4%)	(4%)	(1%)
Press	1	5	6	5	7	24
	(0%)	(3%)	(3%)	(4%)	(5%)	(3%)
TOTAL	249	175	236	122	136	918

B. Inside Pages

	NYT	WP	SLPD	CT	SFEx	TOTAL
Foreign	341	248	143	175	160	1067
	(64%)	(56%)	(54%)	(52%)	(48%)	(56%)
Official U.S.	142	141	82	101	115	581
	(26%)	(32%)	(31%)	(30%)	(35%)	(30%)
Domestic pol.	20	23	18	34	24	119
	(4%)	(5%)	(7%)	(10%)	(7%)	(6%)
Interest group	11	9	6	10	8	44
	(2%)	(2%)	(2%)	(3%)	(2%)	(2%)
Public opinion	11	3	7	10	15	46
	(2%)	(1%)	(3%)	(3%)	(5%)	(2%)
Press	11	15	10	9	8	53
	(2%)	(3%)	(4%)	(3%)	(2%)	(3%)
TOTAL	536	439	266	339	330	1910

C. Front and Inside Pages Combined

	NYT	WP	SLPD	CT	SFEx	TOTAL
Foreign	468	333	261	225	219	1506
	(60%)	(54%)	(52%)	(49%)	(47%)	(53%)
Official U.S.	246	213	174	152	166	951
	(31%)	(35%)	(35%)	(33%)	(36%)	(34%)
Domestic pol.	36	34	36	43	32	181
	(5%)	(6%)	(7%)	(9%)	(7%)	(6%)
Interest group	12	10	6	12	14	54
	(2%)	(2%)	(1%)	(3%)	(3%)	(2%)
Public opinion	11	4	9	15	20	59
	(1%)	(1%)	(2%)	(3%)	(4%)	(2%)
Press	12	20	16	14	15	77
	(2%)	(3%)	(3%)	(3%)	(3%)	(3%)
TOTAL	785	614	502	461	466	2828

Appendix II.
Distribution of Front-Page Sources by Period for Each Crisis

1. LAOS

A. Laos, 22–31 January

	NYT	WP	SLPD	CT	SFEx	TOTAL
Foreign	2	2	2	2	0	8
	(22%)	(40%)	(50%)	(100%)		(40%)
Official U.S.	7	2	2	0	0	11
	(78%)	(40%)	(50%)			(55%)
Domestic pol.	0	0	0	0	0	0
Interest group	0	0	0	0	0	0
Public opinion	0	0	0	0	0	0
Press	0	1	0	0	0	1
		(20%)				(5%)
TOTAL	9	5	4	2	0	20

B. Laos, February

	NYT	WP	SLPD	CT	SFEx	TOTAL
Foreign	7	1	1	0	0	9
	(50%)	(33%)	(25%)			(43%)
Official U.S.	7	2	3	0	0	12
	(50%)	(67%)	(75%)			(57%)
Domestic pol.	0	0	0	0	0	0
Interest group	0	0	0	0	0	0
Public opinion	0	0	0	0	0	0
Press	0	0	0	0	0	0
TOTAL	14	3	4	0	0	21

C. Laos, 1–15 March

	NYT	WP	SLPD	CT	SFEx	TOTAL
Foreign	6	4	0	0	0	10
	(75%)	(57%)				(56%)
Official U.S.	1	2	2	0	0	5
	(13%)	(29%)	(67%)			(28%)
Domestic pol.	0	1	0	0	0	1
		(14%)				(6%)
Interest group	0	0	0	0	0	0
Public opinion	0	0	0	0	0	0
Press	1	0	1	0	0	2
	(13%)		(33%)			(11%)
TOTAL	8	7	3	0	0	18

D. Laos, 16–31 March

	NYT	WP	SLPD	CT	SFEx	TOTAL
Foreign	22	17	33	6	31	109
	(50%)	(40%)	(52%)	(46%)	(55%)	(50%)
Official U.S.	16	24	24	7	22	93
	(36%)	(57%)	(38%)	(54%)	(39%)	(43%)
Domestic pol.	6	1	6	0	3	16
	(14%)	(2%)	(10%)		(5%)	(7%)
Interest group	0	0	0	0	0	0
Public opinion	0	0	0	0	0	0
Press	0	0	0	0	0	0
TOTAL	44	42	63	13	56	218

E. Laos, 1–15 April

	NYT	WP	SLPD	CT	SFEx	TOTAL
Foreign	11	12	25	2	15	65
	(52%)	(52%)	(56%)	(29%)	(58%)	(53%)
Official U.S.	9	10	15	5	11	50
	(43%)	(43%)	(33%)	(71%)	(42%)	(41%)
Domestic pol.	1	1	5	0	0	7
	(5%)	(4%)	(11%)			(6%)
Interest group	0	0	0	0	0	0
Public opinion	0	0	0	0	0	0
Press	0	0	0	0	0	0
TOTAL	21	23	45	7	26	122

2. BERLIN

A. Berlin, 1–23 June

	NYT	WP	SLPD	CT	SFEx	TOTAL
Foreign	18	14	18	4	20	74
	(43%)	(38%)	(53%)	(80%)	(49%)	(47%)
Official U.S.	16	16	11	1	12	56
	(38%)	(43%)	(32%)	(20%)	(29%)	(35%)
Domestic pol.	7	6	5	0	9	27
	(17%)	(16%)	(15%)		(22%)	(17%)
Interest group	0	0	0	0	0	0
Public opinion	0	0	0	0	0	0
Press	1	1	0	0	0	2
TOTAL	(2%)	(3%)				(1%)
	42	37	34	5	41	159

B. Berlin, 24–30 June

	NYT	WP	SLPD	CT	SFEx	TOTAL
Foreign	9	11	5	4	0	29
	(64%)	(55%)	(42%)	(100%)		(48%)
Official U.S.	5	8	7	0	3	23
	(36%)	(40%)	(58%)		(30%)	(38%)
Domestic pol.	0	1	0	0	4	5
		(5%)			(40%)	(8%)
Interest group	0	0	0	0	0	0
Public opinion	0	0	0	0	0	0
Press	0	0	0	0	3	3
					(30%)	(5%)
TOTAL	14	20	12	4	10	60

C. Berlin, July

	NYT	WP	SLPD	CT	SFEx	TOTAL
Foreign	37	11	33	11	12	104
	(32%)	(17%)	(31%)	(19%)	(24%)	(27%)
Official U.S.	54	38	37	11	30	170
	(47%)	(60%)	(35%)	(19%)	(61%)	(43%)
Domestic pol.	24	14	34	35	6	113
	(21%)	(22%)	(32%)	(61%)	(12%)	(29%)
Interest group	0	0	0	0	0	0
Public opinion	1	0	0	0	0	1
	(1%)					(0%)
Press	0	0	2	0	1	3
			(2%)		(2%)	(1%)
TOTAL	116	63	106	57	49	391

D. Berlin, August

	NYT	WP	SLPD	CT	SFEx	TOTAL
Foreign	94	59	158	58	28	397
	(60%)	(56%)	(68%)	(70%)	(42%)	(62%)
Official U.S.	54	42	59	24	34	213
	(35%)	(40%)	(25%)	(29%)	(51%)	(33%)
Domestic pol.	7	1	9	1	2	20
	(4%)	(1%)	(4%)	(1%)	(3%)	(3%)
Interest group	0	0	2	0	0	2
			(1%)			(0%)
Public opinion	1	0	1	0	0	2
	(1%)		(0%)			(0%)
Press	0	3	3	0	3	9
		(3%)	(1%)		(4%)	(1%)
TOTAL	156	105	232	83	67	643

E. Berlin, September

	NYT	WP	SLPD	CT	SFEx	TOTAL
Foreign	64	14	32	14	17	141
	(71%)	(35%)	(51%)	(39%)	(40%)	(52%)
Official U.S.	24	24	26	14	21	109
	(27%)	(60%)	(41%)	(39%)	(50%)	(40%)
Domestic pol.	0	1	2	8	1	12
		(3%)	(3%)	(22%)	(2%)	(4%)
Interest group	0	0	0	0	0	0
Public opinion	1	0	1	0	0	2
	(1%)		(2%)			(1%)
Press	1	1	2	0	3	7
	(1%)	(3%)	(3%)		(7%)	(3%)
TOTAL	90	40	63	36	42	271

F. Berlin, 1–6 October

	NYT	WP	SLPD	CT	SFEx	TOTAL
Foreign	15	1	10	2	3	31
	(68%)	(33%)	(45%)	(50%)	(50%)	(54%)
Official U.S.	7	2	10	2	3	24
	(32%)	(67%)	(45%)	(50%)	(50%)	(42%)
Domestic pol.	0	0	2	0	0	2
			(9%)			(4%)
Interest group	0	0	0	0	0	0
Public opinion	0	0	0	0	0	0
Press	0	0	0	0	0	0
TOTAL	22	3	22	4	6	57

3. CUBA

A. Cuba, 25–31 August

	NYT	WP	SLPD	CT	SFEx	TOTAL
Foreign	6	2	5	3	1	17
	(35%)	(50%)	(31%)	(27%)	(13%)	(30%)
Official U.S.	8	0	9	3	4	24
	(47%)		(56%)	(27%)	(50%)	(43%)
Domestic pol.	0	0	0	0	0	0
Interest group	3	2	2	5	3	15
	(18%)	(50%)	(13%)	(45%)	(38%)	(27%)
Public opinion	0	0	0	0	0	0
Press	0	0	0	0	0	0
TOTAL	17	4	16	11	8	56

B. Cuba, September

	NYT	WP	SLPD	CT	SFEx	TOTAL
Foreign	36	8	31	10	20	105
	(27%)	(22%)	(21%)	(29%)	(22%)	(24%)
Official U.S.	49	11	53	9	35	157
	(37%)	(31%)	(36%)	(26%)	(38%)	(35%)
Domestic pol.	41	15	62	12	30	160
	(31%)	(42%)	(42%)	(35%)	(32%)	(36%)
Interest group	6	2	3	2	7	20
	(5%)	(6%)	(2%)	(6%)	(8%)	(4%)
Public opinion	0	0	0	0	0	0
Press	1	0	0	1	1	3
	(1%)			(3%)	(1%)	(1%)
TOTAL	133	36	149	34	93	445

C. Cuba, 1–19 October

	NYT	WP	SLPD	CT	SFEx	TOTAL
Foreign	23	9	11	4	4	51
	(30%)	(33%)	(25%)	(15%)	(15%)	(26%)
Official U.S.	31	7	18	7	12	75
	(41%)	(26%)	(41%)	(26%)	(46%)	(38%)
Domestic pol.	13	5	7	9	8	42
	(17%)	(19%)	(16%)	(33%)	(31%)	(21%)
Interest group	9	5	8	7	2	31
	(12%)	(19%)	(18%)	(26%)	(8%)	(16%)
Public opinion	0	0	0	0	0	0
Press	0	1	0	0	0	1
		(4%)				(1%)
TOTAL	76	27	44	27	26	200

D. Cuba, 20–22 October

	NYT	WP	SLPD	CT	SFEx	TOTAL
Foreign	4	0	0	0	0	4
	(44%)					(14%)
Official U.S.	3	3	6	2	2	16
	(33%)	(60%)	(75%)	(100%)	(50%)	(57%)
Domestic pol.	1	0	2	0	0	3
	(11%)		(25%)			(11%)
Interest group	1	0	0	0	0	1
	(11%)					(4%)
Public opinion	0	0	0	0	0	0
Press	0	2	0	0	2	4
		(40%)			(50%)	(14%)
TOTAL	9	5	8	2	4	28

E. Cuba, 23–29 October

	NYT	WP	SLPD	CT	SFEx	TOTAL
Foreign	100	23	70	39	32	264
	(51%)	(35%)	(44%)	(48%)	(34%)	(44%)
Official U.S.	74	37	77	33	37	258
	(38%)	(57%)	(49%)	(41%)	(39%)	(43%)
Domestic pol.	8	1	5	4	19	37
	(4%)	(2%)	(3%)	(5%)	(20%)	(6%)
Interest group	14	4	4	4	4	30
	(7%)	(6%)	(3%)	(5%)	(5%)	(5%)
Public opinion	0	0	1	0	3	4
			(1%)		(3%)	(1%)
Press	0	0	1	1	0	2
			(1%)	(1%)		(0%)
TOTAL	196	65	158	81	95	595

4. VIETNAM

A. Vietnam, 1–20 August

	NYT	WP	SLPD	CT	SFEx	TOTAL
Foreign	13	9	9	3	5	39
	(72%)	(75%)	(75%)	(60%)	(71%)	(72%)
Official U.S.	5	3	3	2	2	15
	(28%)	(25%)	(25%)	(40%)	(29%)	(28%)
Domestic pol.	0	0	0	0	0	0
						(0%)
Interest group	0	0	0	0	0	0
						(0%)
Public opinion	0	0	0	0	0	0
						(0%)
Press	0	0	0	0	0	0
						(0%)
TOTAL	18	12	12	5	7	54

B. Vietnam, 21 August–2 September

	NYT	WP	SLPD	CT	SFEx	TOTAL
Foreign	39	32	29	24	22	146
	(53%)	(53%)	(53%)	(69%)	(65%)	(57%)
Official U.S.	33	25	24	10	10	102
	(45%)	(42%)	(44%)	(29%)	(29%)	(40%)
Domestic pol.	0	0	0	0	0	0
						(0%)
Interest group	1	0	0	0	0	1
	(1%)					(0%)
Public opinion	0	0	0	0	0	0
						(0%)
Press	0	3	2	1	2	8
		(5%)	(4%)	(3%)	(6%)	(3%)
TOTAL	73	60	55	35	34	257

C. Vietnam, 3 September–2 October

	NYT	WP	SLPD	CT	SFEx	TOTAL
Foreign	33	29	31	4	4	101
	(44%)	(46%)	(48%)	(25%)	(14%)	(41%)
Official U.S.	33	25	26	11	19	114
	(44%)	(40%)	(40%)	(69%)	(66%)	(46%)
Domestic pol.	9	7	8	0	3	27
	(12%)	(11%)	(12%)		(10%)	(11%)
Interest group	0	1	0	0	1	2
		(2%)			(3%)	(1%)
Public opinion	0	1	0	1	0	2
		(2%)		(6%)		(1%)
Press	0	0	0	0	2	2
					(7%)	(1%)
TOTAL	75	63	65	16	29	248

D. Vietnam, 3 October–1 November

	NYT	WP	SLPD	CT	SFEx	TOTAL
Foreign	18	3	24	5	18	68
	(43%)	(17%)	(39%)	(19%)	(37%)	(35%)
Official U.S.	19	11	26	13	16	85
	(45%)	(61%)	(42%)	(50%)	(33%)	(43%)
Domestic pol.	4	3	8	2	5	22
	(10%)	(17%)	(13%)	(8%)	(10%)	(11%)
Interest group	0	0	0	1	5	6
				(4%)	(10%)	(3%)
Public opinion	0	0	2	1	5	8
			(3%)	(4%)	(10%)	(4%)
Press	1	1	2	4	0	8
	(2%)	(6%)	(3%)	(15%)		(4%)
TOTAL	42	18	62	26	49	197

E. Vietnam, 2–10 November

	NYT	WP	SLPD	CT	SFEx	TOTAL
Foreign	24	12	25	14	10	85
	(59%)	(55%)	(60%)	(35%)	(59%)	(52%)
Official U.S.	14	8	13	15	4	54
	(34%)	(36%)	(31%)	(38%)	(24%)	(33%)
Domestic pol.	3	1	2	7	0	13
	(7%)	(5%)	(5%)	(18%)		(8%)
Interest group	0	0	0	1	0	1
				(3%)		(1%)
Public opinion	0	0	0	1	0	3
				(8%)		(2%)
Press	0	1	2	0	3	6
		(5%)	(5%)		(18%)	(4%)
TOTAL	41	22	42	40	17	162

Appendix III.
Front-Page Breakdown of the Three Major Source Categories for Each Crisis

1. LAOS

A. Foreign (all periods combined)

	NYT	WP	SLPD	CT	SFEx	TOTAL
Great Britain	8	7	12	3	9	39
	(17%)	(19%)	(20%)	(30%)	(20%)	(19%)
France	2	0	4	0	0	6
	(4%)		(7%)			(3%)
Nonspecified	17	2	6	0	3	28
Western	(35%)	(6%)	(10%)		(7%)	(14%)
Warsaw Pact	1	0	0	0	1	2
nations	(2%)				(2%)	(1%)
Russia	1	7	7	5	8	28
	(2%)	(19%)	(11%)	(50%)	(17%)	(14%)
Pro-Western Asian	4	5	15	0	3	27
	(8%)	(14%)	(25%)		(7%)	(13%)
U.S.-backed	6	8	7	2	8	31
Laotian	(13%)	(22%)	(11%)	(20%)	(17%)	(15%)
Other Laotian	4	3	0	0	5	12
	(8%)	(8%)			(11%)	(6%)
North Vietnam	1	0	2	0	1	4
	(2%)		(3%)		(2%)	(2%)
P. R. China	0	1	4	0	6	11
		(3%)	(7%)		(13%)	(6%)
Neutral nations	4	3	3	0	2	12
	(8%)	(8%)	(5%)		(4%)	(6%)
Other	0	0	1	0	0	1
			(2%)			(1%)
TOTAL	48	36	61	10	46	201

B. Official U.S. (all periods combined)

	NYT	WP	SLPD	CT	SFEx	TOTAL
White House	15	9	10	5	10	49
	(38%)	(23%)	(22%)	(42%)	(30%)	(29%)
Diplomatic	19	14	20	4	12	69
	(48%)	(35%)	(43%)	(33%)	(36%)	(40%)
Unidentified	5	15	16	3	10	49
	(13%)	(38%)	(35%)	(25%)	(30%)	(29%)
Military	1	1	0	0	1	3
	(3%)	(3%)			(3%)	(2%)
Other federal	0	1	0	0	0	1
		(3%)				(1%)
TOTAL	40	40	46	12	33	171

C. Domestic Political (all periods combined)

	NYT	WP	SLPD	CT	SFEx	TOTAL
National	5	1	4	0	1	11
Democrat	(71%)	(33%)	(36%)		(33%)	(46%)
National	2	2	6	0	2	12
Republican	(29%)	(67%)	(55%)		(67%)	(50%)
Other	0	0	1	0	0	1
congressional			(9%)			(4%)
TOTAL	7	3	11	0	3	24

2. BERLIN

A. Foreign (all periods combined)

	NYT	WP	SLPD	CT	SFEx	TOTAL
West Germany	52	26	79	36	23	216
	(22%)	(24%)	(31%)	(39%)	(29%)	(28%)
Great Britain	21	9	21	12	1	64
	(9%)	(8%)	(8%)	(13%)	(1%)	(8%)
France	13	10	10	3	3	39
	(5%)	(9%)	(4%)	(3%)	(4%)	(5%)
Other West	4	1	12	2	5	24
European	(2%)	(1%)	(5%)	(2%)	(6%)	(3%)
Nonspecified	44	15	39	3	10	111
Western	(19%)	(14%)	(15%)	(3%)	(13%)	(14%)
Russia	60	32	26	23	22	163
	(25%)	(29%)	(10%)	(25%)	(28%)	(21%)
East Germany	40	12	58	14	11	135
	(17%)	(11%)	(23%)	(15%)	(14%)	(17%)
Other communist	2	2	7	0	2	13
	(1%)	(2%)	(3%)		(3%)	(2%)
Latin America	0	0	1	0	0	1
			(0%)			(0%)
United Nations	0	0	1	0	0	1
			(0%)			(0%)
Pro-Western Asian	0	0	2	0	0	2
			(1%)			(0%)
Neutral nations	0	3	0	0	3	6
		(3%)			(4%)	(1%)
Other	1	0	0	0	0	1
	(0%)					(0%)
TOTAL	237	110	256	93	80	776

B. Official U.S. (all periods combined)

	NYT	WP	SLPD	CT	SFEx	TOTAL
White House	25	19	32	16	27	119
	(16%)	(15%)	(21%)	(31%)	(26%)	(20%)
Diplomatic	44	27	42	10	13	136
	(28%)	(21%)	(28%)	(19%)	(13%)	(23%)
Unidentified	52	53	47	5	41	198
	(33%)	(41%)	(31%)	(10%)	(40%)	(33%)
Military	37	29	24	21	22	133
	(23%)	(22%)	(16%)	(40%)	(21%)	(22%)
Other federal	2	2	5	0	0	9
	(1%)	(2%)	(3%)			(2%)
TOTAL	160	130	150	52	103	595

C. Domestic Political (all periods combined)

	NYT	WP	SLPD	CT	SFEx	TOTAL
National Democrat	19	4	29	16	7	75
	(50%)	(17%)	(56%)	(36%)	(32%)	(42%)
National Republician	18	13	21	24	7	83
	(47%)	(57%)	(40%)	(55%)	(32%)	(46%)
Leaders of both parties	0	3	0	2	0	5
		(13%)		(5%)		(3%)
Cong. action	1	1	0	0	4	6
	(3%)	(4%)			(18%)	(3%)
Other cong.	0	2	2	2	4	10
		(9%)	(4%)	(5%)	(18%)	(6%)
TOTAL	38	23	52	44	22	179

3. CUBA

A. Foreign (all periods combined)

	NYT	WP	SLPD	CT	SFEx	TOTAL
West Germany	4	0	4	2	1	11
	(2%)		(3%)	(4%)	(2%)	(2%)
Great Britain	21	5	10	4	8	48
	(12%)	(12%)	(9%)	(7%)	(14%)	(11%)
France	3	0	0	2	0	5
	(2%)			(4%)		(1%)
Other West	3	0	5	2	0	10
European	(2%)		(4%)	(4%)		(2%)
Nonspecified	19	4	4	1	4	32
Western	(11%)	(10%)	(3%)	(2%)	(7%)	(7%)
Russia	37	10	40	12	20	119
	(22%)	(24%)	(34%)	(21%)	(35%)	(27%)
Other communist	6	1	2	2	1	12
	(4%)	(2%)	(2%)	(4%)	(2%)	(5%)
Cuba	24	10	25	16	14	89
	(14%)	(24%)	(21%)	(29%)	(25%)	(20%)
Cuban	1	0	1	1	0	3
opposition	(1%)		(1%)	(2%)		(1%)
Other Latin	31	6	9	5	1	52
America	(18%)	(14%)	(8%)	(9%)	(2%)	(12%)
Turkey	1	0	1	0	0	2
	(1%)		(1%)			(0%)
United Nations	9	4	7	0	6	26
	(5%)	(10%)	(6%)		(11%)	(6%)
Pro-Western Asian	0	0	0	0	1	1
					(2%)	(0%)
Neutral nations	6	0	7	7	1	21
	(4%)		(6%)	(13%)	(2%)	(5%)
Canada	3	2	0	1	0	6
	(2%)	(5%)		(2%)		(1%)
Other	1	0	2	1	0	4
	(1%)		(2%)	(2%)		(1%)
TOTAL	169	42	117	56	57	441

B. Official U.S. (all periods combined)

	NYT	WP	SLPD	CT	SFEx	TOTAL
White House	27	20	40	16	18	121
	(16%)	(34%)	(25%)	(30%)	(20%)	(23%)
Diplomatic	38	9	52	17	21	137
	(23%)	(16%)	(32%)	(31%)	(23%)	(26%)
Unidentified	54	17	36	4	21	132
official U.S.	(33%)	(29%)	(22%)	(7%)	(23%)	(25%)
Military	37	11	29	13	24	114
	(22%)	(19%)	(18%)	(24%)	(27%)	(22%)
Other federal	7	1	5	4	5	22
	(4%)	(2%)	(3%)	(7%)	(6%)	(4%)
Local officials	2	0	1	0	1	4
	(1%)		(1%)		(1%)	(1%)
TOTAL	165	58	163	54	90	530

C. Domestic Political (all periods combined)

	NYT	WP	SLPD	CT	SFEx	TOTAL
National Democrat	21	9	29	10	23	92
	(33%)	(43%)	(38%)	(40%)	(40%)	(38%)
National Republican	32	9	40	11	23	115
	(51%)	(43%)	(53%)	(44%)	(40%)	(48%)
Cong. action	4	3	4	3	2	16
	(6%)	(14%)	(5%)	(12%)	(4%)	(7%)
Other cong.	4	0	2	1	3	10
	(6%)		(3%)	(4%)	(5%)	(4%)
Local Democrat	1	0	1	0	4	6
	(2%)		(1%)		(7%)	(2%)
Local Republican	0	0	0	0	2	2
					(4%)	(1%)
Unspecified local	1	0	0	0	0	1
	(2%)					(0%)
TOTAL	63	21	76	25	57	242

4. VIETNAM

A. Foreign (all periods combined)

	NYT	WP	SLPD	CT	SFEx	TOTAL
Great Britain	1	0	1	0	0	2
	(1%)		(1%)			(0%)
France	5	1	0	1	2	9
	(4%)	(1%)		(2%)	(3%)	(2%)
Russia	4	0	2	0	0	6
	(3%)		(2%)			(1%)
South Vietnam officials	73	57	77	31	43	281
	(57%)	(67%)	(65%)	(62%)	(73%)	(64%)
South Vietnam Catholics	2	2	2	1	0	7
	(2%)	(2%)	(2%)	(2%)		(2%)
South Vietnam Buddhists	13	5	7	6	8	39
	(10%)	(6%)	(6%)	(12%)	(14%)	(9%)
South Vietnam exiles	1	0	2	1	0	4
	(1%)		(2%)	(2%)		(1%)
National Lib. Front	1	0	1	0	0	2
	(1%)		(1%)			(0%)
South Vietnam— other	10	12	12	6	5	45
	(8%)	(14%)	(10%)	(12%)	(8%)	(10%)
North Vietnam	2	1	2	1	0	6
	(2%)	(1%)	(2%)	(2%)		(1%)
P. R. China	1	2	1	1	0	5
	(1%)	(2%)	(1%)	(2%)		(1%)
Pro-Western Asian	2	3	2	2	0	9
	(2%)	(4%)	(2%)	(4%)		(2%)
Neutral Asian	1	0	1	0	0	2
	(1%)		(1%)			(0%)
United Nations	3	0	4	0	0	7
	(2%)		(3%)			(2%)
Vatican	2	2	2	0	0	6
	(2%)	(2%)	(2%)			(1%)
Other	6	0	2	0	1	9
	(5%)		(2%)		(2%)	(2%)
TOTAL	127	85	118	50	59	439

B. Official U.S. (all periods combined)

	NYT	WP	SLPD	CT	SFEx	TOTAL
White House	6	5	11	8	6	36
	(6%)	(7%)	(12%)	(16%)	(12%)	(10%)
Diplomatic	35	31	33	11	10	120
	(34%)	(43%)	(36%)	(22%)	(20%)	(32%)
Unidentified	47	19	23	14	13	116
official U.S.	(45%)	(26%)	(25%)	(27%)	(25%)	(31%)
Military	12	15	23	17	21	88
	(12%)	(21%)	(25%)	(33%)	(41%)	(24%)
Other federal	4	2	2	1	1	10
officials	(4%)	(3%)	(2%)	(2%)	(2%)	(3%)
TOTAL	104	72	92	51	51	370

C. Domestic Political (all periods combined)

	NYT	WP	SLPD	CT	SFEx	TOTAL
National	11	5	11	2	2	31
Democrat	(69%)	(45%)	(61%)	(22%)	(25%)	(50%)
National	3	5	5	6	3	22
Republican	(19%)	(45%)	(28%)	(67%)	(38%)	(35%)
Cong. action	0	0	1	0	0	1
			(6%)			(2%)
Other cong.	2	1	1	0	1	5
	(13%)	(9%)	(6%)		(13%)	(8%)
Local	0	0	0	1	2	3
Democrat				(11%)	(25%)	(5%)
TOTAL	16	11	18	9	8	62

Appendix IV.
Editorials: Precipitating Events and Interests Criticized for Each Crisis

1. LAOS

A. Precipitating Events

	22–31 Jan.	Feb.	1–15 Mar.	16–31 Mar.	1–15 Apr.	Total
NYT						
U.S. official	–	3	–	3	–	6
SEATO	–	–	–	1	–	1
Soviets	–	–	–	–	1	1
Pro-Western Laotian	–	1	–	–	–	1
Other Laotian	–	–	–	–	1	1
Pathet Lao	–	–	–	1	1	2
Communist China	–	1	–	–	1	2
Britain	–	–	–	2	–	2
TOTAL	–	5	–	7	4	16
WP						
U.S. official	–	–	–	1	1	2
SEATO	–	–	–	1	–	1
Soviets	2	–	–	1	1	4
Other Laotian	–	–	–	–	1	1
Britain	–	–	–	–	1	1
TOTAL	2	–	–	3	4	9
SFEx						
U.S. official	–	–	–	1	2	3
Soviets	–	–	–	1	–	1
Britain	–	–	–	–	1	1
TOTAL	–	–	–	2	3	5
CT						
U.S. official	–	–	2	1	1	4
Soviets	–	–	–	–	1	1
TOTAL	–	–	2	1	2	5
SLPD						
U.S. official	1	1	–	2	1	5
Pro-Western Asian	–	–	–	–	1	1
SEATO	–	–	–	1	–	1
Soviets	–	–	1	2	–	3
Pro-Western Laotian	–	1	1	–	–	2
Other Laotian	1	–	2	–	–	3
France	–	–	–	1	–	1
TOTAL	2	2	4	6	2	16

B. Interests Criticized

	22–31 Jan.	Feb.	1–15 Mar.	16–31 Mar.	1–15 Apr.	Total
NYT						
Communist China	–	1	–	–	–	1
"Communists"	–	–	–	1	–	1
TOTAL	–	1	–	1	–	2
WP						
U.S. official	2	–	–	–	1	3
Soviets	2	–	–	2	–	4
France	–	–	–	1	–	1
TOTAL	4	–	–	3	1	8
SFEx						
U.S. official	–	–	–	–	1	1
Soviets	–	–	–	1	2	3
TOTAL	–	–	–	1	3	4
CT						
U.S. official	–	–	2	–	2	4
Democrats	–	–	–	1	–	1
TOTAL	–	–	2	1	2	5
SLPD						
Soviets	–	–	–	2	–	2
Pro-Western Laotian	–	1	–	–	–	1
TOTAL	–	1	–	2	–	3

2. BERLIN

A. Precipitating Events

	1–23 June	24–30 June	July	Aug.	Sept.	1–6 Oct.	Total
NYT							
U.S. official	3	2	6	6	2	–	19
Republicans	–	–	–	1	–	–	1
Soviets	4	2	1	8	4	1	20
Britain	–	–	–	1	–	–	1
West	–	–	4	4	1	–	9
Congress	–	=	1	–	–	–	1
Neutrals	–	–	–	–	1	–	1
Canada	–	–	–	–	1	–	1
France	–	–	1	1	–	–	2
UN	–	–	–	1	–	–	1
TOTAL	7	4	13	22	9	1	56
WP							
U.S. official	3	1	2	4	–	–	10
Republicans	1	–	1	–	–	–	2
W. Germany	–	–	1	1	–	–	2
E. Germany	–	1	1	1	1	–	4
Soviets	2	2	2	5	1	–	12
West	–	–	1	1	–	–	2
Congress	–	–	1	–	–	–	1
Neutrals	–	–	–	2	1	–	3
Canada, Italy	–	–	–	1	–	–	1
France	–	–	–	–	1	–	1
TOTAL	6	4	9	15	4	–	38
SFEx							
U.S. official	2	2	9	6	3	–	22
Republicans	1	–	–	–	2	–	3
Democrats	–	–	2	–	–	1	3
W. Germany	–	–	1	1	–	–	2
E. Germany	–	–	1	–	–	–	1
Soviets	2	1	–	6	2	–	11
Press	1	1	1	1	–	–	4
Britain	–	–	–	1	1	–	2
West	–	–	–	–	2	–	2
Neutrals	–	–	1	–	–	–	1
Canada	–	–	–	1	–	–	1
UN	–	–	–	–	1	–	1
TOTAL	6	4	15	16	11	1	53

CT

U.S. official	4	1	6	4	7	–	22
Republicans	–	–	–	1	1	–	2
Democrats	1	–	–	2	1	1	5
W. Germany	–	–	1	–	–	–	1
E. Germany	–	–	1	–	–	–	1
Soviets	1	–	2	7	3	–	13
Press	–	1	–	2	–	–	3
Britain	1	2	3	–	–	–	6
West	–	–	1	–	2	–	3
Congress	–	–	–	1	–	–	1
Neutrals	–	–	–	–	1	–	1
France	–	–	–	–	1	–	1
TOTAL	7	4	14	17	16	1	59

SLPD

U.S. official	4	1	3	2	2	2	14
Democrats	1	1	–	1	1	1	5
W. Germany	–	2	–	–	–	–	2
Soviets	1	1	–	5	2	2	11
Press	–	–	–	–	1	–	1
Interest groups	–	–	–	–	1	–	1
West	–	–	1	1	–	–	2
France	1	–	–	–	–	–	1
Canada	–	–	–	–	1	–	1
TOTAL	7	5	4	9	8	5	38

B. Interests Criticized

	1–23 June	24–30 June	July	Aug.	Sept.	1–6 Oct.	Total
NYT							
U.S. official	–	1	–	1	–	–	2
Republicans	–	–	–	1	–	–	1
Soviets	5	1	8	11	6	1	32
W. Germany	–	1	–	–	–	–	1
E. Germany	–	–	1	1	–	1	3
West	–	–	–	1	–	–	1
Neutrals	–	–	1	–	–	–	1
TOTAL	5	3	10	15	6	2	41
WP							
U.S. official	–	–	–	1	–	–	1
Republicans	1	–	–	–	–	–	1
E. Germany	–	1	1	2	1	–	5
Soviets	4	1	4	9	3	–	21
West	1	–	–	1	–	–	2
Neutrals	–	–	–	1	–	–	1
France	–	–	–	1	–	–	1
TOTAL	6	2	5	15	4	–	32

SFEx

U.S. official	3	1	4	1	1	–	10
Republicans	–	–	–	–	1	–	1
Democrats	–	–	–	–	–	1	1
Soviets	2	2	7	9	2	–	22
W. Germany	–	–	–	1	–	–	1
E. Germany	–	–	2	2	–	–	4
Britain	1	–	1	–	–	–	2
Neutrals	–	–	1	–	2	–	3
TOTAL	6	3	15	13	6	1	44

CT

U.S. official	4	1	3	3	2	–	13
Republicans	–	–	–	1	–	–	1
Democrats	–	–	–	1	1	1	3
E. Germany	–	–	1	1	–	–	2
Soviets	2	–	2	9	2	–	15
Britain	–	2	2	–	–	–	4
West	–	–	–	–	1	–	1
Neutrals	–	–	–	–	1	–	1
TOTAL	6	3	8	15	7	1	40

SLPD

U.S. official	–	–	3	2	–	–	5
Republicans	–	–	–	–	–	1	1
Interest groups	–	1	–	–	–	–	1
Soviets	–	–	1	2	1	–	4
West	–	–	1	4	–	–	5
W. Germany	–	–	1	5	–	1	7
France	–	–	–	–	–	1	1
TOTAL	–	1	6	13	1	3	24

3. CUBA

A. Precipitating Events

	25–31 August	1–30 September	1–22 October	23–29 October	Total
NYT					
U.S. official	–	4	4	6	14
Cong. action	–	1	–	–	1
Republicans	–	2	–	–	2
Cuba	–	1	–	–	1
Cuban exiles	–	1	–	–	1
Soviets	–	4	–	5	9
West	–	–	1	–	1
UN	–	–	–	2	2
TOTAL	–	13	5	13	31

WP

U.S. official	–	2	1	4	7
Republicans	–	–	2	–	2
Democrats	–	–	2	–	2
Cuba	1	1	1	–	3
OAS	–	–	2	1	3
Cuban exiles	1	–	–	–	1
Soviets	–	2	–	3	5
Canada	–	–	–	1	1
UN	–	–	–	1	1
TOTAL	2	5	8	10	25

SFEx

U.S. official	1	5	2	4	12
Cuba	–	1	–	–	1
Other Lat. Amer.	–	2	1	–	3
OAS	–	1	–	–	1
Press	–	–	–	1	1
Cuban exiles	1	2	–	–	3
Other int. groups	–	1	–	–	1
Neutrals	–	–	1	–	1
Soviets	1	3	–	1	5
West	–	1	–	–	1
TOTAL	3	16	4	6	29

CT

U.S. official	–	3	1	5	9
Cong. action	–	2	–	–	2
Other Lat. Amer.	–	1	–	–	1
Press	–	1	–	–	1
Cuban exiles	1	–	–	–	1
Soviets	–	1	–	1	2
TOTAL	1	8	1	6	16

SLPD

U.S. official	–	4	6	1	11
Republicans	–	1	–	–	1
Democrats	1	–	–	–	1
Cong. action	2	1	–	–	3
Cuba	–	–	1	–	1
OAS	–	–	1	–	1
Press	–	–	–	1	1
Cuban exiles	1	–	–	–	1
Soviets	–	1	–	–	1
West	–	–	1	–	1
TOTAL	4	7	9	2	22

B. Interests Criticized

	25–31 August	1–30 September	1–22 October	23–29 October	Total
NYT					
Republicans	–	2	–	–	2
Congress	–	1	–	–	1
Cuba	–	2	1	–	3
Cuban exiles	–	1	–	–	1
Soviets	–	6	1	5	12
UN	–	–	–	2	2
TOTAL	–	12	2	7	21
WP					
Republicans	–	–	1	1	2
Democrats	–	–	2	–	2
Cuba	–	–	1	–	1
Soviets	–	1	2	2	5
TOTAL	–	1	6	3	10
SFEx					
U.S. official	1	5	–	–	6
Other Lat. Amer.	–	–	1	–	1
Press	–	1	–	1	2
Soviets	–	2	–	2	4
OAS	–	–	1	–	1
West	–	1	–	–	1
Neutrals	–	–	1	–	1
TOTAL	1	9	3	3	16
CT					
U.S. official	–	7	1	–	8
Congress	–	1	–	–	1
Cuba	–	–	–	1	1
Cuban exiles	1	–	–	–	1
Soviets	–	1	–	2	3
UN	–	–	–	2	2
OAS	–	1	–	–	1
TOTAL	1	10	1	5	17
SLPD					
Republicans	–	8	2	1	11
Congress	–	–	1	–	1
Cuba	–	–	1	–	1
Cuban exiles	1	–	–	–	1
Soviets	–	–	–	1	1
TOTAL	1	8	4	2	15

4. VIETNAM

A. Precipitating Events

	1–20 Aug.	21 Aug.– 2 Sept.	3 Sept.– 2 Oct.	3 Oct.– 1 Nov.	2–10 Nov.	Total
NYT						
U.S. official	–	1	3	5	1	10
South Viet. offs.	2	3	2	2	3	12
South Viet. Buddhists	1	–	–	1	–	2
France	–	1	1	–	–	2
Cambodia	–	1	–	–	–	1
Democrats	–	–	2	1	–	3
TOTAL	3	6	8	9	4	30
WP						
U.S. official	–	1	4	2	–	7
South Viet. offs.	1	3	–	1	2	7
South Viet. Buddhists	1	–	–	–	–	1
TOTAL	2	4	4	3	2	15
SFEx						
U.S. official	–	–	–	3	–	3
South Viet. offs.	–	1	–	4	2	7
South Viet. Buddhists	–	–	–	1	–	1
Press	–	–	2	2	–	4
UN	–	–	1	–	–	1
TOTAL	–	1	3	10	2	16
CT						
U.S. official	–	–	4	2	2	8
South Viet. offs.	–	1	–	2	1	4
France	–	–	1	–	–	1
Cong. report	–	–	1	–	–	1
Chicago Charity Campaign	–	–	–	1	–	1
TOTAL	–	1	6	5	3	15
SLPD						
U.S. official	1	1	6	2	–	10
South Viet. offs.	1	4	1	4	3	13
South Viet. Buddhists	–	–	–	1	–	1
France	–	1	–	–	–	1
Democrats	–	–	1	–	–	1
Republicans	–	–	1	1	–	2
Vatican	–	–	1	–	–	1
South Viet. exiles	–	–	–	1	–	1
TOTAL	2	6	10	9	3	30

B. Interests Criticized

	1–20 Aug.	21 Aug.– 2 Sept.	3 Sept.– 2 Oct.	3 Oct.– 1 Nov.	2–10 Nov.	Total
NYT						
U.S. official	–	2	2	4	–	8
South Viet. offs.	3	5	5	4	3	20
France	–	1	–	–	–	1
Cambodia	–	1	–	–	–	1
Democrats	–	–	1	–	–	1
TOTAL	3	9	7	8	3	31
WP						
U.S. official	–	1	3	3	1	8
South Viet. offs.	2	3	2	1	2	10
France	–	1	–	–	–	1
Congress	–	–	–	1	–	1
TOTAL	2	5	5	5	3	20
SFEx						
U.S. official	–	–	–	3	1	4
South Viet. offs.	–	1	1	4	–	6
South Viet. Buddhists	–	–	–	1	–	1
U.S. liberals	–	–	1	–	–	1
UN	–	–	1	–	–	1
Press	–	–	–	1	–	1
TOTAL	–	1	3	9	–	14
CT						
U.S. official	–	–	7	3	3	13
South Viet. offs.	–	1	–	1	–	2
Democrats	–	–	–	1	–	1
Movie actors	–	–	–	1	–	1
Press	–	–	–	–	1	1
TOTAL	–	1	7	6	4	18
SLPD						
U.S. official	1	2	2	2	–	7
South Viet. offs.	1	4	6	8	3	22
France	–	1	1	–	–	2
Republicans	–	–	–	1	–	1
U.S. conservatives	–	–	–	–	2	2
TOTAL	2	7	9	11	5	34

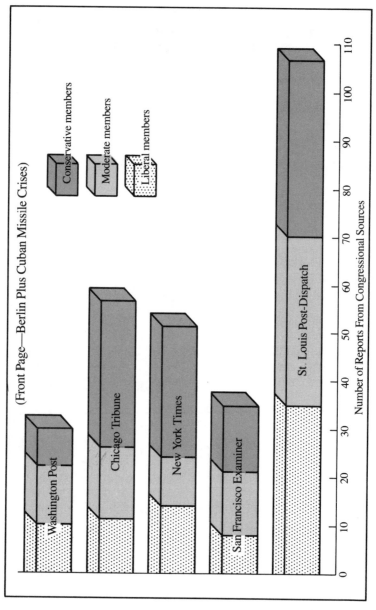

(Front Page—Berlin Plus Cuban Missile Crises)

Conservative members

Moderate members

Liberal members

Washington Post

Chicago Tribune

New York Times

San Francisco Examiner

St. Louis Post-Dispatch

Number of Reports From Congressional Sources

0   10   20   30   40   50   60   70   80   90   100   110

Figure 9. Breakdown of Congressional Sources by Ideological Reputation*

Appendix V.
Breakdown of Congressional
Sources by Ideological Reputation

Figure 9 illustrates the five papers' usage of congressional sources by ideological reputation for the two crises that most concerned the members of Congress. The figure specifically illustrates ideological balance on the part of two newspapers, the *Post-Dispatch* and the *Examiner*. In contrast, the *Tribune* and the *Times* quoted more conservatives. In their adversarial role during the Berlin and Cuban crises, congressional conservatives were clearly making news, though certainly not on the same level as the president.

Clear tilting in the sense of giving favored front-page treatment to congressional sources of a particular ideological reputation occurred most markedly in the case of the *Tribune*, in which conservatives nearly equaled the combined total of moderates and liberals (twenty-seven out of a total of fifty-six sources). The *Post* displayed a less marked tendency to lean in the opposite direction during this period; conservatives received little front-page coverage.

Some of the differences between ideological source usage in the *Post* and *Tribune* could certainly have occurred because more politicians of the various persuasions were making news in the vastly different political environments of Washington and Chicago. It is unlikely that this factor explains all the difference, however, because many of the senators and congressmen were quoted making statements in Washington over the five-month period included in this analysis. They were frequently covered by Washington-based reporters seeking a reaction to presidential initiatives.

Figure 9 also illustrates another phenomenon, the fact that, except for the

*(note to figure) For this graph, the authors formulated an ideological index based on the indices of the leading conservative and liberal interest groups that rated senators and representatives at the time. These were, on the conservative side, the Civic Affairs Associates (CAA) and the Americans for Constitutional Actions (ACA). On the liberal side, the rating organizations were the Americans for Democratic Action (ADA) and the Committee on Political Education, AFL-CIO (COPE). Each group gave members of Congress a rating based on the percentage of times he or she voted on the side of an issue the group favored.

The authors have attached a label to each senator and representative rated during the 1961–62 period. A *conservative* was considered to be one whose average CAA and ACA rating was 70 percent or over; a *liberal*, one whose ADA and COPE rating was 70 percent or over; and a *moderate*, one who did not have 70 percent on either side.

Except for COPE, all these organizations included foreign policy issues in their indices. For an enumeration of the issues, see "Roll Call Used, Positions Taken by Groups Rating Congress," *Congressional Quarterly Fact Sheet, On Groups Rating Congressmen*, week ending 26 October 1962, page 2019. For the indices themselves, see "How Special Interest Groups Rate Representatives" and "How Special Interest Groups Rate Senators," ibid., pages 2022 and 2024, respectively.

Examiner, the outlying papers turned to congressional sources more frequently than did the *Washington Post* and the *New York Times*. The outlying *Post-Dispatch* used congressional sources twice as frequently as its nearest competitor, which gave it a unique status as the newspaper most reliant on congressional sources in its foreign policy coverage.

Note on Methodology

To assess the extent of presidential influence on the press, this study uses a content analysis of the coverage of foreign policy issues for selected periods in five newspapers: *New York Times, Washington Post, Chicago Tribune, St. Louis Post-Dispatch*, and *San Francisco Examiner*. All front-page and inside-page stories that contained some comment about the relevant issue, though the whole story need not have been about it, have been analyzed. Sources—the best available measure of influence on news coverage—have been counted. Many stories had more than one source.

Page-one sources, separated from inside-page sources for purposes of the analysis, have a special importance both in terms of the editorial values they suggest and in terms of probable impact on the public and officials. Because page-one stories usually continue and conclude on inside pages, their sources were considered page-one sources whether they appeared at the beginning of the story on page one or at the end on the inside page.

Inside-page sources were counted and evaluated as well, however, because they also convey information about journalistic judgments and because knowing what information about an issue was available on inside pages is also important. It has thus been possible to learn a good deal about why a foreign policy issue becomes a page-one story, whether as a result of presidential initiative or for other reasons.

Sources were divided into the following categories:

1. *Foreign*—foreign government officials in other nations or in embassies in the United States; international agencies; and nongovernmental foreign sources, such as religious leaders and newspapers. Western European sources include officials from unspecified "Western" nations, and could thus include some U.S. officials.

2. *Official U.S.*—White House personnel, including the president and his staff; diplomatic personnel, including State Department officials in the United States or in its embassies abroad; the military, including Defense Department officials and military officers both active and retired; "others," including officials in such agencies as CIA, VOA, and AID; and unidentified sources, often designated by such terms as "high American officials" and "administration sources."

3. *Domestic Political*—includes such categories as Democrats—national; Democrats—state and local; Republicans—national; Re-

publicans—state and local; unspecified members of Congress; and congressional action. This category also includes political figures who were out of office (e.g., former President Eisenhower).

4. *Interest Groups*—includes such categories as business, labor, religious, patriotic, and peace groups. Includes groups of exiles seeking to influence U.S. foreign policy who live in America, such as the Cuban exiles.

5. *Public Opinion*—includes such categories as polls, nonsystematic random interviews, statements by academics, and individual statements of opinion.

6. *Press* (U.S.)—includes reporters' personal experiences and quotations from other newspapers, periodicals, or journalists.

These categories were mutually exclusive, and it was usually possible to include almost all sources in one of them. This was possible because editors require source specification, if not by name, as closely by institutional affiliation as possible. It was thus usually possible even to determine whether an unidentified source was an unidentified foreign source or an unidentified U.S. official or domestic political source. In cases where this was not possible, checks were made through interviews to determine source categories, and source figures were adjusted accordingly. In cases where no checks were possible and where a term such as "informed sources" was used in a context that allowed no determination of source category to be made, the decision was made not to include the source.

The approach that has been used differs from the frequently used symbol and line measurement approaches to newspaper content analysis. Line measurement has not been used because it would be extremely difficult to assign an accurate numerical value to each source in an article that includes a multiplicity of them. It has also been assumed that space-related values will average out in a study that includes a large number of sources and makes a clear distinction between page-one and inside-page sources. A total of 4,224 front-page and 7,024 inside-page sources have been analyzed; these appeared in 1,819 page-one and 4,675 inside-page news stories in the five newspapers. Given its detailed coverage of foreign and official news, it is not surprising that the *Times* had nearly twice the number of stories as any of the other papers: 2,116 in the *Times*, 1,254 in the *Examiner*, 1,127 in the *Post*, 1,030 in the *Tribune*, and 967 in the *Post-Dispatch*. For a breakdown of the 4,224 page-one and 7,024 inside-page sources into categories, see appendixes I–III.

The symbol approach has been used in other studies to document the flow of ideas. By recording a symbol, such as "democracy," and determining whether it is used in a context of "for," "against," or "neutral," studies such as those by Ithiel de Sola Pool provide a record of newspaper attitudes. One of the assumptions of such studies has been accepted for this study: frequency of occurrence is a significant measure. Sources rather than symbols have been selected for this analysis of news coverage, however, because what is significant about news coverage in it is more where reporters obtained their material than how they felt about it.

For purposes of editorial analysis, in contrast, the concern was with how the editors felt about the issues; thus their attitudes were measured. Rather than using the categories "for," "against," and "neutral," which are sometimes used, editorials were analyzed in only one dimension: whether or not they were critical of a particular individual or institution's position. This approach simplifies comparison and reflects the primary reason why many editorials are written: to criticize someone at home or abroad. To determine influence affecting editorial decisions, there was noted for each editorial what was called the *precipitating event*, the event or events that spurred its writing. These events were delineated into categories: whether they were official American actions, foreign ones, domestic political ones, and so on. Just how each newspaper expressed its position and how that changed over time were analyzed in the context of changing policy positions on the part of the policy-making and evaluating institutions to which the newspapers responded.

Finally, every column relating to each of the crises was considered in relation to the kinds of pressure the columnist was trying to bring to bear on the president for a preferred course of action. Unlike the news stories and editorials, these were not analyzed quantitatively, partly because the nationally syndicated columnists did not represent any one newspaper's editorial viewpoint. But columnists like Joseph Alsop, Walter Lippmann, and James Reston were quite important both in official Washington and among other Americans interested in foreign affairs in the early 1960s, and their views formed an integral part of this study.

Notes

Chapter 1

1. Letters and Memoranda for Theodore C. Sorensen Papers, JFK Speech Files, 1961–63, University of North Carolina Speech, 12 October 1961, John F. Kennedy Library. For further discussion of this incident, see Montague Kern, "The Presidency and the Press: John F. Kennedy's Foreign Policy Crises and the Politics of Newspaper Coverage" (Ph.D. diss., Johns Hopkins University School of Advanced International Studies, 1979), pp. 290–92. This dissertation established the basic framework for this book, including initial detailed analyses of the Laotian, Berlin, and Cuban crises.

2. Sylvester is quoted in Sorensen, *Kennedy*, p. 359. Two of the journalists who criticized the administration for "news management" were Hanson Baldwin and Arthur Krock, both of the *New York Times*. See Baldwin, "Managed News," *Atlantic* 211 (April 1963): 53–59; and Krock, "Mr. Kennedy's Management of the News," *Fortune* 67 (March 1963): 82, 199–202. Other critics were James Colburn of the Committee on the Freedom of Information of the American Society of Newspaper Editors and Clark Mollenhoff of the Cowles papers. Otherwise, the press tended to follow Reston's support for the president. The Reston quote appears in "How to Make Things Worse than They Really Are," *New York Times*, 21 November 1962, p. 30.

3. See a letter to the president from Douglass Cater, 29 October 1962 and the president's reply of 30 October 1962, P.O.F. Special Correspondence No. 28, Douglass Cater, Kennedy Library. The "now-it-can-be-told" articles appeared first in the *New York Times*, then in the *Washington Post, Time, Life, Readers Digest, Look*, and the *Saturday Evening Post*. See also Memorandum to Theodore C. Sorensen from C. J. Lewin, 5 November 1962, Sorensen Papers, Box 37, Kennedy Library.

4. Shannon, "The Censors," *New York Post*, 4 November 1962, op ed page. For a detailed discussion of Kennedy's overall press strategies and of his specific policies following the Cuban missile crisis, see Kern, "The Presidency and the Press," chapter 2 and pp. 397–411. On Kennedy's careful preparation for news conferences, see Pierre Salinger, *With Kennedy*, p. 140.

5. Schneider is quoted in Presidential Office File #15 503–1/ST #1 ST 40–ST 42, Kennedy Library.

6. Chalmers M. Roberts, comments at conference of the Society for Historians of American Foreign Relations, Washington, D.C., 1 August 1981.

7. Krock used the term "assiduousness" to sum up Kennedy's relationship with the press. Krock, *Memoirs*, p. 181. On attitudes toward presidential authority during the 1950s and early 1960s, see Arthur M. Schlesinger, Jr., *The Imperial Presidency*, pp. 127–76.

8. Bundy, interview in New York, N.Y., 9 July 1978.

9. Two recent references to what political scientist Robert Locander calls "John Kennedy's press management successes" are in Locander, "The Adversary Relation-

ship: A New Look at an Old Idea," *Presidential Studies Quarterly* 9 (Summer 1979): 267–68; and David Halberstam, *The Powers That Be*, p. 352, passim.

10. Cater, *The Fourth Branch of Government*; Reston, *The Artillery of the Press*, pp. 42–59. The Alsop quote is from "Options: Joseph Alsop Interview with Barbara Newman," National Public Radio, 1975 (transcript).

11. Recent books on Roosevelt's and Nixon's often stormy relationships with the press are Graham J. White, *FDR and the Press*; and William E. Porter, *Assault on the Media*. The quote is from Hilsman, *The Politics of Policymaking in Defense and Foreign Affairs*, p. 114.

12. For foreign coverage, see John A. Lent, "Foreign News in the American Media," *Journal of Communication* 27 (Winter 1977): 46–51; and Barry Rubin, "International News and the American Media," in Dante B. Fascell, ed., *International News*. See also Bernard C. Cohen, *The Press and Foreign Policy*.

For a challenge to the view of presidential dominance in the domestic area, see David L. Paletz and Robert M. Entman, "Presidents, Power, and the Press," *Presidential Studies Quarterly* 10 (Summer 1980): 416–26. For a recent view emphasizing cycles in the relationship, see Michael Baruch Grossman and Martha Joynt Kumar, *Portraying the President*.

13. The Korean example is cited in James Aronson, *The Press and the Cold War*, p. 107. He states: "Not one major daily newspaper opposed the intervention in Korea or disputed the official version that the North Koreans had instigated the fighting." In *The Press and Foreign Policy*, Bernard C. Cohen also succumbs frequently to the tendency toward overgeneralization in analyzing press coverage of foreign affairs.

14. For elucidation of these five groupings and also the administration, or "official U.S.," category, see the Note on Methodology, which also discusses the types of content analysis used in analyzing news stories and editorials.

15. For a fuller discussion of the problem of proving press influence on presidential decision making, see Kern, "The Presidency and the Press," pp. 5–7.

16. Bundy interview.

17. For leading examples of organizational theory, see Edward J. Epstein, *News from Nowhere*; and Leon V. Sigal, *Reporters and Officials*. For pack journalism, see Doris A. Graber, "Press Coverage Patterns of Campaign News: The 1968 Presidential Race," *Public Opinion Quarterly* 48 (Autumn 1971): 502–11; and for another example of writing which assumes that the press is a homogeneous entity, see American Enterprise Institute Forum, *The Press and Public Policy*.

18. Cohen, *The Press and Foreign Policy*, pp. 124–30.

19. Wiggins, interview in Ellsworth, Maine, 24 August 1978.

20. Sigal's pioneering *Reporters and Officials* is an example of a study that is based almost exclusively on the two leading Washington-oriented papers, the *Times* and *Post*.

21. Grossman and Kumar, *Portraying the President*, p. 209.

22. According to the frequent Gallup polls relating to presidential popularity, Kennedy dropped below 61 percent in public approval only once during his administration, only to 59 percent in October 1963. None of Kennedy's four successors was able to maintain even a 50-percent approval rating throughout his service as president. For Kennedy's ratings, see George H. Gallup, *The Gallup Poll*, 3: 1707–1850.

23. Concern about a Soviet threat had been the basis of American foreign policy since the Truman years, and this continued to be true in 1961–62. This apprehension was shared by the two segments of the American public that have been isolated by public opinion analysts: the elite and mass. Indicating the cold war attitudes of the time, the dominant foreign policy issues, according to the American Institute of Public Opinion survey of 8 February 1961, were the threat of war and relations with the Soviet Union. See Ralph B. Levering, *The Public and American Foreign Policy*, pp. 111–16.

Chapter 2

1. In the *Saturday Review* poll, the *Times* finished first, the *Post-Dispatch* fourth, the *Post* sixth, and the *Tribune* ninth. In the Bernays poll of publishers, the *Times* again finished first, the *Post-Dispatch* second, the *Post* seventh, and the *Tribune* again was ninth. See John Tebbel, "Rating the American Newspaper—Part I," *Saturday Review* 44 (13 May 1961): 59–61; and Ernest C. Hynds, *American Newspapers in the 1970s*, p. 257.

2. For the number of each newspaper's foreign correspondents, see John Wilhelm, "The Reappearing Foreign Correspondent," *Journalism Quarterly* 40 (Spring 1963): 150.

3. Wicker, interview in New York, N.Y., 28 June 1978. Elucidation of Rovere's views can be found in Richard H. Rovere, *The American Establishment*, pp. 3–21. Ithiel de Sola Pool, who compared the *Times* with other newspapers such as *Pravda* and the *Times* of London, views it as an "establishment" newspaper because of its relationship to government. He described the *Times* as having "some of the traits of the semiofficial papers in more politicized countries." Its reporters have special entree to key political figures, and its columns are often used for covert propaganda or for trial balloons in statements commonly attributed to "an official source" or "usually reliable sources." See de Sola Pool, *The Prestige Papers*, p. 62.

4. The reporters, columnists, and editors of the *Times* who wrote on national and international affairs in the early 1960s were almost exclusively male; hence the contemporary use of "*Times*men." A rare exception was Marjorie Hunter of the Washington bureau. The staffs of other papers were also overwhelmingly male.

5. Szulc said both in his testimony to a Senate committee in 1975 and in an interview with the authors at Washington, D.C., 3 February 1978, that he went to the White House on the morning of 9 November 1961 with Richard Goodwin of the State Department to talk about a job in the administration. Szulc's recollection of Kennedy's asking him whether or not Castro should be assassinated appears in the report of the Senate's Select Committee to Study Governmental Operations, *Alleged Assassination Plots Involving Foreign Leaders*, p. 138.

6. Wallace Carroll, interview in Sparta, N.C., 11 June 1977; E. W. Kenworthy, interview in Washington, D.C., 15 July 1978.

7. Carroll, in his interview with the authors, commented that the *Times* did not have to worry about being cut off because "officials want their views to appear in the *Times*"; Karl Meyer, interview in New York, N.Y., 29 June 1978.

8. Robert Estabrook, interview in Lakeville, Conn., 30 June 1978. For additional information on the *Post* during these years, see Chalmers M. Roberts, *The Washington Post*; and Halberstam, *The Powers That Be*.

9. Wiggins interview; Meyer interview.

10. Kenworthy interview; Philip Graham appointment book; Roberts, interview in Washington, D.C., 19 June 1978; Alfred Friendly, interview in Washington, D.C., 7 July 1978. The authors are grateful to Roberts for helping obtain access to the appointment book through Katherine Graham.

11. Friendly interview; Estabrook interview. Estabrook, who became chief foreign correspondent after leaving the position of editor of the editorial page in 1961, stressed the *Post*'s financial constraints, as did Friendly and Wiggins.

12. Meyer interview; Dean Rusk, interview in Athens, Ga., 23 March 1979.

13. The total number of sources cited by the *Times* during the four crises—3,472—was much higher than the *Post-Dispatch*'s 2,178. This difference in depth of coverage largely resulted from the *Times*'s greater resources, especially for covering foreign news.

14. Dudman, interview in Washington, D.C., 2 February 1978. For examples of the *Post-Dispatch*'s hard-hitting reporting, see Dudman's series on Latin America in 1962 and on Vietnam in 1963.

15. Childs, interview in Washington, D.C., 2 February 1978; Robert Lasch, telephone interview, 24 June 1978.

16. Childs interview.

17. Lasch interview; Childs interview; "Cuba Conference Notes and Doodles," October 1962 to 12 November 1962, and Note by Major General Chester "Ted" Clifton, 22 October 1962, P.O.F., Countries No. 115, Kennedy Library.

18. Robert Young, interview in Washington, D.C., 2 February 1978.

19. Young interview; Laurence Burd, interview in Bethesda, Md., 1 April 1978.

20. Trohan, interview in Columbia, Md., 6 April 1978; William F. Anderson, telephone interview, 23 January 1978.

21. George Morgenstern, telephone interview, 17 June 1978.

22. Trohan, "Report from Washington," *Chicago Tribune*, 1 February 1961, p. 10.

23. Burd interview; Young interview.

24. Susan C. Clemmer, interview in Washington, D.C., 15 June 1978. She served on the editorial staff of the *Chicago Daily Calumet*.

25. For a discussion of the hostility between the *Tribune* and Democratic administrations and of the press rivalry in Chicago, see "Field Bids to Fan Chicago Newspaper War," *Business Week* (28 February 1959): 56–58, 63. Anderson and Trohan also discussed this subject in their interviews.

26. While the *Tribune* was being cut off, William Stoneman of the *Daily News* received an interview with Kennedy before leaving to become his paper's correspondent in West Germany. The able chief Washington correspondent, Peter Lisagor, grew in importance during the Kennedy years. See Lisagor, oral history interview with Ronald J. Grele in Washington, D.C., 22 April 1966, Kennedy Library.

27. *Selections from the Writings and Speeches of William Randolph Hearst*, p. 308. This book was loaned to the authors by Charles L. Gould, the *Examiner*'s publisher during the early 1960s and a strong admirer of Hearst.

28. Gould, written response to authors' questions, 1 August 1978; Hearst, interview

in New York, N.Y., 28 June 1978; Hearst oral history interview with James A. Oesterle in New York, N.Y., 25 March 1971, Kennedy Library. Hearst's education in a military academy and his work as a military correspondent during World War II may have contributed to his predisposition to consult the military in times of crisis, an approach that emerged clearly in his editorials. In such a situation, he told the authors, "our military should be consulted damn well."

29. Means, interview in Washington, D.C., 2 June 1978; Eastham, interview in Washington, D.C., 17 July 1978; Gould written response. Fierce competition in circulation with the *San Francisco Chronicle* may also have been a factor.

30. The two popular papers, the *Tribune* and *Examiner*, were the lowest in total sources used: 1,640 for the former and 1,884 for the latter. The *Examiner*, reflecting its constituency's lack of interest in foreign news, had the lowest overall percentage of foreign sources for each of the four crises. Because it did not attempt a great deal of independent foreign coverage and because it was not as avowedly antiadministration as the *Tribune*, its official U.S. source usage was relatively high, the sources frequently derived from news service stories. Like the *Tribune* an outlying paper more conservative than the administration, the *Examiner*'s percentage of domestic political sources was second only to the *Tribune*. The third outlying paper, the *Post-Dispatch*, was more liberal than the administration and also used more nongovernment domestic sources than the two Washington-oriented papers. See tables 1 and 2.

31. For a detailed discussion of overall differences in source usage, see Kern, "The Presidency and the Press," pp. 79–96. For an analysis of official U.S. source usage by newspaper, see especially pages 86–92.

Chapter 3

1. See Charles A. Stevenson, *The End of Nowhere*, pp. 130–77, for a useful analysis of United States policy during this period.

2. Undated transition letter from Alsop to "Jack," P.O.F., Special Correspondence No. 27, Joseph Alsop, Kennedy Library.

3. Alsop, interview in Washington, D.C., 29 April 1978.

4. In his interview, Alsop discussed his involvement with the president during critical periods.

5. Alsop interview.

6. Alsop interview; Childs, interview in Washington, D.C., 8 February 1978.

7. Sorensen, *Kennedy*, p. 722.

8. "New Peace Moves for Laos Near," *San Francisco Examiner*, 18 February 1961, p. 2; "King of Laos Proclaims Neutrality, Asks Peace," ibid., 20 February 1961, p. 13; "Reds Cut Key Laos Road in Big Victory," ibid., 12 March 1961, p. 1.

9. Pearce, telephone interview, 14 July 1978.

10. Wood, "Rugged Country Confronts American Troops if Called to Laos: Reporter Recalls Three Visits to Nation," *Chicago Tribune*, 7 January 1961, p. 9.

11. "Laos Admits Lying for Aid; Premier Says Wolf Cry Is Propaganda," *Chicago Tribune*, 27 January 1961, p. 1; "Neutral Laos Bid Discussed by Rusk, Red," ibid., 21 February 1961, p. 8; "Communist Threats in Cuba and Laos," ibid., 6 March 1961, p. 6. The *Tribune*'s only other editorial of the period is also critical of American diplo-

matic efforts: "If these people (Ambassador Harriman in particular) were kept at home, their capacity for imprudent statements and mischief making would be substantially reduced." Last week, Ambassador Thompson "chased off through the snows of Siberia after Premier Khrushchev in order to hand the Soviet dictator a personal note from Kennedy." "Itinerant Diplomacy," ibid., 12 March 1961, p. 20.

12. Morgenstern interview.

13. Reston expressed this view in "The Biggest Story in the World," *New Republic* 148 (4 May 1963): 15–17. He was published in this periodical because of the *Times* newspaper strike.

14. Jorden, "U.S. Envoy Briefs Kennedy on Laos," *New York Times*, 4 February 1961, p. 1.

15. Winthrop Brown, oral history interview with Larry T. Hackman in Washington, D.C., 1 February 1968, Kennedy Library.

16. Nevard, "Laos Rebel Move Linked to Parley, Forming of a Rival Regime Viewed as Step Toward Peace Negotiations," *New York Times*, 5 February 1961, p. 30.

17. "Crisis in Laos," *New York Times*, 4 February 1961, p. 18.

18. Kenworthy interview. Indicating the cold war attitudes of the time, the dominant foreign policy issues according to the American Institute of Public Opinion (#641) as of 8 February 1961 were the threat of war and relations with the Soviet Union. On 3 November 1961, the question was asked (#651) in Great Britain and the United States: Would the respondent prefer to fight an all-out nuclear war or live under Communist rule? Eighty-one percent of the respondents in the United States said "fight a nuclear war" as compared with 21 percent in Great Britain.

19. Wilde, "Russian Arms Go to Laos in Huge Build-up; Artillery, Armor," *New York Times*, 3 March 1961, p. 1. "Hundreds of tons" of material were involved. Souvanna Phouma's government was seen as a front for communists intent on taking over the country. Wilde, however, based the article on a visit to Phong Savan with Souvanna Phouma, who insisted that two Western journalists accompany him despite Soviet objections. "Red Gains in Laos," ibid., 3 March 1961, p. 26.

20. See Kern, "The Presidency and the Press," p. 432.

21. Alsop, "The Crunch," *Washington Post*, 6 March 1961, p. 13.

22. Beech, interview in Washington, D.C., 28 March 1978; Beech, "Villain Role Seen Certain for U.S. in History of Laotian Civil War," *Washington Post*, 22 January 1961, p. 14.

23. Estabrook interview.

24. Estabrook interview.

25. Estabrook interview.

26. Dudman interview.

27. Dudman interview.

28. "Time for a New Laos Policy," *St. Louis Post-Dispatch*, 24 January 1961, p. B2.

29. "Progress on Laos," *St. Louis Post-Dispatch*, 23 February 1961, p. B2.

30. "Russians on the Spot in Laos," *St. Louis Post-Dispatch*, 13 March 1961, p. C2; Lasch interview.

Chapter 4

1. Bundy interview.

2. Carroll, "U.S. Ready to Face All Risks to Bar Red Rule of Laos," *New York Times*, 21 March 1961, p. 1; Kenworthy interview.

3. Jorden, "West Will Offer New Plan to Test Moscow on Laos; U.S. Revises Stand; Backs Control Unit—Kennedy Will Make Statement Today," *New York Times*, 23 March 1961, p. 1

4. Roberts, "Big Stick Policy: Kennedy Ties Negotiations to Reds' Behavior," *Washington Post*, 18 March 1961, p. 11.

5. Alsop, "Behind the Public Face," *Washington Post*, 22 March 1961, p. 15.

6. Childs, "Russia Is Told U.S. Can't Accept Military Takeover in Laos: Decision Now Up to Khrushchev," *St. Louis Post-Dispatch*, 20 March 1961, p. C1.

7. Laos ranked second in terms of official sources to the *Washington Post* on page one and first on the inside pages. See appendix II for page-one comparisons for the 16–31 March period.

8. During the final Eisenhower crisis, the *Examiner* editorially favored a "solid, pro-Western" Laos as opposed to the "neutralist" Laos supported by the Allies, but urged that intervention be limited to money, transportation, and supplies. If SEATO should become involved, the paper argued, the Asian nations that had more to lose should supply the troops. Earlier, Hearst had stated his view that United States aid money was being wasted in Laos. After the president's speech on 23 March Hearst did not revive these reservations in his front-page editorials. See his front-page editorials: "Toast to an End and a Beginning," *San Francisco Examiner*, 1 January 1961; and "Laos a 'Domino' in Asian Crisis," ibid., 26 March 1961. See also "No U.S. Troops" ibid., 5 January 1961, sec. II, p. 2.

9. Baldwin, "The Position of Laos," *New York Times*, 6 January 1961, p. 1; Baldwin, "Troubled Laos Now the Vortex of the East-West Struggle," ibid., 26 March 1961, sec. 4, p. 3.

10. "A New War for Laos?" *Chicago Tribune*, 24 March 1961, p. 10.

11. Murray Ilson, "Goldwater Supports President in Firm Stand on Laos Crisis," *New York Times*, 25 March 1961, p. 2.

12. "Poll Shows Chicagoans Fear of War in Laos: Chicagoans Hope for a Solution," *Chicago Tribune*, 25 March 1961, p. 4; Morgenstern interview. Morgenstern did not believe that constituency pressure contributed to the *Tribune*'s stance.

13. Roberts, unpublished article written 9 April 1961, based on talks with President Kennedy, 6 April 1961, loaned to the authors by Roberts; Stevenson, *End of Nowhere*, p. 47.

14. Lawrence, "Kennedy and Macmillan Appeal to Soviets to Back Neutral Laos; Rusk Asks SEATO to Meet Crisis; Full Agreement; President Holds Talks with British Chief at Key West," *New York Times*, 27 March 1961, p. 4.

15. Ibid.

16. Burd interview; "Four Newsmen Kept from 'Briefing'; Explanation Is Asked after Meeting with Bohlen," *Baltimore Sun*, 28 March 1961, p. 2.

17. Trohan, "Report from Washington," *Chicago Tribune*, 3 April 1961, p. 3.

18. A fuller discussion of source usage on Laos is included in chapter 5.

Chapter 5

1. Murray Marder, "GOP Wants No Reds in Any Laos Regime," *Washington Post*, 30 March 1961, p. 10; "Peiping to Send Troops if SEATO Does, Foreign Minister Says," *St. Louis Post-Dispatch*, 3 April 1961, p. 1.

2. Marder, "GOP Wants No Reds."

3. Robert C. Albright, "GOP Mapping Stand on Laos," *Washington Post*, 8 April 1961, p. 2; Warren Duffee, "Senator Scott Raps Laos Coalition," ibid., 9 April 1961, p. 6; "House GOP Back 'Ev and Charlie' Views," ibid., 12 April 1961, p. 2.

4. "Background Dinner with General Lyman L. Lemnitzer," 29 March 1961, and "Background Luncheon with Charles E. Bohlen," 27 March 1961, Estabrook Papers, loaned to the authors by Estabrook.

5. Schlesinger, *Robert Kennedy and His Times*, p. 703.

6. Brown oral history interview.

7. "The Thaw," *Chicago Tribune*, 8 April 1961, p. 10.

8. "How Bad Is Bad," *San Francisco Examiner*, 6 April 1961, p. 30. See appendix IV for a breakdown of *Examiner* editorials, including events which precipitated the editorials and interests criticized during this period.

9. "Dallying on Laos," *Washington Post*, 28 March 1961, p. 10; Estabrook interview.

10. Roberts, " 'Solution' for Laos Carries Stiff Price," *Washington Post*, 28 March 1961, p. 1.

11. Roberts, *First Rough Draft*, p. 192.

12. Ibid., pp. 192, 193.

13. "O Souvanna," *Washington Post*, 13 April 1961, p. 18; "Three Months of Kennedy," ibid., 20 April 1961, p. 18.

14. Roberts, "An Eisenhower Domino Plagues His Successor," *Washington Post*, 9 April 1961, p. E1.

15. Alsop, "Marshal Sarit's Fears," *Washington Post*, 3 April 1961, p. 11; Alsop, "Colonel Thao's Election Day," ibid., 11 April 1961, p. 13; Alsop, "April Fool for Col. Hung," ibid., 12 April 1961, p. 17. See also Alsop, "Colonel Thao's War," ibid., 14 April 1961, p. 15.

16. J. William Fulbright, Memorandum to the President 24 March, received 27 March 1961, Box 128, P.O.F., Vietnam, 1961, Kennedy Library.

17. The percentages of total coverage represented by domestic political sources during the latter March period are for page one and inside pages, respectively 7 and 14 percent; for 1–15 April they are, respectively, 6 and 9 percent. See appendix II for page-one breakdown by newspaper.

18. There were a total of sixteen front-page sources for 16–31 March and six for 1–15 April. The inside-page sources numbered thirty-eight for 16–31 March and twelve for the later period.

19. "Laos Deal Critics Still Sound Off," *San Francisco Examiner*, 7 April 1961, p. 2.

20. Official U.S. sources ran a strong second to foreign sources, especially on page one, but domestic political never reached 10 percent on page one or 15 percent on inside pages. See appendixes II and III for more detailed breakdowns.

21. "Background Luncheon with Charles E. Bohlen at the Invitation of Ernest Lindley," 27 March 1961, Estabrook Papers.

22. Alsop, "On the Razor's Edge," *Washington Post*, 13 March 1961, p. 13; Alsop interview; Jorden, "Laos and the West," *New York Times*, 8 January 1961, p. E11.

23. Herbert S. Dinerstein, *The Making of a Missile Crisis*.

Introduction to Part Three

1. See such straw polls as the "Listening Post: Fight for Berlin—if We Must . . . ," *Newsweek* 58 (17 July 1961): 18–20; Paul Olsen, "Should America Risk War in Berlin?" *San Francisco Examiner*, 19 July 1961, p. 14; and Samuel Lubell, "U.S. Public Firm on Berlin," *New York World Telegram and Sun*, 5 July 1961, p. 30. See also pages 61–62 in this book for discussion of a Gallup poll on the issue of general attitudes toward the Berlin issue as well as differences across the country. Pearce interview; Gallup, *The Gallup Poll*, 3:1729, 1734.

2. See the AP stories: "Legion Head Sees War Threat in '61," *New York Times*, 27 June 1961, p. 2; and "Legion Says War Is Inevitable," *San Francisco Examiner*, 29 June 1961, p. 11. See also Kern, "The Presidency and the Press," pp. 186–89, for a more detailed discussion of interest groups.

Chapter 6

1. See Llewellyn Thompson, oral history interview with Elizabeth Donohue in Washington, D.C., 25 March 1964, Kennedy Library.

2. Trohan, "Report from Vienna," *Chicago Tribune*, 10 June 1961, p. 4.

3. Salinger, *With Kennedy*, p. 182; Reston, "Kennedy and Khrushchev Find Limited Laos Accord but Split on Berlin and Key Arms Issues," *New York Times*, 5 June 1961, p. 1; Alsop interview.

4. Bell, oral history interview with Joseph E. O'Connor in Washington, D.C., 16 April 1966, Kennedy Library.

5. Bell, "Vienna Flareup by Khrushchev Set Off by Berlin Issue," *Washington Post*, 9 June 1961, p. 14.

6. "Fear Berlin Showdown by Next Winter," *Chicago Tribune*, 9 June 1961, p. 1; "Reds Set Berlin Deadline; Khrushchev Demands on Kennedy Told; Wanted 3 Power Test Ban Rule," ibid., 11 June 1961, p. 1. Contrast the three page-one stories on 11 June 1961: "Kennedy Proposes Parley on Germany Now," *Washington Post*; Sydney Gruson, "Soviet Proposed Six-Month Delay to U.S.," *New York Times*; and "Reds Set Berlin Deadline, Khrushchev Demands on Kennedy Told, Wanted Three-Power Test Ban Rule," *Chicago Tribune*.

7. "Firm Stand on Berlin Urged by Goldwater," *Chicago Tribune*, 16 June 1961, p. 4; "After Vienna, Berlin," ibid., 10 June 1961, p. 12; "Betrayal at Teheran," ibid., 21 June 1961, p. 10.

8. Roberts interview.

9. Graham appointment book, entry for 10–11 June 1961; Roberts, "Kennedy Courage: President Reflects on the Kind Needed," *Washington Post*, 10 June 1961, p. 9.

10. "Adenauer and Brandt Unite against Nikita, Reject Red Plan for German Pact," *Chicago Tribune*, 12 June 1961, p. 6.

11. For details of how foreign sources influenced each newspaper, see Kern, "The Presidency and the Press," pp. 216–25.

12. Gruson, "U.S. Said to Aim at German Talks," *New York Times*, 14 June 1961, p. 1; Kenworthy interview.

13. See the *San Francisco Examiner* articles based on the interviews: Bob Considine, "Khrushchev's Power—How Far Does It Go?," 9 June 1961, p. 1; Considine, "Task Force Interview: Red China Menaces Russia—Adenauer," 11 June 1961, p. 1; and Serge Fliegers and Pierre J. Huss, "Task Force Berlin Talks," 12 June 1961, p. 1. See also Huss, "Blunt New Khrushchev Orders in Cold War; Blueprint from Russia for Remaking Germany," *San Francisco Examiner*, 14 June 1961, p. 1.

14. Hearst, "Nation's Life at Stake in Six Months," *San Francisco Examiner*, 26 June 1961, p. 1. The article was based on a speech he delivered to the B'nai B'rith.

15. Childs, "Berlin Crisis Has a Time Limit," *Washington Post*, 21 June 1961, p. 18.

16. Alsop, "Chilling—Yet Invigorating," *Washington Post*, 12 June 1961, p. 13.

17. Baker, "British Declare Berlin Stand Is as Firm as Any in West," *Washington Post*, 15 June 1961, p. 12.

18. "Home Warns Reds: U.S.-Britain United," *Chicago Tribune*, 17 June 1961, p. 1. Compare the *Chicago Tribune* editorial "Where Angels Fear to Tread," 2 June 1961, p. 12, which remarks that the British will probably "cut and run," with its assessment in "Lord Home in Chicago," 17 June 1961, p. 12.

19. "British Intentions," *Chicago Tribune*, 28 June 1961, p. 10, which quotes a Reuters 27 June London dispatch that relates this "authoritative" *Times* (London) story; "What's That Again, Lord Home?" *Chicago Tribune*, 27 June 1961, p. 18; "Briton 'Amazed,'" *Chicago Tribune*, 27 June 1961, p. 1. Prime Minister Macmillan took a position before Parliament that, while mentioning "negotiations," referred to the proposals of the Geneva foreign ministers' conference of 1959 as "just and equitable" and reiterated that there was "no question whatever of any modification of British commitments on Berlin." Any talks over Berlin and Germany, he noted in response to a question by British Socialist Desmond Donnelly, must be "real negotiation. We must not be asked to submit to blackmail." See Baker, "Macmillan Is Cheered for Firm Berlin Stand," *Washington Post*, 28 June 1961, p. 15; and Arthur Veysey, "Firm on Berlin: Britain," *Chicago Tribune*, 28 June 1961, p. 1.

20. Macmillan, *Pointing the Way*, pp. 391–92. Another indication of the intensity of the British feeling is found in Baker, "Beleaguered Bastion, IX: British Resent Charge of 'Softness' on Berlin," *Washington Post*, 4 July 1961, p. 1. He reported that the British government was "harassed over continuing reports, mostly in the American press, alleging British weakness."

21. Like those of Alsop and Lippmann, her columns were widely syndicated through the *New York Herald-Tribune*, appearing for example in the *Post-Dispatch* and Hearst papers.

22. Higgins, "The Next to the Last Straw," *New York Herald Tribune*, 19 June 1961, p. 20. See also her comments in "Bonn Puts Faith in JFK Firmness," ibid., 27 June 1961, p. 2. She had a reputation among German journalists in Washington of being "hard to resist" because of her "journalistic intensity." Jan Reifenberg, interview in Washington, D.C., 26 January 1978.

23. William Atwood, "Visit with Walter Lippmann," *Look* 25 (25 April 1961): 100–102 ff. Lippmann, oral history interview with Mrs. Farmer, no place or date,

Kennedy Library. See also Roberts, "Lippmann, on TV, Views the World with Wisdom, Calm Advice," *Washington Post*, 17 June 1961, p. 11.

24. Kissinger to Schlesinger, Arthur Schlesinger File, Kennedy Library.

25. Lisagor oral history interview.

26. Lippmann, "Kennedy Shows Berlin's Importance," *St. Louis Post-Dispatch*, 9 June 1961, p. 3B.

27. Lippmann, "The Problem of Berlin," *St. Louis Post-Dispatch*, 29 June 1961, p. 3B.

28. Three additional op ed pieces by Roberts brought the total to fourteen during this period.

29. "Vienna to Berlin," *New York Times*, 11 June 1961, sec. 4, p. 19; "Khrushchev's Time Limit," ibid., 17 June 1961, p. 29.

30. David Klein, interview in New York, N.Y., 27 June 1978; and Nathaniel Gerstenzang, interview in Maplewood, N.J., 27 June 1978.

31. Sulzberger, "How to Slice the Salami in Berlin," *New York Times*, 19 June 1961, p. 26; Sulzberger, "No Status in the Status Quo," 21 June 1961, ibid., p. 36.

32. Krock, "Berlin Enigma," *New York Times*, 18 June 1961, sec. 4, p. 8; Reston, "Enter 'Naughty Nik' and Exit 'Sweet Nikita,'" ibid., 23 June 1961, p. 28; Schwartz, "The Communist Line Now—Moscow View: Strength of Soviet Indicates That Communism Is the 'Wave of the Future,'" ibid., 18 June 1961, sec. 4, p. 3.

33. "Somber Indeed," *St. Louis Post-Dispatch*, 16 June 1961, p. B2; "Negotiating on Berlin," ibid., 23 June 1961, p. B2.

34. Sulzberger, "Bargaining Points on Berlin," *St. Louis Post-Dispatch*, 13 July 1961, p. B3; "British View on Berlin," (an editorial from the *Manchester Guardian*), ibid., 3 July 1961, p. B2; "Before a Dead End in Berlin: Inflexible Policy Could Mean War—British Editorial Offers Three Points for Negotiation," ibid., 16 July 1961, p. B2. French sources were little used on the Berlin issue, so this point of view has not been discussed in detail.

35. Klein interview; "Bridges Wants U.S. to Reaffirm Policy on Berlin," *St. Louis Post-Dispatch*, 20 June 1961, p. 6; "Lord Home's Message," *Chicago Tribune*, 16 June 1961, p. 12.

36. "Convince Khrushchev We Would Fight for Freedom, Nixon Says," *Washington Post*, 21 June 1961, p. 1.

37. Ibid.; "Salesman for a Cause," *Time*, 23 June 1961, pp. 12–16.

38. The two *Post-Dispatch* editorials favorable to Mansfield were "Negotiating on Berlin," 23 June 1961, p. B2; and "Key to National Survival," 25 June 1961, p. D2. The page-one story in the *Times* on the Mansfield proposal was Baker, "Mansfield Suggests Berlin Be Free City Trusteeship," 15 June 1961.

39. These percentages derive from a total of 27 senators and congressmen quoted on page one and on the inside pages of all newspapers during 1–23 June.

Chapter 7

1. "Kennedy Sees Top Aides in Long Meeting on Berlin," *New York Times*, 24 June 1961, p. 1. In the *Post-Dispatch* of the same day, this meeting drew a three-column headline, "U.S. Firm on Berlin But Not Belligerent," and an article, based largely

on statements by Secretary of Defense Robert McNamara that hinted at a military buildup.

2. Jack Raymond, "Kennedy Calls upon Khrushchev to Let Berlin Decide Its Future; Both Stress Peril, Offer to Talk," *New York Times*, 29 June 1961, p. 1.

3. "Replying to Khrushchev," *New York Times*, 1 July 1961, p. 16; Rusk interview. Rusk indicated the president was interested in negotiations during this period—at least up until 22 June. On this date, Rusk made a public statement designed to encourage the Soviets to "talk some of the fever out of it" which he said had been cleared with Kennedy.

4. The following were the questions and answers: On the question of Berlin, do you think the United States plans to stand firm, or will make further concessions to Russia? Stand firm 68.5%; Make concessions 7.9%; Don't know 23.6%; If it were up to you, would you have the United States stand firm or make concessions to Russia? Stand firm 85.4%; Make concessions 3.5%; Don't know 11.1%; (Asked only of those answering "Stand firm" in Question 2) Would you have the United States go to war if necessary to maintain the status quo in Berlin? Yes 54.6%; No 20.4%; Don't know 25.0%; Has your feeling about the ability of the present Kennedy Administration increased, remained the same, or decreased since January? Increased 30.8%; Remained the same 41.6%; Decreased 17.6%; Don't know, 10%. This poll is located in White House Central File 840-PR-16, Public Opinion Polls, Kennedy Library.

5. "A Policy of Preparedness," *New York Times*, 25 June 1961, p. 8E.

6. "If You Want Peace . . . ," *Newsweek* 58 (3 July 1961): 13–16.

7. David Wise, *New York Herald Tribune*, 5 July 1961, p. 7. Wise received support from "angry military officers" who predicted that the leak would not be traced to uniformed personnel. They pointed out that the published material had been discussed before a large audience in a State Department briefing. Baldwin, "FBI Inquiry into Alleged Leak Viewed as Slap at Pentagon," *St. Louis Post-Dispatch*, 6 July 1961, p. B1. See also T. R. Phillips, "President's Brother Enters Case of Pentagon Leak," ibid., 15 July 1961, p. B1; and John D. Norris, "U.S. Call-up of Reserves Is Considered," *Washington Post*, 12 July 1961, p. 1.

8. Klein interview.

9. For a discussion of the Acheson proposal and who in the government opposed and favored it, see Curtis Cate, *The Ides of August*, pp. 84–85.

10. Memorandum to the president from Senator Mike Mansfield, 17 July 1961, Kennedy Library.

11. Alsop, "Room to Plan," *Washington Post*, 7 July 1961, p. 11. Higgins, "Decision Not to Call National Emergency Now Practical One," *St. Louis Post-Dispatch*, 24 July 1961, p. C1.

12. For a description of O'Donnell's position and of his meeting with Sorensen, see Cate, *Ides of August*, pp. 108–12.

13. Higgins, "Berlin—Crisis for Russians, Too; East German Loyalty Shaky," *San Francisco Examiner*, 3 July 1961, p. 1. The other front-page articles were: Gaston Coblentz, "East Germany—A Fuse That May Backfire on Khrushchev," ibid., 4 July 1962, p. 1; "Khrushchev Orders Hike in Russian War Budget," ibid., 9 July 1962, p. 1; F. H. Bartholomew, "Red Units Roll in Eastern Reich," ibid., 10 July 1962, p. 1; and Coblentz, "Peace Treaty-War Move: Russians Threaten to Mass on West German Border," ibid., 23 July 1962, p. 1.

14. Alsop, "Berlin Viewpoints Swirl about JFK," *San Francisco Examiner*, 26 June 1961, p. 30; Alsop, "A Nuclear War over Berlin?" ibid., 28 June 1961, p. 30; Alsop, "Waiting for a Sign," ibid., 3 July 1961, p. 14; Alsop, "Nikita and Adolf—A Comparison," ibid., 12 July 1961, p. 32; Alsop, "Berlin Decisions Take Too Long," ibid., 14 July 1961, p. 32; Alsop, "Berlin-Last Act Curtain Rising," ibid., 17 July 1961, p. 28; Alsop, "New U.S. Defense Plan for Berlin," ibid., 24 July 1961, p. 32; Alsop, "Odd Episode with a Russ Diplomat," ibid., 26 July 1961, p. 32; Alsop, "New Approach to Berlin Crisis," ibid., 28 July 1961, p. 32. William White, "The Berlin Issue," ibid., 26 June 1961, p. 31; Eric Sevareid, "Russians in a Jam over Berlin," ibid., 8 July 1961, p. 14; White, "Silence on Berlin," ibid., 19 July 1961, p. 31; Kenneth Rexroth, "Facing Up to Berlin," ibid., 23 July 1961, sec. 2, p. 3.

15. The group was the Committee in Support of the Psychological Offensive. Hearst, "Bold Policy Best in Facing Reds" (editorial), *San Francisco Examiner*, 16 July 1961, p. 1. For the percentage of Hearst criticisms as compared with those of other papers, see appendix IV. See also "Support JFK on Berlin, Nixon Urges," *Washington Post*, 1 July 1961, p. 14.

16. Graham appointment book.

17. See, for example, Flora Lewis, "Veiled Bid for Berlin Deal Seen in K Memo," *Washington Post*, 28 June 1961, p. 1; Waverly Root, "Paris Shifts Concern from Africa to Berlin," ibid., 30 June 1961, p. 1; Murray Marder, "East German Air Decree Is Seen as Stage 1 of Pressure Buildup," ibid., 1 July 1961, p. 1; Hans J. Morgenthau, "K Seeks to Make a Legalism of Berlin Issue," ibid., 2 July 1961, "Outlook" section, p. 1; Marder, "Moscow Plays 'Sad Sack' Game in Berlin in Move to Inflict Degrading Blow on West," ibid., 3 July 1961, p. 1.

18. Reston, "Enter 'Naughty Nik' and Exit 'Sweet Nikita,'" *New York Times*, 23 June 1961, p. 28.

19. John Hightower, "Kennedy and Advisors Meeting to Decide What to Do in Berlin Crisis," *St. Louis Post-Dispatch*, 29 June 1961, p. 1.

20. Trohan interview. The dropped sentence read: "I am confident that, given a sincere desire to achieve a peaceful settlement of the issues which still disturb the world's tranquility we can, in our time, reach that peaceful goal which all peoples so ardently desire."

21. Adenauer, "ridiculing" a Brandt suggestion that the Allies invite all countries that fought Germany in World War II to a peace conference, made page one, while the Brandt speech was covered at the end of the article and thus captured the attention only of readers who followed the story to its conclusion on page two. Larry Rue, "Peace Party Plan Spurned by Adenauer," *Chicago Tribune*, 10 July 1961, p. 1.

22. Alsop, "Seeming in Earnest," *Washington Post*, 23 June 1961, p. 15; Alsop, "Peering into the Inferno," ibid., 28 June 1961, p. 17. Undated letter from Alsop to Kennedy on Berlin, P.O.F., Special Correspondence No. 24, Joseph Alsop, Kennedy Library, was labeled only "Tuesday," but it squares with the views of several administration sources that fear in the White House about war over Berlin was greatest during this pre-Wall period.

23. Marcy, interview in Washington, D.C., 20 March 1978.

24. Childs, "Fulbright, Quiet Critic, Making Influence Felt as Shaper of Foreign Policy," *St. Louis Post-Dispatch*, 9 July 1961, p. F1.

25. Childs, "Humphrey Says Berlin Answer Is Negotiation, Urges U.S. Act; Amer-

ica Must Offer Proposals As Quickly As Possible, Senator Declares after German Visit," *St. Louis Post-Dispatch*, 15 July 1961, p. B1.

26. Childs, "War Psychosis Grows in U.S., Inflamed by Soviet Statements; As This Country Retorts Similarly to Khrushchev, Area for Berlin Negotiations Diminishes," *St. Louis Post-Dispatch*, 18 July 1961, p. 1; Childs, "Kennedy Must Look beyond Defense Plans in Berlin Crisis," ibid., 24 July 1961, p. C1. See also T. R. Phillips, "Military Men Would Mobilize 400,000 Men in Berlin Crisis; Russian Counter-Action Feared; Both Nations Could Reach Such Threatening Postures That Compromise Would Be Impossible Without Sustaining Loss of Prestige," ibid., 19 July 1961, p. C3.

27. Childs interview.

28. Childs interview.

29. Childs, "Kennedy Berlin Talk Tonight Is Expected to Be Calm in Tone; Broadcast to Nation Will Stress Long-Term Build-up to Meet Communists' Global Challenge," *St. Louis Post-Dispatch*, 25 July 1961, p. 1; Childs interview.

30. Childs, "Kennedy Berlin Talk Tonight."

31. "Firmness with Moderation," *St. Louis Post-Dispatch*, 26 July 1961, p. C2; "Prudence and Candor," ibid., 20 July 1961, p. B2.

32. Lasch interview.

Chapter 8

1. Brandt, *People and Politics*, p. 27.

2. "Red Tanks Move into East Zone of City," *Chicago Tribune*, 14 August 1961, p. 1; Larry Rue, "Brandt Asks Firm Steps to Free Traffic," ibid., 14 August 1961, p. 1.

3. John Hightower, "Kennedy Sees Rusk, Possibility of Retaliation by the Allied Bloc; Diplomats Indicate Travel Ban from West to East Germany Is One Step under Consideration," *St. Louis Post-Dispatch*, 14 August 1961, p. 1; Sydney Gruson, "Soviet Troops Encircle Berlin to Back up Sealing of Border; U.S. Is Drafting Vigorous Protest," *New York Times*, 14 August 1961, p. 1; Gerd Wilcke, "Adenauer Is Sure Allies Will React," ibid., 14 August 1961, p. 1; "Calls West Envoys," *Chicago Tribune*, 14 August 1961, p. 1; Fred Farris, "JFK, Rusk Charge 'Flagrant Violation,'" *San Francisco Examiner*, 14 August 1961, p. 1; Warren Rogers, Jr., "JFK Readies Tough Protest," ibid., 15 August 1961, p. 1.

4. See, for example, "Not Wholly Wishful Thoughts on Berlin," *Chicago Tribune*, 16 August 1961, p. 16.

5. Bundy interview; Klein interview; Brandt, *People and Politics*, p. 19.

6. Max Frankel, "U.S. Holds 26,000 in Navy to Raise Armed Strength," *New York Times*, 15 August 1961, p. 1.

7. Ibid.

8. Marder, "Reds Tighten Seal-Off in Berlin; U.S. Officials Minimize Danger of War Over Communist Clampdown; Kennedy Confers with Aides about Counter Measures," *Washington Post*, 15 August 1961, p. 1; Roberts, "On Duty 24 Hours: New Operations Unit Is Crisis News Center," ibid., 15 August 1961, p. 1. The third page-one story that day was Flora Lewis, "Mail and Traffic Links Severed in Divided City," ibid., 15 August 1961, p. 1. See also "Rivets in the Curtain," *Washington Post*, 15

August 1961, p. A12; and "Brandt Bids U.S. Act on Berlin Now," *Washington Post*, 17 August 1961, p. 1.

9. "Nothing to Lose but Chains," *New York Times*, 16 August 1961, p. 30; "Protest Over Berlin," ibid., 16 August 1961, p. 30; "Berlin: First Round," ibid., 19 August 1961, p. 16.

10. Alsop, "The Jail-Gate Closes," *Washington Post*, 16 August 1961, p. 17.

11. "Willy Brandt's Boot," *San Francisco Examiner*, 18 August 1961, p. 30.

12. "The Barbarian," *Chicago Tribune*, 15 August 1961, p. 16; "One Weapon We Shoot Off," ibid., 23 August 1961, p. 16.

13. "Spokesman without a Mandate," *Chicago Tribune*, 19 August 1961, p. 12.

14. "Quandary at the Gate" (cartoon), *Chicago Tribune*, 20 August 1961, p. 5.

15. Cate, *Ides of August*, pp. 350–51.

16. Ibid., pp. 403–5.

17. "Wisely Thinking Twice," *St. Louis Post-Dispatch*, 14 August 1961, p. B1; "Not Only Demands," ibid., 29 August 1961, p. B2; Lasch interview.

18. "Morale Builder," *San Francisco Examiner*, 23 August 1961, p. 26.

19. Higgins, "Help Khrushchev Club," *New York Herald Tribune*, 14 August 1961, p. 16; Higgins, "No Genius for Retreat," ibid., 21 August 1961, p. 14.

20. Holborn interview, 7 October 1977; David Wise, "Advisors in Crisis Failed to Alert Kennedy, Forced Hand, Upset Plan," *New York Herald Tribune*, 26 August 1961, p. 1. Wise provided some of the best investigative journalism of the period in the liberal Republican *New York Herald Tribune*. The *Post* and the *Times* did not pick up on the story.

21. See a copy of the complete Gallup poll that was sent to Walt Rostow, 31 July 1961, by C. D. Jackson of *Time-Life*. The poll was published in bits and pieces in the press, notably in the *Post* and the *Post-Dispatch* during late July and August. Jackson was interested in furthering the then growing psychological warfare campaign that he, like William Randolph Hearst, Jr., was promoting and that he felt the State Department was opposing. He felt this poll supported his views. No. 117, P.O.F., Germany, Berlin Crisis, Polls, Kennedy Library.

Public support for the president continued during August. Sixty-six percent of the American public was satisfied with his Berlin policies, according to a Gallup poll (AIPO, No. 649, Roper Center for Public Opinion Research) taken between 24 and 29 August 1961.

The *Chicago Tribune* reported that few of the fifty passersby at State and Randolph streets interviewed in their straw poll said they would change the administration's policies, which were "firm but not aggressive." "Government Berlin Stand Backed Here; Chicagoans Tell Worry, Hope Over Berlin," *Chicago Tribune*, 27 August 1961, p. 3.

22. For details of the press-presidential relationship during September and early October, see Kern, "The Presidency and the Press," pp. 286–94.

23. Bundy interview.

Introduction to Part Four

1. Dinerstein, *The Making of a Missile Crisis*, pp. 138–41.

2. See chapter 24, "The Confrontation in Cuba," in Theodore C. Sorensen, *Ken-*

nedy (New York: Doubleday, paperback ed., 1965), pp. 667–718. See also Louis Harris, Study No. 1082, December 1961 (Florida), P.O.F., No. 105, "Political Climate in Florida," and article and editorial from the *San Francisco Chronicle* (2 and 18 January 1962) sent to TCS from OB in the executive office of the president, Theodore Sorensen File, Box 36, Kennedy Library.

Poll AIPO, No. 663, 18 September 1962, Roper Center, asked the question: "Taking everything into account what action, if any, do you think the United States should take at this time in regard to Cuba?" Responses were:

Bomb, invade, belligerent act	10%
Trade embargo, starve them out	13%
Do something short of actual war	26%
Keep out, hands off	22%
Other action	4%
Don't know	25%

See also AIPO, No. 660, 26 June 1962, Roper Center.

Chapter 9

1. The story in the *Post-Dispatch* ran under a four-column headline: "Castro Charges Vessels Fired on Havana Suburb, Blames United States, Washington Denies Flatly Involvement in an Attack," *St. Louis Post-Dispatch*, 25 August 1962, p. 1. In the *Chicago Tribune*, 26 August 1962, p. 1, two AP stories and a Jules Dubois story ran under the banner headline "Seize Two, Cubans Raid Boats! Castro Accuses U.S.; Student Tells Story," along with a picture of the three jubilant "student leaders." See also "U.S. Says Cuban Exiles Shelled Havana, Orders Seizure of Attack Boats," *St. Louis Post-Dispatch*, 26 August 1962, p. 1.

2. See Kern, "The Presidency and the Press," figures 1 and 2, pp. 306–7, for a breakdown of interest group coverage during the Cuban crisis, the one that produced the greatest interest group coverage. See also "The Cuban Raid," *Chicago Tribune*, 28 August 1962, p. 12; Dubois, "Castro Cuts Link to United States for Ten Hours; Seen as Cover to Display Troops," *Chicago Tribune*, 27 August 1962, p. 1. During Karl Meyer's interview with the authors, he described Dubois's relationship with and attitude toward Castro. Dubois was an opponent of Latin American dictators and supported Romulo Betancourt of Venezuela as his model.

3. For a description of the president's November 1961 decision to overthrow Castro by means of a "people's" revolution and the subsequent Operation Mongoose program, see Schlesinger, *Robert Kennedy*, pp. 474–80. For a description of agreements with Florida institutions, including the press, to keep the matter quiet—despite the extensive nature of the program in southern Florida—see Columbia Broadcasting System, "CBS Reports: The CIA's Secret Army," produced by Judy Crichton and George Crile, 10 June 1977 (transcript).

4. Dubois, "Hear Russia Builds Sub Bases in Cuba," *Chicago Tribune*, 9 September 1962, p. 1; "Demands U.S. Aid for Cuban Student Unit; Borja Sees Possibility of Castro Overthrow," ibid., 3 September 1962, p. 2; "Ask Military Intervention against Cuba," ibid., p. 1.

5. Wise, "President Believes Rising Cuba Unrest May Topple Castro," *New York Herald Tribune*, 22 June 1962, p. 14. See also the transcript of the 29 August news conference in *Public Papers of the Presidents*, 1962, p. 652.

6. "Pitiful Plight of Cubans," *San Francisco Examiner*, 29 August 1962, p. 3.

7. The Cuban exile group, the Student Revolutionary Directorate, was led by Juan Manuel Salvat. See the following editorials: "A Brave Group," *San Francisco Examiner*, 10 September 1962, p. 32; and "The Silent Pundits," ibid., 14 September 1962, p. 32.

8. "The Cuban Choices," *Washington Post*, 28 August 1962, p. 12.

9. Frank C. Porter, "U.S. Warns It Can't Stop Ship Raids; Cites Impossibility of Patrolling Every Mile of Coastline," *Washington Post*, 13 October 1962, p. 1. The question of whether or not the United States was encouraging an armed assault was left to the *New Republic*, which editorialized that "one ought to know whether or not this government is committed to encouraging or arming an assault on another country." "Which Cuba Policy?" *New Republic* 147 (27 October 1962): 3–4.

10. Szulc interview. Szulc cited Jonathan Daniels of the *Times*. See also Szulc, "The *New York Times* and the Bay of Pigs," in David Brown and W. Richard Bruner, eds., *How I Got That Story*, pp. 315–29.

11. Szulc interview.

12. Szulc interview.

13. Wiggins assumed responsibility from Estabrook, who became chief European correspondent in the fall of 1961. Meyer felt that the Cuban communists had an affinity with the communist Chinese. Their counterparts, the right-wing Cuban exiles, "would like nothing better than to sink a Soviet ship and thereby force the United States into war." The solution was for the United States to "give plenary authority to someone who actually knows something about Cuba and who would be shrewd enough to frame and carry out a policy aimed at encouraging internal change. . . . It would mean acceptance of the fact that a post-Castro regime would be Socialist and nationalist, and that American properties would remain nationalized. It would involve attacking Castro not from the Right, but from the Left in the name of the revolution Castro aborted." Meyer felt this might be difficult for the United States to manage because the "prevailing attitude of CIA operatives in Miami" was "against encouraging any internal sabotage that might damage properties once owned by Americans." Meyer, "The Cuban Torment," *The New Leader* 45 (1 October 1962): 3–4. This story was reprinted from the British *New Statesman*. Meyer interview.

14. Higgins, "Cuba: A Finger on Kennedy," *New York Herald Tribune*, 28 August 1962, p. 1.

15. *Public Papers of the Presidents*, 1962, pp. 674–81.

16. Pat Holt, interview in Bethesda, Md., 21 July 1978.

17. For the text of the resolution, see U.S., Congress, Senate, *Situation in Cuba*, 87th Cong., 2d sess., 1962, S. Rept. 2111, Calendar No. 2077, p. 85006.

18. The criticisms of U.S. officials totaled 56 percent of all criticisms in *Examiner* editorials on Cuba. This was six percentage points higher than during the 1–23 June period of the Berlin crisis.

19. "A Cuba Blockade," *San Francisco Examiner*, 6 September 1962, p. 34; Hearst, "When Is Red Buildup a Threat to Safety?" ibid., 16 September 1962, p. 1.

20. "Kennedy on Cuba," *Chicago Tribune*, 6 September 1962, p. 16. See also the

Tribune's five other critical editorials during September: "Khrushchev's Threat," 12 September 1962, p. 16, which the paper blames on Kennedy's weakness; "Kennedy's Patience," 15 September 1962, p. 10, which questions his intelligence on the question of "defensive" weapons in the light of his Bay of Pigs performance; "Be It Resolved," 28 September 1962, p. 12, which reviews his "fateful and inadequate decisions" during that operation on the basis of a September issue of *Newsweek*; "Our Baby," 26 September 1962, p. 12, which blames the "spineless administration" for failure to obtain Allied support on the shipping blockade from Britain and Norway; and "The Senators Huff and Puff," 21 September 1962, p. 14.

On 10 September 1962, Trohan concluded that the "Reds have set up 9 of 24 missile bases promised Castro. . . . In addition, Russia has supplied Russian bombers and fighters to Cuba." Trohan, "Report from Washington," *Chicago Tribune*, 10 September 1962, p. 2.

21. See Goldwater in the *San Francisco Examiner*: "Military Aid in Latin America," 6 September 1962, p. 34; "Policy of Victory Over Reds," 16 September 1962, p. 3; "Soviets Using Cuba as Canaveral Threat?" 18 September 1962, p. 28; "Bold Red Move in Cuba," 20 September 1962, p. 34; "Monroe Doctrine Gutted?" 25 September 1962, p. 38; "Are We Encouraging Khrushchev to Miscalculate?" 28 September 1962, p. 38. See also David Lawrence in the *San Francisco Examiner*: "Soviet Defiance of the Monroe Doctrine," 10 September 1962, p. 32; "A Repeat of History?" 12 September 1962, p. 34; "Inaction Breeding War?" 19 September 1962, p. 32; and "A Strategy of Vacillation," 26 September 1962, p. 34.

22. Eisenhower said he broke his silence on foreign policy issues on 15 October because of a Kennedy "engines-were-idling" speech on 20 September "in my own home state of Pennsylvania." Eisenhower said that Kennedy's foreign policy was "too sad to talk about," and spoke of his own record: "In those eight years we lost no such ground to tyranny. . . . We witnessed no abdication of responsibility. . . . No walls were built. No threatening foreign bases were established." His crises—Korea, Trieste, Quemoy and Matsu, Lebanon, and Guatemala—all resulted in defeat of communist efforts. Robert Hartman, "Ike Hits Kennedy Foreign Record," *Washington Post*, 16 October 1962, p. 1. Why "has this extreme danger (a nation divided by partisanship) been risked?" William S. White asked three days after Eisenhower's speech. For a "bare hope by President Kennedy that he might just bring to Congress a few more Democrats who would favor those domestic welfare programs that were denied by the old Congress." White, "A Strange Equation on the Cuban Issue," *San Francisco Examiner*, 21 September 1962, p. 34; White, "An Involuntary Isolation," ibid., 28 September 1962, p. 36; "National Unity Is in Danger," ibid., 18 October 1962, p. 34.

23. Having gone from the presidency of Brown University to the Council on Foreign Relations, Wriston wrote occasional columns that appeared in the *Post*. During this period, the *Post* thus turned to the foreign policy establishment for commentary supporting the president's position. State Department, "American Opinion Situation," 24 September 1962, Arthur Schlesinger Subject Files, 1961–64, Box No. 5, Cuba, 2 January to 29 September 1962, Kennedy Library.

24. Krock, "Mr. Kennedy's Management of the News," *Fortune* 67 (March 1963): 82.

25. Krock had attended the insider "bull sessions" during the Roosevelt years with key New Deal figures—Roosevelt's wrinkle in press communication. Like other *Times*

bureau chiefs before and after him, Krock had been privy to secrets that he did not reveal for reasons of national security. He knew, for example, of the North African invasion as well as of the U-2 flights over Soviet territory long before they became public knowledge when Powers was shot down. Krock, *Memoirs*, pp. 171, 181, 366; Wicker interview; Holborn interview.

26. Krock, "But a Naval Patrol Is Not an 'Invasion,'" *New York Times*, 30 August 1962, p. 28.

27. Krock, "Effect of the Missile Age on Historic Doctrines," *New York Times*, 4 September 1962, p. 32; Krock, "Cuba and Politics: Democrats Hope to Contain Debate and GOP Must Treat Warily," ibid., 9 September 1962, sec. 4, p. 12.

28. Krock, "Contrast between Sources of Foreign Policy," *New York Times*, 14 September 1962, p. 30. He said, "A comparison between extracts from the transcripts of the last two White House news conferences demonstrates his [Kennedy's] continued reluctance to concede publicly, as Senator Humphrey has, that the Monroe Doctrine isn't what it used to be." Krock then turned to a Bundy article in the October 1962 issue of *Foreign Affairs* that noted: "when the same treaty is used to cover everyone, we must look past the paper to the facts." Krock concluded, "How about trying the experiment of conceding the results of these looks as they occur?" Krock, "A New Name for the Monroe Doctrine," *New York Times*, 18 September 1962, p. 38.

29. Barth, "Freedom and the Press," *Progressive* 26 (June 1962): 29–33.

30. In his interview with the authors, Estabrook contended that Barth was not a foreign policy expert.

31. "Talks on Cuba," *Washington Post*, 7 September 1962, p. 7.

32. Meyer interview. Adolph A. Berle had had a distinguished government career as a Latin Americanist and published a book in 1962 for the Council on Foreign Relations, *Latin America*, which was quite influential.

33. "The Cuban Problem," *New York Times*, 6 September 1962, p. 30; "Moscow Beats the Drum," ibid., 12 September 1962, p. 38.

34. Sokolsky was a conservative columnist carried by the *Washington Post* as a holdover from the *New York Herald Tribune*. He died in 1963 and was replaced on the *Post* op ed page by Max Freedman, the friend of both Vice-President Johnson and President Kennedy. Sokolsky felt that Cuba is "burned in the hearts of the American people, like Calais, 1588." Sokolsky, "Always Cuba," *Washington Post*, 15 October 1962, p. 13. His solution in September was to invoke the Monroe Doctrine and the Platt Amendment, which are "as binding as the Ten Commandments," and "then go into Cuba and take it over, as we did before." Sokolsky, "The Monroe Doctrine," ibid., 17 September 1962, p. 13. Sokolsky blamed the victory of communism in Cuba on the *New York Times*, which had undermined United States support for Batista, and on the State Department and the Kennedy administration; the latter two had failed to respond to the implication of Castro's ample warning. Sokolsky gave play to the ambassadors' views that were appearing in "Who Lost Cuba?" books and that reinforced the Republican critique. Sokolsky, "Two Military Fronts," *Washington Post*, 15 September 1962, p. 12; Sokolsky, "The Bay of Pigs," ibid., 19 September 1962, p. 17. See also Frankel, "As United States Allies See Cuba," *New York Times*, 30 September 1962, sec. 4, p. 4; Baldwin, "U.S. and USSR: The Danger Points and Heightened Tension," ibid., 16 September 1962, sec. 4, p. 3; Reston, "How About a Blockade on Nonsense?" ibid., 16 September 1962, sec. 4, p. 19.

35. Dudman, interview in Washington, D.C., 2 and 8 February 1978. Grant had apparently obtained permission to visit Cuba through contacts with the Cuban delegation at the United Nations.

36. For an analysis of Cuban and Soviet perceptions before the introduction of missiles into Cuba and of the significance of the Guatemalan experience and the Bay of Pigs to these perceptions, see the skillful narrative in Dinerstein, *Making of a Missile Crisis*. See also Grant, "Policy of U.S. toward Cuba Said to Be Counted a Failure If It Is Judged by Its Results," *St. Louis Post-Dispatch*, 25 July 1962, p. E1.

37. See the retitled *Times* editorial "Cuban Invasion: Course of Folly; Hysteria Over Soviet Aid to Cuba Does Not Justify 'Utter Madness' of Armed Attack," *St. Louis Post-Dispatch*, 6 September 1962, p. 2B; Reston, "Proposal for Blockading Cuba Would Involve Act of War; That Course Is Advocated Out of Frustration as a Kind of Bargain-Basement Solution to Castro, Reds," ibid., 17 September 1962, p. 1 ES; and "Clear Words on Cuba," ibid., 6 September 1961, p. 2 ES. See also "No to the Warhawks," ibid., 14 September 1962, p. 2 ES; and "For Standby Powers," ibid., 9 September 1962, p. 2 ES.

38. Holt interview; "Clear Words on Cuba"; "For Standby Powers."

Chapter 10

1. See "Meeting with Latin American Foreign Ministers, Official Use Only, Washington, October 2–3, 1962—The Status of Agriculture, Industry, and Medical Services," Schlesinger Subject Files, 1961–64, Box No. 5, Cuba 1/2/62–9/29/62, Kennedy Library; and Kurzman, "Hemispheric Stand on Cuba Stiffens—with Reservations," *Washington Post*, 2 October 1962, p. 20.

2. "The Embargo on Castro," *New York Times*, 5 October 1962, p. 32.

3. Memorandum to the President from Louis Harris, "The Shape of this Campaign," 4 October 1962, P.O.F., No. 105, Polls, General, Kennedy Library.

4. Carl Brockdorf, "United States Troops Occupy Crossings as Deadline Nears," *Washington Post*, 4 September 1962, p. 1; Carl Hartman, "Soviets Yield on Route, Stir New Berlin Tension," ibid., 5 September 1962, p. 1; Roberts, "Soviets Believed Testing U.S. Determination on West Berlin," ibid., 5 September 1962, p. 6; Don Cook, "Reds Spur West Berlin Armor Ban," ibid., 12 September 1962, p. 13; Alsop, "A Very Cold Autumn," *Washington Post*, 15 September 1962, p. 13.

5. Roberts, "Flareup of Berlin Issue Is Expected after November 6," *Washington Post*, 9 October 1962, p. 8; Marder, "U.S. Getting Ready for a Worsening of Berlin Crisis," ibid., 12 October 1962, p. 7.

6. Roberts, "Talking Up a Crisis Might Avert One," *Washington Post*, 18 October 1962, p. 21. Berlin was the lead issue in the "News of the Week in Review," *New York Times*, 14 October 1962, p. 2E. See also the lead editorial, "Berlin Drama," *Washington Post*, 17 October 1962, p. 17; Lippmann, "Showdown at Berlin," *Washington Post*, 16 October 1962, p. 17; and Lippmann, "Toward a German Policy," ibid., 18 October 1962, p. 27.

7. Alsop, "Cuba and Public Opinion," *San Francisco Examiner*, 8 October 1962, p. 14. See also his other October columns that dealt with Cuba as a political rather than

a strategic problem: "Cuba and the California Voters," ibid., 3 October 1962, p. 32; and "Warmth But No Flame," ibid., 15 October 1962, p. 34.

8. Alsop interview.

9. Quoted in Robert A. Divine, ed., *The Cuban Missile Crisis*, p. 14.

10. Reston, "On Cuba and Pearl Harbor—the American Nightmare," *New York Times*, 12 October 1962, p. 30; Kenworthy interview.

11. Reston, "On Cuba and Pearl Harbor."

12. Donovan, interview in Falls Church, Va., 17 August 1978. In the *Tribune*, however, Keating was accorded ten paragraphs on page 2: "Warns of Peril," *Chicago Tribune*, 11 October 1962.

13. "Something to Watch," *Chicago Tribune*, 3 October 1962, p. 14. "The present Administration seems to have altogether too great an attachment to the procedure of railroading people into psychiatric wards. . . . If General Walker has committed an offense, his right is to be tried in a court, not to be humiliated." Krock, "Kennedy and Eisenhower Intensify Partisanship as Election Nears," *New York Times*, 14 October 1962, sec. 4, p. 8.

14. "Congressmen and Editors Choose Cuba as the Main Campaign Issue," *Congressional Quarterly* report published in the *Washington Post*, 18 October 1962, p. 2. See also "GOP Campaign Chiefs Say Cuba Is Top Issue," ibid., 17 October 1962, p. 5.

Chapter 11

1. Sorensen, *Kennedy*, pp. 682–92.

2. Salinger, *With Kennedy*, p. 151.

3. Ibid., p. 253.

4. Ibid., p. 261; Kenworthy interview.

5. Alsop interview.

6. Roberts, "Marine Moves in South Linked to Cuban Crisis; High Official Sees Situation 'Tense, Tight,'" *Washington Post*, 21 October 1961, p. 1.

7. *Public Papers of the Presidents*, 1962, pp. 806–9.

8. Neustadt Memorandum for Theodore C. Sorensen, "Subject: The President's *Next* TV Address," 27 October 1962, Sorensen Files, Box 36, Kennedy Library.

9. Salinger later said that the number of correspondents in attendance was "surpassed only [by] the weekend of President Kennedy's assassination and funeral." Salinger, *With Kennedy*, pp. 266, 288.

10. Sorensen, "Notes to Speech Draft," 20 October 1962, Cuba Classified Subject Files, October 1962, Sorensen Files, Kennedy Library.

11. Pentagon "Background Briefing on Cuban Situation," 22 October 1962, 8:00 P.M., p. 19, Kennedy Library.

12. This undated article ("An Intelligence Gap: Experts Ask if Reports on Cuba Were Poor or Adapted to Policy") is in the Cuban newspaper and periodical clippings file of Paul Sakwa, who was Chief of Covert Operations for the CIA in Vietnam, 1959–61, and in charge of intelligence at the State Department's Bureau of Intelligence and Research (INR) during the years 1962–64. In an interview with the authors, he noted that, because of the poor CIA intelligence on Cuba during this period,

he gleaned material from domestic and foreign periodicals and newspapers in libraries. Sakwa, interview in Washington, D.C., 3 April 1978. At INR in 1962 he wrote a lengthy research piece about Republican statements on Castro that was designed to make the party look bad and that is still in his possession. The authors are grateful to him for the use of his files.

13. Pentagon "Background Briefing on Cuban Situation."

14. This argument appeared as the result of a later backgrounder. See Robert C. Hartmann, "U.S. Claims Major Differences between Cuban, Turkish Bases," *Washington Post*, 24 October 1962, p. 23.

15. Max Frankel, "The State Secrets Myth," *Columbia Journalism Review* 10 (September/October 1971): 22–26.

16. Lasch interview. See also "Limited Blockade," *St. Louis Post-Dispatch*, 23 October 1961, p. 2ES.

17. Lippmann, "Blockade Proclaimed," *Washington Post*, 25 October 1962, p. 25. See also Dean Acheson, "Homage to Plain Dumb Luck," reprinted in Divine, *Cuban Missile Crisis*, pp. 196–206.

18. Salinger, *With Kennedy*, p. 279.

19. "Cuba Conference Notes and Doodles," October 1962 to 12 November 1962; and Note by Major General Chester ("Ted") Clifton, 22 October 1962, P.O.F., Countries No. 115, Kennedy Library. Childs reported that Clifton had briefed him during the missile crisis week. Childs interview, 8 February 1978. Luce had always been considered particularly important by the Kennedys. The White House had been aware of and disappointed by his failure to support the president's Cuban policies in September. Presidential Diary, 24 October 1962, off-the-record meeting from 4:05–4:33 with Henry Luce and Otto Feuerbringer, Kennedy Library.

20. Reston, "Khrushchev's Miscalculation on Cuba," *New York Times*, 24 October 1962, p. 38.

21. Reston, "Kennedy's New Diplomacy in Cuba," *New York Times*, 26 October 1962, p. 30; Reston, "To Deal or Not to Deal: That's the Question," ibid., 28 October 1962, sec. 4, p. 10. See also Acheson, "Homage to Plain Dumb Luck"; and Root, "France Is Expected to Give U.S. Public Support, Private Warning," *Washington Post*, 24 October 1962, p. 13. Root's article from Paris, two days before Reston's 26 October column, gave a clear indication of what the real French feelings were on the matter. Reston was one of the journalists who could have responded to these had he so chosen. The fact that the *Post* also saw no reason to give major play to the French position was evidenced by its publication of Root's article on page 13 of the newspaper.

22. Reston, "The President's View—Kennedy Rejects Thesis That Outcome on Cuba Shows 'Tough Line' is Best," *New York Times*, 29 October 1962, p. 1.

23. Means interview.

24. Salinger, *With Kennedy*, p. 301.

25. Ibid., p. 272.

26. Ibid., p. 301.

27. Sorensen, *Kennedy*, p. 805.

28. Elie Abel, oral history interview with Dennie O'Brien in New York, 18 March 1970, Kennedy Library. According to Abel, Rusk, "at a number of crucial points in the missile crisis—had very often, not on a Friday afternoon, but on say, a Saturday morning, a group of us in and kind of gave us the line. A crucial point, I remember, was the

Sunday when the crisis was defused, to everyone's enormous relief and the surprise of many . . . he appealed to us, 'When you're writing about this, don't make this appear to be a capitulation on the part of the Russians.'" Warren Unna, interview in Washington, D.C., 2 July 1979.

29. See table 3 (Laos), table 4 (Berlin), table 5 (Cuba).

30. In the authors' interview with Wicker, he mentioned Reston's quip.

31. "Yahooing through Life," *San Francisco Examiner*, 25 October 1962, p. 34; "Ominous Turn in Cuba Crisis," ibid., 27 October 1962, p. 16; Hearst, "Tough Line with Soviets Pays Off," ibid., 28 October 1962, p. 1.

32. "The Cuban Lesson," ibid., 29 October 1962, p. 16. The *Examiner*'s publisher, Charles L. Gould, substituted for Admiral Arleigh Burke at the San Francisco Commercial Club on Navy Day, 25 October. In his speech, Gould said that the president was finally standing up to the "Godless hordes" of Russians and Chinese after decades of appeasement.

33. It is unfortunate that manhood was involved in domestic thinking about strategic issues. It was mentioned specifically by William S. White, the columnist closest to Lyndon B. Johnson, the consummate politician and the next president of the United States. Robert Young, *Chicago Tribune* reporter who was also later close to Johnson, told about President Johnson's criticism of Kennedy's manhood: Johnson would fall down on his hands and knees in dramatic replication of Kennedy's weak-kneed begging of Khrushchev at Vienna. This, Johnson stated, he would never do over Vietnam. Young interview. See also White, "Finally the U.S. Draws the Line," *San Francisco Examiner*, 25 October 1962, p. 34.

34. Lawrence, "The Blockade of Cuba," *San Francisco Examiner*, 24 October 1962, p. 34; Lawrence, "Why Did Mr. Kennedy Wait So Long?" ibid., 25 October 1962, p. 34; Lawrence, "Blockade Is Insufficient," ibid., 26 October 1962, p. 36.

35. Trohan noted that he had used the term "our president" advisedly "because Mr. Kennedy has made himself president of all Americans by returning to standards of traditional pride and courage." Trohan, "Report from Washington," *Chicago Tribune*, 27 October 1962, p. 4. See also the *Times* reprint in the *Tribune* that was given space on page 1; "'Sudden' Cuba Crisis a Puzzle in Deception," *Chicago Tribune*, 25 October 1962; "Our Course Is Set," ibid., 23 October 1962, p. 18; "Getting Back on Our Own Feet," ibid., 25 October 1962, p. 18; and "Why Cuba Isn't Like Turkey," ibid., 24 October 1962, p. 16.

36. Salinger, *With Kennedy*, p. 293.

37. Adam Yarmolinsky, oral history interview with Daniel Ellsberg in Washington, D.C., 11 November 1964, Kennedy Library.

38. For a discussion of the news management controversy and of Kennedy's continuing efforts after the crisis to enhance the public image of his leadership during the crisis week, see Kern, "The Presidency and the Press," pp. 397–411.

The issue of whether or not the president should be free to lie to the press in foreign policy crisis situations arose in November 1962 and continued into the following year. Trohan, Krock, Baldwin, James Colburn of the Committee on the Freedom of Information of the American Society of Newspaper Editors, and Clark Mollenhoff of the Cowles papers opposed the practice.

Reston and Markel of the *Times* defended it. Reston thought the press "could scarcely apply normal procedures to the actions of the first American government ever engaged in facing up to the possibility of nuclear war." Markel argued that the success of the president's handling of the crisis was sufficient justification for his methods. The administration argued that the cold war situation required a suspension of normal standards of accountability, and Markel agreed. This argument, however, turned out to be a dangerous one, as the press was to learn during the Vietnam War. Reston, "How to Make Things Worse than They Really Are," *New York Times*, 21 November 1962, p. 30; Markel, "Management of News," *Saturday Review* 46 (9 February 1963): 51.

Introduction to Part Five

1. For an analysis of policy toward Vietnam during the Kennedy years, see for example Weldon A. Brown, *Prelude to Disaster*, pp. 173–227; Chester L. Cooper, *The Lost Crusade*, pp. 204–70; Leslie H. Gelb with Richard K. Betts, *The Irony of Vietnam*, pp. 69–95; George C. Herring, *America's Longest War*, pp. 73–107; George McFurnan Kahin and John W. Lewis, *The United States in Vietnam*, pp. 127–46; Guenter Lewy, *America in Vietnam*, pp. 22–29; and Geoffrey Warner, "The United States and the Fall of Diem," *Australian Outlook* 28 (December 1974): 245–58. Still the most detailed and authoritative study of Kennedy's policy is *The Pentagon Papers: The Defense Department History of United States Decision Making on Vietnam*, 2:1–276.

2. For the split within the U.S. government, see for example John Mecklin, *Mission in Torment*, pp. 204–24; David Halberstam, *The Best and the Brightest*, pp. 296–358; and William Colby, *Honorable Men*, pp. 205–7. Particularly helpful on the divisions within the administration was James Thomson, Jr., interview in Cambridge, Mass., 28 June 1979.

3. Halberstam, telephone interview, 2 August 1979; Neil Sheehan, interview in Washington, D.C., 2 July 1979.

4. *Pentagon Papers*, 2:455–58. In their interviews with the authors, Halberstam and Sheehan emphasized that their major sources were anti-Diem American and South Vietnamese officials in Vietnam.

5. Sheehan interview.

6. Beech interview.

7. Rusk interview; Salinger, *With Kennedy*, p. 326; Ball, interview in New York, N.Y., 29 June 1979.

8. Salinger, *With Kennedy*, p. 324.

9. Thomson, interview in Cambridge, Mass., 28 June 1979.

10. For Vietnam's relative lack of importance as a news story in 1961 and 1962, see appendix V; Browne, *The New Face of War*, pp. 177–82; and Halberstam, *The Making of a Quagmire*, p. 210. Sheehan, in his interview, provided further affirmation.

11. Sheehan interview; Halberstam, *The Making of a Quagmire*, p. 195; Frederick E. Nolting, Jr., "The Turning Point: The Origin and Development of United States Commitment in Vietnam," *Foreign Service Journal* 45 (July 1968): 18–20.

Chapter 12

1. *Pentagon Papers*, 2:232–47.

2. Dudman's ten-part series on Asia appeared in the *Post-Dispatch* between 3 and 13 February 1963. Senator Mansfield subsequently placed the entire series in the *Congressional Record.* U.S. Congress, Senate, 88th Cong., 1st sess., 4 March 1963, *Congressional Record* 109:3452–65.

3. Halberstam interview; Sheehan interview.

4. Halberstam, "Mrs. Nhu Denounces U.S. for 'Blackmail' in Vietnam," *New York Times*, 8 August 1963, p. 1.

5. Halberstam, " 'Blackmailed' by U.S. Embassy, Mme. Nhu Says," *St. Louis Post-Dispatch*, 8 August 1963, p. 1; "Let the Buddhists Burn—Mrs. Nhu," *San Francisco Examiner*, 9 August 1963, p. 2; "State Department Gives Back of Its Hand to Madame Nhu's Blackmail Charge," *Washington Post*, 9 August 1963, p. 15.

6. "Mrs. Nhu Speaks Out," *New York Times*, 9 August 1963, p. 22; "Sputtering Darkness," *Washington Post*, 9 August 1963, p. 16.

7. "Intemperate Attack," *St. Louis Post-Dispatch*, 9 August 1963, p. 2C; "The Nhus and the Buddhists" (*New York Times* editorial), *Chicago Tribune*, 10 August 1963, p. 8.

8. "Crisis in Vietnam 'Distresses' U.S.," *New York Times*, 17 August 1963, p. 1.

9. Halberstam, *Making of a Quagmire*, pp. 190–92; Carroll interview; Rusk interview.

10. Szulc, "Concern Rises on Diem," *New York Times*, 8 August 1963, p. 1.

11. Higgins, *Our Vietnam Nightmare*, pp. 56–203. The quote is from page 131.

12. Higgins, "Diem Warns Buddhists against Hope of Coup," *Washington Post*, 9 August 1963, p. 15; Higgins, "Diem Asserts Firm Stand in Effort to End Religious Woes Peacefully," *Washington Post*, 15 August 1963, p. E14.

13. Higgins, "Buddhist Publicity Mill," *San Francisco Examiner*, 14 August 1963, p. 38.

14. Conniff, "Conflicting Views on Vietnam," *San Francisco Examiner*, 17 August 1963, p. 18.

15. Robert Donovan, Higgins's superior in the Washington bureau of the *Herald-Tribune*, recalled that he and others had serious reservations about her reporting. Donovan interview.

16. Halberstam, "The Buddhist Crisis in Vietnam: A Collision of Religion, World Politics, and Pride," *New York Times*, 11 September 1963, p. 14; *Pentagon Papers*, 2:203.

17. *Pentagon Papers*, 2:232–42; Colby, *Honorable Men*, p. 209.

18. Halberstam, "Vietnam Orders Schools Closed in Rising Unrest," *New York Times*, 25 August 1963, p. 1; Robert Trumbull, "Americans in Saigon Turn against Diem Regime," ibid., 26 August 1963, p. 3; Higgins, "U.S. Advisers in South Viet-Nam See Favorable Turn in War on Reds," *Washington Post*, 28 August 1963, p. 12; Beech, "Censorship in Saigon Is a Failure," ibid., 30 August 1963, p. 15; Higgins, "Vietnam's Buddhist Strategy," *San Francisco Examiner*, 27 August 1963, p. 1.

19. *Pentagon Papers*, 2:232–40; Szulc, "Vietnam's Army Absorbed by U.S. in Pagoda Raids," *New York Times*, 27 August 1963, p. 1; Szulc, "Long Crisis Seen

on Vietnam Rule," ibid., 28 August 1963, p. 1; Szulc, "U.S. Spurns Denial by Diem on Crisis," ibid., 29 August 1963, p. 1.

20. Unna interview.

21. Unna, "Chuong Quits as Viet Ambassador; Hits Diem's 'Totalitarian Tactics,'" *Washington Post*, 23 August 1963, p. 1; Unna, "U.S. Weighs Move in Viet-Nam: American Interests Facing Double Danger," ibid., 24 August 1963, p. 7.

22. Roger Hilsman, *To Move a Nation*, p. 496.

23. "Crisis in South Vietnam," *New York Times*, 22 August 1963, p. 26; "Fresh Approach in Saigon," ibid., 28 August 1963, p. 32; "Desperation in Saigon," *Washington Post*, 22 August 1963, p. 20.

24. "Another Fumble in Viet Nam," *St. Louis Post-Dispatch*, 29 August 1963, p. D2; "Which Policy in Viet Nam?" ibid., 3 September 1963, p. C2.

25. South Vietnamese sources, like all references to foreign sources, include only nationals of that country, not U.S. officials or journalists living there. These are included under "official U.S." and "press." For additional explanation of the categories, see the Note on Methodology.

26. Alsop interview.

27. "Mao Forecasts U.S. Pullout in South Viet-Nam," *Washington Post*, 30 August 1963, p. 17; Szulc, "Peking and Hanoi Differ on Saigon," *New York Times*, 30 August 1963, p. 2; "Hanoi Hints Paris Role as Unifier," *Washington Post*, 2 September 1963, p. 17; M. S. Handler, "Neutral Vietnam Held North's Aim," *New York Times*, 5 November 1963, p. 12.

28. Peter Grose, "De Gaulle Offers to Help Vietnam End Foreign Role," *New York Times*, 30 August 1963, p. 1; "Washington Is Annoyed," ibid., p. 2; Root, "France May Get Soviet Support on Plan to Neutralize Viet-Nam," *Washington Post*, 1 September 1963, p. 9.

29. "De Gaulle's Blast at U.S.," *San Francisco Examiner*, 31 August 1963, p. 1; Root, "France Seen Aiming to 'Regain' Indochina," *Washington Post*, 31 August 1963, p. 1; Szulc, "Paris Premature on Vietnam Unity, Washington Says," *New York Times*, 31 August 1963, p. 1; "An Offer to Consider," *Chicago Tribune*, 4 September 1963, p. 10.

30. Thomson interview; Hilsman, *To Move a Nation*, p. 505.

Chapter 13

1. Sorensen, *Kennedy*, p. 323.

2. *Public Papers of the Presidents*, 1963, p. 652. Frank Cormier of the AP recalled that Ted Clifton told him on 1 September that Kennedy planned to make a "major policy statement" on Vietnam in the interview; when Cronkite saw Cormier's story the next day, he was angry and told Salinger that he did not intend to ask a single question about Vietnam. "You'd be well advised if you did," Salinger responded. Cormier to the authors, 28 June 1978.

3. Salinger, *With Kennedy*, p. 114; *Public Papers of the Presidents*, 1963, p. 659.

4. Sidey's views on Kennedy's declining interest in print journalists are discussed in Halberstam, *Best and the Brightest*, pp. 361–62. In Alsop's interview with the authors, he described his conversation with Kennedy about Vietnam.

5. *Public Papers of the Presidents*, 1963, pp. 673–77.

6. Ibid.

7. Bundy interview.

8. Sheehan, "U.S. Accused of Plotting Coup d'Etat," *Washington Post*, 3 September 1963, p. 1; Szulc, "Washington Officials Accuse Nhu of Blackmail," *New York Times*, 5 September 1963, p. 5; "Mrs. Nhu Calls Kennedy Appeaser," ibid., 12 September 1963, p. 1; "Diem Denounces TV," ibid., 22 September 1963, p. 3.

9. Halberstam interview.

10. "Vietnam's Pagoda Raiders Reported on C.I.A. Payroll," *New York Times*, 9 September 1963, p. 1; Reston, "Washington Is Privately Upset but Is Publicly Silent on Financing," ibid., p. 1.

11. Sheehan, "U.S. Acts to End Dispute Among Its Viet Missions," *Washington Post*, 15 September 1963, p. 1; Halberstam, "U.S. Civilian Aides in Vietnam Press for a Decision on Diem," *New York Times*, 15 September 1963, p. 4.

12. Hilsman, *To Move a Nation*, pp. 508–9; *Pentagon Papers*, 2:243–52; Halberstam, *Best and the Brightest*, pp. 333–50; Unna, "McNamara-Taylor Viet Trip Aimed at Healing U.S. Civilian-Military Rift," *Washington Post*, 4 October 1963, p. 1; "White Hot Wrangle on Vietnam," *San Francisco Examiner*, 24 September 1963, p. 1; Unna interview.

13. Halberstam, "Anguish in Vietnam: Americans with a Mission Weigh Emotions against Policies of U.S.," *New York Times*, 3 September 1963, p. 4; Browne, "U.S. Is Losing Many Friends in S. Viet-Nam," *Washington Post*, 8 September 1963, p. 21.

14. Roy Essoyan, "Nhu Dominates Brother Diem; Is Strongly Anti-Communist But Admires Red Techniques," *St. Louis Post-Dispatch*, 3 September 1963, p. 1C; Robert Trumbull, "Youth of Saigon Count on Future," *New York Times*, 8 September 1963, p. 2; Trumbull, "U.S. Prestige Tied to Saigon Dispute," ibid., 3 September 1963, p. 2.

15. "22 Senators Call for Viet Reforms or End of Aid," *Washington Post*, 13 September 1963, p. 12; Dudman, "Move in Senate to End U.S. Aid Believed Useful to Kennedy as Lever against Viet Nam Regime," *St. Louis Post-Dispatch*, 2 October 1963, p. 1C; "Aid Bill Amendment Authorizes President to Withhold Vietnam Funds," *New York Times*, 16 October 1963, p. 7; Hilsman, *To Move a Nation*, p. 505.

16. J. William Fulbright, interview in Washington, D.C., 10 July 1978; Bryce Nelson, telephone interview, 10 July 1979; Means, "Stop Diem Aid, Urges U.S. Senator," *San Francisco Examiner*, 5 September 1963, p. 2.

17. Harris, "U.S. Public Support of Viet War Continues despite Buddhist Crisis," *Washington Post*, 30 September 1963, p. 1; Harrington, telephone interview, 22 June 1979. A typical advertisement by the committee appears in the *New York Times*, 15 September 1963, p. E5; for a news story on a letter by the committee to Kennedy criticizing American support of Diem, see "Clergymen Score U.S. Aid to Diem," *New York Times*, 15 August 1963, p. 3. See also Kenneth Dole, "U.S. Clergy Seeks to Halt Aid to Viet in Religious Strife," *Washington Post*, 17 August 1963, p. C6, which includes criticism of the Diem regime by the Catholic magazine *Commonweal*.

18. Sydney Kossen, "Young Demos—Militants Win," *San Francisco Examiner*, 9 September 1963, p. 1; "Legion's Head Calls for New Fight on Reds," *Chicago Tribune*, 11 September 1963, p. 5.

19. "An Offer to Consider," *Chicago Tribune*, 4 September 1963, p. 10; Conniff, "Vietnamese Time-Bomb," *San Francisco Examiner*, 5 September 1963, p. 32;

Krock, "U.S. Policy in Asia," *New York Times*, 22 September 1963, p. E11.

20. "Chiding Diem," *Washington Post*, 4 September 1963, p. 14; "Patron and Client," ibid., 11 September 1963, p. A18.

21. "The CIA Again," *Washington Post*, 10 September 1963, p. 18; "Mission to Saigon," ibid., 23 September 1963, p. 16.

22. "The Way to Success in Viet Nam," *St. Louis Post-Dispatch*, 5 September 1963, p. 2B; "Putting Pressure on Diem," ibid., 12 September 1963, p. 2B; "What Goal in Viet Nam?", ibid., 22 September 1963, p. 2C.

23. "Confusion on Vietnam," *New York Times*, 22 September 1963, p. E10.

24. Reston, "How to Make Things Worse than They Really Are," *New York Times*, 4 September 1963, p. 38; Reston, "How to Keep the Budget Up with the Times," ibid., 8 September 1963, p. 10E; Reston, "On Suppressing the News Instead of the Nhus," ibid., 11 September 1963, p. 42.

25. Pearson, "Senators Saw Diem as 'Mandarin,'" *Washington Post*, 14 September 1963, p. D27.

26. Alsop interview.

27. Alsop, "In the Gia Long Palace," *Washington Post*, 20 September 1963, p. 17.

28. Alsop, "The War Can Be Won," *Washington Post*, 25 September 1963, p. 17; Alsop, "The Crusaders," ibid., 23 September 1963, p. 17; Klein interview.

29. Alsop interview.

Chapter 14

1. *Pentagon Papers*, 2:250–63.

2. Ibid.

3. *Public Papers of the Presidents*, 1963, pp. 759–80.

4. Ball interview; Cooper, *Lost Crusade*, p. 265; Schlesinger, *Robert Kennedy*, p. 716; Taylor, *Swords and Plowshares*, p. 299.

5. "Candor Needed on Vietnam," *New York Times*, 4 October 1963, p. 34.

6. "Politics as Usual in Vietnam," *San Francisco Examiner*, 5 October 1963, p. 14; "Clouded Crystal Ball," *Washington Post*, 4 October 1963, p. 20; "Father and Daughter," *St. Louis Post-Dispatch*, 9 October 1963, p. 2C; "Educated Guesses," *Chicago Tribune*, 5 October 1963, p. 10.

7. For the president's comments at the press conference, see *Public Papers of the Presidents*, 1963, pp. 768, 770, 773–74, 828; for the McNamara-Taylor recommendations approved in the 2 October meeting, see *Pentagon Papers*, 2:250.

8. "Mrs. Nhu Is Here; U.S. Cool to Visit," *New York Times*, 8 October 1963, p. 1; William Moore, "Cancel Mme. Nhu's Visa, Senator Asks," *Chicago Tribune*, 8 October 1963, p. 6; "Visa to Mrs. Nhu Is under Inquiry," *New York Times*, 9 October 1963, p. 10.

9. William Fulton, "Mme. Nhu Pledges to Honor U.S. Ties," *Chicago Tribune*, 10 October 1963, p. 3; Unna, "Mme. Nhu Regrets Cool Reception Here," *Washington Post*, 17 October 1963, p. 9; "Dragon Lady S. F. Date," *San Francisco Examiner*, 4 October 1963, p. 1.

10. Upon her arrival in New York, Madame Nhu said she hoped during her visit "to

try to understand why we can't get along better." "Mrs. Nhu Is Here; U.S. Cool to Visit," *New York Times*, 8 October 1963, p. 1; "Father and Daughter," *St. Louis Post-Dispatch*, 9 October 1963, p. 2C; "The Nhu Show," *Chicago Tribune*, 16 October 1963, p. 12; "The Visits of Tito and Mme. Nhu," *San Francisco Examiner*, 15 October 1963, p. 32; Hearst, "The White Hats and Black Hats," *San Francisco Examiner*, 20 October 1963, p. 1.

11. William O'Brien, "Miss Nhu and Friend Out on the Town," *San Francisco Examiner*, 29 October 1963, p. 1.

12. "Dragon Lady Faces Rough S.F. Welcome," *San Francisco Examiner*, 21 October 1963, p. 1; Peter Trimble, "Mme. Nhu Arrives, Lively Lady in Pink," ibid., 28 October 1963, p. 1; Trimble, "Students Mob Cops at UC," ibid., 30 October 1963, p. 14; Dan North, "Nhu Pickets on Job Early," ibid., 27 October 1963, p. 24; "Mme. Nhu Picketing Assailed by Dobbs," ibid., 29 October 1963, p. 9.

13. Essoyan, "Sixth Viet Buddhist Burns Self to Death," *Washington Post*, 6 October 1963, p. 1; Hedrick Smith, "Rusk Condemns Attack in Saigon on U.S. Newsmen," *New York Times*, 6 October 1963, p. 1.

14. Hoberecht telephone interview, 18 July 1979; Sheehan interview.

15. Hoberecht interview.

16. Halberstam interview.

17. Halberstam, *Making of a Quagmire*, p. 268; Smith, interview in Washington, D.C., 3 July 1979.

18. Halberstam, *Making of a Quagmire*, p. 276.

19. *Public Papers of the Presidents*, 1963, p. 846; Unna, "U.S. Expected and Desired Saigon Revolt," *Washington Post*, 2 November 1963, p. 1.

20. Unna, "U.S. Indicates Support," *Washington Post*, 3 November 1963, p. 1; Dudman, "Military Rule in Viet Nam," *St. Louis Post-Dispatch*, 10 November 1963, p. 1C; Frankel, "Vietnam Holds Strategic Importance for West," *New York Times*, 3 November 1963, p. 4E.

21. Smith interview; Michael Pakenham, "Kennedy Confers on Viet," *Chicago Tribune*, 3 November 1963, p. 1; Warren Rogers, "U.S. Ready to Grant Viet Ties," *San Francisco Examiner*, 6 November 1963, p. 13. "The American authorities made clear that the No. 1 U.S. priority is to win the war against Communist insurgents," Rogers wrote. "After that, they said, would be soon enough for the normal democratic processes."

22. John D. Morris, "Congress Briefed on Saigon Rising," *New York Times*, 2 November 1963, p. 2; Unna, "Rusk Praises Progress of Rebels' Viet Regime," *Washington Post*, 6 November 1963, p. 18.

23. "Secret Burial Set for Diem, Nhu," *Washington Post*, 4 November 1963, p. 1; Essoyan, "Bare Story behind Coup in Viet Nam," *Chicago Tribune*, 10 November 1963, p. 1.

24. Halberstam, "Coup in Saigon: A Detailed Account," *New York Times*, 6 November 1963, p. 1.

25. Halberstam, "Saigon Coup Gives Americans Hope," *New York Times*, 6 November 1963, p. 16; Halberstam, "Junta Has Brought a New Glimmer of Hope for Vietnam and Its Anti-Communist War," ibid., 10 November 1963, p. E3; Sheehan interview.

26. "Coup in Viet Nam," *St. Louis Post-Dispatch*, 3 November 1963, p. 2B; "Hope in South Vietnam," *Washington Post*, 2 November 1963, p. 10; "Coup in Saigon," *New York Times*, 2 November 1963, p. 24; "Opportunity in Vietnam," ibid., 3 November 1963, p. 8E.

27. Reston, "Where Do We Go from Here in South Vietnam?" *New York Times*, 3 November 1963, p. 4E; Reston, "Why a Truce in Korea and Not in Vietnam?" ibid., 6 November 1963, p. 40.

28. Childs, "Kennedy Initiative in Foreign Affairs Is Not Likely during Year of Presidential Campaign," *St. Louis Post-Dispatch*, 3 November 1963, p. 3B; Drummond, "Turnover in Saigon; New Team, Promising Start," *Washington Post*, 6 November 1963, p. 21; Lerner, "Fall of the Ngos," *San Francisco Examiner*, 10 November 1963, p. C4.

29. Alsop, "Farewell to Diem," *Washington Post*, 4 November 1963, p. 17; Alsop, "Blood on Our Hands?" ibid., 6 November 1963, p. 21.

30. "Who Pulled the Rug?" *Chicago Tribune*, 3 November 1963, p. 24; "Poor Dividends in a Dirty Business," ibid., 5 November 1963, p. 20.

31. "Viet Nam," *San Francisco Examiner*, 3 November 1963, p. A.

32. Conniff, "'Foggy Bottom' and the Viet Revolt," *San Francisco Examiner*, 4 November 1963, p. 13; Conniff, "Dark Chapter in Diplomacy," ibid., 8 November 1963, p. 36.

33. *Pentagon Papers*, 2:261–62.

34. Unna interview; Sheehan interview.

Chapter 15

1. Wicker, quoted in *Commentary* 51 (July 1971): 18, in a response to Daniel P. Moynihan's "The Presidency and the Press," *Commentary* 51 (March 1971): 41–52.

2. For analyses of news coverage of Afghanistan and Iran, see Montague Kern, "The Invasion of Afghanistan: Domestic vs. Foreign Stories," and David Altheide, "Iran vs. U.S. TV News: The Hostage Story Out of Context," in William C. Adams, ed., *Television Coverage of the Middle East*, pp. 106–57.

3. For a study of television that stresses presidential dominance, see Newton Minow, John B. Martin, and Lee Mitchell, *Presidential Television*.

4. Jim Karayn, president of television station KHYY, spoke of television as a national institution in competition with the presidency at the Center for the Study of the Presidency's Annual Student Symposium in Washington, D.C., on 14 March 1982. For an analysis that suggests that opinion follows television coverage during elections, see Weaver, Gruber, McCombs, and Eyal, *Media Agenda-Setting in a Presidential Election*. For public opinion and Middle East coverage, see Adams, ed., *Television Coverage of the Middle East*; for a discussion of media diplomacy, see Doris A. Graber, *Mass Media and American Politics*, pp. 252–53.

5. For a listing of studies of various parts of the world based on content analysis, see William C. Adams, "Covering the World in Ten Minutes: Network News and International Affairs," in William C. Adams, ed., *Television Coverage of International Affairs*, pp. 3–15. For coverage of Carter and Reagan administration policy issues, see

Montague Kern, *Television and Middle East Diplomacy*; and "Television, The Reagan Administration and El Salvador: Was There a Policy Role for the Media?" (Paper delivered at the annual meeting of the International Association for Mass Communication Research, Paris, France, 6 September 1982). For newspaper coverage of other Carter issues, see Bruce Miroff, "The Media and the Woes of Jimmy Carter" (Paper delivered at the annual meeting of the American Political Science Association, New York, 3–6 September 1981).

Bibliography

Interviews

Kennedy Administration Officials
George W. Ball, undersecretary of state, 29 June 1979.
McGeorge Bundy, White House, national security adviser, 11 July 1978.
Frederick L. Holborn, Senator John F. Kennedy's staff before the 1960 election,
    Bundy's White House staff after 1961, 7 October 1977, 6 February 1978.
Paul M. Kattenburg, Southeast Asia Division, Department of State, written response
    to questions, 27 July 1979.
David Klein, State Department, and, subsequently Bundy's White House staff, 27
    June 1978.
Richard I. Phillips, Public Affairs Division, Department of State, 1 June 1979.
Dean Rusk, secretary of state, 23 March 1979.
Paul Sakwa, Bureau of Intelligence and Research, State Department, 3 April, 8 May
    1978.
James C. Thomson, Jr., Far East Bureau, Department of State, 28 June 1979.

Congress
Martin J. Clancy, Senate Republican Policy Committee, 28 July 1978.
J. William Fulbright, chairman, Senate Foreign Relations Committee, 10 July 1978.
Pat M. Holt, Latin American specialist, Senate Foreign Relations Committee, 21
    July 1978.
Carl M. Marcy, chief of staff, Senate Foreign Relations Committee, 20 March 1978.
Bryce Nelson, Senator Frank Church's foreign affairs adviser, telephone interview,
    10 July 1979.
Francis R. Valeo, Senator Mike Mansfield's foreign policy adviser, 20 March 1978.

Chicago Tribune
William Anderson, congressional reporter, 23 January 1978.
Laurence Burd, White House correspondent, 1 April 1978.
George Morgenstern, editorial page editor, 17 June 1978.
Walter Trohan, chief, Washington bureau, 6 April 1978.
Robert Young, Washington bureau reporter, 2 February 1977.

New York Times
Wallace Carroll, Washington bureau news editor, 11 June 1977.
Nathaniel Gerstenzang, assistant foreign news editor, 27 June 1978.
David Halberstam, correspondent in South Vietnam, telephone interview, 2 August
    1979.
E. W. Kenworthy, State Department and congressional reporter, 27 March 1978.

Hedrick Smith, State Department reporter, 3 July 1979.
Tad Szulc, Washington bureau reporter, 3 February 1978.
Seymour Topping, chief of the Moscow bureau, 11 July 1978.
Tom Wicker, White House reporter, 28 June 1978.

St. Louis Post-Dispatch
Marquis W. Childs, Washington bureau chief and columnist, 2 and 8 February 1978.
Irving Dilliard, editor, editorial page until 1957, 20 June 1978.
Richard B. Dudman, Washington bureau reporter, 2 and 8 February 1978.
Robert N. Lasch, editor, editorial page after 1957, 24 June 1978.

San Francisco Examiner
Tom Eastham, editor of the Hearst afternoon paper in San Francisco, the *News Call Bulletin*, 17 July 1978.
Charles L. Gould, publisher of the *San Francisco Examiner*, written response to questions, 1 August 1978.
William Randolph Hearst, Jr., editor and publisher of the Hearst chain, 28 June 1978.
Marianne Means, White House reporter for the Hearst chain, 2 June 1978.
Richard Pearce, editorial page editor, *San Francisco Examiner*, 14 July 1978.

Washington Post
Robert H. Estabrook, editor, editorial page, and foreign correspondent, based in London, 30 June 1978.
Alfred W. Friendly, managing editor, 7 July 1978.
Karl E. Meyer, editorial page, 29 June 1978.
Chalmers M. Roberts, chief foreign policy reporter and analyst, 19 June 1978.
Warren Unna, Washington bureau reporter, 2 July 1979.
J. R. Wiggins, editor, 24 August 1978.

Other Journalists
Joseph W. Alsop, columnist, 29 April 1978.
Keyes Beech, Far East correspondent, *Chicago Daily News*, 28 March 1978.
Henry O. Brandon, Washington correspondent, *London Sunday Times*, 24 January 1978.
Susan Clemmer, city editor, *Chicago Daily Calumet*, 1966–67, 15 July 1978.
Robert J. Donovan, Washington bureau chief, *New York Herald-Tribune*, 17 August 1978.
Ernest Hoberecht, Tokyo bureau chief, UPI, telephone interview, 18 July 1979.
Jan Reifenberg, Washington correspondent, *Frankfurter Allgemeine Zeitung*, 26 January 1978.
Richard H. Rovere, Washington correspondent, *New Yorker*, 30 June 1978.
William V. Shannon, columnist, *New York Post*, 9 April 1978.
Neil Sheehan, UPI correspondent in South Vietnam, 2 July 1979.

Kennedy Library Materials

Oral History Interviews
Government: Richard M. Bissell, Winthrop G. Brown, Lucius D. Clay, W. Averell
  Harriman, Roger Hilsman, George F. Kennan, James Loeb, Frank F. Man-
  kiewicz, William R. Tyler, Adam Yarmolinsky.
Press: Elie Abel, Jack L. Bell, Charles L. Bartlett, Gilbert A. Harrison, William
  Randolph Hearst, Jr., Carroll Kilpatrick, Joseph Kraft, William H. Lawrence,
  Walter Lippmann, Peter Lisagor, Henry R. Luce, Edward P. Morgan, Hugh S.
  Sidey.

Other Manuscript Sources
In addition to oral history interviews, the Kennedy Library presidential office files
and diaries were examined. So were the appointment diaries of Dean Rusk and Theodore Sorensen, along with the files of a number of the president's advisers. Subject
category files relating to the conduct of his foreign policy were also reviewed.

Newspapers and Periodicals

All articles pertaining to the subject matter of this book—editorials, columns, and
news stories—were read on both page one and inside pages of the *Washington Post*,
the *New York Times*, the *San Francisco Examiner*, the *St. Louis Post-Dispatch*, and
the *Chicago Tribune* for the following periods:
  1 January through 15 April 1961
  1 June through 6 October 1961
  24 August through 29 October 1962
  1 August through 10 November 1963
  In addition, a number of articles from these newspapers were read for other periods during 1961, 1962, and 1963. These were found either in the Arthom Collection
at Wake Forest University, Winston-Salem, North Carolina, or on microfilm at the
Library of Congress. A number of articles from other newspapers and periodicals as
well as government press releases were also used from the Arthom Collection, together with the following:

Atwood, William. "Visit with Walter Lippmann." *Look* 25 (25 April 1961):
  100–102 ff.
Bagdikian, Ben H. "Washington Letter: The Morning Line." *Columbia Journalism
  Review* 1 (Fall 1962): 26–28.
Baldwin, Hanson W. "Managed News: Our Peacetime Censorship." *Atlantic* 211
  (April 1963): 53–59.
Balutis, Alan P. "The Presidency and the Press: The Expanding Presidential Image."
  Presidential Studies Quarterly 7 (Fall 1977): 244–51.
Barth, Alan. "Freedom and the Press." *Progressive* 26 (June 1962): 29–33.
Bethell, Tom, and Peters, Charles. "The Imperial Press." *Washington Monthly* 8
  (November 1976): 28–34.

Bingham, W., and Just, Ward S. "The President and the Press." *Reporter* 26 (12 April 1962): 18–23.

Evans, Rowland, and Novak, Robert. "How Carter Views the World." *Washington Post*, 31 January 1979.

"Field Bids to Fan Chicago Newspaper War." *Business Week* (28 February 1959): 56–58.

"Fight for Berlin?—If We Must. . . ." *Newsweek* 58 (17 July 1961): 18–20.

Frankel, Max. "The 'States Secrets' Myth." *Columbia Journalism Review* 10 (Sept./ Oct. 1971): 22–26.

Graber, Doris A. "Press Coverage and Voter Reaction in the 1968 Presidential Election." *Political Science Quarterly* 87 (March 1974): 68–100.

———. "Press Coverage Patterns of Campaign News: The 1968 Presidential Race." *Public Opinion Quarterly* 48 (Autumn 1971): 502–11.

Gerbner, George. "Ideological Perspectives and Political Tendencies in News Reporting." *Journalism Quarterly* 41 (Autumn 1964): 495–508.

Grossman, Michael, and Kumar, Martha Joynt. "The White House and the News Media: The Phases of Their Relationship." *Political Science Quarterly* 94 (Spring 1979): 37–53.

———, and Rourke, Francis. "The Media and the Presidency: An Exchange Analysis." *Political Science Quarterly* 91 (Fall 1976): 455–70.

Hamilton, Lee H., and Van Dusen, Michael H. "Making the Separation of Powers Work." *Foreign Affairs* 57 (October 1978): 17–39.

Hart, Jim A. "The Flow of International News into Ohio." *Journalism Quarterly* 38 (Autumn 1961): 541–43.

Hutchison, Earl R. "Kennedy and the Press: The First Six Months." *Journalism Quarterly* 38 (Autumn 1961): 453–59.

"If You Want Peace. . . ." *Newsweek* 58 (3 July 1961): 13–16.

Krock, Arthur. "Mr. Kennedy's Management of the News." *Fortune* 67 (March 1963): 82, 199–202.

Lee, Jong R. "Rallying around the Flag: Foreign Policy Events and Presidential Popularity." *Presidential Studies Quarterly* 7 (Fall 1977): 252–56.

Lent, John A. "Foreign News in American Media." *Journal of Communication* 27 (Winter 1977): 46–51.

Locander, Robert. "The Adversary Relationship: A New Look at an Old Idea." *Presidential Studies Quarterly* 9 (Summer 1979): 266–74.

Markel, Lester. "Management of News." *Saturday Review* 46 (9 February 1963): 51 ff.

Meyer, Karl E. "The Cuban Torment." *New Leader* 45 (1 October 1962): 3–4.

Molotch, Harvey, and Lester, Marilyn. "News as Purposive Behavior: On the Strategic Use of Routine Events, Accidents, and Scandals." *American Sociological Review* 39 (February 1974): 101–12.

Moynihan, Daniel P. "The Presidency and the Press." *Commentary* 51 (March 1971): 41–52.

Mueller, John. "Presidential Popularity from Truman to Johnson." *American Political Science Review* 64 (March 1970): 18–23.

Nolting, Frederic E., Jr. "The Turning Point: The Origin and Development of United

States Commitment in Vietnam." *Foreign Service Journal* 45 (July 1968): 18–20.

Paletz, David L., and Entman, Robert M. "Presidents, Power, and the Press." *Presidential Studies Quarterly* 10 (Summer 1980): 416–26.

Patrick, Richard. "Leadership in Foreign Affairs Reexamined: Kennedy and Laos without Radical Revisionism." *World Affairs* 140 (Winter 1978): 245–58.

Reston, James. "The Biggest Story in the World." *New Republic* 148 (4 May 1963): 15–17.

Sempel, Guido H., III. "The Prestige Press Covers the 1960 Presidential Campaign." *Journalism Quarterly* 38 (Spring 1961): 157–63.

Tebbel, John. "Rating the American Newspaper—Part I." *Saturday Review* 44 (13 May 1961): 59–61.

Tichenor, Philip; Donohue, George; and Olien, Clarice. "Mass Communication Research: Evolution of a Structural Model." *Journalism Quarterly* 50 (Autumn 1973): 419–23.

Warner, Geoffrey. "The United States and the Fall of Diem." *Australian Outlook* 28 (December 1974): 245–58.

"Which Cuba Policy?" *New Republic* 147 (27 October 1962): 3–4.

Wildavsky, Aaron. "The Two Presidencies." *Transaction* 4 (December 1966): 7–14.

Wilhelm, John. "The Re-appearing Foreign Correspondent." *Journalism Quarterly* 40 (Spring 1963): 147–68.

Wilhoit, C. Cleveland. "Political Symbol Shifts in Crisis News." *Midwest Journal of Political Science* 13 (May 1969): 313–19.

Books and Other Materials

Adams, William C., ed. *Television Coverage of the Middle East*. Norwood, N.J.: Ablex, 1981.

———, ed. *Television Coverage of International Affairs*. Norwood, N.J.: Ablex, 1982.

Allison, Graham. *Essence of Decision: Explaining the Cuban Missile Crisis*. Boston: Little, Brown, 1971.

Alsop, Joseph. "Options." Transcript. National Public Radio, 1975.

———. "Reporting Politics." In *The Press in Perspective*, edited by Ralph D. Casey. Baton Rouge: Louisiana State University Press, 1963.

Alsop, Stewart. *Stay of Execution: A Sort of Memoir*. Philadelphia: Lippincott, 1973.

American Enterprise Institute Forum. *The Press and Public Policy*. Washington, D.C., 1979.

Aronson, James. *The Press and the Cold War*. Indianapolis: Bobbs-Merrill, 1970.

Baldwin, Hanson W. *The Great Arms Race: A Comparison of U.S. and Soviet Power Today*. New York: Praeger, 1958.

Benjamin, Gerald, ed. *The Communications Revolution in Politics*. New York: Academy of Political Science, 1982.

Berelson, B. R. *Content Analysis in Communication Research*. Glencoe, Ill.: Free Press, 1952.

Berle, Adolph A. *Latin America: Diplomacy and Reality*. New York: Harper and Row, 1962.

Best, James A. *Public Opinion: Micro and Macro*. Homewood, Ill.: Dorsey Press, 1973.

Betts, Richard K. *Soldiers, Statesmen, and Cold War Crises*. Cambridge, Mass.: Harvard University Press, 1977.

Bonsal, Philip W. *Castro, Cuba, and the United States*. Pittsburgh: University of Pittsburgh Press, 1971.

Braestrup, Peter. *Big Story*. New York: Doubleday, 1978.

Brandt, Willy. *People and Politics: The Years 1960–1975*. Boston: Little, Brown, 1978.

Broder, David S. "Political Reporters in Presidential Politics." In *Inside the System*, edited by Charles Peters and John Rothchild. New York: Praeger, 1972.

Brown, David, and Bruner, W. Richard, eds. *How I Got That Story*. New York: Dutton, 1967.

Brown, Weldon A. *Prelude to Disaster: The American Role in Vietnam, 1940–1963*. Port Washington, N.Y.: Kennikat Press, 1975.

Browne, Malcolm W. *The New Face of War*. Indianapolis: Bobbs-Merrill, 1965.

Carney, Thomas F. *Content Analysis: A Technique for Systematic Inference from Communication*. Winnipeg: University of Manitoba Press, 1972.

Cate, Curtis. *The Ides of August: The Berlin Wall Crisis, 1961*. New York: M. Evans, 1978.

Cater, Douglass. *The Fourth Branch of Government*. Boston: Houghton Mifflin, 1959.

Catudal, Honoré. *Kennedy and the Berlin Wall Crisis: A Case Study in U.S. Decision Making*. Berlin: Verlag, 1980.

Childs, Marquis. *Witness to Power*. New York: McGraw-Hill, 1975.

Chittick, William O. *State Department, Press, and Pressure Groups: A Role Analysis*. New York: Wiley, 1970.

Clausen, Aage R. *How Congressmen Decide: A Policy Focus*. New York: St. Martin's Press, 1973.

Cohen, Bernard C. *The Political Process and Foreign Policy: The Making of the Japanese Peace Treaty*. Princeton: Princeton University Press, 1957.

————. *The Press and Foreign Policy*. Princeton: Princeton University Press, 1963.

————. *The Public's Impact on Foreign Policy*. Boston: Little, Brown, 1976.

Colby, William. *Honorable Men: My Life in the CIA*. New York: Simon and Schuster, 1978.

Committee of Concerned Asian Scholars. *Laos: War and Revolution*. Edited by Nina S. Adams and Alfred W. McCoy. New York: Harper and Row, 1970.

Cooper, Chester L. *The Lost Crusade: America in Vietnam*. Greenwich, Conn.: Fawcett, 1972.

Cornwall, Elmer. *Presidential Leadership of Public Opinion*. Bloomington: Indiana University Press, 1965.

Cronin, Thomas E. "The Textbook Presidency." In *Inside the System*, edited by Charles Peters and John Rothchild. New York: Praeger, 1972.

Crouse, Timothy. *The Boys on the Bus*. New York: Ballantine, 1972.

Dahl, Robert A. *After the Revolution? Authority in a Good Society*. New Haven: Yale University Press, 1970.

——— . *Who Governs?* New Haven: Yale University Press, 1961.

Davison, W. Phillips, and Yu, Frederick T. C., eds. *Mass Communication Research: Major Issues and Future Directions*. New York: Praeger, 1974.

Dinerstein, Herbert S. *Intervention against Communism*. Baltimore: Johns Hopkins University Press, 1967.

——— . *The Making of a Missile Crisis, October 1962*. Baltimore: Johns Hopkins University Press, 1976.

Divine, Robert A., ed. *The Cuban Missile Crisis*. Chicago: Quadrangle Books, 1971.

Dolce, Philip C., and Skau, George H. *Power and the Presidency*. New York: Scribner's, 1976.

Dommen, Arthur J. *Conflict in Laos: The Politics of Neutralization*. New York: Praeger, 1971.

Dunn, Delmer D. *Public Officials and the Press*. Reading, Mass.: Addison-Wesley, 1969.

Epstein, Edward J. *News from Nowhere*. New York: Vintage, 1973.

Fall, Bernard. *Anatomy of a Crisis*. Garden City, N.Y.: Doubleday, 1969.

Fascell, Dante B., ed. *International News: Freedom Under Attack*. Beverly Hills, Calif.: Sage Publications, 1979.

Field, Michael. *The Prevailing Wind: Witness in Indochina*. London: Metheun, 1965.

Fisher, Glen H. *Public Diplomacy and the Behavioral Sciences*. Bloomington: Indiana University Press, 1972.

Fox, Douglas M., ed. *The Politics of U.S. Foreign Policy Making: A Reader*. Pacific Palisades, Calif.: Goodyear, 1971.

Gallup, George H. *The Gallup Poll: Public Opinion, 1935–1971*. 3 vols. New York: Random House, 1972.

Gelb, Leslie H., with Betts, Richard K. *The Irony of Vietnam: The System Worked*. Washington, D.C.: Brookings Institution, 1979.

Gould, Charles L. "Navy Day Remarks before the San Francisco Commercial Club." Mimeographed. 23 October 1962.

Graber, Doris A. *Mass Media and American Politics*. Washington, D.C.: Congressional Quarterly Press, 1980.

——— . *Verbal Behavior and Politics*. Urbana: University of Illinois Press, 1976.

Graham, Phillip. Appointment Book (Datebook). In the possession of Katherine Graham.

Grossman, Michael Baruch, and Kumar, Martha Joynt. *Portraying the President: The White House and the News Media*. Baltimore: Johns Hopkins University Press, 1981.

Halberstam, David. *The Best and the Brightest*. New York: Random House, 1972.

——— . *The Making of a Quagmire*. New York: Random House, 1965.

——— . *The Powers That Be*. New York: Knopf, 1979.

Halper, Thomas. *Foreign Policy Crises: Appearance and Reality in Decision Making*. Columbus: Charles E. Merrill, 1971.

Halperin, Morton H. *Bureaucratic Politics and Foreign Policy*. Washington, D.C.:
    Brookings Institution, 1974.
Hearst, William Randolph, Jr. *Selections from the Writings and Speeches of William
    Randolph Hearst*. San Francisco: privately published, 1948.
Herring, George C. *America's Longest War: The United States and Vietnam,
    1950–1975*. New York: Wiley, 1979.
Hess, Stephen. *The Washington Reporters*. Washington, D.C.: Brookings Institution,
    1981.
Higgins, Marguerite. *Our Vietnam Nightmare*. New York: Harper and Row, 1965.
Hilsman, Roger, *To Move a Nation*. Garden City, N.Y.: Doubleday, 1967.
———— . *The Politics of Policymaking in Defense and Foreign Affairs*. New York:
    Harper and Row, 1971.
Holsti, Ole R. *Content Analysis for the Social Sciences and Humanities*. Reading,
    Mass.: Addison-Wesley, 1969.
Hynds, Ernest C. *American Newspapers in the 1970s*. New York: Hastings House,
    1975.
Kahin, George McFurnan, and Lewis, John W. *The United States in Vietnam*. New
    York: Dell, 1967.
Kattenburg, Paul. *The Vietnam Trauma in American Foreign Policy, 1945–1975*.
    New Brunswick, N.J.: Transaction Books, 1980.
Kennedy (John F.) Library. "The Presidency and the Press: A Selection of Books."
    Mimeographed. July 1973.
Kennedy, Robert F. *Thirteen Days*. New York: Norton, 1969.
Kern, Montague. "The Afghan Invasion Crisis: Domestic vs. Foreign Stories. In
    Television Coverage of the Middle East, edited by William C. Adams. Nor-
    wood, N.J.: Ablex, 1981.
———— . "The Presidency and the Press: John F. Kennedy's Foreign Policy Crises
    and the Politics of Newspaper Coverage." Ph.D. dissertation, Johns Hopkins
    University School of Advanced International Studies, 1979.
———— . "Television, The Reagan Administration and El Salvador: Was There a
    Policy Role for the Media?" Paper delivered at the annual meeting of the Inter-
    national Association for Mass Communication Research, 6 September 1982, at
    Paris, France.
———— . *Television and Middle East Diplomacy: Jimmy Carter's Fall 1977 Peace
    Initiative*. Washington, D.C.: Georgetown University, Center for Contemporary
    Arab Studies, 1983.
Knightly, Philip. *The First Casualty*. New York: Harcourt Brace Jovanovich, 1975.
Kohler, Foy D. *Understanding the Russians*. New York: Harper and Row, 1970.
Kraft, Joseph. *Profiles in Power: A Washington Insight*. New York: New American
    Library, 1966.
Krieghbaum, Hillier. *Pressures on the Press*. New York: Crowell, 1972.
Krock, Arthur. *Memoirs: Sixty Years on the Firing Line*. New York: Funk and Wag-
    nalls, 1968.
Levering, Ralph B. *The Cold War, 1945–1972*. Arlington Heights, Ill.: Harlan Da-
    vidson, 1982.
———— . *The Public and American Foreign Policy, 1918–1978*. New York: Morrow,
    1978.

Lewy, Guenter. *America in Vietnam.* New York: Oxford University Press, 1978.

Lippmann, Walter. *U.S. Foreign Policy: Shield of the Republic.* Boston: Little, Brown, 1943.

McCartney, James. "Vested Interests of the Reporter." In *Reporting the News,* edited by Louis M. Lyons. Cambridge, Mass.: Harvard University Press, 1965.

McGraffin, William, and Knoll, Erwin. *Anything But the Truth.* New York: Putnam, 1968.

Macmillan, Harold. *Pointing the Way, 1959–71.* New York: Harper and Row, 1972.

McNamara, Robert S. *The Essence of Security: Reflections in Office.* New York: Harper and Row, 1968.

Mecklin, John. *Mission in Torment.* Garden City, N.Y.: Doubleday, 1965.

Mendelsohn, Harold A., and Crespi, Irving. *Polls, TV, and the New Politics.* Scranton, Pa.: Chandler Publishing, 1970.

Meyer, Karl E., and Szulc, Tad. *The Cuban Invasion: The Chronicle of a Disaster.* New York: Atheneum, 1962.

Minow, Newton; Martin, John B.; and Mitchell, Lee. *Presidential Television.* New York: Basic Books, 1973.

Miroff, Bruce. "The Media and the Woes of Jimmy Carter." Paper delivered at the annual meeting of the American Political Science Association, 3–6 September 1981, at New York.

——— . *Pragmatic Illusions: The Presidential Politics of John F. Kennedy.* New York: David McKay, 1976.

Neustadt, Richard. *Presidential Power.* New York: Wiley, 1960.

New York Times. *The Mass Media and Politics.* New York: *New York Times,* 1972.

Nimmo, Dan D. *Newsgathering in Washington.* New York: Atherton, 1964.

——— . *The Political Persuaders.* Englewood Cliffs, N.J.: Prentice-Hall, 1970.

Paletz, David L., and Entman, Robert N. *Media Power Politics.* New York: Free Press, 1981.

The Pentagon Papers: The Defense Department History of United States Decision Making on Vietnam (Senator Gravel Edition). 5 vols. Boston: Beacon Press, 1971.

Planck, Charles H. *The Changing System of German Reunification in Western Diplomacy, 1955–66.* Baltimore: Johns Hopkins University Press, 1967.

Pollard, James E. *The Presidents and the Press.* New York: Macmillan, 1947.

Polsby, Nelson W. *The Modern Presidency.* New York: Random House, 1973.

Pool, Ithiel de Sola. *The Prestige Papers: A Comparative Study of Political Symbols.* Cambridge, Mass.: MIT Press, 1970.

——— . "Trends in Content Analysis Today: A Summary." In *Trends in Content Analysis,* edited by Ithiel de Sola Pool. Urbana: University of Illinois Press, 1959.

Porter, William E. *Assault on the Media: The Nixon Years.* Ann Arbor: University of Michigan Press, 1976.

Presidential Press Secretaries Forum. "The Presidential Press Secretaries' Forum." Mimeographed. Gonzaga University, 1 April 1978.

Public Papers of the Presidents: John F. Kennedy, 1961–63. Washington: U.S. Government Printing Office, 1962–64.

Reedy, George E. *The Twilight of the Presidency.* New York: Mentor, 1970.

Relyea, Harold C. *The Presidency and Information Policy*. New York: Center for the Study of the Presidency, 1981.

Reston, James. *The Artillery of the Press: Its Influence on American Foreign Policy*. New York: Harper and Row, 1967.

Rienow, Robert, and Rienow, Leona Train. *The Lonely Quest: The Evolution of Presidential Leadership*. Chicago: Follett, 1966.

Rivers, William L. *The Opinionmakers*. Boston: Beacon Press, 1965.

Roberts, Chalmers M. *First Rough Draft*. New York: Praeger, 1973.

————— . *The Washington Post: The First 100 Years*. Boston: Houghton Mifflin, 1977.

Rourke, Francis E. *Bureaucracy and Foreign Policy*. Baltimore: Johns Hopkins University Press, 1972.

Rovere, Richard H. *The American Establishment*. New York: Harcourt, Brace and World, 1962.

St. Louis Post-Dispatch. "The Story of the *St. Louis Post-Dispatch*." 11th ed., revised by Harry Wilensky. St. Louis: Pulitzer Publishing Company, 1973.

Salinger, Pierre. *With Kennedy*. New York: Doubleday, 1966.

Salisbury, R. "Interest Groups." In *Handbook of Political Science*, vol. 4, edited by F. Greenstein and N. Polsby. Boston: Addison-Wesley, 1975.

Schick, Jack M. *The Berlin Crisis: 1958–1962*. Philadelphia: University of Pennsylvania Press, 1971.

Schlesinger, Arthur M., Jr. *The Imperial Presidency*. Boston: Houghton Mifflin, 1973.

————— . *Robert Kennedy and His Times*. Boston: Houghton Mifflin, 1978.

————— . *A Thousand Days: John F. Kennedy in the White House*. Boston: Houghton Mifflin, 1965.

Sharp, Harry Wall, Jr. "The Kennedy News Conference." Ph.D. dissertation, Purdue University, 1967.

Shepardson, Whitney H. *Early History of the Council on Foreign Relations*. Stamford, Conn.: Overbrook Press, 1960.

Sigal, Leon V. *Reporters and Officials: The Organization and Politics of Newsmaking*. Lexington, Mass.: D. C. Heath, 1973.

Slüsser, Robert M. *The Berlin Crisis of 1961*. Baltimore: Johns Hopkins University Press, 1973.

Smith, Earl E. T. *The Fourth Floor: An Account of the Castro Communist Revolution*. New York: Random House, 1962.

Sorensen, Theodore C. *Kennedy*. New York: Bantam, 1966.

Steel, Ronald. *Walter Lippmann and the American Century*. Boston: Little, Brown, 1980.

Stevenson, Charles A. *The End of Nowhere*. Boston: Beacon Press, 1973.

Szulc, Tad. "The *New York Times* and the Bay of Pigs." In *How I Got That Story*, edited by David Brown and W. Richard Bruner. New York: Dutton, 1967.

Talese, Gay. *The Kingdom and the Power*. New York: World, 1969.

Taylor, Maxwell D. *Swords and Plowshares*. New York: Norton, 1972.

Toye, Hugh. *Laos: Buffer State or Battleground?* London: Oxford University Press, 1968.

Trask, David T. "The Congress as Classroom: J. William Fulbright and the Crisis of American Power." In *Makers of American Diplomacy from Benjamin Franklin to Henry Kissinger*, edited by Frank J. Merli and Theodore A. Wilson. New York: Scribner's, 1974.

Trice, Robert H. *Interest Groups and the Foreign Policy Process: U.S. Policy in the Middle East*. Beverly Hills, Calif.: Sage Publications, 1976.

Tucker, Robert W.; Watts, William; and Free, Lloyd A. *The United States in the World: New Directions for the Post-Vietnam Era?* Washington, D.C.: Potomac Associates, 1976.

Turnstall, Jeremy, ed. *Media Sociology*. London: Constable, 1970.

United States Congress. Senate. Select Committee to Study Governmental Operations. *Alleged Assassination Plots Involving Foreign Leaders*. 94th Cong., 2d sess., S. Rept. 94–465, 1975.

Viser, Festus J., ed. *The News Media: A Service and a Force*. Memphis: Memphis State University Press, 1970.

Watts, William, and Dominguez, Jorge I. *The United States and Cuba: Old Issues and New Directions*. Washington, D.C.: Potomac Associates, 1977.

——— , and Free, Lloyd A. *State of the Nation, III*. Lexington, Mass.: D. C. Heath, 1978.

——— ; Packard, George R.; Clough, Ralph N.; and Oxnam, Robert B. *Japan, Korea, and China: American Perceptions and Policies*. Lexington, Mass.: Lexington Books, 1979.

Weaver, David H.; Graber, Doris A.; McCombs, Maxwell E.; and Eyal, Chaim H. *Media Agency-Setting in a Presidential Election: Issues, Images and Interest*. New York: Praeger, 1981.

White, Graham J. *FDR and the Press*. Chicago: University of Chicago Press, 1979.

Wicker, Tom. *On Press*. New York: Viking Press, 1978.

Wiggins, James Russell. "Prior Restraint." In *Mass Media and the Law: Freedom and Restraint*, edited by David G. Clark and Earl R. Hutchison. New York: Wiley-Interscience, 1970.

Wilcox, Francis O., and Frank, Richard A. *The Constitution and the Conduct of American Foreign Policy*. New York: Praeger, 1976.

Wise, Kenneth Lloyd. "The War News System." Ph.D. dissertation, American University, 1967.

Wolfson, Lewis W. "A Report on the State of the Presidential News Conference." New York: National News Council, 1975.

Zeigler, L. Harmon, and Peak, G. Wayne. *Interest Groups in American Society*. Englewood Cliffs, N.J.: Prentice-Hall, 1972.

Index